THE NEW YORK TIMES

Dictionary of Money and Investing

THE NEW YORK TIMES

Dictionary of Money and Investing

- THE ESSENTIAL
A-TO-Z GUIDE
TO THE LANGUAGE
OF THE NEW MARKET

GRETCHEN MORGENSON

and CAMPBELL R. HARVEY, Ph.D.

TIMES BOOKS

Henry Holt and Company • New York

Times Books
Henry Holt and Company, LLC
Publishers since 1866
115 West 18th Street
New York, New York 10011

Henry Holt® is a registered trademark
of Henry Holt and Company, LLC.

Library of Congress Cataloging-in-Publication Data

The New York times dictionary of money and investing :
the essential A-to-Z guide to the language of the new market.—1st ed.
   p. cm.
  ISBN 0-8050-6933-X (pbk.)
   1. Money—Dictionaries. 2. Investments—Dictionaries. I. New York times.

HG216.N49 2002
332'.03—dc21   2002018964

First Edition 2002

Designed by Victoria Hartman

Printed in the United States of America
1 3 5 7 9 10 8 6 4 2

With gratitude to Paul, Conor, and Mize

—G. M.

To my wife, Susana, and my children,

Cassandra, Catriona, and Campbell

—C. H.

PREFACE
How to Use This Dictionary

More Americans than ever are investing in the stock market today.

In the mid-1990s, employers shifted the management of workers' retirement plans to self-directed plans—particularly 401(k)s—that require people to make their own investment decisions. Perhaps as a result of this shift, throngs of investment firms have sprung up to serve these retail investors (see page 280 to learn what makes individuals retail, as compared to institutional, investors), offering greater and faster access to the markets. The number of media outlets devoted to investing, personal finance, and other business topics has swelled, supplying a dizzying mass of information to investors. The Internet only adds to the cacophony, with hundreds of chat rooms abuzz with stock, bond, and mutual fund tips and tidbits.

How can anyone make sense of it all, especially when Wall Street often dresses up its investment offerings in unintelligible lingo that seems designed to obfuscate, despite recent SEC regulations that require "plain language"? Investors, if they are to be successful in the markets, need help deciphering the information overload and cutting through the jargon and the hype.

We came to this project after years of studying and reporting on the markets. Having long thought about the need for a handy desk reference that could serve this purpose, we have identified the terms that may crop up, either frequently or infrequently, in the prospectuses, business news, finance primers, SEC reports, Web sites and search engines, and other sources that investors turn to on a regular basis.

To make the dictionary as useful as possible to investors, we have focused primarily on terms dealing with securities, exchanges, and trading, whether stocks, bonds, mutual funds, or other assets. To that end, the reader will find definitions for all of the major U.S. markets from the New York Stock Exchange to the Nasdaq—and what it means for a stock to be traded on one versus the other—and indexes, including the Dow Jones Industrial Average, Russell 2000, S&P 500, Wilshire 5000, and more. With options and derivatives, there seem to be an endless range of investing choices for any security, and the dictionary will guide the reader through the labyrinth of puts, calls, and exercises. We decode P/E ratios, EPS, REITs, 10-Ks, 13-Ds, and the rest of the alphabet soup as well as figures of speech from the Street. Since an understanding of the basics of corporate governance is essential for sound investing, the reader will find explanations of the role of the board of directors, the difference between chapter 7 and chapter 11 bankruptcy, and related terms. With retirement accounts, estates, trusts, and taxes taking on larger and larger roles in an investor's bottom line, many of the most important terms dealing with these issues are included in the dictionary as well.

For each term, we have included the primary definition or definitions pertaining to money and investing. Because there are so many abbreviations, acronyms, and colloquialisms in the markets, we have cross-referenced terms to help readers track down information and identify synonyms, antonyms, and related terms. These references are noted at the end of definitions prefaced by "See" for abbreviations, acronyms, and slang; "Also known as" and "Also called" for synonyms; "See also" and "Compare to" for related terms; and "Opposite of" for antonyms and antithetical methods. Web addresses are included, when available, for exchanges, indexes, associations, and government departments and agencies.

THE NEW YORK TIMES

Dictionary of Money
and Investing

A

AAII *See* American Association of Individual Investors.

above par *See* par.

absolute priority Rule in bankruptcy proceedings requiring senior creditors to be paid in full before junior creditors receive any payment.

abusive tax shelter A limited partnership that the IRS judges to be claiming tax deductions illegally.

accelerated depreciation Any method of depreciating an asset that produces larger deductions from its value in the early years of its life.

acceleration clause A contract stating that the unpaid balance becomes due and payable if specific actions transpire, such as failure to make interest payments on time.

accommodative monetary policy Federal Reserve System policy to increase the amount of money available to banks for lending. When the economy falters, the Fed often makes its policies more accommodating to help increase economic activity. *See also* monetary policy.

account What an investor must have at a brokerage firm before he or she can trade securities. In the context of bookkeeping, refers to the ledger pages upon which various assets, liabilities, income, and expenses are represented. In the context of investment banking, refers to the status of securities sold and owned or the relationship between parties to an underwriting syndicate.

account balance Credits minus debits held in an account at the end of a reporting period.

account executive The brokerage firm employee who handles securities orders for clients. *See also* broker.

account reconciliation The reviewing and adjusting of the balance in a personal checkbook to match a bank statement.

account statement A summary of all banking balances or of all securities transactions and positions, both long and short, in a customer's account at a brokerage firm.

accountant's opinion A signed statement from an independent public accountant after examination of a firm's records and accounts, usually stating that the presentation of the company's financial position is fair and accurate. If the accountant is uncertain that the records accurately reflect the company's position, then his opinion is qualified. Although qualified opinions are rare, investors should watch for them. *See also* qualified opinion.

accounts payable Money owed by a company to its suppliers.

accounts receivable Money owed to a company by its customers.

accounts receivable financing A short-term financing method in which accounts receivable are pledged as collateral for cash advances from a lender. *See also* factor.

accounts receivable turnover ratio The ratio of sales to average accounts receivable, which measures how quickly a company's customers pay their bills.

accredited investor Wealthy investor with a net worth of $1 million or more or an annual income of at least $200,000 who can invest in a private-placement investment or other offering not sold to the public and not registered with the SEC.

accretion The accumulation of capital gains in a discount bond as it approaches maturity and a value of par or $10,000. Even though these gains are not received until maturity, they are considered income by the IRS and are taxed as such each year.

accrual accounting convention An accounting system that tries to match the recognition of revenues a company has earned with the expenses it incurred in generating those revenues.

accrual basis An accounting practice in which expenses and income are treated as if they are earned or incurred, whether or not they have been received or paid. *Opposite of* cash basis.

accrual bond A bond on which interest accrues but is not paid to the investor during the time of accrual. The amount of accrued interest is added to the remaining principal of the bond and is paid at maturity.

accrued benefits The pension benefits earned by an employee according to years of service.

accrued discount Interest that accumulates on U.S. savings bonds from the date of purchase until the date of redemption or final maturity, whichever comes first. Series A, B, C, D, E, EE, F, I, and J are discount or accrual bonds, meaning principal and interest are paid when the bonds are redeemed. Series G, H, HH, and K are current-income bonds, and the semiannual interest paid to their holders is not included in accrued discount.

accrued interest Amount that has accumulated between the most recent interest payment and the sale of a bond or other fixed-income security. At the time of sale, the buyer pays the seller the bond's price plus "accrued interest," calculated by multiplying the coupon rate by the fraction of the coupon period that has elapsed since the last payment. For example if a bondholder receives $40 in coupon payments semi-annually and sells the bond one-quarter of the way into the coupon period, the buyer pays the seller $10.

accrued market discount The rise in the market value of a discount bond as it approaches maturity and becomes redeemable at par.

accumulated dividend A dividend that has reached its due date, but is not paid out. *See also* cumulative preferred stock.

accumulated-profits tax A tax on earnings kept in a firm to prevent the higher personal income tax rate that would result if profits were paid out as dividends to the owners.

accumulation In the context of mutual funds, refers to the regular investing of a fixed amount while reinvesting dividends and capital gains. In the context of corporate finance, refers to profits that are plowed back into the capital base of the company rather than paid out as dividends.

ACH *See* automated clearing house.

acid-test ratio The ratio of a company's current assets minus its inventories, accruals, and prepaid items to current liabilities. *Also called* quick ratio.

acquiree A firm that is being acquired.

acquirer A firm or individual that is acquiring something.

acquisition When a firm buys another firm.

acquisition cost For an investor, the price plus brokerage commissions of a security, or the sales charge applied to load funds. *See also* tax basis.

acquisition of assets A merger or consolidation in which an acquirer purchases the selling firm's assets.

acquisition of stock A merger or consolidation in which an acquirer purchases the acquiree's stock.

active Describes a market in which there is frequent trading.

active account Refers to a brokerage account in which many transactions occur. Brokerage firms may levy a fee if an account generates an inadequate level of activity.

active fund management An investment approach that purposely shifts funds either between different asset classes or between individual securities or industry groups. *Opposite of* passive investment management.

active income Income from an active business as opposed to passive investment income according to the U.S. tax code.

active investor An investor who takes a large stake in a corporation and takes an active role in its management.

active management The pursuit of investment returns in excess of a specified benchmark.

active return Return relative to a benchmark. If a portfolio's return is 5 percent, and the benchmark's return is 3 percent, then the portfolio's active return is 2 percent.

active portfolio strategy A strategy that uses available information and forecasting techniques to seek better performance than a buy-and-hold or passive portfolio strategy.

actuals The physical commodity (such as pork bellies or silver) underlying a futures contract.

A-D Advance-decline, or measurement of the number of issues trading above their previous closing prices less the number trading below their previous closing prices over a particular period. As a technical measure of market breadth, the steepness of the A-D line indicates whether a strong bull or bear market is under way or when a market is being broken.

ADB *See* adjusted debit balance.

adjustable rate Refers to an interest rate that is adjusted periodically, usually according to a standard market rate, such as that prevailing on Treasury bonds or LIBOR. Typically, such issues have a set floor or ceiling, called a cap or collar, which limits the adjustment over the life of the loan.

adjustable-rate mortgage (ARM) A mortgage that features predetermined adjustments of the interest rate at regular intervals based on an established index. The interest rate is adjusted at each interval to a rate equivalent to the index value plus a predetermined spread, or margin, over the index. These spreads are usually subject to per-interval and to life-of-loan interest-rate or payment-rate caps.

adjustable-rate preferred stock (ARPS) Publicly traded issues that may be collateralized by mortgages and mortgaged-backed securities.

adjusted basis Price from which to calculate and derive capital gains or losses upon sale of an asset. Account actions, such as any stock splits that have occurred since the initial purchase, must be accounted for. *See also* cost basis.

adjusted debit balance (ADB) The loan balance in a margin account that is calculated by combining the balance owed to a broker with any outstanding balance in the special miscellaneous account, and any paper profits on stocks that have been sold short.

adjusted gross income (AGI) Gross income less allowable deductions is the income on which an individual is taxed by the federal government.

adjusted-balance method Method of calculating finance charges on a loan that uses as its basis the account balance remaining after adjusting for all transactions posted during the given billing period. *See also* average-daily-balance method; previous-balance method.

ADR *See* American depositary receipt.

ADS *See* American depositary share.

advance Increase in the market price of stocks, bonds, commodities, or other assets.

advance refunding In the context of municipal bonds, refers to the sale of new bonds, known as the refunding issue, before the first date on which the old bonds can be retired. The refunding issue usually specifies a rate lower than the issue to be refunded, and the proceeds are invested, usually in government securities, until the higher-rate bonds can be retired. Such a strategy reduces the borrowing costs of the issuer.

advancement Money or property given to a person by the deceased before death and intended as an advance against the beneficiary's share in the will.

adverse opinion An independent auditor's opinion expressing that a firm's financial statements do not reflect the company's position accurately. *See also* qualified opinion.

advisory letter A newsletter offering financial advice to its readers.

affiliate Relationship between two companies when one company owns a substantial interest but less than a majority of the voting stock of another company. Also when two companies are both subsidiaries of a third company. *See also* subsidiary; parent company.

affiliated person An individual who possesses enough influence and control in a corporation as to be able to alter the actions of the corporation. Can also be considered an insider. *Also known as* control person.

affirmative covenant A bond covenant that specifies certain actions the firm must take to remain within the terms of its contract with the lender. *Also known as* positive covenant.

affordability index An index that measures the financial ability of consumers to purchase a home.

after-acquired clause A contractual clause in a mortgage agreement stating that any additional mortgageable property attained by the borrower after the mortgage is signed will be regarded as additional security for the obligation addressed in the mortgage.

after-hours dealing or trading Securities trading after regular trading hours, usually between 9:30 A.M. and 4:00 P.M. on organized exchanges.

aftermarket *See* secondary market.

after-tax basis The comparison basis used to analyze the net after-tax returns on a corporate taxable bond and a municipal tax-free bond.

after-tax profit margin The ratio of net income to net sales.

after-tax real rate of return The after-tax rate of return on an investment, minus the inflation rate.

against the box *See* selling short against the box.

agency A broker acting as intermediary between buyer and seller, taking no financial risk personally or as a firm, and charging a commission for the service. *Opposite of* principal.

agency bank A form of organization commonly used by foreign banks to enter the U.S. market. An agency bank cannot accept deposits or extend loans in its own name; it acts as agent for the parent bank. It is also the financial institution that issues American depositary receipts (ADRs) to the general market.

agency securities Securities issued by federally related institutions and U.S. government–sponsored entities. Such agencies were created to reduce borrowing costs for certain sectors of the economy, such as agriculture. Securities issued by agencies such as the Government National Mortgage Association (Ginnie Mae), Federal Home Loan Mortgage Corporation (Freddie Mac), and Federal National Mortgage Association (Fannie Mae) are not backed by the full faith and credit of the U.S. government, but by the agencies themselves. Therefore, these securities carry slightly more risk than Treasury bills, notes, or bonds.

agent The decision-maker in a principal-agent relationship.

aggressive-growth mutual fund A mutual fund designed for maximum capital appreciation which invests in companies with high growth rates.

AGI *See* adjusted gross income.

aging schedule A table of accounts receivable broken down into age categories, such as zero to thirty days, thirty to sixty days, and sixty to ninety days, which is used to determine if customers are paying bills on schedule.

agreement among underwriters A contract among members of a syndicate underwriting a security that defines the members' proportionate liability, which is usually limited to and based on the participants' level of involvement. The contract outlines the payment schedule on the settlement date. *Compare to* underwriting agreement.

ahead of itself In context of general equities, refers to stocks that are overbought or oversold on a fundamental basis.

ahead of you An order for a stock at the same price as another customer but entered ahead of that order. When a customer's order goes unfilled, it is often because other orders were placed first.

AIBD Association of International Bond Dealers.

AIMR Association for Investment Management and Research, an organization that administers standards of conduct for investment analysts. www.aimr.org

air pocket Often referred to as a cause of a stock's precipitous price drop, typically on the unexpected news of poor results.

All Ordinaries Index The major index of Australian stocks, comprising 330 of the major companies listed on the Australian Stock Exchange. www.asx.com.au

all-in cost Total costs, explicit and implicit.

all-or-none order (AON) An order for stock that is to be executed at a specified price in its entirety or not at all, and thus is testing the strength/conviction of the counterparty. An AON order remains alive until executed or canceled. *Opposite of* any-part-of order.

all-or-none underwriting An arrangement whereby a security issue is canceled if the underwriter is unable to sell the entire issue to investors.

allotment The number of securities assigned to each of the participating firms in an underwriting syndicate.

alpha Used with beta as a measure of risk-adjusted performance. An alpha is usually generated by comparing the excess return of the security or mutual fund to the S&P 500's excess return. Suppose a mutual fund has a return of 25 percent, and the risk-free return as found in a short-term interest rate is 5 percent; that means the fund's excess return is 20 percent. During the same time, the market excess return is 9 percent. If the beta of the mutual fund is 2.0, making it twice as risky as the S&P 500, the expected excess return, given the risk, is 2×9 percent or 18 percent. But the actual excess return is 20 percent; hence, the alpha is 2 percent. A positive alpha means the security has outperformed the benchmark on a risk-adjusted basis.

alphabet stock Categories of common stock of a corporation that track the performance of a particular subsidiary. The various alphabetical categories have different voting rights and pay dividends tied to the operating performance of the particular divisions. But although some investors like these issues because they reflect a particular aspect of a company's business and allow investors to focus on those operations, these stocks do not give their holders ownership of the business's assets. Those assets belong to the holders of the parent company's shares. This means that owners of alphabet, or tracking stocks, can never profit from a takeover in which a premium to the prevailing market is paid.

alternative investments Refers to the strategy of investing in hedge funds.

alternative minimum tax (AMT) A federal tax aimed at ensuring that wealthy individuals, estates, trusts, and corporations pay a minimal level of income tax. For individuals, the AMT is calculated by adding adjusted gross income to tax-preference items. Because the level of income at which the AMT kicks in has not been increased to account for inflation, the AMT applies to more middle-income taxpayers each year.

American Association of Individual Investors (AAII) A not-for-profit organization located in Chicago, Illinois, that educates individual investors about stocks, bonds, mutual funds, and other financial instruments. www.investware.com/aaii.stm

American depositary receipt (ADR) Certificates issued by a U.S. bank that represent foreign shares of a company held by the bank in the country of issue. One ADR may represent a portion of a foreign share, one share, or a bundle of shares of a foreign corporation. If the ADRs are "sponsored," the corporation provides financial information and other assistance to the bank and may subsidize the administration of the ADR. "Unsponsored" ADRs do not receive such assistance. ADRs are subject to the same currency, political, and economic risks as the underlying foreign share. The price of ADRs and underlying foreign shares is essentially equal. American depositary shares (ADS) are a similar form of certification.

American depositary receipt fees Fees associated with the creating or releasing of ADRs from ordinary shares, charged by the commercial banks that maintain them.

American depositary receipt ratio The number of ordinary shares into which an ADR can be converted.

American depositary share (ADS) Foreign stock issued in the United States and registered in the ADR system.

American shares Securities certificates issued in the United States by a transfer agent acting on behalf of the foreign issuer. The certificates represent claims to foreign equities.

American Stock Exchange (AMEX) Stock exchange with the third highest volume of trading in the United States, located in New York. Much of the trading on AMEX is in index options (computer technology index and major-market index), but shares of small- to medium-sized companies are also traded there. The exchange was founded as an alternative to the NYSE. In 1998, the AMEX merged with the NASD. Under the merger, the NASD assumes the role of parent company, with AMEX operating as an independent entity within the larger NASD family of companies. www.amex.com. *See also* Curb, the.

American-style option An option contract that can be exercised at any time between the date of purchase and the expiration date. Most exchange-traded options are American-style.

AMEX *See* American Stock Exchange.

Amman Stock Exchange The only agency authorized as a formal market for trading securities in Jordan. www.ammanstockex.com

amortization The repayment of a loan by installments.

amount outstanding and in circulation All currency issued by the Bureau of the Mint and intended as a medium of exchange. Coins sold by the Bureau of the Mint at premium prices are not included; uncirculated coin sets sold at face value plus handling charge are included.

AMT *See* alternative minimum tax.

analyst Employee of a brokerage or fund-management house who studies companies and makes buy-and-sell recommendations on stocks of these companies to clients or to internal investment managers. Most specialize in a specific industry.

angel In the context of venture capital, the first investor to provide financing to a start-up company.

announcement date Date on which particular news concerning a given company is announced to the public. Used in event studies, which researchers use to evaluate the economic impact of events of interest.

annual basis The technique of taking a figure covering a period of less than one year and extrapolating it to cover a full one-year period. The process is known as annualizing. If an investment returned 5 percent in six months, its annualized return would be 10 percent. Does not take compounding into account.

annual effective yield *See* annual percentage yield.

annual fund operating expenses For mutual funds, the management fee and "other expenses" charged to investors, including the expenses for maintaining shareholder records, providing shareholders with financial statements, and providing custodial and accounting services. For funds with charges, selling and marketing costs are also included.

annual meeting Meeting of a company's stockholders held once a year at which its managers report on the year's results. It is at the annual meeting that shareholders can ask questions of management.

annual percentage rate (APR) The periodic rate times the number of periods in a year. For example, a 5 percent quarterly return has an APR of 20 percent. Does not take compounding into account.

annual percentage yield (APY) The effective, or true, annual rate of return. The APY is the rate actually earned or paid in one year, taking into account the effect of compounding. The APY is calculated by taking one plus the periodic rate and raising it to the number of periods in a year. For example, a 1 percent per month rate has an APY of 12.68 percent $(1.01^{12} - 1)$.

annual rate of return There are several ways of calculating an investment's annual rate of return. If the rate of return is calculated on a monthly basis, we sometimes multiply this number by twelve to express an annual rate of return. This is often called the annual percentage rate (APR). The annual percentage yield (APY) includes the effect of compounding interest.

annual renewable term insurance *See* term life insurance.

annual report Yearly record of a publicly held company's financial condition. It includes a description of the firm's operations, management's discussion of the year's results, as well as balance sheet, income statement, and cash flow statement information. SEC rules require that it be distributed to all shareholders. A more detailed annual report called a 10-K is filed with the SEC.

annualized gain If a stock appreciates 1.5 percent in one month, the annualized gain for that stock over a twelve-month period is 12×1.5 percent or 18 percent. Compounded over the twelve-month period, the gain is $1.015^{12} - 1$, or 19.6 percent.

annuitant An individual who receives benefits from an annuity.

annuitize To commence a series of payments from the capital that has been invested or has accumulated in an annuity. The payments may be a fixed amount, for a fixed period of time, or for a lifetime.

annuity A regular, periodic payment made by an insurance company to a policyholder for a specified period of time.

annuity certain An annuity that pays a specific amount on a monthly basis for a set amount of time.

annuity in arrears An annuity with a first payment one full period hence, rather than immediately.

annuity starting date The date when an annuitant starts receiving payments from an annuity.

anticipated holding period The period of time an individual expects to hold an asset.

antidilutive effect Result of a transaction that increases earnings per common share by decreasing the number of shares outstanding. Companies may buy back their own shares to make earnings on a per-share basis look higher.

antitrust laws Legislation established by the federal government in the late nineteenth century to prevent the formation of monopolies and to regulate trade.

any-or-all bid Often used in risk arbitrage. Takeover bid in which the acquirer offers to pay a set price for all outstanding shares of the target company, or any part thereof. *Compare to* two-tier bid.

any-part-of order In context of general equities, order to buy or sell a quantity of stock in multiple transactions if necessary. *Opposite of* all-or-none order.

AON *See* all-or-none order.

AOS *See* automated order system.

appreciation Increase in the value of an asset.

approved list A list of equities and other investments that a financial institution or mutual fund is approved to make.

APR *See* annual percentage rate.

APY *See* annual percentage yield.

arbitrage The simultaneous buying and selling of a security at two different prices, resulting in small profits without a great deal of risk. Perfectly efficient markets present no arbitrage opportunities. Perfectly efficient markets seldom exist, but arbitrage opportunities are often precluded because transaction costs reduce the profits from the trades.

arbitrage bonds Municipality-issued bonds intended to save costs by refunding or retiring a higher-rate bond. Lower-rate refunding issue proceeds are invested in Treasuries until the higher-rate issue can be retired.

arbitrage-pricing theory An asset-pricing theory pioneered by Stephen Ross in 1976 that says the expected return on a security is related to its risk exposures to a number of factors.

arbitrageur One who profits from the differences in price when the same, or an extremely similar, security, currency, or commodity is traded in two or more markets. The arbitrageur profits by simultaneously purchasing and selling these securities to take advantage of pricing differentials or spreads created by market conditions.

Arizona Stock Exchange A single price auction exchange for equity trading that allows anonymous buyers and sellers to trade at low transaction costs. www.azx.com

ARM *See* adjustable-rate mortgage.

arms index An advance-decline (A-D) market indicator that is computed by dividing the ratio of advances to declines by the ratio of advancing volume to declining volume. Usually a moving average is applied to this index. An index above 1.0 suggests that more volume is moving toward declining stocks. An index level below 1.0 suggests that volume is concentrating on advancing stocks. *Also known* as TRIN.

arm's-length transaction A trade between unrelated parties that represents the prevailing market for an asset or service. Or a trade between related parties that is conducted as if they were unrelated so that there is no conflict of interest in the transaction.

ARPS *See* adjustable-rate preferred stock.

ARR *See* average rate of return.

arrearage In the context of investments, the amount of interest on bonds or dividends on cumulative preferred stock that is due but unpaid.

articles of incorporation Legal document establishing a corporation and its structure and purpose. *Also known as* charter.

ascending tops A bullish chart pattern depicting ever-rising peaks in a security's price over a period of time. *Opposite of* descending tops.

Asian option Option based on the average price of the underlying assets during the life of the option.

ask price The lowest price an investor will accept to sell a stock, also called an offer. Practically speaking, this is the price at which a dealer often buys shares of stock. *Compare to* bid price.

assay Metal-purity test to confirm that a metal meets the standards for trading on a commodities exchange.

assessed valuation The value assigned to property by a municipality for the purpose of tax assessment. Such an assessed valuation is important to investors in municipal bonds that are backed by property taxes.

asset Any possession that has value in an exchange.

asset class Category of assets, such as stocks, bonds, real estate, and foreign securities.

asset play A company with assets that are believed to be not accurately reflected in its stock price, making it an attractive buy or undervalued.

asset stripper A corporate raider that takes over a target company in order to sell large assets of the acquired company to repay debt. The net selling of the assets and the payment of the debt can leave the raider with assets that are worth more than what it cost to make the acquisition.

asset substitution Occurs when a firm invests in assets that are riskier than those that the debt-holders expected.

asset turnover The ratio of a company's net sales to its total assets.

asset value The net market value of a corporation's assets on a per-share basis. Not to be confused with the market value of the shares, which is computed by multiplying its share price by the number of shares outstanding. A company is undervalued in the market when its asset value exceeds its market value.

asset-allocation decision The decision regarding how an investor's funds should be distributed among the major classes of assets in which it may invest. Money managers can decide between bond, stock, real estate, or commodity investments.

asset-allocation mutual fund A mutual fund that rotates its trades among stocks, bonds, and money market securities to maximize return on investment and minimize risk.

asset-backed security A security that is collateralized by loans, leases, receivables, or installment contracts on personal property, not real estate.

asset-based financing Method of financing in which lenders and equity investors look principally to the cash flow from a particular asset or set of assets for a return on, and the return of, their financing.

asset-coverage test A bond-indenture restriction that permits additional borrowing if the ratio of a company's assets to its debt does not fall below a specified minimum.

asset-management account Account at a brokerage house, bank, or savings institution that incorporates banking services and brokerage features.

asset-pricing model A model for determining the required or expected rate of return on an asset. *See also* capital asset pricing model; arbitrage-pricing theory.

assets A firm's productive resources.

assets-in-place Property in which a firm has already invested.

assimilation The public absorption or acceptance of a new issue of stocks once the stock has been completely sold by the underwriter.

Association for Investment Management and Research *See* AIMR.

assumption Becoming responsible for the liabilities of another party.

asymmetric information Information that is known to some people but not to others and that may affect security prices. *See also* lemon problem.

at par A price equal to nominal or face value of a security.

at risk The danger of economic loss.

at the bell The opening or close of a market.

at the market   An order to buy or sell a security at the prevailing market price. *See also* market order.

at-the-close order   An order to buy or sell that is to be executed in its entirety at the closing price of the security on the exchange. If the execution cannot be made under this condition, the order is canceled.

at-the-money   An option is at-the-money if the strike price of the option is equal to the market price of the underlying security. For example, if a stock is trading at 54, then the option with the strike price of 54 is at-the-money.

at-the-opening order   An order to buy or sell that is to be executed at the opening and corresponding price of the stock or not at all. Any such order or portion thereof that is not executed is canceled.

Athens Stock Exchange   Greece's only major securities market. www.ase.gr/default_en.asp

auction market   Market in which the prevailing price of a security is determined through the free interaction of prospective buyers and sellers, as on the floor of the New York Stock Exchange. The Nasdaq market, by contrast, is a dealer market, meaning that intermediaries, called market makers, act on behalf of investors, executing their trades and often increasing investors' costs of trading.

audit   An examination of a company's accounting records and books conducted by an outside professional accountant to determine whether the company is maintaining records and reporting financial results according to generally accepted accounting principles. *See also* accountant's opinion.

audit trail   Resolves the validity of an accounting entry by a step-by-step record by which accounting data can be traced to their source. Audit trails can also trace securities transactions.

auditor's report   Section of an annual report that includes the auditor's opinion about the veracity of a company's financial statements.

Australian Stock Exchange   Australia's major securities market, formed when the six state stock exchanges (Adelaide, Brisbane, Hobart, Melbourne, Perth, and Sydney stock exchanges) were merged in 1987. www.asx.com.au/asx/homepage/index.jsp

authority bond   A bond issued by a government agency or a corporation created to manage a revenue-producing public enterprise such as a toll bridge or transit operation.

authorized shares   Shares authorized for issuance by a firm's corporate charter. Increasing the number of authorized shares must be agreed to by a company's shareholders because new shares dilute existing shareholders' stake in the company.

automated clearinghouse (ACH) A collection of thirty-two regional, electronic, interbank networks used to process transactions electronically with a guaranteed one-day bank collection float. www.nacha.org

automated customer account transfer For transfers of securities from a nonequity trading account to your equity trading account with your broker.

automated order system (AOS) Computerized order-entry system that sends orders to investment banks or floor brokers on an exchange.

automatic extension An automatic extension of time granted to a taxpayer to file a tax return.

automatic funds transfer An electronic transfer of funds from one account or investment vehicle to another.

automatic investment program A program in which an investor can invest or withdraw funds automatically. In a mutual fund, for example, an investor can automatically withdraw a specified amount from his bank account on a regular basis to be invested in the fund.

automatic stay A restriction on debt-holders from collection efforts related to collateral or asset seizure. Automatically imposed when a firm files for bankruptcy under Chapter 11.

automatic withdrawal A mutual fund that gives shareholders the right to receive a fixed payment from dividends on a quarterly or monthly basis.

availability float Checks deposited by a company that have not yet been cleared by a bank.

average An arithmetic mean return of selected stocks intended to represent the behavior of the market or some component of it. One example is the widely quoted Dow Jones Industrial Average (DJIA), which adds the current prices of the thirty DJIA stocks and divides the results by a predetermined number, the divisor.

average age of accounts receivable The weighted-average age of all the firm's invoices before they are paid.

average collection period, or days' receivables A company's accounts receivable divided by its sales, or the total amount of credit extended per dollar of daily sales. If this figure rises, investors could view it negatively as an indication that a company's customers are not paying their bills as promptly as they previously did. If the figure falls, the company would be perceived as managing its customers' accounts more efficiently.

average cost Refers to the average cost of securities bought at different prices over time.

average down A strategy used by investors to reduce the average cost of shares, in which the investor purchases more shares as the price of the stock decreases. The investor receives more shares per dollar and decreases the average price per share. *Also known as* double up.

average equity A customer's average daily balance in a trading account at a brokerage firm.

average life The average number of years that each dollar of unpaid principal due on the mortgage remains outstanding. *Also known as* weighted-average life.

average maturity The average time to maturity of securities held by a mutual fund. Changes in interest rates have greater impact on funds with longer average maturity because those funds will be subject to greater interest rate risk.

average rate of return (ARR) The ratio of the average cash inflow to the amount invested.

average tax rate Taxes as a fraction of income; total taxes divided by total taxable income.

average-daily-balance method A method for calculating interest in which the balance owed each day by a customer is divided by the number of days. *See also* adjusted-balance method; previous-balance method.

away A trade, quote, or market that does not originate with the dealer in question but at another firm.

axe The most influential firm in the trading of an over-the-counter stock, or the firm that trades the greatest number of its shares. This firm is presumed by investors to be particularly knowledgeable about the company's prospects, and its trading in the shares is watched closely. Axe also refers to a brokerage firm analyst who appears to be closest to the company and whose recommendations to investors therefore are scrutinized.

B

baby bond A bond with a face value of less than $1,000.

back away In the financial markets, when a buyer or seller withdraws from a previously declared interest or transaction. Among brokerage firms executing trades for their customers, a trader who backs away fails to make good on a standing bid or offer for a minimum quantity, such as one hundred shares, of a stock.

back months In the context of futures and options trading, refers to the months of contracts with expiration dates farthest away.

back office Brokerage house clerical operations that support but do not include the trading of stocks and other securities. All written confirmation and trade settlements, record keeping, and regulatory compliance occur in the back office. *Also known as* operations department.

back taxes Taxes due that have not been paid on time.

backdating In the context of mutual funds, a feature allowing fund holders to use an earlier date on a letter of intent to invest in a mutual fund in exchange for paying a reduced sales charge.

back-end-load fund A mutual fund that charges investors an exit fee fee to sell or redeem shares, often ranging from 4 percent to 6 percent. Some back-end-load funds impose a full commission if the shares are redeemed within a designated length of time, such as one year. The commission decreases the longer the investor holds the shares. The formal name for a back-end load or exit fee is the contingent deferred sales charge.

backlog Value of orders a company has received from customers but that have not yet been filled. Changes in a company's backlog can be a clue to its future results. Investors like to see rising backlogs as it represents an increase in orders.

bad debt A debt that is written off and deemed uncollectible.

bad title Title to property that does not distinctly confer ownership, usually in the context of real estate.

bailout Refers to relieving an individual, corporation, or government entity in financial trouble. The 2001 effort to provide financial help to airlines after the September 11 terrorist attacks, which caused Americans to cancel travel plans, is an example of a government-sponsored bailout.

balance of payments A compilation of all economic transactions between residents of one nation and those of all other nations during a period of time, usually a calendar year.

balance of trade Net flow of goods, exports minus imports, between two countries.

balance sheet A summary of a company's assets, liabilities, and net worth at a moment in time. *Also called* statement of condition.

balanced budget A budget in which the income equals the expenditures.

balanced fund A mutual fund that invests in both stocks and bonds, thereby balancing the investment risks in each type of security.

balloon payment The final and usually large payment that repays all remaining principal and interest on a loan. So-called balloon mortgages often carry lower interest rates than those without a balloon-payment feature.

bank anticipation note (BAN) Note issued by states and municipalities to obtain interim financing for a project that will eventually be funded through the sale of a public bond issue.

Bank for International Settlements (BIS) An international bank headquartered in Basel, Switzerland, that serves as a forum for monetary cooperation among several European central banks, the Bank of Japan, and the U.S. Federal Reserve System. Founded in 1930 to handle the German payment of World War I reparations, it now monitors and collects data on international banking activity and promulgates rules concerning international bank regulations. www.bis.org

bank holding company A company that owns or has controlling interest in two or more banks and/or other bank holding companies.

Bank Insurance Fund (BIF) A unit of the Federal Deposit Insurance

Corporation (FDIC) that provides deposit insurance for banks but not savings and loan associations. www.fdic.gov

bank trust department Bank department that deals with estates, administers trusts, and provides services such as estate planning to its clients.

banker's acceptance A short-term credit investment created by a nonfinancial firm and guaranteed by a bank as to payment. Acceptances are traded at discounts to face value in the secondary market. These instruments have been a popular investment for money market funds. They are commonly used in international transactions.

bankruptcy Inability to pay debts. In bankruptcy of a publicly owned enterprise, the ownership of the firm's assets is transferred from its stockholders to its bondholders. There are several types of bankruptcy; the most common type for public companies is chapter 11, which allows a company to keep operating as it reorganizes.

barbell strategy An investing strategy popular among bond investors in which the maturities of the securities included in the portfolio are concentrated at two extremes, short-term and long-term. Such a strategy would be appealing if the manager believes the long end of the bond market is set to outperform the middle end. And in the short-term, the cash provided by the investments help the manager to fund operations.

barter The trading or exchange of goods or services without using currency.

base rate British equivalent of the U.S. prime rate.

Basel Accord Agreement concluded in 1988 to develop standardized capital requirements for banks across countries based on the riskiness of their loans.

basis The price an investor pays for an asset plus any out-of-pocket expenses. It is used to determine capital gains or losses for tax purposes when the investment is sold. *Also known as* cost basis.

basis point In the bond market, the smallest measure used for quoting yields is a basis point. Each percentage point of yield in bonds equals one hundred basis points. Basis points also are used for interest rates. An interest rate of 5 percent is fifty basis points higher than an interest rate of 4.5 percent.

basket trades *See* program trades.

B-D form A document required by the SEC to be filed by brokerage houses, broker/dealers, that outlines the firms' finances and officers. It is not readily available to investors, but may be obtained from the SEC or the NASD, both in Washington, D.C.

bear An investor who believes a security or the overall market in one asset class will decline. A bear market is a prolonged period of falling stock or bond prices, usually by 20 percent or more.

bear hug Hostile takeover attempt in which the acquirer offers an exceptionally large premium over the market value of the target's share to squeeze the target into acceptance.

bear market An overall downward trend in securities prices that reflects slower economic activity or investors' anticipation of it. In the post–World War II period, bear markets typically last just under twelve months.

bear raid An attempt by investors to depress the price of a stock by selling large numbers of shares short. The investors pocket the difference between the initial price and the new, lower price after this maneuver. The technique is illegal under SEC rules, which stipulate that every short sale must be made when a stock's price is rising or stable but not falling.

bear trap The predicament facing short sellers when a bear market reverses its trend and becomes bullish. Short sellers then are forced to buy back the shares they have sold short at higher prices.

bearer bond Bonds that are not registered on the books of the issuer. Such bonds are held in physical form by the owner, who receives interest payments by physically detaching coupons from the bond certificate and delivering them to the paying agent. *See also* registered bond.

bearish A way to describe a conservative or gloomy investor attitude.

before-tax contributions The portion of an employee's salary contributed to a retirement plan before federal income taxes are deducted; this reduces the individual's gross income for federal tax purposes.

bell Signal on a stock exchange to indicate the open and close of trading.

bellwether issues Securities that are widely watched by investors or are the most popular among buyers and sellers. *Also known as* benchmark issues. *Opposite of* off-the-run issues, which are more obscure and less popular.

below par Less than the nominal or face value of a security.

benchmark A predetermined set of securities whose performance is used for comparison purposes by professional money managers or individual investors. Such sets may be based on published indexes, such as the S&P 500 Composite Index, or may be customized to suit a particular investment strategy.

benchmark interest rate Also referred to as the base interest rate, it is the minimum interest rate investors will demand for investing in a non-Treasury security.

benchmark issues *See* bellwether issues.

beneficial ownership Person or entity that enjoys the benefits of ownership even though title to the security is in another name.

beneficiary A person who receives the benefits, usually money or other property, of a trust or will or the recipient of the proceeds of a life insurance policy. *Compare to* heir.

bequest Property left to an heir under the terms of a will.

best-efforts sale An arrangement made by investment banks underwriting a company's securities to sell only those securities that it has lined up investors to buy. In more common underwritings, the investment bank agrees to buy the entire issue of securities, taking on the risk that it will not be able to sell it to investors. *Opposite of* purchase and sale

best-efforts test One of two tests that a debtor must meet in order to file for chapter 13 bankruptcy. The debtor must make his or her best effort to repay debts by making structured payments drawing on all disposable income for at least three and up to five years. *See also* best-interest test.

best-interest test One of two tests that a debtor must meet in order to file for chapter 13 bankruptcy. The debtor must pay creditors at least as much as the creditors would have received if he or she had filed chapter 7 bankruptcy. *See also* best-efforts test.

beta The measure of a fund's or stock's movement in relation to the overall market or to an alternative benchmark. A beta of 1.5 means that a stock is expected to return approximately 1.5 times the market's gain. If the market's return is 10 percent, then a stock's expected return would be 15 percent. Conversely, if the market drops 5 percent, a stock with a beta of 1.5 is expected to fall 7.5 percent. Investors who buy high-beta stocks should be prepared for higher-than-typical volatility and should be able to sustain steep declines.

bid/price The price that a potential buyer is willing to pay for a security. Sometimes used in the context of takeovers where one corporation is trying to buy another. In stock trading, the bid-ask spread is the difference between what buyers are willing to pay for shares and what sellers are asking for in terms of price. Such spreads are shown on brokers' computers but also are available for investors trading from home from sources offering Nasdaq level-two trading data.

bid wanted Notice by a potential seller of a security that he or she is looking for a potential buyer of a security. *Opposite of* offer wanted.

BIF *See* Bank Insurance Fund.

Big Board A nickname for the New York Stock Exchange (NYSE), where approximately three thousand common and preferred stocks are traded. Founded in 1792, the NYSE is the oldest exchange in the United States and the largest. It is located at the corner of Broad and Wall Streets in Manhattan. *See* New York Stock Exchange.

binder An amount of money paid to indicate good faith in a transaction before it is completed.

BIS *See* Bank for International Settlements.

Black Friday A reference to September 24, 1869, when the financial markets experienced a precipitous drop. Another Black Friday occurred in October 1929 when the biggest bear market in history began; stocks lost on average 86 percent of their value over a period of two years.

Black Monday A reference to October 19, 1987, when the Dow Jones Industrial Average fell 508 points, losing 25 percent of its value.

Black-Scholes option-pricing model A model for pricing equity options that uses a combination of the stock price, the exercise price of the option, the risk-free interest rate that prevails, the time that the option has to expiration, and the expected volatility of the stock return. Developed by Fischer Black and Myron Scholes in 1973.

blind pool A limited partnership or public company that does not announce its intentions as to what businesses or properties it will acquire. A highly speculative instrument.

blind trust A trust in which a third party has total discretion to make investments on behalf of a beneficiary while the beneficiary is uninformed about the holdings of the trust. When individuals go into public service, they typically put their assets into blind trusts so that they cannot be viewed as benefiting in their portfolio from their positions of power.

block Large quantity of stock or large dollar amount of bonds held or traded. As a rule of thumb, ten thousand shares or more of stock and $200,000 or more worth of bonds would qualify as a block.

blocked currency A currency that is not convertible into another currency owing to exchange controls.

blue list Daily financial publication featuring bonds offered for sale by dealers and banks. www.bluelist.com.

blue-chip company A large and creditworthy company known for the quality and wide acceptance of its products or services, its ability to make money and pay dividends. Blue-chip shares refer to stock in these companies.

board of directors Individuals elected by a company's shareholders who carry out certain tasks established in its charter. Boards are usually composed of a combination of inside and outside directors. The inside directors may include certain key executives, such as the chief executive officer, as well as directors who are considered close to the firm, such as representatives from firms that do a substantial amount of business with the company. Outside directors, on the other hand, have no direct connection with the firm. Members of the board serve on various committees created to rule on significant issues at the company. For example, the audit committee oversees the company's accounting methods and the compensation committee rules on executive pay at the company. Good corporate governance involves having strong, independent outside directors and a chairman of the board who is an outside director.

Board of Governors of the Federal Reserve System The seven-member managing body of the Federal Reserve System, the United States' central bank, which sets policies on bank practices, interest rates, and the supply of money in the financial system. Appointed by the U.S. president and confirmed by the Senate for staggered terms of seven years. *See* Federal Reserve Board.

boardroom A room where meetings of a company's directors take place. Also refers to the room at a brokerage firm office where its clients can watch an electronic board displaying stock prices and trades.

bogey The return an investment manager's portfolio is compared to for performance evaluation; similar to a benchmark. If the bogey is met, the manager is retained. Those who do not meet these hurdles are likely to be replaced.

boiler room A brokerage firm where unscrupulous salespeople try to sell investors speculative, even fraudulent, securities over the telephone.

boilerplate Standard terms and conditions.

bolsa Spanish and Portuguese for stock exchange.

Bombay Stock Exchange India's major securities market. *Also known as* Mumbai Stock Exchange. www. bseindia.com

bond Debt instruments that are issued by companies or countries for a period of more than one year. The U.S. government, local governments, water districts, companies, and many other types of institutions sell bonds. When an investor buys a bond, he or she is lending money to the entity backing the bond. The seller of the bond agrees to repay the principal amount of the loan at a specified time. Interest-bearing bonds pay interest periodically.

bond broker A broker on the floor of an exchange who trades bonds.

Bond Buyer A daily publication featuring many essential statistics and index figures relevant to the fixed-income markets. www.bondbuyer.com

bond covenant A contractual provision in a bond indenture. Such covenants may require certain actions of the company floating the bond and may limit other actions. For example, in a corporate bond, a covenant may state what earnings level the company must make before it can pay out dividends to investors.

bond fund A mutual fund that invests for steady income rather than capital gain by purchasing corporate, municipal, or U.S. government debt obligations or some combination of them.

bond indenture Contract that sets forth the promises of a corporate-bond issuer and the rights of investors buying the bond.

bond market The group of investors, traders, and brokers that buys and sells bonds, including Treasury securities, corporate issues, mortgage-backed securities, and others. *Also known as* debt market.

Bond Market Association Business association that represents the bond industry before governments, regulators, and businesses. Members include securities firms and banks that underwrite debt securities. www.bondmarkets.com

bond rating A rating based on the possibility of default by a bond issuer. Typical ratings range from AAA (highly unlikely to default) to D (in default). The best-known rating agencies are Moody's and Standard & Poor's.

bond value Calculated as the discounted present value of all expected coupons on a bond and the expected final principal. The calculation of expected coupons and principal takes into account the probability of default and expected recovery rates. The bond value would also take into account convertibility options.

bondholder A firm often has both stockholders and bondholders. When a company is liquidated, the bondholders have first call on its assets.

book A trader's security positions.

book cash *See* ledger cash.

book runner The managing underwriter for a new issue. The book runner maintains the book of securities sold.

book value A company's total assets minus intangible assets and liabilities, such as debt. Companies whose shares trade below their book values are considered a bargain and are sought by so-called value investors.

book value per share A company's book value divided by its shares outstanding. Book value per share reflects accounting valuation but not necessarily market valuation.

book-to-bill The book-to-bill ratio is the ratio of orders taken (booked) to products shipped and bills sent (billed). The ratio measures whether the company has more orders than it can deliver. This monthly figure is of major interest to investors in technology stocks who look for any indication of future profits. These figures are found in a company's financial statements.

bottom fisher An investor seeking stocks that have fallen significantly in price.

bottom line A company's net earnings. *See* profit.

bottom-up equity investment style An investment strategy that de-emphasizes the significance of economic and market cycles, focusing instead on the analysis of individual companies and stocks. *Opposite of* top-down equity investment style.

bourse French for stock exchange.

bracket creep The gradual movement into a higher tax bracket when income increases as a result of inflation.

Brady bond Bond issued by an emerging country under a debt-reduction plan that gives certain guarantees to greatly reduce the investment's risk.

breadth The percentage of stocks or other assets advancing relative to those unchanged or declining. When more stocks are rising than falling, the market's breadth is considered strong.

break-even point Refers to the price at which a transaction produces neither a gain nor a loss.

breakout A rise in a security's price above a resistance level, commonly its previous high price. Also a drop below a level of support, commonly the former lowest price. A breakout is taken to signify a security's likelihood to continue moving in the same direction and used by technical analysts as a buy or sell indicator. *See* technical analysis.

breakpoint sale For mutual funds, refers to the investment amount necessary to make the fund holder eligible for a reduced sales charge.

breakup value The value of a company if its various operations or assets are split up and sold. Often calculated by professional investors seeking undervalued stocks.

Bretton Woods agreement An agreement signed by the original United Nations members in 1944 that established the International Monetary Fund and the post–World War II international monetary system of fixed exchange rates.

bridge financing Interim financing used until more permanent financing is arranged.

broad tape An expanded version of the ticker tape, displayed on a screen in the boardroom of a brokerage firm's office, showing constantly updated financial information and news.

broker An individual who is paid a commission for executing customer orders. Either a floor broker, who executes orders on the floor of an exchange, or an upstairs broker, who handles retail customers' orders. Also, a person who acts as an intermediary between a buyer and seller, usually charging a commission. A broker must be registered with the exchange where securities are traded. *Opposite of* dealer.

broker loan rate The interest rate a brokerage firm charges its clients when they borrow money to buy stocks. *Also known as* call-money rate.

brokerage firm A company that conducts various aspects of securities trading, analysis, and advisory services. Such firms employ brokers who buy and sell securities for customers' accounts, and investment bankers who provide advice on acquisitions and restructurings to corporate clients. These firms also trade securities for their own profit. Most are publicly traded companies.

brokered CD A certificate of deposit issued by a bank or thrift institution bought by a brokerage firm in bulk to be resold to brokerage customers. A brokered CD features a higher interest rate than bank CDs.

brought over the wall Compelling a research analyst of an investment bank to work in the underwriting department for a corporate client, therefore allowing for the transmission of private information. Sometimes referred to as bringing someone "over the Chinese Wall." *See* Chinese wall.

B2B An Internet strategy known as business to business in which a company sells its products to other companies rather than to consumers.

bucket shop A fraudulent brokerage firm that accepts customers' orders but does not execute those trades immediately. A bucket-shop broker promises a customer a certain price, but waits until prices move favorably for the brokerage firm before excuting the order. Alternatively, the broker may never fill the customer's order but keep the money until the customer wants to sell the security.

Budapest Stock Exchange Established in 1864, the major securities market of Hungary. www.bse.hu

budget A detailed schedule of financial activity, such as an advertising budget, a sales budget, or a capital budget.

budget deficit The amount by which government spending exceeds government revenues.

budget surplus The amount by which government revenues exceed government spending.

Buenos Aires Stock Exchange (Bolsa de Comercio de Buenos Aires) Argentina's major securities market. Spanish language only. www.bcba.sba.com.ar

bull An investor who thinks the market or a particular stock will rise.

bull market A market characterized by generally rising security prices. Historically, at least in the postwar period, bull markets have lasted longer than bear markets. The longest bull market in history began in late 1990 and lasted until March 2000.

bulldog bond A bond denominated in British pounds by a corporation that is not based in the United Kingdom.

bullion coins Metal coins consisting of gold, silver, platinum, or palladium that are actively traded. American eagle and Canadian maple leaf coins are examples. Their prices are directly connected to the underlying price of their metal.

bullish A characterization of positive investor attitudes on stocks, bonds, or any financial instrument.

bundling Creation of securities either by combining primitive and derivative securities into one composite hybrid or by separating returns on an asset into classes. *See also* unbundling.

burn rate The rate at which a start-up or fledgling company expends capital to finance costs prior to its generation of positive cash flow. Companies that burn through their investors' or lenders' capital before they are able to independently generate cash flow go out of business or are acquired, unless they can raise additional capital.

Bureau of the Mint Office of the U.S. government where paper money is printed and coins minted.

business cycle Repetitive cycle of economic expansion and contraction also referred to as boom and bust. The official peaks and troughs of the U.S. cycle are identified by the National Bureau of Economic Research in Cambridge, Massachusetts. www.nber.org

business risk The risk that the cash flow of an issuer will be impaired because of adverse economic conditions, making it difficult for the issuer to meet its obligations.

business-segment reporting Reporting the results of a company's separate divisions or subsidiaries.

buy in To cover, offset, or close out a short position.

buy on close Buying at the end of a trading session at a price within the closing range.

buy on margin Borrowing to buy additional shares using the shares purchased as collateral.

buy on opening Buying at the beginning of a trading session at a price within the opening range.

buy recommendation A recommendation to buy a stock usually made by a security analyst employed by a major investment bank.

buy them back To cover a short position in a stock or to reverse a sale transaction. *Opposite of* trade me out.

buy-and-hold strategy An investment strategy with little active buying and selling of stocks from the time the portfolio is created until the end of the investment horizon. Investors who adhere to this strategy do so to reduce their trading costs, thereby generating more net income, it is hoped.

buy-and-write strategy An options strategy that involves the purchase of stocks and other assets along with the writing of covered call options on them to create additional income.

buyback The repurchase by a company of its own shares in the open market. Buybacks reduce the number of shares outstanding and therefore make earnings per share rise even if overall income has stayed the same. But buybacks can be considered an inefficient use of share-holder capital, especially when they are made at times when stock prices are high.

buyer's market Market in which supply exceeds demand, creating lower prices. *Opposite of* seller's market.

buying power The amount of money available to buy securities, determined by adding the total cash held in brokerage accounts and the amount that could be spent if securities were borrowed against the limit.

buy-limit order Conditional trading order that indicates that a security may be bought at the designated price or lower. *Opposite of* sell-limit order.

buyout Purchase of controlling interest in a company's stock. A leveraged buyout is conducted with borrowed money.

buy-side analyst A financial analyst employed by a money management firm that purchases securities for its clients. *Opposite of* sell-side analyst.

bylaws Rules and practices that govern management of an organization. These can often be found in a company's financial statements. Changes in company bylaws may be reported on form 8-K filed with the SEC.

C

CAC-40 index A broad-based index of common stocks composed of forty of the hundred largest French companies listed on the forward segment of the Paris Stock Exchange.

cage A section of a brokerage firm used for receiving and disbursing funds.

calendar List of new issues scheduled to come to market shortly.

calendar effect Describes the tendency of stocks to perform differently at different times during a year, including performance anomalies like the January effect (when stocks have higher historical returns), day-of-the-week effect, month-of-the-year effect, and holiday effect.

calendar spread An option strategy in which there is a simultaneous purchase and sale of options of the same class and strike prices, but with different expiration dates.

call date A date before maturity, specified at issuance, when the issuer of a bond may retire part of the bond for a specified call price. If the bond is retired, or called, the yield to an investor who purchased the bond will be less than if the investor received income for the period until maturity. For this reason, investors calculate what a bond's rate of interest would be until its call date, known as its yield to call.

call feature Part of the indenture agreement between the bond issuer and buyer describing the schedule and price of redemptions prior to maturity.

call loan A loan repayable on demand. Sometimes used as a synonym for broker loan.

call option An option contract that gives its holder the right to purchase a specified number of shares of the underlying stock or other asset at the given strike price, on or before the expiration date of the contract. Investors who buy call options generally do so because they believe the price of the underlying stock or asset will rise and their option will increase in value. *Opposite of* put option.

call premium Premium in price above the par value of a bond or share of preferred stock that must be paid to holders to redeem the bond or share of preferred stock before its scheduled maturity date.

call price The price, specified at issuance, at which the issuer of a bond may retire part of the bond at a specified call date. *Also known as* redemption price.

call protection A feature of some callable bonds that establishes an initial period, usually two to three years, when the bonds may not be called.

call provision A provision granting a bond issuer the right to buy back all or part of an issue prior to maturity.

called away In convertible bonds, when they are redeemed before maturity. In options, when a call or put option is exercised against the stockholder or asset holder. In a sale, when delivery is required on a short sale.

call-money rate The interest rate that banks charge brokers to finance margin loans to investors. The broker loan rate is usually calculated by adding a percentage point or more to the prime rate. *Also known as* broker loan rate.

Canadian Venture Exchange An association among the Toronto Stock Exchange, the Montreal Exchange, the Vancouver Stock Exchange, the Alberta Stock Exchange, and the Winnipeg Stock Exchange for the purpose of providing Canadian market data to customers outside Canada. www.cdnx.com

cap An upper limit on the interest rate on a floating-rate note or on an adjustable-rate mortgage. Caps are usually related to an underlying interest rate, say one percentage point over the six-month T-bill rate.

capital Money invested in a firm.

capital appreciation *See* capital growth.

capital asset A long-term asset, such as land or a building, not purchased or sold in the normal course of business.

capital asset pricing model An economic theory that describes the relationship between risk and expected return, and serves as a model for the pricing of risky securities. The model asserts that the only risk that is priced by rational investors is systematic risk, because that risk cannot be eliminated by diversification. The model says that the expected return of a security or a portfolio is equal to the rate on a risk-free security plus a risk premium related to the asset's systematic risk. The model was invented by William Sharpe in 1964 and John Lintner in 1965.

capital budget A company's planned capital expenditures.

capital budgeting The process of choosing a company's long-term capital assets.

capital expenditure Amount used during a particular period to acquire or improve long-term assets such as property, plant, or equipment.

capital flight The movement of capital away from a country in response to fears of economic uncertainty and other risk factors.

capital formation Expansion of capital or capital goods through savings, which leads to economic growth.

capital gain When a stock is sold for a profit, the capital gain is the difference between the net sales price of the securities and their net cost, or original basis price. If a stock is sold below cost, the difference is a capital loss.

capital gains distribution A distribution to the shareholders of a mutual fund of its profits from selling stocks or bonds that is subject to capital gains taxes for the shareholders. Even if a shareholder has not sold shares and realized the gain, he or she must pay the taxes on the gains realized by the fund. This makes mutual funds less tax-efficient than individual stocks, where gains are only taxed when shares are sold.

capital gains tax The tax levied on profits from the sale of capital assets. A long-term capital gain, which is achieved once an asset is held for at least twelve months, is taxed at a maximum rate of 20 percent for taxpayers in the 28 percent tax bracket and 10 percent for taxpayers in the 15 percent tax bracket. Assets held for less than twelve months are taxed at regular income tax levels, which are considerably higher. Since January 1, 2001, assets held for at least five years are taxed at 18 percent and 8 percent, respectively.

capital goods Goods used by firms to produce other goods, e.g., office buildings, machinery, equipment.

capital growth The increase in an asset's market price. *Also called* capital appreciation.

capital loss The difference between the net cost of a security at purchase and the net sales price, if the security is sold at a loss.

capital rationing Placing limits on the amount of new investment undertaken by a firm, either by using a higher cost of capital, or by setting a maximum on the entire capital budget or parts of it.

capital requirement Financing required for the successful operation of a business.

capital stock Stock authorized by a firm's charter. The number and the value of issued shares are usually shown, together with the number of shares authorized, in the capital accounts section of the balance sheet. *Also known as* common stock.

capital structure The makeup of the liabilities and stockholders' equity side of the balance sheet, especially the ratio of debt to equity and the mixture of short and long maturities. A firm's capital structure is extremely important in economic downturns when revenues may fall but obligation to pay off debts remains high.

capital-appreciation fund A mutual fund that invests in companies with anticipated maximum growth rates.

capital-intensive Used to describe industries that require large investments in capital assets to produce their goods, such as the automobile or aerospace industries. These firms require large profit margins and/or low costs of borrowing to survive.

capitalization The debt and/or equity mix that funds a firm's assets.

capitalization ratio This ratio compares a company's debt to total capitalization and reflects the extent to which a corporation is trading on its equity. Capitalization ratios can be interpreted only in the context of the stability of industry and company earnings and cash flow. *Also called* financial leverage ratio.

capitalize The accounting treatment of an asset that is depreciated or amortized, such as a plant or piece of property. Capitalizing assets can affect earnings because the depreciation reduces net profits.

capital-market efficiency The degree to which the present asset price accurately reflects current information in the marketplace.

captive finance company A company, usually a subsidiary that is wholly owned by a parent company, whose main function is financing consumer purchases from the parent.

Caracas Stock Exchange Originally established in 1947, it merged with a competitor in 1974 to become the only securities exchange of Venezuela. www.caracasstock.com/bvc-eng/index.jsp

carry The cost of financing, or carrying, an investment position.

carryforward Tax loss that can be applied to offset future income in some specified number of future years.

carrying value Book value, or the net value at which an asset is carried on a firm's balance sheet.

cartel A group of businesses or nations that act together as a single producer of a good to obtain market control and to influence prices on that item in their favor by limiting its production. The United States has laws prohibiting cartels. The most famous cartel is OPEC, a group of oil-producing nations.

cash The value of assets that can be converted into cash immediately, as reported by a company. Usually includes bank accounts and marketable securities, such as government bonds and banker's acceptances. Cash equivalents on balance sheets include securities that mature within ninety days.

cash account A brokerage account in which an investor pays cash to settle trades rather than borrows to pay for them.

cash basis An accounting method that recognizes revenues and expenses when cash is actually received or paid out.

cash budget A forecasted summary of a firm's expected cash inflows and cash outflows as well as its expected cash and loan balances.

cash cow A company that pays out most of its earnings per share to stockholders as dividends. Or a company or division of a company that generates a steady and significant amount of free cash flow.

cash delivery The provision of some futures contracts that requires delivery not of underlying assets but settlement according to the cash value of the asset.

cash dividend A dividend paid in cash to a company's shareholders. The amount is normally based on profitability and is taxable as income.

cash earnings A firm's cash revenues less cash expenses, which excludes the costs of depreciation.

cash flow In investments, cash flow represents earnings before depreciation and amortization, known as noncash charges. Sometimes called cash earnings. Cash flow from operations (called funds from operations by real estate and other investment trusts) is important because it indicates the ability to fund ongoing operations and pay dividends.

cash flow break-even point The point below which the firm will need either to obtain additional financing or to liquidate some of its assets to meet its fixed costs.

cash flow coverage ratio The number of times that financial obligations such as interest or principal payments, preferred stock dividends, and rental payments are covered by earnings before interest, taxes, rental payments, and depreciation.

cash flow from operations A firm's net cash inflow resulting directly from its regular operations (disregarding extraordinary items such as the sale of fixed assets or transaction costs associated with issuing securities), calculated as the sum of net income plus noncash expenses such as depreciation that are deducted in calculating net income.

cash flow per common share Cash flow from operations minus preferred stock dividends, divided by the number of common shares outstanding.

cash investment Short-term debt instrument—such as commercial paper, banker's acceptances, and Treasury bills—that matures in less than one year. *Also known as* money market instrument.

cash management Refers to the efficient management of cash in a business in order to put the cash to work more quickly and to keep the cash in applications that produce income.

cash market This is a currency or commodity market that involves the immediate delivery of a security or instrument. *Also called* spot market.

cash offer A proposal, either hostile or friendly, to acquire a target company through the payment of cash for the stock of the target. *Compare to* exchange offer (where a company is purchased using stock.)

cash on delivery (COD) The practice of institutional investors paying the full purchase price for securities in cash.

cash position The percentage of a mutual fund's assets invested in short-term securities, such as U.S. Treasury bills or other money market instruments.

cash ratio The proportion of a firm's assets composed of cash.

cash transaction A transaction in which exchange is immediate in the form of cash, unlike a forward contract, which calls for future delivery of an asset at an agreed-upon price.

cash-conversion cycle The length of time between a firm's purchase of inventory and the receipt of cash from customers buying the product.

cash-equivalent item Examples include Treasury bills and banker's acceptances, securities easily converted into cash.

cashier's check A check drawn directly on a customer's account, making the bank the primary obligor, and assuring that the amount will be paid.

cash-management bill Very short-maturity bills that the Treasury occasionally sells because its cash balances are down and it needs money for a few days.

cash-on-cash return A method used to find the return on investments for which there is no active secondary market. The return is determined by dividing the annual cash income by the total investment.

cash-plus convertible Convertible bond that requires cash payment upon conversion.

cash-settlement contract Futures contract such as stock-index futures that settles for cash and does not involve delivery of the underlying stock or other asset.

cash-surrender value The amount an insurance company will pay if the policyholder tenders or cashes in a whole life insurance policy. The value depends upon how long the policyholder has paid into the policy.

casualty insurance Insurance protecting a firm or home owner against loss of property, damage, and other liabilities.

casualty loss A financial loss caused by damage, destruction, or loss of property as a result of an unexpected or unusual event.

catastrophe call Early redemption of a municipal revenue bond because a catastrophe has destroyed the project that provided the revenue source backing the bond.

CATS *See* Certificate of Accrual on Treasury Securities.

caveat emptor Latin expression meaning "buyer beware," which warns that an investor should conduct due diligence on an investment before proceeding.

CBO *See* collateralized bond obligation.

CBOE *See* Chicago Board Options Exchange.

CBOT *See* Chicago Board of Trade.

CD *See* certificate of deposit.

ceiling The highest level of an interest rate on a mortgage, for example, or other numerical factor allowable in a financial transaction.

central bank A country's main bank whose responsibilities include the issue of currency, the administration of monetary policy, engaging in transactions designed to facilitate healthy business interactions and orderly capital markets. The Federal Reserve System is the U.S. central bank.

certainty equivalent return The certain return that carries no risk an investor would trade for a larger return with an associated risk. For example, a particular investor might trade an uncertain 4 percent return with 6 percent risk for a certain return of 1.5 percent.

certificate A formal document used to record ownership, such as stock certificates, that proves ownership of stock in a corporation.

Certificate of Accrual on Treasury Securities (CATS) A U.S. Treasury issue that generates no interest but is sold at a significant discount from its value at maturity. Therefore an investor receives the difference between the discount and the maturity value. The value of the security increases as it gets closer to maturity; those incremental changes in value are taxed as income to the holder. As a result, most discounted Treasuries are held in tax-deferred accounts so that taxes owed on the changes in the securities' values are deferred until the holder is in a lower tax bracket.

certificate of deposit (CD) This is a certificate issued to an investor by a bank or thrift that indicates a specified sum of money has been deposited. A CD has a maturity date and a specified interest rate, and can be issued in any denomination. The duration can be up to five years. The certificate is backed by the bank or thrift up to the limits specified by law. *Also called* time deposit.

certified check A bank-guaranteed check for which funds are immediately withdrawn, and for which the bank is legally liable.

certified financial planner (CFP) A person who has passed examinations accredited by the Certified Financial Planner Board of Standards, showing that the person is able to manage a client's banking, estate, insurance, investment, and tax affairs. www.cfp-board.org

certified financial statement Financial statement that includes an accountant's opinion indicating that it has or has not been prepared in accordance with generally accepted accounting principles.

certified public accountant (CPA) An accountant who has met certain standards of the accounting profession, including experience, age, and licensing, and has passed exams in a particular state.

CFA *See* chartered financial analyst.

CFP *See* certified financial planner.

CFTC *See* Commodity Futures Trading Commission.

chairman of the board The man or woman who is the highest-ranking member of a board of directors, presides over its meetings, and is often the most powerful person in a corporation.

change in financial position Source of funds provided from operations, and uses of those funds, that alters a company's cash flow position. These include depreciation costs, deferred taxes, capital expenditures, and other items.

chapter 11 bankruptcy Named for section 11 of the U.S. bankruptcy code, under which a business is allowed to keep operating as it reorganizes and receives debt relief. The debtor firm is reorganized under court supervision because the estimated value of the reorganized firm exceeds the expected proceeds from its liquidation. If the company continues to do business after filing for chapter 11 bankruptcy, its operations are overseen by a bankruptcy trustee appointed by the court. *Also called* reorganization.

chapter 7 bankruptcy Named for section 7 of the U.S. bankruptcy code, under which a debtor's property, whether a firm or an individual, is sold and the proceeds are split among creditors. For firms, a chapter 7 bankruptcy indicates that the court has decided that reorganization under chapter 11 would fail to establish a profitable business. *Also called* liquidation; straight bankruptcy.

chapter 13 bankruptcy Named for section 13 of the U.S. bankruptcy code, under which a debtor can retain assets while paying off all or part of his or her debts under a structured repayment plan lasting three to five years. Individuals filing for chapter 13 bankruptcy must meet the best-efforts and best-interest tests. *Also called* wage-earner's bankruptcy.

chapter 12 bankruptcy Named for section 12 of the U.S. bankruptcy code, which sets rules for bankruptcy of family farms. The rules are similar to those under chapter 13.

charge off The writing off of a bad debt.

charitable lead trust A trust that pays income to a designated charity for a specified period of years or until the grantor's death, when the remaining income is then passed to beneficiaries, specified by the grantor, who are usually family members. The gifts to the charity through the trust are tax deductible. *Compare to* charitable remainder trust.

charitable remainder trust An irrevocable tax-exempt trust that pays income to a designated person or persons, often the grantor, until the grantor's death, when the remainder is passed on to a designated charity. In addition, the grantor may claim an income tax deduction at the time the trust is established for the future charitable gift. *Compare to* charitable lead trust.

charter The bylaws of a corporation. *Also known as* articles of incorporation.

chartered financial analyst (CFA) An experienced financial analyst who has passed rigorous examinations given by the Association for Investment Management and Research in economics, financial accounting, portfolio management, security analysis, and standards of conduct. www.aimr.org

chartist A technical analyst who charts the movements in stocks, bonds, and commodities to find trends in patterns of trading that can then be used to predict where securities' prices will go.

chasing the market Purchasing a security at a higher price than expected because prices are rapidly climbing, or selling a security at a lower level when prices are quickly falling. This kind of indiscriminate buying or selling is not advised.

chastity bond Bond redeemable at par value in the case of a takeover. Chastity refers to the deleterious effect that would result if a company had to pay more for the bond in an acquisition than it would have in the open market.

chattel mortgage A loan agreement that grants to the lender a lien on property other than real estate. Chattel is personal or movable property.

cheapest-to-deliver issue The Treasury security with the highest rate that a seller of a futures contract can earn by buying an issue and then delivering it at the settlement date.

check A bill of exchange representing a draft on a bank from deposited funds that pays a certain sum of money to a certain person or party.

checking the market Searching for bid and offer prices from market makers to find the best deal.

Chicago Board of Trade (CBOT) The largest futures exchange in the United States. www.cbot.com

Chicago Board Options Exchange (CBOE) A securities exchange created in the early 1970s for the public trading of option contracts. The primary place where stock options, foreign currency options, and index options (S&P 100, S&P 500, and OTC 250 indexes) are traded. www.cboe.com

Chicago Mercantile Exchange (CME) An exchange for trading futures and options that collects and disseminates market information and maintains a clearing mechanism while enforcing trading rules. Futures (such as the S&P 100 and S&P 500) and futures options (such as the S&P 500 stock index) are traded here. www.cme.com

Chicago Stock Exchange (CHX) A major exchange trading only stocks, with 90 percent of transactions taking place on an automated execution system called MAX. www.chicagostockex.com

chief executive officer (CEO) The person who is principally responsible for the activities of a company. Sometimes the CEO is also chairperson of the board.

chief financial officer (CFO) The officer of a firm who is responsible for handling its financial affairs. Chief financial officers are the corporate executives most likely to deal with Wall Street analysts and institutional investors regarding companies' prospects.

chief operating officer (COO) The officer of a firm responsible for day-to-day management, often the president or an executive vice president.

Chinese hedge Applies mainly to convertible securities. A strategy involving shorting a convertible bond and buying a larger number of underlying shares. *Opposite of* setup.

Chinese wall Communication barrier between investment bankers at a firm and its traders or brokers. This barrier is erected to prevent the sharing of inside information about companies that bankers are likely to have.

churning Excessive trading of a client's account in order to increase the broker's commissions. Churning is a violation of U.S. securities laws.

Cincinnati Stock Exchange (CSE) Stock exchange based in Cincinnati that is the only fully automated stock exchange in the United States. It has no trading floor and handles all members' transactions using computers. www.cincinnatistock.com

circle Underwriters of a company's shares or bonds often seek out and "circle" investor interest in a new issue before final pricing. The customer circled has basically made a commitment to purchase the issue if it is available at an agreed-upon price. If the actual price is other than that stipulated, the customer supposedly has first offer at the actual price but does not have to purchase.

circuit breaker Measure instituted by exchanges to stop trading temporarily when the market has fallen by a certain percentage in a specified period. It is intended to prevent a market free fall by permitting buy and sell orders to rebalance during the hiatus.

claimant A party to an explicit or implicit contract.

class Generally refers to a category of assets such as stocks, fixed-income securities, or commodities. But there are also classes within each category. For example, shares of foreign companies are a class of equities. Investors speak of the different asset classes when they are trying to decide how to allocate their holdings for the best possible return.

class A/class B share *See* classified stock.

class-action lawsuit A legal complaint filed by a lawyer or group of lawyers for a group of petitioners with an identical grievance, often with an award proportionate to the number of shareholders involved. Class-action lawsuits, also referred to as strike suits, may be filed after a company's stock price has dropped precipitously.

classified stock The division of stock into more than one class of shares, usually called class A and class B. The specific features of each class, which are set out in the charter and bylaws, usually give certain advantages to the class A shares, such as increased voting power. For instance, one share of class A stock may be equal in voting power to ten shares of class B.

clean opinion An auditor's opinion reflecting an unqualified acceptance of a company's financial statements.

clean price Bond price excluding interest that has accrued since the payment of the last coupon.

clean up In the context of general equities, the purchase or sale of all the remaining supply of stock, or the last piece of a block, which leaves a net zero position.

clear To settle a trade. This can be done by the seller delivering securities to the buyer or the buyer delivering funds in the proper form to the seller. A trade that does not clear is said to fail. The clearing of securities' trades for brokerage firms is often conducted by other firms that specialize in the administration of securities' trading. These firms also provide the capital necessary for smaller brokerages to conduct business.

clear a position To eliminate a long or short position, leaving no ownership or obligation.

clear title Title to ownership that is untainted by any claims on the property or disputed interests, and therefore available for sale. This is usually checked through a title search by a title company.

clearing corporation Organization that is affiliated with exchanges and used to complete securities transactions by taking care of validation, delivery, and settlement. The largest in the United States is the National Securities Clearing Corporation (NSCC). www.nscc.com

clearing member A member firm of a clearinghouse. While each clearing member must also be a member of the exchanges, not all members of the exchange belong to the clearing organization. All trades of a nonclearing member must be registered with and settled through a clearing member.

clearinghouse An adjunct to a futures exchange through which transactions executed on its floor are settled by a process of matching purchases and sales. A clearing organization is also charged with the proper conduct of delivery procedures and the adequate financing of the entire operation.

clearinghouse funds Funds from the Federal Reserve System, requiring three days to clear, that are passed to and from banks.

clone fund A new mutual fund set up within a fund family to emulate a successful fund started by another firm.

close When trading in a security or in a trading session ends. Sometimes used to refer to closing price.

close a position In the context of general equities, eliminate an investment from one's portfolio by either selling a long position or covering a short position.

close market An active market in which there is a narrow spread between bid and offer prices due to a high volume of trading and many competing market makers.

closed corporation A corporation whose shares are owned by just a few people and that has no public market.

closed fund A mutual fund or hedge fund that is no longer issuing shares, mainly because it has grown too large and its managers fear that they will not be able to provide large-enough returns to investors.

closed out Position that is liquidated when the client does not provide additional cash or securities to meet a margin call or when a client cannot cover a short sale.

closed-end fund Mutual fund that sells a set number of shares like any other corporation and usually does not redeem its shares. A publicly traded fund sold on stock exchanges or over the counter that may trade above or below its net asset value depending upon investor interest. *Opposite of* open-end fund.

closed-end mortgage Mortgage against which no additional debt may be issued. *See also* open-end mortgage.

closely held A corporation whose voting stock is owned by only a few shareholders.

closely held company A company that has a small group of controlling shareholders. In contrast, a widely held firm has many shareholders. It is difficult or impossible to wage a proxy battle for closely held firms because the owners are typically a tight-knit group.

closing costs All the expenses involved in transferring ownership of real estate.

closing price Price of the last transaction of a particular stock completed during a day's trading session on an exchange or electronic market. Sometimes also called the closing quote.

closing purchase A transaction in which the purchaser's intention is to reduce or eliminate a short position in a stock, or in a given series of options.

closing range The high and low prices, or bids and offers, for a security that are recorded during the period designated as the official close.

closing sale A transaction in which the seller's intention is to reduce or eliminate a long position in a stock, or a given series of options.

closing tick This data point determines the number of stocks whose closing prices are higher than their previous trades against the number of stocks whose closing prices were lower than their previous trades. *See also* TRIN.

closing transaction Applies to derivative products. Buy-or-sell transaction that eliminates an existing position (selling a long option or buying back a short option). *Opposite of* opening purchase.

closing TRIN *See* TRIN.

cloud on title A claim or encumbrance, usually discovered in a title search, that may impair the title to a property, making its validity questionable and its sale impossible. *Also known as* bad title.

cluster analysis A statistical technique that identifies clusters of stocks whose returns are highly correlated within each cluster and relatively uncorrelated across clusters. Cluster analysis has identified groupings such as growth, cyclical, stable, and energy stocks.

CME   *See* Chicago Mercantile Exchange.

CMO   *See* collateralized mortgage obligation.

coattail investing   A risky trading practice of making trades similar to those of other successful investors, usually institutional investors. This is risky because following other investors usually means buying stocks after they have risen or selling after they have fallen.

COD transaction   A trade in which cash is paid when the security is delivered. *See also* cash on delivery.

code of procedure   The guide of the National Association of Securities Dealers used to adjudicate complaints filed against NASD members.

Coffee, Sugar & Cocoa Exchange (CS&CE)   The New York–based commodity exchange trading futures and options. The CS&CE shares the trading floor at the Commodities Exchange Center with other members of the New York Board of Trade. www.csce.com

cofinancing agreements   Joint participation of the World Bank and other agencies or lenders in providing funds to developing countries.

coincident indicators   Economic indicators that give an indication of the status of the economy. These differ from leading or lagging indicators in that coincident indicators show what is happening currently, not in the past or future.

coinsurance effect   Refers to the fact that the merger of two firms lessens the probability of default on either firm's debt.

cold-calling   A practice in which brokers call potential customers in the hope of selling stocks, bonds, or other financial products and reaping commissions.

collar   An upper and lower limit on the interest rate on a floating-rate note or an adjustable-rate mortgage (ARM). Collars are also used when executives want to lock in a certain price for their shares if they decline but limit their upside potential. Collars are arranged for executives by brokerage firms.

collateral   Asset that backs a loan and that can be repossessed if a borrower defaults.

collateral trust bond   A bond in which the issuer grants investors a lien on stocks, notes, bonds, or other financial assets as security. A mortgage bond is an example.

collateralized bond obligation (CBO)   An investment-grade security consisting of a collection of mainly corporate bonds with different levels of risk, called tiers, that are determined by the quality. CBOs backed by highly risky junk bonds receive higher interest rates than other CBOs.

collateralized mortgage obligation (CMO) A security, backed by a pool of mortgages, structured so that there are several classes of bond-holders with varying maturities called tranches. The principal payments from the underlying pool of pass-through securities are used to retire the bonds on a priority basis as specified in the prospectus. *Also known as* mortgage pass-through security.

collection The presentation of a negotiable instrument for payment, or the conversion of any accounts receivable into cash.

collection float The period between the time a check is deposited in an account and the time the funds are made available to the account holder.

collection policy Procedures a firm follows in attempting to collect its accounts receivable or what its customers owe.

collection ratio The ratio of a company's accounts receivable to its average daily sales, which gives the average number of days it takes the company to convert receivables into cash. Investors watch collection ratios for signs of change. When collection ratios rise, investors may grow concerned that the company is having trouble securing payments from its customers and could be stuck with bad debts.

collective wisdom The combination of all the individual opinions about a stock's or security's value.

Colombo Stock Exchange Established in 1984, the only public stock exchange of Sri Lanka. www.cse.lk

COLT (continuous on-line trading system) Computerized over-the-counter (OTC) traders assistance system that provides for trade entry and position monitoring, among other functions.

comanager A bank that ranks just below a lead investment banking firm in a security offering. Comanagers may assist the lead manager bank in the pricing and issue of the security.

combination A strategy using options involving two long or two short positions with different expiration dates or exercise prices. *Also known as* straddle.

combination bond A bond backed by the government unit issuing it as well as by revenue from the project that is to be financed by the bond. These two elements make the bond safer.

come in, get hit When one investor's price to buy or sell a security is accepted by another and the trade is executed. *Opposite of* on the take.

COMEX A division of the New York Mercantile Exchange (NYMEX). Formerly known as the Commodity Exchange, COMEX is the leading U.S. market for metals futures and options trading. www.comex.com

comfort letter A letter from an independent auditor in securities underwriting agreements to assure that information in the registration statement and prospectus delivered to prospective investors is correctly prepared to the best of the auditor's knowledge.

commercial draft Demand for payment.

commercial hedger Company that takes futures position in commodities so that it can guarantee prices at which it will buy raw materials or sell its products. Gold producers hedge their production in this way.

commercial letters of credit Trade-related agreement that a certain amount of bank funds is available to an entity.

commercial loan A short-term loan, typically ninety days, used by a company to finance seasonal working-capital needs.

commercial mortgage-backed securities Similar to other mortgage-backed securities but backed by loans secured with commercial rather than residential property. Commercial property includes multifamily dwellings, shopping malls, office buildings, etc. They are not standardized so there are many details associated with structure, credit enhancement, and diversification that need to be understood when valuing these instruments.

commercial paper Short-term unsecured promissory notes issued by a corporation. The maturity of commercial paper is typically less than nine months; the most common maturity range is thirty to fifty days or less.

commercial property Real estate that produces an income.

commercial risk The risk that a debtor will be unable to pay his or her debts because of business events, such as bankruptcy.

commingling In the context of securities, this involves mixing customer-owned securities with brokerage firm–owned securities. This process is referred to as rehypothecation, which is the use of customers' collateral to secure their loans. This is legal only with customer consent, although some securities and collateral must be kept separately.

commission The fee paid to a broker to execute a trade, based on number of shares, bonds, options, and/or their dollar value. In 1975, deregulation led to the establishment of discount brokers, which charge lower commissions than full-service brokers. Full-service brokers offer advice and usually have a staff of analysts who follow specific industries. Discount brokers simply execute a client's order and usually do not offer an opinion on a stock.

commission broker A broker on the floor of an exchange who acts as agent for a particular brokerage house and buys and sells stocks for the brokerage house on a commission basis.

commission-only compensation Payment to a financial adviser of only commissions on investments purchased when the client implements the recommended financial plan. Differs from fee-only compensation, in which an adviser earns a flat fee based on the amount of assets under management.

commitment A trader's obligation to accept or make delivery on a futures contract.

commitment fee A fee paid to a commercial bank in return for its legal commitment to lend funds that have not yet been advanced. Often used in risk arbitrage. In the United Kingdom, refers to payments to institutional investors, pension funds, and life insurance companies by the lead underwriter of a takeover that takes place when the underwriter provides the target company's shareholders with a cash alternative for a target company's shares in exchange for the bidding company's shares. The payment is typically 0.5 percent for the first thirty days, 1.25 percent for each week thereafter, and a final 0.75 percent acceptance payment when the takeover is completed.

Committee on Uniform Securities Identification Procedures (CUSIP) Committee that assigns identifying numbers and codes for all securities. These "CUSIP" numbers and symbols are used when recording all buy or sell orders.

Commodities Exchange Center (CEC) The location of five New York futures and commodities exchanges: Commodity Exchange, Inc. (COMEX); the New York Mercantile Exchange (NYMEX); New York Cotton Exchange; Coffee, Sugar & Cocoa Exchange (CS&CE); and New York Futures Exchange (NYFE). The exchanges share a trading floor.

commodity A commodity is a food, metal, or another physical substance that investors buy or sell, usually via futures contracts.

commodity bundle One unit of collection of the complete set of goods produced and sold in the world market.

commodity futures contract An agreement to buy a specific amount of a commodity at a specified price on a particular date in the future, allowing a producer to guarantee the price of a product or raw material used in production.

Commodity Futures Trading Commission (CFTC) An agency created by the U.S. Congress in 1974 to regulate exchange trading in futures. Investors with complaints about their commodities accounts take them to this organization. www.cftc.gov

commodity indices Indices measuring the price and performance of physical commodities, often by the price of futures contracts for the commodities that are listed on commodity exchanges.

commodity paper A loan or advance secured by commodities.

commodity-backed bond A bond with interest payments tied to the price of an underlying commodity.

common factor An element that influences many assets. According to multiple-factor risk models, the common factors determine correlations between asset returns. Common factors include size of the company (often measured by market capitalization), valuation measures (such as price to book value ratio), and dividend yield.

common market An agreement between two or more countries that permits the free movement of capital and labor as well as goods and services.

common property Assets held by two or more people or organizations under an agreement of co-ownership such as joint tenancy or community property.

common shares In general, a public corporation has two types of shares, common and preferred. The common shares usually entitle the shareholders to vote at shareholder meetings. Common shares have a discretionary dividend, while preferreds have an obligatory dividend.

common stock Securities that represent equity ownership in a company. Common stocks let an investor vote on such matters as the election of directors. They also give the holder a share in a company's profits via dividend payments or the capital appreciation of the security. Common stockholders have junior status to the claims of secured/unsecured creditors, bondholders, and preferred shareholders in the event of a company's liquidation.

common-size analysis The representing of balance-sheet items as percentages of assets and of income-statement items as percentages of sales. This allows investors to compare companies of different sizes.

common-size statement A statement in which all items are expressed as a percentage of a base figure, useful for purposes of analyzing trends and changing relationships among financial-statement items. For example, all items in each year's income statement could be presented as a percentage of net sales.

common-stock fund A mutual fund investing only in common stock.

common-stock market The market for trading equities, not including preferred stock.

community property Under the laws of some states, assets that are acquired by legal spouses during marriage, giving each a one-half interest in the property. In estates, only one-half of community property can be granted by each spouse in a will.

companion bonds A class of a collateralized mortgage obligation (CMO) whose principal is paid off first when the underlying mortgages are prepaid due to falling interest rates. When interest rates rise, there will be lower prepayments of the principal; companion bonds therefore absorb most of the prepayment risk of a CMO.

company A proprietorship, partnership, corporation, or other form of enterprise that engages in business.

company doctor An executive brought in to turn a troubled company around and make it profitable.

company-specific risk The risk associated with an investment in a particular company that is not associated with broad factors such as interest rates or the performance of the economy.

comparative statements Financial statements from different periods that allow the comparison of figures to illustrate trends in a company's performance.

comparison universe A group of money managers employing a similar investment style that is used to assess relative performance of a portfolio manager.

compensatory financing facility Entity that attempts to reduce the impact of import costs and export instability on a country's economy.

competition Rivalry between or among businesses trying to obtain a larger piece of the same market share.

competitive bidding A process that takes place prior to a securities offering in which different investment firms submit competing bids to the company issuing the securities for the right to sell them to investors.

competitive offering An offering of securities through c [...] ding.

complete To fill an order.

completion risk The risk that a project will not be brought into ope[...] tion or completed successfully.

compliance department A department in all organized stock exchanges and brokerage firms that ensures that all companies, traders, members, and employees comply with securities laws and regulations.

composite tape *See* tape; consolidated tape.

compound annual return *See* annual percentage yield.

compound growth rate The rate of growth of a figure, compounded over some period of time. Returns in an investment are typically figured using compound growth rates.

compound interest Interest paid on previously earned interest as well as on the principal.

compounding The process of accumulating the value of money forward in time. For example, interest earned in one period earns additional interest during each subsequent time period. *Opposite of* discounting.

compounding frequency The number of compounding periods in a year. For example, quarterly compounding has a compounding frequency of four times in one year.

compounding period The length of the time period that elapses before interest compounds, such as a quarter in the case of quarterly compounding.

comprehensive due-diligence investigation The investigation of a firm's business in conjunction with a securities offering to determine whether the firm's business and financial situation and its prospects are adequately disclosed in the offering's prospectus.

comptroller The corporate manager responsible for the firm's accounting activities. Sometimes spelled "controller."

comptroller of the currency A government official, appointed by the president, who oversees all national banks and receives and publishes reports from the banks at least quarterly. This department also supervises federal branches and agencies of foreign banks. The office of the comptroller is headquartered in Washington, D.C., and has six district offices as well as a London office to oversee international activities of national banks. The comptroller also serves as a director of the Federal

Deposit Insurance Corporation (FDIC). The office was established in 1863. www.occ.treas.gov.

computerized market-timing system A computer trading system that compiles large amounts of data on securities in search of patterns and trends in price action that may indicate when to buy or sell.

concession The per-share or per-bond compensation paid to members of a selling group for participating in a corporate underwriting.

concession agreement An understanding between a company and the host government that specifies the rules under which the company can operate locally.

conditional call Applies mainly to convertible securities. Circumstances under which a company can retire some of its securities early, usually stated as percentage of a stock's trading price during a particular period, such as 140 percent of the exercise price during a forty-day trading span.

conditional call option A protective guarantee that in the event a high-yield bond is retired or called, the issuing corporation will replace the bond with a noncallable bond of the same life and terms as the bond that is being called.

conduit IRA *See* roll-over IRA.

conduit theory The theory that because investment companies are merely conduits for capital gains, dividends, and interest, which are in fact passed along to shareholders, the investment company should not be taxed as a corporation.

confidence indicator A measure of investors' faith in the economy and the securities market. A low or deteriorating level of confidence is considered by many analysts as a negative or bearish sign.

confidence letter Statement by an investment bank that it is confident that the financing for an acquirer's takeover can and will be obtained. Often used in risk arbitrage.

confidence level In risk analysis, the degree of assurance that a specified failure rate is not exceeded.

confirmation The written statement sent to an investor that follows any "trade" in the securities markets. Confirmation is issued immediately after a trade is executed. It spells out the security bought or sold, settlement date, terms, and commissions.

conflict between bondholders and stockholders Bondholders and stockholders may have interests in a corporation that conflict, largely because stockholders want a company to manage itself for growth while bondholders are more conservative and want executives to generate enough cash flow to cover debt costs. Sources of conflict include dividends, which may drain corporate coffers. Protective covenants in bonds work to resolve these conflicts.

conforming loan Mortgage loan that meets the qualifications of Freddie Mac or Fannie Mae and is bought from a lender and issued as a pass-through security.

conglomerate A firm engaged in two or more unrelated businesses.

conglomerate merger A merger involving two or more firms that are in unrelated businesses.

consensus forecast The mean (average) of all financial analysts' forecasts for a company.

consignment Transfer of goods to a seller while title to the merchandise is retained by the owner.

consolidated financial statement A financial statement that shows all the assets, liabilities, and operating accounts such as the income statement of a parent company and its subsidiaries.

consolidated mortgage bond A bond that covers several units of property, sometimes refinancing mortgages on the properties.

consolidated tape Combined ticker tapes registering trades performed on the NYSE and the AMEX. Network A covers the NYSE-listed securities and is used to identify the originating market. Network B does the same for AMEX-listed securities and also reports on securities listed on regional stock exchanges. *Also known as* tape; ticker tape.

consolidated tax return A tax return combining the reports of affiliated companies that are at least 80 percent owned by a parent company.

consolidation The combining of two or more firms to form an entirely new entity.

consolidation loan A loan that is used to combine and finance payments on other loans.

consortium A group of companies or entities that cooperate and share resources in order to achieve a common objective.

consortium banks A merchant banking subsidiary set up by several banks that may or may not be of the same nationality. Consortium banks are common in the Euromarket and are active in loan syndication.

constant dollars Dollars of a base year used as a general measure of purchasing power. Sometimes called real dollars. *Opposite of* nominal dollars.

constant-dollar plan Method of purchasing securities by investing a fixed amount of money at set intervals. The investor buys more shares when the price is low and fewer shares when the price is high, thus reducing the overall cost. *Also known as* dollar-cost averaging.

constant-ratio plan An investment strategy that maintains a predetermined ratio between stock and fixed-income investments through regular adjustments of distribution of funds into different investments. *Also known as* formula investing.

construction loan A short-term loan to finance building costs.

constructive receipt The date a taxpayer receives dividends or other income, for use in determining taxes.

consumer confidence A gauge of consumer optimism that is used by investors as an indicator of future business and stock market trends. There are two popular measures: that of the Conference Board, which surveys five thousand households, and the University of Michigan's index. Both indices are published monthly.

consumer credit Credit a firm grants to consumers for the purchase of goods or services. *Also called* retail credit.

Consumer Credit Counseling Services Nonprofit state-by-state organizations created by large institutional creditors, such as credit card companies, that help individuals and families set up debt repayment plans.

Consumer Credit Protection Act of 1968 Federal legislation establishing rules for the disclosure of the terms of a loan to protect borrowers. *Also known as* truth-in-lending act.

consumer durable Consumer product that is expected to last three years or more, such as an automobile or a home appliance. Also referred to as consumer cyclical because it is usually bought during an economic boom period rather than during a downturn. Therefore, sale of these goods is dependent upon the economic cycle.

consumer finance company A bank subsidiary or corporation that lends money to consumers for purchase of goods.

consumer interest Interest paid on consumer loans, such as interest on credit cards and retail purchases.

consumer price index (CPI) The CPI measures the prices of consumer goods and services and is a measure of the pace of U.S. inflation. The Department of Labor publishes the CPI every month. www.dol.gov

consumer staples Goods not used in production but bought for personal or household use, such as food, clothing, cosmetics, and entertainment products.

consumption tax Also referred to as value-added tax, this levy is added to all purchases made by consumers, except for food. Some value-added taxes are focused on luxury items, such as boats and furs.

contagion When the returns of different types of securities or different markets are unusually similar or correlative. For example, under usual conditions a certain level of correlation of market returns is typical. But a period of contagion would be associated with much higher-than-expected correlation. An example was the conjectured contagion in East Asian markets that began in July 1997 when the value of the Thai currency plummeted, followed by the economic collapse of other emerging markets, and culminating in Russian default on its short-term debt. Contagion is difficult to identify because correlations are known to change through time, and during periods of negative returns correlations are known to increase. As a result, what might appear to be excessive similarities may not be contagion.

contingent claim A claim that can be made only if one or more specified outcomes occur.

contingent deferred sales charge The formal name for a fee levied on holders of a mutual fund when they sell their shares.

contingent pension liability Under the Employee Retirement Income Security Act, a firm is liable to its pension plan participants for up to 39 percent of the net worth of the firm.

contingent voting power Enables preferred stockholders to vote when the company fails to satisfy the agreement between itself and the preferred stockholders.

continuous compounding The process of accumulating the time value of money forward in time on a continuous, or instantaneous, basis. Interest is earned constantly, and at each instant the interest that accrues immediately begins earning interest as well.

continuous net settlement Method of securities' clearing and settlement using a clearinghouse that matches transactions to securities available, resulting in one receive or deliver position at the end of the day.

contra broker The broker on the buy side of a sell order or on the sell side of a buy order.

contract A term describing a unit of trading for a financial or commodity future. Also, the actual bilateral agreement between the buyer and seller of a transaction as defined by an exchange.

contract month The month in which futures contracts may be satisfied by making or accepting a delivery of the underlying asset.

contractual claim An amount that by legal agreement must be paid periodically to the buyer of a security; contractual claim may also specify the time at which the principal must be repaid and other details.

contractual plan A plan in which fixed dollar amounts of mutual-fund shares are purchased through periodic investments, usually featuring some sort of additional incentive for the fixed-period payments.

contramarket stock In the context of general equities, stock that tends to go against the trend of the market as a whole, such as a commodities-related stock or one in an industry out of favor with investors in a bull market. Such a stock allows investors with large exposure to the overall market to hedge their bets.

contrarian An investment style that leads one to buy assets that have performed poorly and sell assets that have performed well. There are two possible reasons this strategy might work. The first is the belief that if an asset has deviated from its usual level, it should eventually return to that level. The second reason has to do with overreaction: investors might have overreacted to bad news, sending the asset price lower than it should be.

contrarian investing Ignoring market trends by buying securities that the investor considers undervalued and out of favor with other investors.

contribution Money placed in an individual retirement account (IRA), an employer-sponsored retirement plan, or other retirement plan for a particular tax year. Contributions may be deductible or nondeductible, depending on the type of account.

control In corporations, control is achieved with 50 percent of the outstanding votes plus one vote.

control person Anyone with the potential to exert pressure or influence on a company's operations. A control person might sit on a company's board or run one of its significant operations. Under securities laws, control persons must disclose changes in their holdings of company stock. *Also known as* affiliated person.

control stock The shares owned by the controlling shareholders of a corporation.

controlled commodity Commodity regulated by the Commodities Exchange Act of 1936 in order to prevent fraud and manipulation in commodities futures markets.

controlled foreign corporation A foreign corporation whose voting stock is more than 50 percent owned by U.S. stockholders.

controller *See* comptroller.

convention statement An annual statement filed by a life insurance company in each state where it does business. The statement and supporting documents show, among other things, the assets, liabilities, and surplus of the reporting company.

conventional mortgage A loan based on the credit of the borrower and on the collateral for the mortgage.

conventional option An option contract arranged off the trading floor and not traded regularly.

conventional pass-through Any mortgage pass-through security that is not guaranteed by a government agency such as Freddie Mac or Fannie Mae. *Also called* private-label pass-through.

conventional project A project with a negative initial cash flow that is expected to be followed by one or more positive cash flows.

convergence The movement of the price of a futures contract toward the price of the underlying cash commodity. The futures price is equal to the spot price plus the cost of carry. The cost of carry is usually positive and includes items like the storage cost plus the cost of the money tied up. At the start, the futures price is higher, but as the contract nears expiration, and time value decreases, the futures price and the cash price converge.

conversion In the context of securities, refers to the exchange of a convertible security such as a bond into stock. In the context of mutual funds, refers to the free exchange of mutual fund shares from one fund to another in a fund family.

conversion feature Specification of the right to transform a particular investment to another form of investment, such as switching between mutual funds or converting preferred stock or bonds to common stock.

conversion parity The price at which a convertible bond or convertible preferred stock equals the market value of the stock it can be converted into. *Also known as* market conversion price.

conversion parity/value Applies mainly to convertible securities. Common-stock price at which a convertible bond can become exchangeable for shares of equal value; value of a convertible bond based solely on the market value of the underlying equity. Par value plus conversion ratio. *See also* bond value; parity.

conversion period The time period during which an investor can exchange a convertible security for common stock.

conversion premium The extent by which the conversion price of a convertible security exceeds the prevailing common-stock price at the time the convertible security is issued.

conversion price Dollar value at which convertible bonds, debentures, or preferred stock can be converted into common stock, as specified when the convertible is issued.

conversion ratio The relationship that determines how many shares of common stock will be received in exchange for each convertible bond or preferred stock when conversion takes place. Determined at the time of issue, it is expressed either as a ratio or as a conversion price from which the ratio can be figured by dividing the par value of the convertible by the conversion price.

conversion value The value of a convertible security if it is converted immediately. *Also called* parity.

convertibility The ability to exchange a currency without government restrictions or controls.

convertible adjustable preferred stock The interest rate on such shares is adjustable and is usually pegged to Treasury rates. They can be exchanged at par value for common stock or cash after the next period's dividend rates are revealed.

convertible arbitrage A practice, usually of buying a convertible bond and shorting a percentage of the equivalent underlying common shares, to create a positive return above the riskless rate. The strategy shoots for capital appreciation if the convertible's premium rises. This form of investing is far from riskless and requires constant monitoring.

convertible bond General debt obligation of a corporation that can be exchanged for a set number of common shares of the issuing corporation at a prestated conversion price. Convertible bonds carry lower interest rates than conventional bonds because they have a greater potential for capital appreciation than conventional bonds.

convertible exchangeable preferred stock Convertible preferred stock that may be exchanged, at the issuer's option, into convertible bonds that have the same conversion features as the convertible preferred stock.

convertible preferred stock Preferred stock that can be converted into common stock at the option of the holder.

convertible price The contractually specified price per share at which a convertible security can be converted into shares of common stock.

cook the books To deliberately falsify the financial statements of a company. An illegal practice under U.S. securities laws.

cooling-off period The period of time between the filing of a preliminary prospectus with the Securities and Exchange Commission and the actual public offering of the securities. This period gives investors the time they need to evaluate an offering.

cooperative An organization owned by its members. Examples are agriculture cooperatives that assist farmers in selling their products more efficiently, and apartment buildings owned by the residents, who have full control of the property.

core capital The capital required of a savings and loan institution, which must be at least 2 percent of assets to meet the rules of the Federal Home Loan Bank.

core competence Primary area of expertise. Narrowly defined fields or tasks at which a company or business or manager excels.

cornering the market Purchasing a security or commodity in such volume as to achieve control over its price. An illegal practice under U.S. securities laws.

corporate bond Debt obligation issued by a corporation.

corporate charter A legal document creating a corporation.

corporate finance One of the three areas of the discipline of finance, dealing with the operation of a firm including both the investment decisions made by management and the financing decisions.

corporate financial management The application of financial principles within a corporation to create and maintain value through decision-making and proper resource management.

corporate financial planning Financial planning conducted by a firm that encompasses preparation of both long- and short-term financial plans.

corporate financing committee A committee of the National Association of Securities Dealers that reviews underwriters' SEC-required documents to ensure that proposed markups charged to customers in the offerings are fair and in the public interest.

corporate repurchase Active buying by a corporation of its own stock in the marketplace. Reasons for repurchase include putting idle cash to use, returning cash to shareholders, raising earnings per share because the number of shares outstanding declines, creating support for a stock price that might be perceived as undervalued, or increasing internal control that would help repel a takeover. Repurchase is subject to rules, such as that buying must be on a zero minus or a minus tick, after the opening and before 3:30 P.M. Buybacks are generally viewed positively by investors but are sometimes frowned upon if a company uses borrowed funds to buy the shares.

corporate tax view The argument that double levying taxation of equity returns (corporate and individual taxes) makes debt a cheaper financing method.

corporate-income fund A unit investment trust featuring a fixed portfolio of high-grade corporate securities, usually with monthly distribution of income.

corporation A legal entity that is separate and distinct from its owners. A corporation is allowed to own assets, incur liabilities, and sell securities, among other things.

corpus *See* principal.

correction Downward movement in the price of an individual stock, bond, commodity, or index. If prices have been rising on the market as a whole and then fall dramatically, it is known as a correction within an upward trend. *Opposite of* rally. *Also known as* dip.

correlation Statistical measure of the degree to which the movements of two variables such as stock and bond returns are related. *See also* correlation coefficient.

correlation coefficient A standardized statistical measure of the dependence of two random variables, defined as the covariance divided by the product of the standard deviations of two variables.

correspondent A financial organization that acts as an intermediary in a market for another organization that does not have access to that market.

cost accounting A branch of accounting that provides information to help the management of a firm evaluate production costs and efficiency.

cost basis The original price of an asset, used to determine capital gains or losses generated in an investment.

cost company arrangement Arrangement whereby the shareholders of a project receive output free of charge but agree to pay all operating and financing charges of the project.

cost of capital Usually the weighted average of the cost of equity and debt capital. It is used to discount cash flows of capital budgeting projects to determine whether the value of the future cash flows exceeds the costs. *Also known as* required rate of return.

cost of carry Out-of-pocket costs incurred while an investor has an investment position. Examples include interest paid to hold long positions in a margin account, dividend lost on short positions, and incidental expenses. *Also known as* net financing cost.

cost of equity The required rate of return or cost of capital for an investment of 100 percent equity.

cost of funds Interest rate associated with borrowing money.

cost of goods sold The total cost of buying raw materials and paying for all the factors that go into producing finished goods.

cost/benefit ratio The net present value of an investment divided by the investment's initial cost. *Also called* profitability index.

cost-plus contract A contract in which the selling price is based on the total cost of production plus a fixed amount.

cost-push inflation Inflation caused by rising prices, usually from increased raw material or labor costs that push up the costs of production. Different from demand-pull inflation, in which costs rise because of increased demand.

cost-recovery period The number of years it takes to fully depreciate a capital asset. This time period is based on classification of the depreciable life of an asset. For instance, computers are written off over five years.

Council of Economic Advisers A group of economists appointed by the president of the United States to provide economic counsel and help prepare the president's budget presentation to Congress.

countercyclical stock Stock whose price tends to rise when the economy is in recession or the market is bearish, and fall during expansions.

counterparty Party on the other side of a trade or transaction.

counterparty risk The risk that the other party to an agreement will default. In an options contract, the risk to the option buyer that the option writer will not buy or sell the underlying asset as agreed. *Also known as* settlement risk.

counterpurchase Exchange of goods between two parties under two distinct contracts expressed in monetary terms.

countertrade The exchange of goods for other goods rather than for cash. *Also called* barter.

country allocation The percentage of a fund's net assets invested in securities of various countries. The percentage serves as an indicator of a fund's diversification and its vulnerability to fluctuations in foreign financial markets or currency exchange rates.

country economic risk Developments in a national economy that can affect the outcome of an international financial transaction.

country risk General level of political, financial, and economic uncertainty in a country that may affect the value of loans to or investments in that country.

country selection A type of active international management that measures the contribution to performance attributable to investing in the better-performing stock markets of the world.

coupon The periodic interest payment made to the bondholders during the life of the bond.

coupon bond A bond featuring coupons that must be presented to the issuer in order to receive interest payments.

coupon payment A bond's interest payment.

coupon rate In bonds, notes, or other fixed-income securities, the stated percentage rate of interest, usually paid twice a year.

coupon-equivalent yield True interest cost expressed on the basis of a 365-day year.

covariance A statistical measure of the degree to which random variables move together. A positive covariance implies that one variable is, on average, above its mean value when the other variable is above its mean value, and vice versa.

covenant Provision in a bond indenture or preferred-stock agreement that requires the bond or preferred-stock issuer to take a certain specified action (*see* affirmative covenant) or to refrain from taking a certain specified action (*see* negative covenant).

cover The purchase of a contract or security to offset a previously established short position.

coverage initiated When analysts at a brokerage firm begin following a particular security, they initiate coverage of it. This usually happens when there is enough trading in it to warrant attention by the investment community or after a company has issued public shares for the first time.

coverage ratio Ratio used to test the adequacy of cash flows generated through earnings for the purpose of meeting debt and lease obligations, including the interest coverage ratio, which addresses a company's interest expenses, and the fixed-charge coverage ratio, which relates to the ability to meet fixed costs.

covered call A position in which an investor who owns a number of shares of a stock sells a call option for shares owned to generate additional income from the stockholding. If the stock appreciates in value, then the investor, known as the writer of the covered call, loses upside gains; that is, the writer has let someone else buy a now-valuable stock at a low price. If the stock falls in value, the writer pockets the premium paid to purchase the call, softening the blow of the stock's lost value. The opposite of a covered call is a naked call. Note that with a naked call, the investor does not own the underlying security, making it a very risky strategy. If the stock rises in value, the writer of the call may be forced to go into the market and purchase the underlying security at a greatly inflated price in order to make good on a naked call. The covered call is not risky in this sense, because the investor already owns the stock.

covered foreign currency loan A loan denominated in a currency other than that of the borrower's home country, for which repayment terms are prearranged through the use of a forward currency contract.

covered interest arbitrage Occurs when a portfolio manager invests dollars in an instrument denominated in a foreign currency and hedges the resulting foreign exchange risk by selling the proceeds of the investment in a forward currency contract denominated in dollars. For example, suppose the U.S. ninety-day Treasury bill rate is 2 percent and the U.K. ninety-day Treasury rate is 4 percent. If you purchased the U.K. bill and at the same time hedged the currency component by selling forward the U.K. pounds you will receive in ninety days, the rate of return will be 2 percent—the same as keeping your investment in the United States.

covered option   Option position that is offset by an equal and opposite position in the underlying security. *Opposite of* naked option.

covered- or hedge-option strategy   Strategy that involves a position in an option as well as a position in the underlying stock or other asset, designed so that one position will help offset any unfavorable price movement in the other. Such strategies include covered call writing and protective put buying. *Opposite of* naked-option strategy.

covered position   Selling an option in a trading strategy when the underlying stock or other asset is already owned.

covered put   A written put-option position in which the option seller is also short the underlying stock or has deposited, in a cash account, funds or assets equal to the cost of exercising the option. This limits the option seller's risk because money or stock that may have to be delivered under the terms of the option is already set aside. If the buyer of the put option decides to exercise the option, the writer's risk is more limited than it would be if no cash or assets were set aside to pay for the transaction. If no such funds are set aside, the option is considered "naked" or "uncovered."

covered writer   An investor who writes options only on stock that he or she owns.

covering   Using forward currency contracts to predetermine the amount in domestic currency of an expected future foreign receipt or payment.

CPA   *See* certified public accountant.

CPI   *See* consumer price index.

cramdown   The ability of the bankruptcy court to confirm a plan of reorganization over the objections of some classes of creditors.

cram-down deal   A merger in which stockholders are forced to accept undesirable terms, such as junk bonds instead of cash or equity, due to the absence of any better alternatives.

crash   Significant loss in market value. The last great crash was in 1929. Some refer to October 1987 as a crash but the market return for the entire year was positive.

crawling peg   An automatic system for revising the exchange rate of a country. It involves establishing a par value around which the rate can vary up to a given percent. The par value is revised regularly according to a formula determined by monetary authorities.

credit Money loaned.

credit analysis Evaluating information on companies and bond issues in order to estimate the ability of the issuer to live up to its future contractual obligations. This analysis tries to determine a company's default risk and determine expected recovery in the event of the default.

credit balance The surplus in a cash account held at a brokerage after purchases have been paid for.

credit bureau An agency that researches the credit history of consumers so that creditors can make decisions about granting of loans.

credit enhancement Purchase of the financial guarantee of a large insurance company in order to reduce the risk of the stock or portfolio with the goal of increasing the chance of raising funds.

credit insurance Insurance against abnormal losses due to unpaid accounts receivable.

credit period The length of time for which a firm's customer is granted credit.

credit quality A measure of a bond issuer's ability to repay interest and principal in a timely manner. Bonds issued by corporations fall into either investment-grade quality, a higher ranking, or junk or high-yield grade. The lower the credit quality, the higher the interest rate investors will demand.

credit rating An evaluation of an individual's or company's ability to repay obligations or its likelihood of not defaulting. *See also* credit-worthiness.

credit risk The risk that an issuer of debt securities or a borrower may default on its obligations, or that the payment may not be made on a negotiable instrument. *See also* default risk.

credit scoring A statistical technique that combines several financial characteristics to form a single score representing a customer's credit-worthiness.

credit spread Difference between the yield on two different securities such as a government note maturing in ten years and a corporate bond with the same maturity. Credit spreads fluctuate as investors react to risks in stocks and bonds. Spreads are typically quoted off government securities. For example, if a corporate bond has a yield of 7 percent while the equivalent Treasury is yielding 5 percent, the corporate bond is trading at "two hundred over," meaning two hundred basis points, or 2 percentage points, over the Treasury yield. In the context of derivative products, a position in which the price of the option sold exceeds the price of the one bought.

credit standards The guidelines a company follows to determine whether a credit applicant is creditworthy.

credit terms The conditions under which credit will be extended to a customer. The components of credit terms are: cash discount, credit period, and net period.

credit union A not-for-profit institution that is operated as a cooperative and offers financial services, such as low-interest loans, to its members. Federal credit unions provide insurance up to $100,000 to members on their accounts. Recently there were more than six thousand federal credit unions serving 44 million people. www.nafcunet.org

credit watch A warning by a bond-rating firm indicating that a company's credit rating may change after the current review is concluded.

crediting rate The interest rate offered on an investment-type insurance policy.

creditor Lender of money.

creditor's committee A group representing firms that have claims on a company facing bankruptcy or extreme financial difficulty. These people get together to make sure their positions in a company are represented.

credit-policy delay The period between the sale of goods for a credit and the payment for those goods. This lag is determined largely by the selling firm's credit policy.

credit-rating agency Company that compiles information on and issues public credit ratings for a large number of firms to help investors assess the firms' financial conditions. Moody's Investors Service, Standard & Poor's, and Fitch are three of the top rating agencies.

creditworthiness Eligibility of an individual or firm to borrow money.

creeping-tender offer The process by which a group attempting to circumvent certain provisions of the Williams Act gradually acquires shares of a target company in the open market.

cross Securities transaction in which the same broker acts as agent for both sides of the trade—a legal practice only if the broker first offers the securities publicly at a price higher than the bid.

cross rate The exchange rate between two currencies expressed as the ratio of two foreign exchange rates that are both expressed in terms of a third currency; foreign exchange rate between two currencies other than the U.S. dollar, the currency in which most exchanges are usually quoted.

cross-border bond Bond that is issued in the international market.

cross-border factoring Concluding a transaction by a network of factors across borders. The exporter's factor can contact correspondent factors in other countries to handle the collection of accounts receivable.

cross-border risk Describes the volatility of returns on international investments caused by events associated with a particular country as opposed to events associated solely with a particular economic trend.

cross-default A provision under which default on one debt obligation triggers default on another debt obligation.

crossed market In the context of general equities, happens when the highest bid price of a stock is higher than the lowest offer price. Also referred to as a locked market.

crossed trade The prohibited practice of offsetting buy and sell orders without recording the trade on the exchange, thus not allowing other traders to take advantage of a more favorable price.

cross-holdings The holding by one corporation of shares in another firm. One needs to consider cross-holdings when figuring total capitalizations of all firms in a particular market.

crowd trading A group of exchange members with a defined area of function tending to congregate around a trading post, pending execution of orders. Includes specialists, floor traders, odd-lot dealers, and other brokers as well as smaller groups with specialized functions.

crowding out Heavy federal borrowing that drives interest rates up and prevents businesses and consumers from borrowing when they would like to because they have been crowded out from the group of investors.

crown jewel A particularly profitable or otherwise particularly valuable corporate unit or asset. The most desirable entities within a diversified corporation as measured by asset value, earning power, and business prospects; in takeover attempts, these entities typically are the main objective of the acquirer and may be sold by a takeover target to make the rest of the company less attractive.

cum dividend With dividend; said of a stock whose owner is eligible to receive a declared dividend. Stocks are usually "cum dividend" for trades made on or before the fifth trading day preceding the record date, when the register of eligible holders is closed for that dividend period. *Opposite of* ex-dividend.

cum rights With rights. When an owner of a stock is eligible to receive the rights attached to it.

cumulative dividend feature A requirement that any missed preferred or preference stock dividends be paid in full before any common dividend payment is made.

cumulative preferred stock Preferred stock whose dividends accrue, should the issuer not make timely dividend payments. *Opposite of* noncumulative preferred stock.

cumulative total return The actual performance of a fund over a particular period.

cumulative voting A system of voting for directors of a corporation in which shareholders' total number of votes is equal to the number of shares held times the number of candidates. *Compare to* cumulative voting.

Curb, the Another name for the American Stock Exchange (AMEX). It refers to the fact that the AMEX began as an outdoor market where trading took place on the curb in front of the New York Stock Exchange.

currency Money.

currency arbitrage Taking advantage of divergences in exchange rates in different money markets by buying a currency in one market and selling it in another market.

currency basket The value of a portfolio of specific amounts of individual currencies, used as the basis for setting the market value of another currency. Also referred to as a currency cocktail.

currency board Entity charged with maintaining the value of a local currency with respect to some other specified currency.

currency call option Contract that gives the holder the right to purchase a specific currency at a specified price or exchange rate within a specific period of time.

currency diversification Using more than one currency as an investing or financing strategy. Exposure to a diversified currency portfolio typically entails less exchange rate risk than if all the portfolio exposure were in a single foreign currency.

currency exchange risk Uncertainty about the rate at which revenues or costs denominated in one currency can be converted into another currency. Companies conducting business overseas must contend with currency risk.

currency future A financial future contract for the delivery of a specified foreign currency.

currency futures contract Contract specifying a standard volume of a particular currency to be exchanged on a specific settlement date.

currency hedge A hedging technique to guard against foreign exchange fluctuations or risk. For example, an investor might sell forward euro 100 million when holding a long position of euro 100 million in stocks.

currency in circulation Paper money, coins, and demand deposits that constitute all the money circulating in the economy.

currency no longer issued Includes old and new series gold and silver certificates, Federal Reserve notes, national bank notes, and 1890 series Treasury notes.

currency option An option to buy or sell a foreign currency.

currency put option Contract that gives the holder the right to sell a particular currency at a specified price (exchange rate) within a specified period of time.

currency risk Exchange rate risk.

currency selection Asset allocation in which the investor chooses among investments denominated in different currencies.

currency swap An agreement to trade a series of specified payment obligations denominated in one currency for a series of specified payment obligations denominated in a different currency.

current account Net flow of goods and services between countries. Current accounts are either at a surplus or a deficit.

current assets Value of cash, accounts receivable, inventories, marketable securities, and other assets that can be converted to cash in less than one year.

current coupon A bond selling at or close to par, that is, a bond with a coupon close to the yields currently offered on new bonds of a similar maturity and credit risk.

current coupon bond Bond on which the coupon is set approximately equal to the bond's yield to maturity at the time of its issuance.

current income Money that is routinely received from investments in the form of dividends, interest, and other income sources.

current issue In Treasury securities, the most recently auctioned issue. Trading is more active in current issues than in those that have been on the market longer, known as off-the-run issues.

current liability Amount a company owes for salaries, interest, accounts payable, and other debts due within one year.

current market value The value of a client's portfolio at today's market price, as listed in a brokerage statement.

current maturity Current time to maturity on an outstanding debt instrument.

current rate method The translation of all foreign currency balance sheet and income statement items at the current exchange rate.

current ratio Indicator of a company's short-term debt-paying ability. Determined by dividing current assets by current liabilities. The higher the ratio, the more liquid the company.

current yield For bonds or notes, the coupon rate divided by the market price of the bond.

current-income bond Bond paying semiannual interest to holder. Interest is not included in the accrued discount.

cushion The minimum period between the time a bond is issued and the time it is called.

cushion bond High-coupon bond that sells at only a moderate premium because it is callable at a price below that at which a comparable non-callable bond would sell. Cushion bonds offer considerable downside protection in a falling market.

cushion theory The theory that a stock with many short positions taken in it will rise, because these positions must be covered by purchasing shares in the open market.

CUSIP number Unique number given to a security to distinguish it from other stocks and registered bonds. *See also* Committee on Uniform Securities Identification Procedures.

custodial fee Fee charged by an institution that holds securities in safekeeping for an investor.

custodian A bank, agent, trust company, or other organization responsible for safeguarding financial assets, or the individual who oversees the mutual-fund assets of a minor's custodial account.

custodian bank A bank or other financial institution that keeps custody of stock certificates and other assets of a mutual fund, individual, or corporate client.

customer's loan consent Agreement signed by a margin customer that allows a broker to borrow the customer's margined securities up to the level of the customer's debit balance to help cover other customers' short positions.

customer's man Stockbroker.

customers' net debit balance The total amount of credit given by NYSE member firms to finance customers purchasing securities.

customized benchmark A benchmark that is designed to meet a client's requirements and long-term objectives.

cutoff point The lowest rate of return acceptable on investments.

cycles A full orbital period. Boom cycles are usually followed by busts.

cyclical stock Stock that tends to rise quickly when the economy turns up and that falls quickly when the economy turns down. Examples are shares of housing, automobile, and paper companies.

D

daily price limit The level at which many commodity, futures, and options markets are allowed to rise or fall in a day. Exchanges usually impose a daily price limit on each contract. When these prices are met, the commodity is said to be up limit or down limit.

daisy chain Manipulation of the market by traders acting in concert to create the illusion of active volume to attract investors; a violation of U.S. securities laws.

date of record Date on which holders of record in a firm's stock ledger are designated as the recipients of either dividends or stock rights.

day order An order to buy or sell a stock that, if not executed or canceled the day it is placed, expires automatically. All orders are day orders unless otherwise specified. Traders often make calls before the opening to check for renewals. *Opposite of* good-'til-cancelled order.

day trading Establishing and liquidating the same position or positions within one day's trading. In the late 1990s, day trading came to refer to rapid-fire buying and selling of stocks during the course of a day and was a technique taken up by many novices during the technology stock mania. Most amateurs lost money day trading.

days in receivables Average time in days that it takes a company to collect money from its customers. If this figure rises, investors may fear that the customers are holding up their payments.

days'-sales-in-inventory ratio Average number of days' worth of sales that is held in inventory. A rising ratio can indicate slowing sales.

dead-cat bounce An up move in a bear market.

dealer An entity that stands ready to buy a security for its own account or sell from its own account. Individual or firm acting as a principal, rather than an agent, in a securities transaction. Principals are market makers in securities, and thus trade for their own account and at their own risk. *See also* specialist.

dealer market Where traders specializing in particular commodities buy and sell assets for their own accounts. The Nasdaq stock market is a dealer market, while the New York Stock Exchange's specialist system allows investors to meet without the intervention of a dealer.

dear money British term for tight money.

Death Valley curve In venture capital, refers to the period before a new company starts generating revenues, when it is difficult for the company to raise money.

debenture Any debt obligation backed strictly by the borrower's integrity, e.g., an unsecured bond.

debit balance The amount that is owed to a broker by a margin customer for loans the customer uses to buy securities.

debt Money borrowed.

debt capacity Ability to borrow. The amount a firm can borrow up to the point where the firm's value no longer increases.

debt instrument An asset requiring fixed dollar payments, such as a government or corporate bond.

debt limitation A bond covenant that restricts a firm's ability to incur additional indebtedness in some way.

debt market The arena where investors trade debt instruments. *Also known as* bond market.

debt outstanding subject to limitation Obligations incurred by the U.S. Treasury subject to the statutory limit set by Congress. Until World War I, a specific amount of debt was authorized for each separate security issue. Beginning with the Second Liberty Loan Act of 1917, the nature of the limitation was modified until, in 1941, it developed into an overall limit on the outstanding federal debt. The limit may change from year to year.

debt ratio A company's total debt divided by its total assets.

debt relief Reducing the principal and/or interest payments, usually on less-developed or Third World country loans.

debt retirement The complete repayment of debt.

debt securities IOUs created through loan-type transactions including commercial paper, bank CDs, U.S. Treasury bills, corporate bonds, and other instruments.

debt service Interest payments plus repayments of principal to creditors. Investors pay close attention to whether or not a company is making enough money to service its debt.

debt service coverage The cash flow generated by a company compared to the annual interest and principal payments on a debt.

debt/equity ratio Indicator of financial leverage at a company. Compares assets provided by creditors such as banks or bondholders to assets provided by shareholders. The ratio is determined by dividing long-term debt by common stockholder equity.

debt-for-equity swap A swap agreement in which one investor agrees to exchange equity returns for debt returns with another investor over a prearranged length of time.

debt-holder *Also known as* bondholder.

debtor Borrower of money.

debtor in possession A firm that continues to operate under the chapter 11 bankruptcy process, usually under the tutelage of a trustee.

debtor-in-possession financing New debt obtained by a firm during the chapter 11 bankruptcy process.

decimal trading The quotation and trading of stock or bond prices in decimals as opposed to fractions such as ⅛. The U.S. markets use decimal trading.

decimalization The quotation and trading of stock or bond prices in decimals as opposed to fractions such as eighths.

decision tree Schematic way of representing alternative sequential decisions and the possible outcomes from these decisions.

deduction An expense that the IRS allows as a reduction of gross taxable income, e.g., charity donations.

deep-discount bond A bond issued with a very low coupon or no coupon that sells at a price far below par value. A bond that has no coupon is called a zero-coupon bond.

default Failure to make timely payment of interest or principal on a debt security or to otherwise comply with the provisions of a bond indenture.

default risk The risk that an issuer of a bond may be unable to make timely principal and interest payments. *Also known as* credit risk.

defeasance The setting aside by a borrower of cash or bonds sufficient to service the borrower's debt. Both the borrower's debt and the offsetting cash or bonds are removed from the balance sheet.

defensive investing An investment strategy involving the purchase of stocks or bonds that will provide a predictable and safe return on an investor's money. These usually are securities of companies whose products sell in both good and bad times. Defensive stocks often include companies that manufacture food, laundry detergent, and other consumer goods.

deferred account A type of account that delays taxes due on that account until some later date; an individual retirement account, for example.

deferred annuity A life insurance product that offers deferral of taxes over the life of the product.

deferred call A provision that prohibits the company from calling the bond before a certain date. During this period the bond is said to be "call protected."

deferred compensation An amount that has been earned by an employee of a company but is not actually paid until a later date, typically through a payment plan, pension, or stock-option plan.

deficit An excess of liabilities over assets, of losses over profits, or of expenditure over income.

deficit spending When government spending exceeds government revenue resulting in government borrowing.

defined benefit plan A pension plan obliging the company to make specified dollar payments, usually in retirement, to qualifying employees. The pension obligations are a liability of the company.

defined contribution plan A company pension plan in which the sponsor is responsible only for making specified contributions into the plan on behalf of qualifying participants.

deflation Decline in the price of goods and services. *Opposite of* inflation.

deflator A statistical factor used to convert current dollar purchasing power into inflation-adjusted purchasing power, enabling the comparison of prices while accounting for inflation in two different time periods.

delayed opening Postponement of the start of trading in a stock until correction of a gross imbalance in buy and sell orders. Such an imbalance is likely to follow on the heels of significant news about the company, such as a takeover offer.

delayed quote When investors' trades are recorded publicly on the consolidated tape well after they were made. Typically, quotes are delayed when volume is heavy. *See* real time.

delinquency Failure to make a payment on a debt or obligation by the specified due date.

delisting Removal of a company's security from listing on an exchange because the firm has not met specific regulations of the exchange.

delivery versus payment A transaction in which the buyer's payment for securities is due at the time of delivery, usually to a bank acting as agent for the buyer, upon receipt of the securities. The payment may be made by bank wire, check, or direct credit to an account. *See also* receive versus payment. *Opposite of* free delivery.

delta The change in the price of a call or put option for a one dollar increase in the value of the underlying stock or other asset. For a call option, a delta of 0.50 means that the option should increase by $.50 if the underlying asset increases by one dollar. For put options, the delta is always negative. *Also called* hedge ratio.

delta neutral Describes value of a portfolio not affected by changes in the value of the asset on which the options are based.

demand deposit Checking account that pays no interest and from which funds can be withdrawn upon demand.

demand loan A loan that can be called by the lender at any time and carries no set maturity date.

deposit insurance *See* Federal Deposit Insurance Corporation (FDIC).

depositary receipt *See* American depositary receipt (ADR).

Depository Trust Company (DTC) A member of the Federal Reserve System and jointly owned by most of the brokerage houses on Wall Street and the New York Stock Exchange, it is the central securities repository where stock and bond certificates are exchanged. Most exchanges now take place electronically, and few paper certificates actually change hands. dtcservices.dtcc.com

depreciate To allocate the cost of an asset over its life.

depreciation Amount allocated during the period to amortize the cost of acquiring long-term assets over the useful life of the assets. A non-cash expense that provides a source of free cash flow.

depression Period in the economy when excess aggregate supply overwhelms aggregate demand, resulting in falling prices, unemployment problems, and economic contraction.

deregulation The reduction of government's role in controlling a market or service. In recent years, the airline and electric utility industries have been deregulated.

derivative A financial contract whose value is based on, or "derived" from, a traditional security such as a stock or bond, a commodity, or market index.

descending tops A chart pattern in which each peak in a security's price movement is lower than the preceding peak over a period of time. *Opposite of* ascending tops.

designated order turnaround (DOT) Fully automated system introduced to the NYSE in 1976 to electronically route smaller orders.

Deutsche Börse Germany's major securities market, including the Frankfurt Stock Exchange. www.deutsche-boerse.com/INTERNET/EXCHANGE/index_e.htm

devaluation A decrease in the spot price of a currency. Often precipitated by a government's announcement of a new economic policy.

diamonds Refers to a unit investment trust that tracks the performance of the Dow Jones Industrial Average. Its holdings consist of the thirty component stocks of the Dow.

dilution Diminution in the proportion of income to which each share is entitled. When a company issues new shares, existing shareholders experience dilution because their portion of ownership in the enterprise must now be shared.

dip Slight drop in securities' prices after a sustained uptrend. Analysts often advise investors to buy a stock on dips, meaning to buy when its price is momentarily weak.

direct deposit service A service that electronically transfers all or part of any recurring payment—including dividends, paychecks, pensions, and Social Security payments—directly to a shareholder's or bank customer's account.

direct foreign investment (DFI) Investment in real assets, such as land, buildings, or plant, outside one's own country.

direct stock-purchase program Investors purchase securities directly from the issuer. These plans benefit investors because they can buy shares without paying a commission.

director *See* board of directors.

disability insurance An insurance policy that insures a worker in the event of an occupational mishap resulting in disability. Insurance benefits compensate the injured worker for lost pay.

discharge of bankruptcy The termination of bankruptcy proceedings, resulting in cancellation of the debtor's obligations.

disclaimer The decision of a beneficiary or heir to refuse to accept a share in an estate or trust within a certain time, generally nine months, in order to forgo his or her tax liability. Or, a clause in a report or document that attempts to absolve the writer of responsibility if any of the information provided is inaccurate.

disclosure A company's release of all information pertaining to the company's business activity, regardless of how that information may influence investors. The U.S. securities laws are based on the requirement that a company make full disclosure of all facts material to its business so that investors can make informed decisions when they buy and sell securities.

discontinued operation Division of a business that has been sold or written off and that is no longer maintained by the company.

discount bond Debt sold for less than its principal or face value. If a discount bond pays no coupon, it is called a zero coupon bond.

discount broker A brokerage house that charges relatively low commission rates in comparison to a full-service broker. Discount brokers' fees are lower because they do not usually offer services such as client advice and research.

discount rate The interest rate that the Federal Reserve charges a bank to borrow funds. The rate, which fluctuates, is set by the Federal Reserve. During a recession, the Federal Reserve actively cuts the discount rate to spur economic activity.

discount window Facility provided by the Federal Reserve Bank enabling member banks to borrow reserves against collateral in the form of Treasuries or other acceptable securities.

discounted cash flow (DCF) Future cash flows estimated to be generated by a company. The cash flows are discounted by numerous factors, such as expected inflation rates, to arrive at a present value.

discounted dividend model (DDM) A formula to estimate the intrinsic value of a company by calculating the present value of all future dividends it is expected to pay.

discounted in/by market Information that is widely accepted or anticipated, and hence is already taken into account in the pricing of a security or the overall market. An example might be a move by the Federal Reserve to cut interest rates that has not yet occurred but is so widely expected that its impact has already been priced into stocks or bonds.

discounting Calculating the present value of a future amount. *Opposite of* compounding.

discretionary account Accounts over which an individual or organization, other than the person in whose name the account is carried, exercises trading authority or control.

discretionary cash flow Cash flow that is available to a company after the funding of all capital investment projects. It is available for paying cash dividends, repurchasing common stock, and retiring debt.

discretionary income The amount of income a consumer has available after purchasing essentials such as food and shelter.

disinflation A decrease in the rate of inflation.

disintermediation An investor who shifts funds from an institution or fund manager (intermediary) to directly invest in the assets on his own.

disposable income The amount of personal income an individual has after taxes and government fees, which can be spent on necessities, spent on nonessentials, or saved.

distress sale The selling of assets under adverse conditions. An investor who incurs a margin call, because his investment has declined, may have to sell securities to cover the call. Distress sales usually depress the price of the asset being sold because it must be liquidated quickly.

distributing syndicate A number of brokerage firms or investment bankers that work together to sell a large lot of securities.

distribution Payment from a mutual fund or a corporation's cash flow. May include dividends from earnings, capital gains from the sale of portfolio holdings, or return of capital invested. Fund distributions can be made by check or by investing in additional shares. Funds are required to distribute capital gains (if any) to shareholders at least once per year. Some corporations offer dividend reinvestment plans (DRIPs).

divergence When two or more averages or indexes fail to move in the same direction.

diversifiable risk *See* unsystematic risk.

diversification Dividing investment funds among a variety of securities with different risk and reward characteristics so as to minimize a downside risk.

diversified investment company An investment vehicle such as a mutual fund that invests in an array of securities.

divestiture The disposal of an asset or investment.

dividend A portion of a company's profit paid to holders of its common and preferred stocks. A stock selling for $20 with an annual dividend of $1 a share yields the investor 5 percent. Dividends on common stock are discretionary and depend on the company's profit prospects.

dividend payout ratio Percentage of company earnings that is paid out as dividends.

dividend reinvestment plan (DRIP) Automatic reinvestment of shareholder dividends in more shares of a company's stock, often without commissions. Some plans provide for the purchase of additional shares at a discount to the prevailing market price. Dividend reinvestment plans allow shareholders to accumulate stock over the long term. The DRIP is usually administered by the company without charges to the shareholder.

dividend yield Represents annual dividends paid to shareholders divided by the prevailing price of the stock.

dividends payable The declared dividend dollar amount that a company is obligated to pay.

divisor Used in construction of stock indices. Suppose there are 10 stocks in an index, each worth $10, putting the index at 100. Now suppose one of the stocks must be replaced with another that is worth $20. The total value of the index would rise to 110 after the swapping even though it only increased because a higher-priced stock was added to it. To keep the index at 100, the divisor is changed from 1 to 1.10. The value of the index, 110/1.1 is kept at 100.

DJIA *See* Dow Jones Industrial Average.

DM Deutsche (German) marks.

dogs of the Dow The group of stocks within the thirty companies in the Dow Jones Industrial Average with the highest dividend yield, which often reflects depressed prices. The investor buying these stocks speculates that they will bounce back fairly quickly.

dollar bond Municipal revenue bond for which quotes are given in dollar prices. Not to be confused with "U.S. dollar" bond, a common term of reference in the Eurobond market.

dollar price of a bond Percentage of face value at which a bond is quoted.

dollar-cost averaging *See* constant-dollar plan.

domestic bond Bond issued and traded within a country and denominated in the currency of that country.

domestic corporation A corporation that is conducting business and based in the country in which it is established, as opposed to a foreign corporation.

donor One who gives property or assets to someone else through the vehicle of a trust.

don't fight the tape Phrase advising not to trade against the general market trend. If stock prices are rising, do not sell. Tape refers to the ticker tape that reports every stock trade and the price at which the transaction is made.

don't know (DK, DKed) "Don't know the trade." A Wall Street expression used whenever one party disavows knowledge of a trade or receives conflicting instructions from the other party.

DOT *See* designated order turnaround.

double bottom A term used in technical analysis to refer to the drop of a stock's price, a rebound, and then a decline to the same level as the original drop.

double taxation Government taxation of the same money twice; specifically, taxation of earnings at the corporate level and dividends at the stockholder level.

double top A term used in technical analysis to refer to the rise of a stock's price, a drop, and then a jump back to the same level as the original increase.

double up A stock-buying strategy that doubles the amount purchased when the price moves in the opposite direction from the direction the investor hoped for. For example, an investor with confidence in a stock buys a thousand shares at $100 and another thousand shares when the price declines to $90. *Also known as* average down.

double witching day A trading day when two related classes of options and futures expire, resulting in a variety of arbitrage strategies to close out positions. On such days, excessive swings in the underlying securities' prices can occur.

Dow dividend theory *See* dogs of the Dow.

Dow Jones Industrial Average (DJIA) The best-known U.S. index of stocks. A price-weighted average of thirty actively traded, well-established companies' shares. The Dow, as it is called, is a barometer of how shares of the largest U.S. companies are performing. There are hundreds of investment indexes around the world for stocks, bonds, currencies, and commodities. Even though the Dow is composed of only thirty stocks, its performance has tracked that of the broader market indexes, such as the S&P 500, remarkably closely.

Dow theory An investment theory that says a major trend in the stock market must be confirmed by simultaneous movement of the Dow Jones Industrial Average and the Dow Jones Transportation Average to new highs or lows.

down round Refers to a round of venture capital financing that is raised at a lower valuation for the company than the previous round. Indicates that a company's fortunes are in decline.

downgrade A negative change in ratings for a stock by a research analyst, or of a bond by an investment rating agency such as Moody's or S&P.

downside risk The risk that a security will decline in value.

downsizing A company's reduction in the number of employees and overall size to increase efficiency and profitability.

downstream The transfer of corporate activity from the larger parent to the smaller subsidiary.

downtick Move down in the price of a particular stock from a previous trade. *Opposite of* uptick.

downturn The transition point between a rising, expanding economy to a falling, contracting one.

draining reserves Federal Reserve System action to tighten the money supply by raising a bank's minimum reserve requirements, selling bonds in the open market, and/or raising the rate that banks must pay to borrow from the Fed.

dressing up a portfolio Money managers' strategy to make transactions for the sole purpose of making a portfolio look good to the investor near the end of a reporting period. Buying stocks to push their prices up at the end of a quarter achieves this. *See also* window dressing.

DRIP *See* dividend reinvestment plan.

dual listing Listing of a security on more than one exchange, thus increasing the competition for bid and offer prices, the liquidity of the securities, and the length of time the stock can be traded daily if listed on both the East and West Coasts.

dual-purpose fund A closed-end fund consisting of two classes of shares. The two classes are preferred shares, on which shareholders receive all the dividends and interest the portfolio collects, and common shares, on which shareholders receive all the capital gains from sales and purchases of securities.

due date Date on which a debt must be paid.

due diligence An internal audit of a target firm by an acquiring firm. Offers are often made contingent upon resolution of the due diligence process. Also refers to the investigation any investor might make before buying a security.

due diligence meeting Usually refers to a meeting held by a brokerage firm that is underwriting a company's shares to allow brokers to question company executives about an upcoming issue. More generally, it could refer to the meeting a potential investor has with a new fund manager or company manager.

dumping Offering large amounts of stock for sale with little or no concern for the effect on the market or the stock price.

duration A common gauge of how much the price of a fixed-income asset such as a bond or mortgage will change owing to a rise or fall in interest rates.

Dutch auction Auction in which the lowest price necessary to sell the entire offering becomes the price at which all securities offered are sold. This technique has been used in Treasury auctions. Auction system in which the price of an item (stock) is gradually lowered until it meets a responsive bid (government Treasury bills) or offer (corporate repurchase) and is sold. When a company repurchases its stocks, it sets a range of prices within which shareholders are invited to sell their shares back to the company. The tender offer is open for a specific period of time at the set price, and the quantity of stock to be purchased is stated as well, subject to proration if more shares are tendered than can be legally purchased under the stated terms.

duty A tax on imports, exports, or consumption goods.

dynamic asset allocation An asset-allocation strategy in which the asset mix is shifted in response to changing market conditions.

dynamic hedging A strategy that involves rebalancing hedged positions in securities as market conditions change, or a strategy that seeks to protect the value of a portfolio using a derivative security that is specifically designed to perform in a manner opposite to the portfolio.

dynasty trust *See* generation-skipping transfer or trust.

E

EAFE Index *See* Europe, Australasia, and Far East Index.

early-withdrawal penalty Penalty paid by the holder of a fixed-term investment, such as a bank certificate of deposit, when he or she withdraws money before the agreed-upon maturity date.

earned income Compensation earned from employment, which includes wages, salary, tips, and compensation.

earned income credit A tax credit for taxpayers based on income and family size.

earnest money Money given to a seller by a buyer to demonstrate the buyer's good faith. If the deal falls through, the deposit is usually forfeited by the party who breaks the contract.

earning asset An asset that generates income, e.g., income from rental property.

earnings Net income for a company during a period of time. Colloquially referred to as the "bottom line" because net earning is the entry at the bottom of the income statement after all expenses are deducted.

earnings before interest after taxes (EBIAT) Operating earnings less taxes.

earnings before interest and taxes (EBIT) *See* operating earnings.

earnings before interest, taxes, depreciation, and amortization (EBITDA) A financial measure defined as revenues less cost of goods sold and selling, general, and administrative expenses. In other words, a company's profit before the deduction of interest, income taxes, depreciation, and amortization expenses. EBITDA became popular in the 1980s when corporate raiders tried to assess what a company's operation generated, not counting interest, taxes, or noncash expenses such as depreciation and amortization which reflect diminished values of a company's assets.

earnings momentum An increase in a company's earnings-per-share growth rate from one reporting period to the next.

earnings per share (EPS) A company's profit divided by the number of shares it has outstanding. If a company earns $2 million in one year and has 2 million shares of stock outstanding, its EPS would be $1 per share. If a company reduces the shares outstanding by buying back its own stock for example, it can make its EPS look better, even if the amount that it earned remains the same.

earnings surprise Positive or negative difference from the consensus forecast of a company's earnings made by brokerage firms. A negative earnings surprise generally has a greater adverse effect on stock prices than a reciprocal positive earnings surprise.

earnings yield The inverse of the price-earnings ratio, it is the ratio of earnings per share to the current share price. It represents what one share of a company's stock has earned.

Easdaq *See* European Association of Securities Dealers Automated Quotation.

easy money A period in which the nation's central bank makes money readily available for banks to lend. *Opposite of* tight money.

EBIAT *See* earnings before interest after taxes.

EBIT *See* earnings before interest and taxes; operating earnings.

EBITDA *See* earnings before interest, taxes, depreciation, and amortization.

economic assumptions General market environment a firm expects to operate in over the life of a financial plan.

economic earnings The real flow of cash that a firm could pay out forever in the absence of any change in the firm's productive capacity.

economic exposure The extent to which the value of a firm will change because of an exchange rate change.

economic growth rate The annual percentage rate of change in a nation's gross national product or total output.

economic indicators Key statistics that indicate the health of a nation's economy. For example, a high unemployment rate indicates a weak economy. A low inflation rate is typical of a strong economy.

economic union An agreement between two or more countries that allows the free movement of capital, labor, and all goods and services, and involves the harmonization and unification of social, fiscal, and monetary policies.

economic value added (EVA) A method of evaluating a company's actual performance against investors' required return on an investment. Suppose a division produces a 12 percent return on capital invested. If investors would usually require a 14 percent return on capital invested, the division destroyed shareholder value under the EVA metric. This description is trademarked by Stern-Stewart. It is analogous to net present value.

economics The study of the economy. There are various economic theories, such as Keynesian economics, monetarist theories, and supply-side economics.

economy of scale Achievement of lower average cost per unit through increased production.

EDGAR The Securities and Exchange Commission (SEC) uses Electronic Data Gathering and Retrieval (EDGAR) to transmit company documents such as annual reports (10-Ks), quarterly reports (10-Qs), and other SEC filings, to investors. www.sec.gov

education IRA A type of individual retirement account allowing parents to contribute up to $500 per year for each child's education up to the child's eighteenth birthday.

effective annual interest rate An annual measure of what an investment is expected to generate that fully reflects the effects of compounding.

effective annual yield Annualized interest rate on a security, computed using compound interest techniques.

effective tax rate The net rate a taxpayer pays on income that includes all forms of taxes. It is calculated by dividing the total tax paid by taxable income.

efficient market A market in which prices of securities quickly and correctly reflect all relevant information.

efficient-market hypothesis States that all relevant information is fully and immediately reflected in a security's market price. The theory implies that an investor should not expect to earn above-market returns utilizing information that is inexpensively available. Under this theory, there are no bargains in financial markets. Three forms of efficient market hypothesis exist: weak form, where stock prices reflect all information on past prices; semistrong form, where stock prices reflect all publicly available information; and strong form, where stock prices reflect all relevant information, including insider information. The theory was pioneered by Eugene F. Fama in 1970.

8-K *See* form 8-K.

elasticity of demand and supply The degree of buyers' responsiveness to price changes. Elasticity is measured as the percentage change in quantity divided by the percentage change in price. A large value (greater than one) of elasticity indicates sensitivity of demand to price, e.g., luxury goods. Goods with a small value of elasticity (less than one) have a demand that is insensitive to price, e.g., food.

electronic communications network (ECN) An alternative trading network that allows investors to post their bids or offers on stocks anonymously. The network essentially eliminates the middleman, allowing investors to meet. Currently these networks do not offer the liquidity that the Nasdaq market provides or that of the NYSE, where specialists are obligated to buy and sell from investors. Therefore, ECNs are not as reliable today as markets for large orders if an investor needs to buy or sell shares immediately. They do, however, offer a cheap alternative to more established markets.

electronic depository transfer The transfer of funds between bank accounts through the automated clearinghouse (ACH) system.

Elliott wave theory Technical market-timing strategy that predicts price movements on the basis of historical price-wave patterns and their underlying psychological motives.

embedded option An option that is part of the structure of a security that gives either the holder or the issuer some rights in addition to the standard terms of the asset.

emergency fund A reserve of cash kept available to meet the costs of any unexpected financial emergencies.

emerging market The national market of a less-developed nation. Examples of emerging markets are Chile, Thailand, and Russia.

Emerging Markets Free (EMF) Index A Morgan Stanley Capital International index created to track stock markets in emerging markets that are open to foreign investment. www.msci.com

emerging-markets fund A mutual fund that invests primarily in countries with economies that are becoming industrialized. Emerging-markets funds tend to carry more risk than domestic stock funds due to currency movements and political instability. Consequently, fund prices can fluctuate dramatically.

EMF Index *See* Emerging Markets Free Index.

employee contribution An employee's own deposit to a company retirement plan.

Employee Retirement Income Security Act (ERISA) The 1974 law that regulates the operation of private pensions and benefit plans. Three federal agencies oversee the enforcement of the law: the Department of Labor, the Internal Revenue Service, and the Pension Benefit Guaranty Corporation. www.dol.gov

employee stock ownership plan A benefit plan for employees in which a company contributes to a trust fund that buys stock.

employee stock-purchase plan A firm-sponsored program that enables employees to purchase shares of the firm's common stock on a preferential basis.

employer matching contribution The amount, if any, a company contributes on an employee's behalf to the employee's retirement account, usually tied to the employee's own contribution.

encumbered A property owned by one party on which a second party has a valid claim. A bank's holding of a home mortgage encumbers the property.

endorse Transferring asset ownership by signing the back of an asset's certificate.

endowment Gift of money or property to a specified institution for a specified purpose.

endowment fund Investment fund established for the support of an institution such as a college, private school, museum, hospital, or foundation. The investment income may be used for the operation of the institution and for capital expenditures.

enhanced indexing An investment strategy whose objective is to exceed the total return of some predetermined index. *Also called* indexing-plus.

entrepreneur A person starting a new company who takes on the risks associated with starting the enterprise, which may require venture capital to cover start-up costs.

environmental fund A mutual fund that invests strictly in stocks of companies that have the goal of bettering the environment. Investors in these funds hope to support and profit from opportunities related to the environmental movement.

EPS *See* earnings per share.

equilibrium price The price when the supply of goods matches the demand for it. Sometimes referred to as the fair price.

equipment trust certificate Certificate issued by a trust that is formed to purchase an asset and lease it out. When the last of the certificates has been repaid, title and ownership of the asset transfer to the leaseholder.

equipment-leasing partnership A limited partnership that receives income and tax benefits such as depreciation costs by purchasing equipment and leasing it to other parties.

equitable owner The beneficiary of property held in a trust.

equity Ownership interest in a firm or asset. In real estate, dollar difference between what a property could be sold for and debts claimed against it, such as a mortgage. In a brokerage account, equity equals the value of the account's securities minus any money borrowed from a brokerage firm in a margin account. "Equities" is another name for stocks or company shares.

equity cap An agreement in which one party agrees to pay another at specific time periods if a designated stock or stock market benchmark tops a predetermined level.

equity claim A claim to a share of company earnings after debt obligations have been satisfied. Sometimes also referred to as a residual claim.

equity collar The simultaneous purchase of an equity floor and sale of an equity cap. This is a hedging device often used by top executives of companies who own many shares of the entity's stock. This protects the purchaser from losing much money if the stock falls but also allows a holder to keep his stock if its price doesn't fall, thereby increasing the chances of gain.

equity floor An agreement in which one party agrees to pay the other at specific time periods if a specific stock or stock market benchmark falls below a predetermined level.

equity funding An investment consisting of a life insurance policy combined with a mutual fund. The insurance policy is paid by the collateral value of fund shares, giving the investor the advantages of insurance protection with the growth potential of a mutual fund.

equity kicker Stock warrants issued attached to privately placed bonds. Warrants give a bondholder the chance for capital appreciation if the warrants rise in price before they expire. Equity kickers are also referred to as sweeteners and are used to attract buyers to a bond.

equity market Stock market.

equity option A security that gives the buyer the right (but not the obligation) to buy or sell a specified number of shares of stock, at a specified price, for a limited time period. The seller of an equity option, in exchange for a premium, takes on the obligation to either sell or buy shares at a specified price for a set period. Equity options provide a low-cost way for buyers to capitalize on significant price moves in a stock and supply sellers with income. Typically one option equals a hundred shares of stock.

equity REIT A real estate investment trust (REIT) that assumes ownership status in the properties it invests in, enabling investors to earn dividends on rental income from the property and appreciation if the property is resold at a profit. *Opposite of* mortgage REIT.

equity swap A swap in which two parties make an exchange based on the performance of a specified stock market index and an interest rate, either a fixed or floating rate. One party to such a trade might believe the stock index would rise and interest rates fall while the counterparty would take the other side of the bet. *Compare to* interest rate swap.

equityholder Stockholder; those holding shares of a company's equity.

equity-linked policy Insurance policy whose interest earned is based upon a stock-index performance.

equivalent taxable yield The yield that must be offered on a bond whose interest is taxable to provide the same after-tax income as a tax-exempt issue.

ERISA *See* Employee Retirement Income Security Act.

escalator clause Provision in a contract allowing cost increases to be passed on to one party. In an employment contract, for example, an escalator clause may call for wage increases to keep up with inflation.

escheatment The process of turning over unclaimed or abandoned property to a state authority. Escheatment laws require mutual funds to turn over uncashed or returned checks or client account fund shares if the owner cannot be located within a length of time determined by each state.

escrow Property or money held by a third party until the agreed-upon obligations of a contract are met.

escrowed to maturity (ETM) Holding of the proceeds from a new bond issue, which are held in escrow, to pay off an existing bond issue at its maturation date.

estate planning The preparation of a plan relating to the administration and disposition of a person's property before or after his or her death. Estate planners pay special attention to reducing taxes owed on an estate.

estate tax A federal or state tax imposed on an individual's assets inherited by heirs. No federal tax is due on an estate with a value of $675,000 or less. The limit is increasing in graduated steps so that after 2005 the floor will be $1,000,000.

estimated tax Tax to be paid quarterly on an individual's income that is not subject to withholding tax, including self-employed income, investment income, alimony, rent, and capital gains.

ETM *See* escrowed to maturity.

EU *See* European Union.

euro The currency of twelve member nations of the European Monetary Union that replaced individual currencies as of January 1, 1999, although the currency was not put into circulation until January 1, 2002. The currencies that were combined to become the euro include the Austrian schilling, Belgian franc, Dutch guilder, Finish markka, French franc, German Deutsche mark, Greek drachma, Irish punt, Italian lire, Luxembourg franc, Portuguese escudo, and Spanish peseta. The three European Union member states that have chosen not to abandon their currencies at this time are Denmark (krone), Sweden (krona), and the United Kingdom (pound sterling).

Eurobond A bond that is underwritten by a syndicate of international banks or brokerage firms and sold to investors in a number of countries. Eurobonds are issued outside the jurisdiction of any single country.

Eurocurrency Financial instruments issued outside a country, but denominated in that country's currency. A Eurodollar is a certificate of deposit in U.S. dollars in some other country (though mainly traded in London). A Euroyen is a CD in yen outside Japan.

Eurocurrency market The money market for borrowing and lending currencies that are held in the form of deposits in banks located outside the countries where the currencies are issued as legal tender.

Eurodollar Refers to a certificate of deposit in United States dollars in a bank that is not located in the United States. Most of the Eurodollar deposits are in London banks, but Eurodeposits may be anywhere other than the United States.

Eurodollar bond Eurobond denominated in U.S. dollars.

Eurodollar certificate of deposit A certificate of deposit paying interest and principal in dollars, but issued by a bank outside the United States, usually in Europe.

Eurodollar obligation Certificate of deposit issued in U.S. dollars by foreign banks and foreign branches of U.S. banks.

Euronext A cross-border European securities market created by the merger of the Amsterdam, Brussels, and Paris exchanges in September 2000 for trading equities, bonds, derivatives, and commodities. www.euronext.com

Europe, Australasia, and Far East (EAFE) Index A stock index, computed by Morgan Stanley Capital International, that includes shares of companies based in twenty-one countries around the world, excluding the United States. This index is the most common benchmark used by investors who put their money in foreign markets. www.msci.com.

European Association of Securities Dealers Automated Quotation (EASDAQ) European version of Nasdaq, a market of stocks in less established companies. www.easdaq.com

European Central Bank (ECB) Bank, located in Frankfurt, Germany, created to monitor the monetary policy of the twelve countries that have converted to the euro from their local currencies. The countries are: Austria, Belgium, Finland, France, Germany, Greece, Ireland, Italy, Luxembourg, the Netherlands, Portugal, and Spain. www.ecb.int

European Currency Unit (ECU) An index of foreign exchange consisting of European currencies, originally devised in 1979. *See also* euro.

European option An option that may be exercised only at the expiration date. *See also* American-style option.

European Union (EU) An economic association of European countries founded by the Treaty of Rome in 1957 as a common market for six nations. It was known as the European Community until January 1, 1994, and currently comprises fifteen countries, those of the European Central Bank as well as Denmark, Sweden, and the United Kingdom.

Its goals are a single market for goods and services without any economic barriers, and a common currency with one monetary authority.

European-style exercise A method of exercising options contracts in which the buyer can exercise the contract on the last day before expiration.

Euroyen *See* Eurocurrency.

EVA *See* economic value added.

even lot *See* round lot.

evening up Buying or selling securities to offset an existing market position.

event risk The risk that the ability of an issuer to make interest and principal payments will change because of a rare, discontinuous, and very large unanticipated change in the market environment such as a natural or industrial accident, regulatory change, takeover, or corporate restructuring.

events of default Contractually specified events that allow a company's lenders to demand immediate repayment of a debt. The most common event is when an interest payment is missed.

evergreen credit Revolving credit line without maturity.

exact interest Interest paid on the basis of a 365-day/year schedule by a bank or other financial institution as opposed to a 360-day basis, which is known as ordinary interest. The difference can be material when large sums are involved.

exact matching A bond portfolio management strategy that involves finding the lowest-cost portfolio generating cash inflows exactly equal to cash outflows that are being financed by investment.

"except for" opinion An incomplete auditor's opinion reflecting an auditor's inability to examine certain areas of the company's operations because of restrictions imposed by management or other conditions. Such an opinion would be viewed by investors as a warning flag.

excess accumulation The amount of a required minimum distribution that an IRA holder fails to remove from the account in a timely manner. Excess accumulations are subject to a 50 percent IRS penalty tax.

excess contribution The amount by which an IRA contribution exceeds the allowable limits. If an excess contribution is not properly corrected, a 6 percent IRS penalty applies.

excess margin Equity present in an individual's brokerage firm margin account above the minimum required by the Federal Reserve or the brokerage firm.

excess return on the market portfolio Difference between the return on a portfolio of securities and the riskless rate.

exchange A place in which shares, options, and futures on stocks, bonds, commodities, and indexes are traded. Principal U.S. stock exchanges are: New York Stock Exchange (NYSE), American Stock Exchange (AMEX), Chicago Board Options Exchange, Philadelphia Stock Exchange, and Pacific Coast Exchange located in San Francisco. Because the shares on the National Association of Securities Dealers Automated Quotation System (Nasdaq) market are not traded in one physical location, it is not called an exchange but instead a stock market.

exchange controls Government restrictions on the purchase of foreign currency by residents and on the purchase of the local currency by nonresidents.

exchange distribution A sale on an exchange floor of a large block of stock in a single transaction. A broker bunches a large number of buy orders and sells the block all at once. The broker receives a special commission for completing the trade.

exchange member Individual or firm that belongs to an exchange. *See* member firm; seat.

exchange of stock Acquisition of another company by purchase of its stock in exchange for cash or shares.

exchange offer A proposal, either hostile or friendly, to acquire a target company through the payment of stock of the acquiring company. *Compare to* cash offer.

exchange privilege A mutual fund shareholder's right to switch from one fund to another within one fund family, usually at no additional charge.

exchange rate The price of one country's currency expressed in another country's currency.

exchange rate risk The risk that an investment's value will change because currency exchange rates rise or fall more than the currency of an investor's home country. *Also called* currency risk.

exchange ratio The number of new shares in an acquiring firm that are offered for each outstanding share of an acquired firm.

Exchange, the A nickname for the New York Stock Exchange. Also known as the Big Board, where common and preferred stocks are traded. The Exchange is the oldest in the United States, founded in 1792, and the largest. It is located at the corner of Broad and Wall Streets in New York City. www.nyse.com

excise tax Federal or state tax placed on the sale or manufacture of a commodity, typically a luxury item, e.g., alcohol.

ex-dividend Literally "without dividend." The buyer of shares when they are quoted ex-dividend will not receive the most recently declared dividend. The interval between the record date and the payment date is usually a few weeks, and it is at this time that the stock trades without its dividend. *Opposite of* cum dividend.

ex-dividend date The first day of trading when the seller, rather than the buyer, of a stock will be entitled to the most recently announced dividend payment. The date set by the New York Stock Exchange (NYSE) (and generally followed on other U.S. exchanges) is currently two business days before the record date. A stock that has gone ex-dividend is denoted by an x in listings on that date. *Also known as* reinvestment date.

execution The process of completing an order to buy or sell securities. Once a trade is executed, a confirmation report is sent to the customer.

execution costs The cost of a transaction excluding commissions but including the movement in the security's price that occurred as a result of the order. Execution costs can rise to high levels in securities that are not widely traded because when an order enters the market, it moves the price up if it is a purchase, down if it is a sale.

executor A person or organization named in a will to oversee the settlement of a deceased person's estate. The executor is responsible for paying debts and taxes, handling any challenges to the will, and distributing property to heirs. State laws often stipulate additional requirements for individuals who serve as executors, such as age and competence. If no will exists at the time of death, an administrator is named by the probate court.

exempt securities Instruments exempt from the registration requirements of the Securities Act of 1933 or the margin requirements of the Securities Exchange Act of 1934. Such securities include government bonds, mortgage-backed securities issued by U.S. government–sponsored enterprises (Ginnie Maes), municipal bonds, commercial paper, and private placements.

exercise To implement the right of the holder of an option to buy, in the case of a call, or sell, in the case of a put, the security underlying the option. *See also* strike price.

exercise limit The cap on the number of option contracts of any one class of contract that can be exercised within a five-day period contract. A stock option's exercise limit is typically two thousand contracts.

exercise notice A notification that an option holder wants to exercise the right to buy or sell (depending on the type of contract) the security underlying the option contract.

exercise price The price at which the security underlying a future or options contract may be bought or sold. *Also known as* strike price.

Ex-Im Bank *See* Export-Import Bank.

exit fee *See* back-end-load fund.

ex-legal A municipal bond offered without a law firm's legal opinion. The majority of bonds are issued with legal opinions.

expansion Phase of the business cycle as it climbs from a trough toward a peak. If an expansion is especially prolonged or if output grows more significantly than is typical, it may be considered a boom period.

expected return on investment Given the risk of the investment, the rate of return that fairly compensates investors for the risk. *See* capital asset pricing model. *Also known as* mean return.

expense ratio The percentage of the assets that are spent to run a mutual fund. This includes expenses such as management and advisory fees, overhead costs, and distribution and advertising fees, also known as 12b-1 fees. The expense ratio does not include brokerage costs for trading the portfolio, although these are reported as a percentage of assets to the SEC by the funds in a statement of additional information (SAI). The SAI is available to shareholders on request. The expense ratio is often termed an operating expense ratio (OER).

expiration The date on which an option contract lapses.

expiration cycle Dates on which options on a particular security expire. A given option will be placed in one of three cycles: the January cycle, the February cycle, or the March cycle. At any time, an option has contracts with four expiration dates outstanding: two in near-term months and two in far-term months.

expiration date The last day, in the case of American-style options, or the only day, in the case of European-style options, on which the option may be exercised. For stock options, this date is the Saturday

immediately following the third Friday of the expiration month; brokerage firms may set an earlier deadline for notification of an option
holder's intention to exercise. If Friday is a holiday, the last trading day
will be the preceding Thursday.

explicit tax A tax specifically collected by a government, including
income, withholding, property, sales, and value-added taxes and tariffs.

Export-Import Bank (Ex-Im Bank) The U.S. federal government
agency that extends trade credits to U.S. companies to facilitate the
financing of U.S. exports. www.exim.gov

expropriation The official seizure by a government of private property.
Any government has the right to seize such property, according to
international law, if prompt and adequate compensation is given.

ex-rights Shares of stock that are trading without rights attached.

extendable bond Bond whose maturity can be extended at the option
of the lender or issuer.

extension Voluntary arrangements to restructure a firm's debt, under
which the immediate payment date is postponed.

external efficiency *See* pricing efficiency; efficient market.

external finance Funding that is not generated by a firm's operations,
usually from borrowing or proceeds of a stock issue.

extinguish Retire or pay off debt.

extra dividend A temporary increase in a firm's dividend beyond the
normal level.

extraordinary call Early redemption of a bond backed by revenue generated by a project. Such an early repayment may be because the revenue source paying the interest on the bond has been eliminated or
has disappeared.

extraordinary item An unusual and unexpected one-time event that
adds to or detracts from earnings and must be explained to shareholders in an annual or quarterly report. A typical item might be costs associated with numerous layoffs of workers when a company downsizes.
Such an event is considered extraordinary because the costs are not
incurred regularly.

ex-warrant Describes a stock sale in which the buyer is not entitled to
the warrant accompanying the stock.

F

face value *See* par value.

factor A financial institution that buys a firm's accounts receivable and collects the accounts from the firm's customers. Factoring is a type of lending, essentially. Retailers often rely on factors to cover the costs of buying merchandise to showcase in a store.

fail A trade is said to fail if on the settlement date either the seller does not deliver securities in proper form or the buyer does not deliver funds in proper form.

fair market price Amount at which an asset would change hands between two unrelated parties that both have knowledge of the relevant facts. *Also known as* market price.

fair rate of return The rate of return that state governments allow a regulated public utility such as an electric company to earn on its investments and expenditures. Utilities then use these profits to pay investors and provide service upgrades to their customers.

fair value An asset at fair value means investors view it as neither underpriced nor overpriced.

fair-and-equitable test A set of requirements for a plan of reorganization to be approved by the bankruptcy court.

fairness opinion An investment bank's professional opinion as to the price an acquiring firm is offering in a takeover or merger. Fairness opinions, because they are paid for by an interested party involved in a merger or business transaction, are not completely reliable.

fallen angel Bond that was considered investment grade when it was issued but dropped below that rating over time because of adverse business conditions or operational trouble. If a bond is expected to fall from investment grade to so-called junk status, its price falls significantly.

family of funds Different mutual funds with varying investment strategies offered by the same investment company.

Fannie Mae *See* Federal National Mortgage Association.

far month The trading month of an option or future contract that is farthest away from the present month. *Opposite of* nearest month.

farther out; farther in Used in the context of options to refer to the relative length of option-contract maturities.

FASB *See* Financial Accounting Standards Board.

fast market Excessively rapid trading in a specific security that causes a delay in the electronic updating of its last sale and market conditions, particularly in options.

FDIC *See* Federal Deposit Insurance Corporation.

Fed *See* Federal Reserve Board.

Fed pass An action taken by the Federal Reserve to make credit easier for borrowers to attain. The Federal Reserve adds more reserves to the banking system and increases the money available for lending.

federal agency securities Securities issued by corporations and agencies created by the U.S. government, such as the Federal Home Loan Bank Board and Ginnie Mae. Unlike U.S. Treasury securities, these so-called agencies are not backed by the full faith and credit of the federal government. But they are backed by the agencies that issue them, which are entities created by the government, and therefore are of lower risk than most securities issued by corporations.

Federal Agricultural Mortgage Corporation (Farmer Mac) A federal agency chartered in 1988 to provide a secondary market for farm mortgage loans.

federal credit agency Agency of the U.S. federal government set up to supply credit to various classes of institutions and individuals, e.g., savings and loans, small businesses, students, farmers, and exporters.

federal deficit When federal government expenditures exceed federal government revenue.

Federal Deposit Insurance Corporation (FDIC) A U.S. federal institution that insures bank deposits up to $100,000 per depositor. The FDIC was created in 1933 following a wave of bank failures in which depositors lost their money. To keep the corporation funded, it charges fees of all member banks that vary according to the relative riskiness of the banks' loans. The FDIC takes over banks that fail and arranges for their loans and deposits to be taken over by another institution, usually ensuring that depositors always have access to their funds. www.fdic.gov

federal farm credit system A system chartered in 1971 through the Farm Credit Act providing U.S. farmers with credit services offered through a federal land bank, a federal intermediate credit bank, and a bank for cooperatives. www.fca.gov

Federal Financing Bank A federal institution that lends money it borrows from the U.S. Treasury to a wide array of federal credit agencies. www.treas.gov/ffb

federal funds Noninterest-bearing deposits held in reserve for depository institutions at their district Federal Reserve Bank. Also, excess reserves loaned by banks to each other.

federal gift tax A federal tax imposed on assets conveyed as gifts to individuals. Gifts of $10,000 or less per person each year are not taxed.

Federal Home Loan Banks (FHLB) The institutions that regulate and lend to savings and loan associations. The Federal Home Loan Banks play a role analogous to that played by the Federal Reserve Bank with its commercial bank members. www.fhlb.gov

Federal Home Loan Mortgage Corporation (Freddie Mac) A congressionally chartered corporation that purchases residential mortgages from savings and loans, banks, and mortgage bankers and compiles portfolios of these mortgages for sale to investors. www.freddiemac.com

Federal Housing Administration (FHA) Federally sponsored U.S. agency chartered in 1934 which buys residential mortgages, sells these mortgages in packages, and insures the lenders against loss if the mortgages are not paid off. www.hud.gov/offices/hsg/hsgabout.cfm

Federal Housing Finance Board (FHFB) U.S. government agency chartered in 1989 to assume the responsibilities formerly held by the Federal Home Loan Bank system. www.fhfb.gov

Federal Intermediate Credit Bank A bank sponsored by the U.S. federal government to provide funds to institutions making loans to farmers.

Federal Land Bank A bank administered under the U.S. Farm Credit

Administration that provides long-term mortgage credit to farmers for agriculture-related expenditures.

Federal National Mortgage Association (Fannie Mae) A publicly owned, U.S. government-sponsored corporation chartered in 1938 to purchase mortgages from lenders and resell them to investors. It packages mortgages backed by the Federal Housing Administration, but also sells some nongovernment-backed mortgages. www.fanniemae.com

Federal Open Market Committee (FOMC) The body that is responsible for setting the interest rates and credit policies of the Federal Reserve System. It consists of the seven members of the Federal Reserve Board as well as five of the twelve reserve-bank presidents. The head of the reserve bank of New York is a permanent member; the remaining presidents serve one-year terms.

Federal Reserve Bank One of the twelve member banks constituting the Federal Reserve System that is responsible for overseeing the commercial and savings banks of its region to ensure their compliance with regulations. Each bank also supplies economic data about its region that the Federal Reserve Board considers when contemplating changes in interest rate policy.

Federal Reserve Board (Fed) The seven-member governing body of the Federal Reserve System, which is responsible for setting reserve requirements and the discount rate, and making other key economic decisions. The chairman of the Federal Reserve Board and the other six members are appointed by the president of the United States. The chairman and vice chairman serve four-year terms; other board members serve for fourteen years. www.federalreserve.gov

Federal Reserve notes The currency of the United States issued by the U.S. government to the public through the Federal Reserve Banks and their member banks. They represent money owed by the government to the public. Currently, the item "Federal Reserve notes amounts outstanding" consists of new-series issues. The Federal Reserve note is the only class of currency currently issued.

Federal Reserve System The monetary authority or central bank of the United States, established in 1913 and governed by the Federal Reserve Board. The system includes twelve Federal Reserve Banks and is authorized to regulate monetary policy in the United States, which includes the setting of interest rates and the expansion or contraction of money that circulates in the nation's banking system, to supervise Federal Reserve member banks, bank holding companies, international operations of U.S. banks, and U.S. operations of foreign banks. www.federalreserve.gov

Federal Savings and Loan Association An institution chartered by the U.S. federal government whose members, also known as thrifts, collect savings deposits and provide mortgage loans.

federal-funds market The market in which banks can borrow or lend reserves, allowing banks temporarily short of their required reserves to borrow reserves from banks that have excess reserves.

federal-funds rate The interest rate that banks with excess reserves at a Federal Reserve district bank charge other banks that need overnight loans. The fed-funds rate, as it is called, often points to the direction of U.S. interest rates because it is set daily by the market, unlike the prime rate and the discount rate. The Federal Reserve does not have a target for the fed-funds rate, which it moves periodically. But in recent years, the fed-funds rate set by the market is followed by moves in the central bank's target rate.

federally related institution Arm of the U.S. federal government that issues securities that are exempt from SEC registration and are backed by the full faith and credit of the U.S. government. Excepted is the Tennessee Valley Authority and its securities.

fedwire A wire transfer system for large amounts of money operated by the Federal Reserve System.

fee table Schedule in a mutual fund's prospectus that discloses what expenses and management fees a shareholder will incur when buying shares.

fee-based compensation Payment to a financial adviser of a set hourly rate, or an agreed-upon percentage of assets under management, for a financial plan. This compensation structure differs from traditional stockbrokers who are paid by commission whenever a trade is conducted. Fee-based compensation is the structure that most encourages advice that benefits the investor since the planner is paid a flat rate regardless of transactions. Also referred to as fee-only compensation.

FHA *See* Federal Housing Administration.

FICA Abbreviation for Federal Insurance and Care for Aged. The Social Security payroll tax.

fiduciary One who must act solely for the benefit of another party, ignoring his own needs entirely. In estates, the person serving as executor holds fiduciary duties.

fill The price at which a stock, bond, or commodity trade is executed.

fill-or-kill order (FOK) A trading order that is automatically canceled unless executed completely within a designated time period. A market or limited price order that is to be executed in its entirety as soon as it is represented in the trading crowd, and if not so executed is to be treated as canceled.

finance A discipline concerned with determining value of an asset and making decisions. The finance function allocates resources, including the acquiring, investing, and managing of resources. To finance a firm is to fund its operations.

finance charge The total cost of credit a customer must pay on a consumer loan, including interest.

finance company A company whose business and primary function is to make loans to individuals, while not receiving deposits like a bank.

Financial Accounting Standards Board (FASB) Board composed of independent members who create and interpret accounting practices known as generally accepted accounting principles (GAAP). www.fasb.org

financial adviser A professional offering financial advice to clients for a fee and/or commission.

financial analysis Analysis of a company's financial statement.

financial analyst Professional who analyzes financial statements, interviews corporate executives, and attends trade shows in order to write reports recommending either purchasing, selling, or holding various stocks. *Also called* securities analyst; investment analyst.

financial distress Events preceding and including bankruptcy, such as violation of loan agreements or dissipation of business.

financial distress costs Legal and administrative costs of liquidation or reorganization. Also includes indirect costs associated with impaired ability to do business.

financial engineering A broad term that can mean combining or carving up existing securities to create new financial products, such as construction of a pool of mortgages to be sold to investors. Financial engineering can also mean achieving a goal—such as increased earnings per share—through accounting gimmicks rather than through growing operations.

financial future A contract entered into now that provides for the delivery of a specified asset, such as a U.S. Treasury security, in exchange for the selling price at some specified future date.

financial guarantee insurance Insurance created to cover losses from specified financial transactions.

financial institution An enterprise such as a bank whose primary business and function is to collect money from the public and invest it in financial assets such as stocks and bonds or lend it out to borrowers.

Financial Institutions Reform, Recovery, and Enforcement Act of 1989 (FIRREA) Legislation that established the Office of Thrift Supervision, which was created in the wake of the savings and loan crisis of the late 1980s. *See* Office of Thrift Supervision (OTS).

financial intermediary Institution that provides the market function of matching borrowers with lenders, or traders with other traders.

financial leverage Use of debt to increase a company's expected return on equity or return on its net worth. Financial leverage is measured by the ratio of a company's debt to its debt plus equity.

financial leverage ratio Common ratio is a company's debt divided by its equity, or debt divided by the sum of its debt plus equity. *Also called* capitalization ratio.

financial market An organized institutional structure or mechanism for creating and exchanging financial assets. The nation's stock, bond, options, and futures markets are known broadly as U.S. financial markets.

financial objectives Goals related to returns that a firm will strive to accomplish during the period covered by its financial plan.

financial plan A blueprint relating to the financial future of a firm that outlines how it expects to fund itself and continue its operations.

financial planner An investment professional who assists individuals with long- and short-term financial goals.

financial planning Evaluating the investing and financing alternatives available to a firm or individuals. Planning for a company includes attempting to make optimal decisions, projecting the consequences of these decisions for the firm in the form of a financial plan, and then comparing future performance against that plan. For individuals, planning usually covers investment strategies for immediate use as well as those designed to achieve long-term goals.

financial policy Criteria describing a corporation's choices regarding how much debt it will amass, its method of financing investment projects, and hedging decisions with a goal of maximizing the value of the firm to stockholders.

financial position The account status of a firm's or individual's assets and liabilities, as reflected on its financial statement.

financial press Media devoted to reporting financial news.

financial price risk The chance there will be a change in a financial price, including changes in currency or foreign exchange rate, a move in interest rates, or a change in a commodity price.

financial public relations Public relations division of a company charged with cultivating positive investor relations and proper disclosure information under securities laws.

financial pyramid A risk structure that spreads investors' risks across low-, medium-, and high-risk vehicles. The bulk of the assets that make up the base of the pyramid are in safe, low-risk investments that provide a predictable return. At the top of the pyramid are a few high-risk ventures that have a modest chance of success. In between are investments with a moderate risk.

financial ratio The result of dividing one financial statement item by another. Ratios help analysts interpret financial statements by focusing on specific relationships. The most common is the price-to-earnings ratio (P/E), which reveals how expensive a stock is. Companies with high P/Es are considered expensive because investors are willing to pay much more than the company earns, on a per-share basis, than investors buying low P/E stocks.

financial risk The risk that the cash flow of an issuer will not be adequate to meet its financial obligations.

financial service income Income from delivery of financial services such as lending, insurance, leasing, or financial service management fees.

Financial Services Modernization Act Enacted in 1999, this act repealed key parts of the Glass-Steagall Act, which prohibits banks affiliating with securities firms. *Also known as* Gramm-Leach-Bliley Act.

financial statement A report of basic accounting data that helps investors understand a firm's financial history and current operations.

financial statement analysis Evaluation of a firm's financial statements in order to assess the firm's worth and its ability to meet its financial obligations.

financial strategy Practices a firm adopts to pursue its financial objectives.

financial structure The way in which a company's assets and operations are financed. Companies can use short-term borrowings, long-term debt, or raise money in the stock markets called equity. Financial structure differs from capital structure in that capital structure accounts for long-term debt and equity only.

financial supermarket A company offering a wide variety of financial services such as banking services, investment advice, and insurance brokerage.

financial tables Tables found in newspapers listing securities prices. The table of stocks lists dividends, yields, price-earnings ratios, trading volume, and price fluctuations for the previous day. Other securities listings are much more abbreviated. For instance, mutual fund tables typically list closing prices and year-to-date percentage gains or losses.

Financial Times Stock Exchange Index (FTSE) Share price index for U.K. companies that is the most widely quoted of British indices. Commonly known as the "Footsie."

financial-needs approach A method of establishing the amount of life insurance required by an individual by estimating the financial needs of his or her dependents in the event of the individual's death.

financing-cost savings A source of competitive advantage to a company that depends on access to a low-cost sources of capital.

finder's fee A fee paid to a person or company for services as an intermediary in a transaction.

Finite-Life Real Estate Investment Trust (FREIT) A real estate investment trust whose priority is to sell its properties within a specified period to realize capital gains.

firewall The barrier between the investment banking and brokerage operations within a financial institution created to prevent the exchange of inside information. Investment bankers are often privy to nonpublic information about companies they are advising, so this information must be kept secret from other parts of the firm where individuals might trade on the information.

firm-commitment underwriting An underwriting in which an investment banking firm commits to buy an entire issue of stock, then sell it to the public, assuming all financial responsibility for any unsold shares.

FIRREA *See* Financial Institutions Reform, Recovery, and Enforcement Act of 1989.

first call date The earliest date stated in a bond indenture on which the issuer may redeem the bond either partially or completely.

first in, first out (FIFO) An accounting method for valuing the cost of goods sold that uses the cost of the oldest item in inventory first. Alternately, last in, first out (LIFO) uses the cost of the newest item produced. Choosing which type of valuation method will be followed can have an impact on a company's financial results in times of inflation when prices are rising rapidly. When prices are stable, whether LIFO or FIFO is used is inconsequential.

first mortgage A lien on a property that gives precedence to the lender of the first mortgage over all other lenders in case of default.

first notice day The first day, varying by contracts and exchanges, on which notices of intent to deliver actual financial instruments or physical commodities against futures are authorized.

fiscal policy Government spending and taxation for the specific purpose of stabilizing the economy.

fiscal year (FY) Accounting period covering twelve consecutive months over which a company determines its earnings and profits. The fiscal year serves as a period of reference for the company and does not necessarily correspond to the calendar year.

fiscal year-end The end of a twelve-month accounting period.

Fisher effect A theory that nominal interest rates in two or more countries should be equal to the required real rate of return to investors plus compensation for the expected amount of inflation in each country.

Fitch One of the United States's top three securities ratings agencies. www.fitchibca.com

five Cs of credit Five characteristics that are used to form a judgment about a customer's creditworthiness: character, capacity, capital, collateral, and conditions.

5 percent rule A guideline of the National Association of Securities Dealers that limits the amount of money a firm can make on a customer's trade to 5 percent of the value of the transaction.

fixed annuity Contract in which an insurance company or issuing financial institution pays a fixed dollar amount of money per period.

fixed asset Long-lived property owned by a firm. Tangible fixed assets include real estate, plant, and equipment. Intangible fixed assets include patents, trademarks, and brand-name recognition.

fixed benefits Payments to a beneficiary that are paid in fixed preset amounts.

fixed cost A cost that does not vary with the level of production.

fixed exchange rate When the value of a country's currency is tied to another country's currency, to a commodity such as gold, or to a basket of currencies. Some countries, for instance, tie their currency to the U.S. dollar.

fixed premium Periodic payments of a fixed, equal amount paid to an insurance company for insurance or an annuity.

fixed-asset turnover ratio The ratio of sales to fixed assets. This helps investors see how productive a company's fixed assets are.

fixed-charge coverage ratio A measure of a firm's ability to meet its fixed-charge obligations. The ratio is earnings before interest and taxes plus lease expenses divided by interest plus lease expenses.

fixed-dollar obligation Conventional bond for which the coupon rate is set at a fixed percentage of the par value.

fixed-for-floating swap An interest rate swap in which one party trades fixed-rate payments for a floating rate, or a rate that fluctuates.

fixed-income instrument Asset that pays a fixed dollar amount, such as bonds and preferred stock.

fixed-income market The market for trading bonds, notes, bills, and preferred stock.

fixed-rate loan A loan whose rate is fixed for the life of the loan.

fixed-term reverse mortgage A mortgage in which the lending institution provides payments to a home owner for a fixed number of years.

flat Most broadly, having neither a short nor a long position in a stock. In market action, characterized by horizontal price movement, usually the result of low activity; in trading equities, to execute without commission or markup.

flat benefit formula Method used to determine a participant's benefits in a defined benefit plan by multiplying months of service by a flat monthly benefit.

flat price The quoted newspaper price of a bond that does not include interest that has accrued since the most recent payment. The price paid by the purchaser is the full price. *Also called* clean price.

flat tax A tax that is levied at the same rate on all levels of income. *Compare to* progressive tax; regressive tax.

flat trades Any security that trades without accrued interest or at a price that includes accrued interest is said to trade flat. A bond in default trades flat; that is, the price quoted covers both principal and unpaid accrued interest.

flatliner *See* horizontal price movement.

flattening of the yield curve A change in the yields of Treasury bonds with various maturities when the difference between the yield on a long-term issue and a short-term issue has decreased. *Opposite of* steepening of the yield curve.

flexible mutual fund Fund that invests in a variety of securities in varying proportions in order to maximize shareholder returns while maintaining a low level of risk.

flight to quality The tendency of investors to move toward safer investments, often government bonds, during periods of high economic uncertainty.

flipping Buying shares in an initial public offering (IPO) and then selling the shares immediately after the start of trading to turn a quick profit.

float As regards equities, the number of shares of a corporation that are outstanding and available for trading by the public, excluding insiders or restricted stock. The more shares a company has in its float, the less the stock will move when a big buyer or seller enters the market.

floater A bond whose interest rate varies with the interest rate of another debt instrument. A bond may have an interest rate of a LIBOR plus a percentage that reflects the risk of a bond.

floating debt Short-term debt that is renewed and refinanced constantly to fund capital needs of a firm or institution.

floating exchange rate A country's decision to allow its currency value to change freely, reflecting trading in the foreign exchange market. The currency is not constrained by central-bank intervention and does not have to maintain its relationship with another currency.

floating lien General attachment against a company's assets or against a particular class of its assets.

floating supply The aggregate of securities believed to be available for immediate purchase, that is, in the hands of dealers and investors wanting to sell.

floating-rate contract A guaranteed investment instrument whose interest payment is tied to some variable, floating interest-rate benchmark, such as a specific-maturity Treasury yield.

floating-rate note Note whose interest payment varies with short-term interest rates.

floating-rate preferred Preferred stock paying dividends that vary with short-term interest rates.

floor The area of a stock exchange where active trading occurs. Also the price at which a stop order is activated in a security, reflecting a drop in price to a certain predetermined level.

floor broker Member of an exchange who is an employee of a member firm and executes orders, as agent, on the floor of the exchange for clients.

floor official An employee of a stock exchange who settles disputes related to the auction process on the floor of the stock exchange.

floor trader A stock exchange member who generally trades only for his own account or for an account controlled by him. Also referred to as a "local."

flow of funds In the context of municipal bonds, refers to the statement displaying the priorities by which municipal revenue will be applied to the debt. With mutual funds, refers to the movement of money into or out of a fund or among various fund sectors.

flower bond Government bonds that, when owned at the time of death, are acceptable at par in payment of federal estate taxes.

fluctuation A change in price or interest rate.

fluctuation limit The limit created by a stock or commodity exchange that halts trading on a future or on all stocks if the price of the future or overall index changes, in either direction, more than a previously set amount. *Also known as* trading curb.

focus list A roster of stocks recommended by an investment bank.

FOK *See* fill-or-kill order.

Forbes 500 *Forbes* magazine's list of the largest publicly owned corporations in the United States according to sales, assets, profits, and market value. www.forbes.com

Forbes 400 A list compiled by *Forbes* magazine of the four hundred wealthiest individuals in the United States. www.forbes.com

force majeure risk The risk that there will be prolonged interruption of operations for an enterprise due to fire, flood, storm, or some other factor beyond the control of the company's sponsors.

forced conversion Occurs when a convertible security is called in by the issuer, usually when the underlying stock is selling well above the conversion price. The issuer thus assures the bonds will be retired without requiring any cash payment. Upon conversion into common stocks, the carrying value of the bonds becomes part of a corporation's equity, thus strengthening the balance sheet.

forecasting Making projections about future performance on the basis of historical and current conditions data.

foreclosure Process by which the holder of a mortgage seizes the property of a home owner who has not made interest and/or principal payments on time as stipulated in the mortgage contract.

foreign bond A bond issued on the domestic capital market of another country.

foreign branch A foreign affiliate that is legally a part of the parent firm.

foreign corporation A corporation conducting business in a country other than the one it is chartered in and that abides by the laws of the other country.

Foreign Corrupt Practices Act An amendment to the Securities Exchange Act created to outlaw bribery of foreign officials by publicly held U.S. companies.

foreign currency Money of a foreign country.

foreign direct investment The acquisition abroad of physical assets such as plant and equipment, with operating control residing in the parent corporation.

foreign equity market Issues floated by foreign companies in the domestic equity market.

foreign exchange (FX) Currency of another country.

foreign holdings The percentage of a portfolio's investments represented by stocks or American Depositary Receipts of companies based outside the United States.

foreign official institutions Central governments of foreign countries, including all departments and agencies of national governments; central banks, exchange authorities, and all fiscal agents of foreign national governments that undertake activities similar to those of a treasury, central bank, or stabilization fund; diplomatic and consular establishments of foreign national governments; and any international or regional organization, including subordinate and affiliate agencies, created by treaty or convention between sovereign states.

foreign tax credit (FTC) Home country credit against domestic income tax, received in return for foreign taxes paid on foreign derived earnings.

foreign-currency forward contract Agreement that obligates its parties to exchange given quantities of currencies at a previously specified exchange rate on a certain future date.

foreign-currency futures contract Standardized and easily transferable obligation between two parties to exchange currencies at a specified rate during a specified delivery month; standardized contract on specified underlying currencies, in multiples of standard amounts. These are bought and sold on a regulated exchange.

foreign-currency option An option that conveys the right (but not the obligation) to buy or sell a specified amount of foreign currency at a specified price within a specified time period.

foreign-currency translation The process of restating income earned by a foreign subsidiary into the currency of the parent company to prepare consolidated financial statements.

foreign-exchange broker Intermediary in the foreign-exchange market who facilitates trading.

foreign-exchange controls Various controls imposed by a government on the purchase or sale of foreign currencies by residents or on the purchase or sale of local currency by nonresidents.

foreign-exchange dealer A firm or individual that buys foreign currency from one party and then sells it to another party. The dealer makes the difference between the buying and selling prices, or the spread.

foreign-exchange market Comprised largely of banks that serve firms and consumers who may wish to buy or sell various currencies.

foreign-exchange risk The risk that a holding in a foreign currency might be impaired by a movement in exchange rates.

foreign-exchange swap An agreement to exchange stipulated amounts of one currency for another currency at one or more future dates.

foreign-source income Income earned from international operations.

forfeiture The loss of rights to an asset outlined in a legal contract if a party fails to fulfill obligations of the contract. A forfeiture clause in a will generally states that any heir who challenges the will's validity would forfeit or reduce their inheritance if the will stands.

form 8-K The form required by the SEC when a publicly held company incurs any event that might affect its financial situation or the value of its stock. Events reported in the 8-K could include acquisitions, bankruptcies, planned—and failed—mergers, resignations from the board of directors, and changes in the corporate bylaws. The 8-K must be filed within one month of the event and therefore provides more current information that the annual 10-K or quarterly 10-Q forms. Foreign firms trading in the United States file form 6-K in place of form 8-K.

form 4 The form required by the SEC for a change in the holdings of an individual owning 10 percent or more of a company's outstanding stock or a change in the holdings of a company officer. Since form 4 indicates whether an insider or large shareholder is buying or selling the company's stock, it can sometimes be a barometer of insiders' feelings about company performance. The form 4 reporting the change must be filed before or on the tenth of the month following the transaction.

form S-4 The form required by the SEC when a publicly held company registers new stock for sale as part of an acquisition plan. The form will often include details about the plan not available in corporate press releases.

form T The form required by the National Association of Securities Dealers (NASD) to report equity transactions after the market's regular hours.

form 10-K The annual report required by the SEC from exchange-listed companies that provides for disclosure of certain audited financial information. The SEC requires that financial statements in the 10-K be audited by an external firm. This is the most common tool used by investors to compare a company's operations from year to year. The 10-K often includes more detailed information than the company's annual report, such as sales by product group, officer compensation, the status of legal proceedings, and the management team's assessment of future risks and opportunities. The "Management Discussion" portion of the 10-K describes the company's performance and strategies in plain English. A related filing, form NT 10-K, notifies the SEC that the company will be late with its 10-K, which must be filed within ninety days of the company's end of fiscal year. The form includes information about why the company will be filing its 10-K late, and may give advance warning of problems.

form 10-Q The quarterly financial report required of public companies by the SEC. The SEC does not require that financial statements in the 10-Q, as compared to the annual 10-K, be audited, but the filing often provides details about a company's announced quarterly earnings.

form 13-D The form required by the SEC when an investor acquires 5 percent or more of the stock of a company, which could signal a takeover attempt. The form must be filed within ten days of the purchase and includes information about the investor's intentions.

form 3 A form required by the SEC and the stock exchange that details securities owned by all holders of 10 percent or more of a company's stock and all company directors and officers.

formula investing *See* constant-ratio plan.

Fortune 500 *Fortune* magazine's listing of the top five hundred U.S. corporations determined by an index of twelve variables. www.fortune.com

forward contract A contract that specifies the price and quantity of an asset to be delivered in the future. Forward contracts are not standardized and are not traded on organized exchanges.

forward cover The purchase in the cash market of the difference between what a seller is obligated to deliver in a forward contract and the amount of the asset the seller owns. For example, if the seller agreed to sell one hundred thousand bushels of corn in September in a forward contract, but only has sixty thousand, he or she would need to purchase forty thousand to cover the obligation.

forward currency contract An agreement to buy or sell a country's currency at a specific price, usually thirty, sixty, or ninety days in the future. This guarantees an exchange rate on a given date.

forward delivery A transaction in which the settlement will occur on a specified date in the future at a price agreed upon on the trade date.

forward differential Annualized percentage difference between current, or spot, prices and forward rates.

forward discount A currency trades at a forward discount when its forward price is lower than its current or spot price.

forward exchange rate Exchange rate fixed today for exchanging currency at some future date. *Opposite of* spot exchange rate.

forward exchange transaction Foreign currency purchase or sale at the current exchange rate but with payment or delivery of the foreign currency at a future date.

forward interest rate Interest rate fixed today on a loan to be made at some future date.

forward market A market in which participants agree to trade some commodity, security, or foreign exchange at a fixed price for future delivery.

forward premium A currency trades at a forward premium when its forward price is higher than its spot or current price.

forward rate agreement Agreement to borrow or lend on a specified future date at an interest rate that is fixed today.

forward-looking multiple An alternate expression for a P/E ratio that is based on expected (forward) earnings rather than on previous reported (trailing) earnings.

401(k) Under section 401(k) of the Internal Revenue Code, a deferred compensation plan set up by an employer so that employees can set aside money for retirement on a pre-tax basis. Employers may match a percentage of the amount that employees contribute to the plan. Contributions by both employees and employers, as well as investment earnings and interest, are not taxed until the employee withdraws the money; if the employee withdraws the money before retirement age, he or she pays an early withdrawal penalty tax. Currently, employees are allowed to annually contribute up to 15 percent of their salary but no more than $11,000 ($12,000 for people fifty or older). Many employers now offer these deferred compensation plans in lieu of or in addition to pensions.

403(b)(7) A tax-deferred annuity that is the equivalent of a 401(k) plan for nonprofit entities. Available to employees of educational institutions, churches, and other employers organized for charitable pursuits. Employees are allowed to annually contribute up to 20 percent of their salary.

fractional share Stocks amounting to less than one full share, usually resulting from splits, acquisitions, exchanges, or dividend reinvestment programs.

franchise agreement Contract by which a domestic company known as a franchiser licenses its trade name or business system for a fee to an independent company or individual, known as the franchisee.

Freddie Mac *See* Federal Home Loan Mortgage Corporation.

free cash flow Cash not required for operations or for reinvestment. Often defined as earnings before interest after taxes (EBIAT) minus capital expenditures less the change in working capital. Formula:

$$\begin{aligned}
\text{Free cash flow} = \ &\text{Sales} \\
&- \text{Cost of goods sold} \\
&\underline{- \text{Selling, general administrative costs}} \\
&(\text{Operating Earnings}) \\
&\underline{- \text{Taxes}} \\
&(\text{Earnings before interest after taxes}) \\
&+ \text{Book depreciation} \\
&- \text{Capital expenditures} \\
&\underline{- \text{Change in working capital}} \\
&(\text{Free cash flow})
\end{aligned}$$

free delivery Securities industry procedure whereby delivery of securities sold is made to the buying customer's bank without requiring immediate payment; thus a credit agreement of sorts. *Opposite of* delivery versus payment.

free right of exchange An investor's right to transfer securities from one name to another name without paying charges that accompany a sales transaction.

free stock A stock that is paid for in full and is not pledged in any way as collateral in a margin account.

free to trade A stock that is not subject to any restrictions on trading. Restricted stock given to corporate executives, by contrast, can only be sold pursuant to SEC rules.

free trade When trade for goods between nations is unrestricted. *Opposite of* protectionism.

free-riding An illegal practice in which the member of an underwriting syndicate retains a portion of an initial public offering (IPO) and resells the securities at a higher price at a later time. Also forbidden is a brokerage customer's rapid buying and selling of a security without putting up money or collateral for the purchase.

FREIT *See* Finite-Life Real Estate Investment Trust.

friction costs Costs, both implicit and explicit, associated with a transaction. Such costs include time, effort, money, and associated tax effects of gathering information and making a transaction.

frictional cost The difference between an index fund return and the index it represents. The typically lower rate of return from the fund results from transactions costs.

frictionless market Ideal trading environment that imposes no costs or restraints on transactions.

friendly merger The merging of two businesses whose managements both believe the new combined operation will be beneficial to stockholders.

friendly takeover Acquisition or merger when the target firm's management and board of directors are in favor of the takeover. *Opposite of* hostile takeover.

front running Buying or selling a security with advance knowledge of a block transaction that will influence the price of the underlying security to capitalize on the block trade. Forbidden by the SEC.

front-end load The fee applied to an investment at the time of initial purchase. A mutual fund purchased from a broker or mutual fund company can deduct a percentage when it is bought, calling it a load.

frozen account A disciplinary action taken by the Federal Reserve Board for a violation of regulation T that prohibits investors from selling securities until they are paid for in full and certificates delivered.

FTC *See* foreign tax credit.

FTSE *See* Financial Times Stock Exchange Index.

full disclosure Describes exchange and government regulations providing for the release and free exchange of all information pertinent to a given security. The U.S. securities laws are based on complete disclosure of all information that is material about a company with the view that investors with a total and accurate picture of a company will be able to make an informed decision about owning its securities.

full trading authorization Indication that a broker can operate free of all trading guidelines from a client. Also referred to as a discretionary account because the broker has discretion over which securities to buy and sell.

full-service broker A broker who provides clients an all-inclusive selection of services such as advice on security selection and financial planning. In contrast to discount brokers, who only execute customers' orders, full-service brokers charge more in commissions, but their extra services are thought by many to compensate for the increased cost.

full-service lease Arrangement in which lessor promises to maintain and insure the equipment leased. *Also called* rental lease.

fully depreciated An asset such as a factory building or a piece of equipment that has already been charged with the maximum amount of depreciation allowed by the IRS for accounting purposes. Depreciation is the accounting for the reduction of an asset's value due to wear and tear.

fully diluted earnings per share Earnings per share expressed as if all outstanding convertible securities and stock options had been exercised.

fully distributed A new stock issue that has been completely resold to the investing public and is no longer held by dealers.

fully invested Used to describe an investor whose assets are totally committed to investments, typically stocks.

fully valued A stock that has reached a price at which analysts think the underlying company's fundamental earning power has been fully recognized by investors.

fund assets The total value of a portfolio's securities, cash, and other holdings, minus any outstanding debts.

fund family A series of funds with different investment objectives offered by one management company. In many cases, investors may move their assets from one fund to another within the family at little or no cost.

fund manager The person charged with overseeing the allocation of the pool of money represented by a particular mutual fund. The fund manager is charged with investing the money to attain the return and level of risk the mutual fund investors desire. *Also called* portfolio manager.

fund of funds A mutual fund or hedge fund that invests in other funds.

fundamental analysis Security analysis that seeks to detect misvalued securities through an analysis of the firm's business prospects. Research often focuses on earnings, revenue, dividend prospects, expectations for future interest rates, and risk evaluation of a company. In macroeconomic analysis, information such as interest rates, gross domestic product, inflation, unemployment, and inventories is used to predict the direction of the economy and, therefore, the stock market. In microeconomic analysis, information such as that found on the balance sheet, income statement, an assessment of products, management, and other market items is used to forecast a company's future success or failure, and expected price action of the stock. *Opposite of* technical analysis.

funded debt Debt maturing after more than one year. *Compare to* unfunded debt. *Also called* long-term debt.

funded pension plan A pension plan in which there is enough money to cover all liabilities, including payments to be made to pensioners in the immediate future.

funding ratio The ratio of a pension plan's assets to its liabilities.

funds from operations (FFO) Used by real estate and other investment trusts to define the cash flow from trust operations; earnings with depreciation and amortization added back.

furthest month In commodities or options trading, refers to the month that is furthest away from the contract's date of settlement.

future A term used to designate a contract covering the sale of financial instruments or physical commodities for future delivery on a commodity exchange.

futures contract A legally binding agreement to buy or sell a security or commodity in a designated future month at a price agreed upon today by the buyer and seller. The contracts themselves are often traded on the futures market. Futures contracts are standardized according to the quality, quantity, and delivery time and location for each commodity. A futures contract differs from an option because an option is the right to buy or sell, while a futures contract is the promise to actually make a transaction. A future is part of a class of securities called derivatives, so named because the securities derive their value from an underlying investment.

futures market A market where contracts for future delivery of a commodity or a security are bought or sold.

futures option An option on a futures contract.

futures price The price at which parties to a futures contract agree to transact on the settlement date. *Opposite of* spot price.

future value The amount of cash at a specified date in the future that is equivalent in value to a specified sum today.

FX *See* foreign exchange.

FY *See* fiscal year.

GAAP *See* generally accepted accounting principles.

gaijin Japanese term used to describe a non-Japanese investor in Japan.

gain A profit on a securities transaction recognized by selling a security for more than it cost the buyer. Depending upon how much time has elapsed since the purchase, the gain will be taxed as ordinary income or capital gains, which have a preferential treatment.

gamma The change in the option delta for a one-dollar increase in the price of the underlying stock or other asset.

gap Financing that is required but for which no provision has been made. The difference in total funding needed for a proposal and the amount of funding already made available. As a company's financial gap increases, so does its reliance on investors or lenders to finance that gap. If investors or lenders choose to reduce their commitments, the company will be caught short and could fail.

gap opening Opening price that is substantially higher or lower than the previous day's closing price, usually because of some extraordinarily positive or negative news.

garage The floor of the NYSE, which is situated on the north side of the main trading floor.

garbatrage Rising stock prices and increased market activity in a sector caused by a major takeover involving large companies in the sector. Speculators feel other takeovers are likely in the sector.

garnishment When a creditor collects debt from a third entity, by requiring an employer to withhold a portion of a debtor's wages for repayment of an unpaid debt.

gather in the stops A market strategy in which investors sell stocks to drive prices to a level that breaks through stop orders known to exist. Once the price is low enough, the stop orders become market orders and are executed, to create snowballing. A manipulative activity that is illegal.

GATT *See* General Agreement on Tariffs and Trade.

GDP *See* gross domestic product.

GDP-implicit price deflator An economic technique used to account for inflation by comparing the current-dollar GDP to constant-dollar GDP as a ratio. The ratio accounts for price changes of goods and services that make up GDP and changes in the composite of GDP.

G-8 *See* Group of Eight.

GEM *See* growing equity mortgage.

general account Federal Reserve Board's term for a margin account provided to a customer by a brokerage firm. Governed by regulation T of the Fed.

General Agreement on Tariffs and Trade (GATT) A treaty adopted by the United Nations in the 1940s aimed at elimination of international trade barriers between member countries. Replaced by the World Trade Organization in 1995.

general cash offer A public offering in cash made to investors at large.

general ledger Accounting records that show all the financial accounts of a business.

general lien An attachment that gives the lender the right to seize the property of a borrower who has not fulfilled the obligations of the loan.

general loan and collateral agreement The agreement governing the broker/dealer's borrowing against listed securities from a bank for the purpose of carrying on business and making trades.

general mortgage A type of obligation that covers all of a borrower's mortgageable properties, not just one specific property.

general obligation bonds Municipal securities secured by the issuer's pledge of its full faith, credit, and taxing power.

general partner A participant who has unlimited liability for the obligations of a partnership.

general partnership A partnership in which all participants are general partners. *Compare to* limited partnership.

general revenue The sum of taxes, charges, and miscellaneous income taken in at the state and local level.

generally accepted accounting principles (GAAP) The overall conventions, rules, and procedures that define accepted accounting practice at a particular time in the United States. These rules are developed by the Financial Accounting Standards Board and are used by the SEC in regulating public companies. www.fasb.org

generation-skipping transfer or trust An irrevocable trust in which a principal amount is placed in a trust on the death of one person, the grantor, and is transferred to the grantor's grandchildren or successive generations when his or her children die. Income from the trust goes to the grantor's children while they are alive, and the grandchildren or other beneficiaries receiving the trust's principal may be able to bypass some estate and transfer taxes.

geographic risk Risk that arises when an insurer issues policies concentrated within certain geographic areas, such as the risk of damage from a hurricane or an earthquake.

geometric mean return Also referred to as the time-weighted rate of return, a measure of the compound rate of growth of the initial portfolio market value during the evaluation period, assuming that all cash distributions are reinvested in the portfolio.

get hit Go lower in price, when bids in the stock or market are hit, causing those bids to vanish and be replaced by lower ones.

G-5 *See* Group of Five.

ghosting The illegal practice whereby one firm drives a stock's price higher or lower, while other conspiring firms follow its lead to influence the price of the stock further.

GIC *See* guaranteed investment contract.

gift inter vivos A piece of property or asset given from one living person to another.

gift splitting A technique used to avoid gift tax in which a sum of money to be given to one person as a gift is halved and given by two people. For example, a husband and wife each donate $10,000 to their child rather than one parent donating $20,000.

gift tax A tax assessed on the giver of a property or asset as a gift. A $10,000 federal gift tax exemption exists per recipient. Some states also tax gifts.

gilt-edged security British and Irish government security. Also referred to as gilt.

Ginnie Mae *See* Government National Mortgage Association.

Ginnie Mae pass-through A security guaranteed by the Government

National Mortgage Association that consists of a collection of mortgages, in which the investor receives, or is passed through, the interest and principal payments of participating home owners.

glamour stock A popular stock characterized by high earnings growth or high expected growth and a price that rises faster than the market average in a bull market.

Glass-Steagall Act Legislation passed in 1933 prohibiting commercial banks from owning, underwriting, or dealing in corporate stock and corporate bonds. A result of the crash of 1929 when banks were found to have improperly peddled securities of companies they owned, benefiting themselves at the expense of investors. The law was largely overturned by the Financial Services Modernization Act of 1999, which eliminated many barriers and allows banks to underwrite securities, for example.

global bond Bond designed to qualify for immediate trading in any domestic capital market and in the Euromarket.

global depositary receipt A receipt denoting ownership of foreign-based corporation stock shares that are traded in numerous capital markets around the world.

global fund A mutual fund that can invest anywhere in the world, including the United States.

globalization Tendency toward a worldwide investment environment, and the integration of national capital markets.

GMC *See* guaranteed mortgage certificates.

GNMA *See* Government National Mortgage Association.

GNMA-I Mortgage-backed securities on which registered holders receive separate principal and interest payments on each of their certificates, usually directly from the servicer of the pool. GNMA-I mortgage-backed securities are single-issuer pools.

GNMA-II Mortgage-backed securities on which registered holders receive an aggregate principal and interest payment from a central paying agent on all their certificates. Principal and interest payments are disbursed on the twentieth day of the month. GNMA-II securities are backed by multiple-issuer pools or custom pools (one issuer but different interest rates that may vary within one percentage point). Multiple-issuer pools are known as "jumbos." Jumbo pools are generally longer and offer mortgages that are more geographically diverse than single-issuer pools.

GNMA midget A GNMA pass-through certificate backed by fixed-rate mortgages with a fifteen-year maturity. GNMA midget is a dealer term and is not used by GNMA in the formal description of its programs.

gnome Freddie Mac's fifteen-year fixed-rate pass-through security issued under its cash program.

GNP *See* gross national product.

go along Used for listed equity securities. Buy or sell at prices that randomly occur on the floor, participating in what trades the specialist and other players will allow.

go around Describes the Federal Reserve Bank of New York's trading-desk practice of communicating with primary dealers to establish a market of bids and offers on behalf of the Federal Open Market Committee.

goal An individual's or institution's financial objective.

godfather offer An aggressive takeover technique, in that the proposed offer of the acquiring company is so large that management of the target company cannot refuse, out of fear of lawsuits or shareholder revolt.

go-go fund A type of mutual fund in highly aggressive growth stocks. The fund has high levels of risk and potential return. *Also known as* momentum fund.

going ahead When a broker-dealer trades in a personal account prior to filling the orders of his or her clients. Prohibited by the NASD rules of fair practice. *Also known as* trading ahead; running ahead.

going away A bond purchased by dealers for immediate resale to investors, as opposed to purchasing a bond to hold for some amount of time, and then reselling it at a future date.

going long Purchase of a security for investment or speculation that the price will rise, resulting in a profit once the security is sold. *Opposite of* going short.

going private When a publicly owned company replaces its stock with ownership by a private group. The firm is delisted on stock exchanges and can no longer be purchased in the open markets.

going public When a private company first offers shares to the public market and investors. *See* initial public offering.

going short Selling stock that an investor does not own by borrowing shares from a broker. The assumption is that the price will fall. The investor then buys the shares for less than they were sold for, recognizing the difference as a profit. *Opposite of* going long.

going-concern accounting opinion A reference to an auditor's opinion of a company's financial condition that questions whether the company is viable and can operate as a "going concern." Such an opinion, often reported in form 10-K, is usually a red flag to investors.

going-concern value The value of a company in terms of its operating business. The difference between a company's going-concern value and its asset or liquidation value is deemed "goodwill" and plays a major role in mergers and acquisitions.

gold bars Bars with a minimum content of 99.5 percent gold, which may be held by central banks or traded by investors.

gold bond Bonds issued by gold-mining companies and backed by gold. The bonds make interest payments based on the level of gold prices.

gold bullion Investment-grade, pure gold, which may be smelted into gold coins or gold bars.

gold certificate Certificate of an investor that shows proof of ownership of gold bullion.

gold coin Coin minted in gold and available for purchase by individuals. Includes the American eagle or the Canadian maple leaf.

gold exchange standard A fixed exchange rate system adopted in the Bretton Woods agreement but later abandoned. It required the United States to peg the dollar to gold, and other countries to peg their currencies to the dollar.

gold fixing The process of determining the price of gold based on supply and demand forces of the market; occurs twice daily in London.

gold mutual fund A mutual fund that primarily invests in gold-mining companies' stock.

gold standard An international monetary system in which currencies are defined in terms of their gold content, and payment imbalances between countries are settled in gold. It was in effect from about 1870 to 1914.

goldbug Analyst who recommends gold as an investment or hedge.

golden handcuffs A contract that binds a broker to a brokerage firm by offering the broker commissions and bonuses, but penalizes the broker if he or she goes to work for another firm.

golden handshake A large payment to a senior employee who is forced into retirement or fired as a result of a takeover or similar development.

golden hello A bonus paid by a securities firm to attract an employee from a competing firm.

golden parachute High level of compensation paid to top management by a target firm if a takeover occurs.

Goldilocks economy A term developed in the mid-1990s to describe the positive performance of the economy as "not too hot, not too cold, just right."

good delivery Delivery of a security with all necessary legal documents attached.

good money Federal funds that clear on the same day, unlike clearinghouse funds, which require three days to clear.

good through/until date order Market or limited price order that remains viable for a stated period of time unless canceled, executed, or changed, after which time such order or the portion thereof not executed is to be treated as canceled.

good-faith deposit Refers to the initial margin-account deposit needed when buying or selling a commodity futures contract—approximately 2 percent to 10 percent of the contract value. Used in the context of securities to describe the deposit required by securities firms engaged in transactions on behalf of a new client. Also used to refer to the deposit with a municipal bond issuer by firms competing for the underwriting business.

good-this-month order (GTM) An order to buy or sell securities that continues to be a valid order until the end of the current month.

good-'til-canceled order (GTC) An order to buy or sell stock that is good until executed or canceled. Brokerages usually set a limit of thirty to sixty days, after which time the order expires if not restated. *Opposite of* day order (which expires at the end of the trading day).

goodwill Excess of purchase price over fair market value of net assets acquired under the purchase method of accounting. Large amounts of goodwill on a company's balance sheet can be dangerous to investors if the high price tags paid in acquiring assets are later written down or off.

government bond Negotiable U.S. Treasury securities.

Government National Mortgage Association (Ginnie Mae or GNMA) A wholly owned U.S. government corporation within the Department of Housing and Urban Development (HUD), Ginnie Mae guarantees the timely payment of principal and interest on securities issued by approved mortgage servicers that are collateralized by Federal Housing

Administration–issued, Veterans Administration–guaranteed, or Farmers Home Administration–guaranteed mortgages. These securities are bought and sold by investors in public markets. www.ginniemae.gov

government obligations U.S. government–backed debt instruments, which are considered among the safest investments possible, including Treasury bonds, bills, and notes, and savings bonds. They are backed by the full faith and credit of the U.S. government.

government securities Negotiable U.S. Treasury securities.

governments U.S. government–issued securities, such as Treasury bills, bonds, and notes, and savings bonds. Governments are considered among the safest investments available as they are backed by the U.S. government. Also used to refer to debt issues of federal agencies, such as Ginnie Maes, which are not directly backed by the U.S. government.

government-sponsored enterprises Privately owned, publicly chartered entities, such as the Student Loan Marketing Association or Fannie Mae, created by Congress to reduce the cost of capital for certain borrowing sectors of the economy including farmers, home owners, and students.

GPM *See* graduated-payment mortgage.

grace period The time period stipulated in most loan contracts and insurance policies during which a late payment will not result in default or cancelation.

graduated call writing Selling covered-call options at incrementally rising exercise prices, so that as the price of the underlying stock rises and the options are exercised, the seller receives a higher average price than the original exercise price.

graduated lease A type of long-term lease whose payments are variable rather than fixed and based upon a benchmark rate, such as changes in the consumer price index.

graduated security A security that has moved from listing on an exchange of less prominence to one of more prominence.

graduated-payment mortgage (GPM) A type of stepped-payment loan in which the borrower's payments are initially lower than those on a comparable rate mortgage. The payments gradually increase over a predetermined period (usually three, five, or seven years), and then are fixed at a higher-level pay schedule. The difference between what the borrower actually pays and the amount required to fully amortize the mortgage is added to the unpaid principal balance.

Graham and Dodd method of investing An investment strategy based on security analysis and identification. Investors buy stocks with undervalued assets speculating that these assets will appreciate to their true value. Refers to the classic investment book *Security Analysis,* by Benjamin Graham and David Dodd, originally published in 1934. The book was the basis of modern securities analysis.

Gramm-Leach-Bliley Act *See* Financial Services Modernization Act.

grandfather clause A provision included in a new rule or regulation that exempts a company that is already conducting business in the area addressed by the regulation from penalty or restriction.

grantor A trader in the options market who makes premium income by selling options. In estates, a person who creates a trust.

grantor retained annuity trust (GRAT) An irrevocable trust for a specified period of years during which the grantor will receive an annuity and after which the remaining assets are transferred to specified beneficiaries outside the grantor's estate. *Compare to* grantor retained income trust.

grantor retained income trust (GRIT) A tax-saving trust in which a grantor transfers property to a beneficiary but receives income until termination, at which time the beneficiary begins receiving the income. *Compare to* grantor retained annuity trust.

grantor trust A mechanism of issuing mortgage-backed securities wherein the mortgages' collateral is deposited with a trustee under a custodial or trust agreement. In estates, a trust that is considered owned by the grantor and therefore all income from the trust is taxed as his or her personal income.

graveyard market Bear market in which investors who sell are faced with substantial losses, while potential investors prefer to stay liquid, that is, to keep their money in cash or cash equivalents until market conditions improve.

GRAT *See* grantor retained annuity trust.

gray knight In a merger or acquisition, a gray knight is an acquiring company that in an unsolicited bid beats a white knight in pursuit of its own best interests, although it is friendlier than a hostile bidder.

gray list Formal roster of stocks that can be traded by a brokerage firm's trading desks, but not in risk arbitrage because an investment bank is involved with the company on nonpublic activity such as mergers and acquisitions advisory. *Also known as* restricted.

gray market Describes the sale of securities that have not officially been issued to firms other than the underwriting syndicate. This type of market serves as a good indicator of demand for a new issue in the public market.

great call Potential customer who may have an interest in participating in a particular equities trade if customer's past inquiry or activity is any indication.

greater-fool theory An investment notion that even when a stock is fully valued by conventional standards, there is room for upward movement because there are enough buyers to push prices further up purely on speculation or hype.

greenmail The holding of a large block of stock of a target company by an unfriendly company, with the object of forcing the target company to repurchase the stock at a substantial premium to prevent a takeover.

greenshoe option Option that allows the underwriter for a new issue to buy and resell additional shares if the deal is popular.

GRIT *See* grantor retained income trust.

gross domestic product (GDP) The market value of goods and services produced over time, including the income of foreign corporations and foreign residents working in the United States, but excluding the income of U.S. residents and corporations overseas. This is the output of a nation that encapsulates economic activity.

gross earnings A person's total taxable income prior to adjustments. *See* adjusted gross income.

gross estate The total value of a person's property and assets before accounting for debts, taxes, and liabilities.

gross income A person's total income prior to exclusions and deductions.

gross interest Interest earned before taxes are deducted.

gross lease A type of property lease in which the lessor (owner of the property being leased) pays expenses associated with ownership such as damages, taxes, and insurance.

gross national product (GNP) Measures an economy's total income. It is equal to GDP plus the income abroad accruing to domestic residents minus income generated in domestic market accruing to nonresidents.

gross per broker The dollar amount of commissions generated by a broker or registered representative over a specific period.

gross profit A company's sales minus its cost of goods sold.

gross profit margin Gross profit divided by sales, which is equal to each sales dollar left over after paying for the cost of goods sold.

gross sales The total of all sales at invoice values, ignoring any adjustments such as customer discounts or returns.

gross spread The fraction of the gross proceeds of an underwritten securities offering that is paid as compensation to the underwriters of the offering.

ground lease A lease of land, as opposed to a lease of a building.

group insurance Insurance coverage for a group, which can usually be obtained at a cheaper rate than insurance for an individual.

Group of Eight (G-8) Refers to economic and political forum of heads of government of eight major industrialized democracies of the world: France, Germany, Italy, Canada, Japan, Russia, United Kingdom, and United States. Before the inclusion of Russia in 1997, it was called the Group of Seven or G-7.

Group of Five (G-5) The five leading countries (France, Germany, Japan, the United Kingdom, and the United States) that meet periodically to cooperate on international economic issues. When currency issues are discussed, the monetary authorities of these nations attend the meeting.

Group of Ten (G-10) A group of ten major industrialized countries whose mission is to create a more stable world economic trading environment through monetary and fiscal policies. The ten countries are Belgium, Canada, France, Germany, Italy, Japan, the Netherlands, Sweden, the United Kingdom, and the United States.

group rotation The tendency of stocks in one sector of the market to outperform and then underperform other industries, usually as a result of economic cycles or the conditions in a particular industry.

group rotation manager A top-down manager who invests in sectors rather than particular firms. Sector investments are determined by sector characteristics such as current price-to-earnings ratios and expected growth prospects.

group sale Block sale of large amounts of securities to institutional investors.

growing equity mortgage (GEM) Mortgage in which annual increases in monthly payments are used to reduce outstanding principal and to shorten the term of the loan.

growing perpetuity A constant stream of cash flow that is expected to increase indefinitely.

growth fund A mutual fund that invests primarily in stocks with a history of and future potential for capital gains. Such funds generally carry more risk than those seeking income.

growth investing An investing style that seeks capital appreciation rather than income. Growth investors assume more risk than income-seeking investors. *Compare to* value investing.

growth manager A money manager who seeks to buy stocks that typically sell at relatively high P/E ratios due to high earnings growth, with the expectation of continued high or higher earnings growth.

growth opportunity Opportunity to invest in profitable projects.

growth phase A phase of development during which a company experiences rapid earnings growth as it produces new products and expands market share.

growth rate Compound annual growth rate for the number of full fiscal years shown. If there is a negative or zero value for the first or last year, the growth is not meaningful.

growth stock Common stock of a company that has an opportunity to invest money and earn more than the opportunity cost of capital.

growth-and-income fund A mutual fund that invests primarily in stocks with a history of capital gains as well as stocks with consistent dividend payments.

GTC *See* good-'til-canceled order.

G-10 *See* Group of Ten.

GTM *See* good-this-month order.

guarantee The assumption of responsibility for payment of a debt or performance of some obligation if the liable party fails to perform to expectations.

guarantee letter A commercial bank's letter assuring payment of the exercise price of a client's put option.

guaranteed bond A type of bond for which a firm other than the issuer guarantees its interest and principal payments.

guaranteed insurability A life and health insurance policy feature that enables the insured to add coverage at future times and at fixed and agreed-upon rates regardless of the health of the policyholder.

guaranteed insurance contract An insurance contract promising a stated nominal interest rate over some specific time period, usually several years. Many retirement accounts invest in these contracts.

guaranteed investment contract (GIC) A pure investment product in which a life insurance company agrees, for a single premium, to pay at a maturity date the principal amount of a predetermined annual interest rate over the life of the investment.

guaranteed mortgage certificates (GMC) First issued by Freddie Mac in 1975, certificates represent undivided interest in specified conventional whole loans and participations previously purchased by Freddie Mac.

guaranteed renewable policy insurance A type of insurance policy that requires the insurer to renew the policy to an individual regardless of health changes. No changes may be made to an individual policyholder unless the same change is applied to all policyholders.

guaranteed replacement-cost-coverage insurance A policy that covers the full cost of replacing damaged property without any allowances or deductions for depreciation or wear and tear.

gun jumping Refers to trading in a security on the basis of information that has not been made available to the public. The illegal solicitation of buy orders in an underwriting before completion and finalization of SEC registration.

gunslinger An aggressive portfolio manager who makes risky investments, typically in margin accounts, in search of high returns.

haircut The margin or difference between the actual market value of a security and the value assessed by the lender in a transaction. Haircut can also refer to a discounted commission or fee.

half-life The point in the life of a mortgage-backed security guaranteed or issued by the Government National Mortgage Association, the Federal National Mortgage Association, or the Federal Home Loan Mortgage Corporation when half of the principal has been repaid.

hammering the market Heavy selling of stocks by speculators who think that a stock or the overall market is overvalued and is about to drop.

hands-off investor An investor who does not play an active role in the management of the corporation. *Also known as* passive investor. *Opposite of* hands-on investor.

hands-on investor An investor who has a large stake in a corporation and takes an active role in its management. *Also known as* active investor. *Opposite of* hands-off investor.

Hang Seng index The major stock index in Hong Kong.

hard asset *See* real asset.

hard capital rationing A capital budget that under no circumstances can be changed.

hard currency A freely convertible currency that is expected to hold its value in the foreseeable future.

hard dollars Actual separate payments made to a brokerage firm by a customer for services, including research. *Opposite of* soft dollars.

harmless warrant Warrant that allows the user to purchase a bond only by surrendering another bond with similar terms.

Hart-Scott-Rodino Act Antitrust act administered by the U.S. Department of Justice and the Federal Trade Commission that requires an investor to file a form with the government before he or she acquires an economic interest in the lesser amount of $15 million or 15 percent of the capitalization of a specific security. The government has thirty days to respond to the filer.

head and shoulders In technical analysis, the pattern that results when a security's price reaches a peak and declines; rises above its former peak and again declines; rises a third time but not to the second peak, and then again declines. The first and third peaks resemble shoulders, while the second peak is the formation's head. Technical analysts generally consider a head and shoulders formation to be a very bearish indication because the security is too weak to rise above its previous highs.

heavy An equities market now dominated by sellers, or oversupply, resulting in falling prices. *See also* overbought; resistance level; tired.

hedge A transaction that reduces the risk of an investment. For example, if an investor owns one hundred shares of IBM but is concerned that the stock might drop, he could purchase a put option that will rise in value if the shares decline. The cost of such a hedge diminishes the potential gains from holding the stock, however.

hedge clause A clause in a research report or any published document that attempts to absolve the writer of responsibility if any of the information provided is inaccurate. *Also known as* disclaimer.

hedge fund An investment strategy that may employ a variety of techniques to enhance returns, such as both buying and shorting stocks according to a valuation model. Hedge funds have become extremely popular in recent years. If the hedge fund is established outside the United States, it is virtually unregulated by the U.S. government. Perhaps the best-known hedge fund was that run by Long Term Capital Management, which nearly failed in the fall of 1998, shaking the financial markets. The $4 billion fund was taken over by a consortium of securities firms and banks, who were organized by the Federal Reserve Bank of New York.

hedge ratio For options, ratio between the change in an option's theoretical value and the change in price of the underlying stock at a given point in time. Investors use such ratios to hedge or protect existing positions. For convertible bonds, the ratio representing the number of underlying common shares sold short compared to the shares into which bonds are convertible. *Also known as* delta.

hedge wrapper An options strategy in which an investor with a long position in an underlying stock buys an out-of-the-money put and sells an out-of-the-money call. The hedge wrapper defines a range where the stock will be sold at expiration of the option, depending upon which way the stock moves.

hedged portfolio A very low-risk portfolio, it may consist of a long position in the stock and a long position in the put option on the stock, so as to produce a return that equals the risk-free interest rate.

hedged tender A strategy to protect an investor who holds shares involved in a partial tender offer, should all shares tendered not be purchased when the offer ends. For example, say an investor owns five thousand shares of a company. An acquiring company makes a tender offer of $100 a share when the shares are currently trading at $80. The investor sells short twenty-five hundred shares after the announcement and the price of the stock has approached $100. The company purchases only twenty-five hundred of the original shares at $100, but the investor has sold the other half of the holding at $100, protecting himself from losses if the price of the stock drops on a post-news dip. The risk in this strategy is that more than twenty-five hundred shares will be accepted in the offer, leaving the investor with a short position in the stock.

hedgie Slang for a hedge fund.

hedging A strategy designed to reduce investment risk using call options, put options, short-selling, or futures contracts. A hedge can help lock in profits. Its purpose is to reduce the volatility of a portfolio by reducing the risk of loss.

heir A person who will inherit the assets of another person when that other person dies without a will. State law determines a person's status as an heir, usually by per capita or per stirpes distribution. *Compare to* beneficiary.

held at the opening A stock that is not open for trading because specialists or regulators have halted all transactions until price imbalances dissipate or significant news is disseminated.

held order An order that must be executed without hesitation.

hell-or-high-water contract A contract that obligates a purchaser of a project's output to make cash payments to the project in all events, even if no product is offered for sale.

Helsinki Exchanges (HEX) Finland's consolidated exchange. The Helsinki Exchanges were formed at the beginning of 1998 following the merger of the Helsinki Stock Exchange Ltd., SOM Ltd., the Securities and Derivatives Exchange, and the Clearing House. www.hse.fi

hemline theory A theory that stock prices move in the same direction as the hemlines of women's dresses. For example, short skirts (1920s and 1960s) are symbolic of bullish markets, and long skirts (1930s and 1940s) are symbolic of bearish markets. Few investors subscribe to the theory.

Herstatt risk The risk of loss in foreign exchange trading whereby one party will deliver foreign exchange but the counterparty financial institution will fail to complete its end of the contract. *Also known as* settlement risk; counterparty risk.

hidden load A sales charge that is not explicitly disclosed or is buried in the fine print of a mutual fund prospectus or life insurance policy.

hidden value Valuable asset owned by a company that is not accurately reflected in its stock price at a particular time. This may happen because a company has written off the value of a physical asset on its books, but because the asset is still productive it has a value.

high current-income mutual fund A mutual fund whose primary goal is to produce a high level of income by making higher-risk investments in instruments such as junk bonds.

high flyer High-priced and highly speculative stock that moves up and down sharply over a short period. Generally glamorous in nature due to the capital gains potential associated with them; also used to describe any high-priced stock. *Opposite of* sleeper.

high price The highest price of a stock over the past fifty-two weeks, adjusted for any stock splits. Can be measured using either closing prices or intraday prices.

high-coupon bond refunding Replace a high-coupon bond with a new, lower-coupon bond.

high-grade bond A bond with AAA, AA, or A rating in Standard & Poor's or Moody's rating system.

highly confident letter An investment banking firm's letter indicating that the firm is highly confident it will be able to arrange financing for a securities deal or a takeover.

highly leveraged transaction Bank loan to a firm with high levels of debt in its capital structure.

highs Stocks that have hit an all-time high for the current fifty-two-week time period. When more stocks are trading at their highs than are trading at their lows, the market is considered bullish.

high-tech stock Stocks of companies operating in high-technology fields. These shares are generally riskier than shares in consumer-oriented goods because technological advancements can make technologies obsolete very quickly. Few high-tech companies remain leaders in their industries for more than ten years.

high-yield bond A bond issued by a company that is less established or less solid financially than those of high-grade issuers. As a result, these companies must pay a higher interest rate to investors than better quality companies. *Also known as* junk bond.

hijacking Japanese term for a takeover.

historical cost Describes the accounting cost carried in the books for an item or asset.

historical cost accounting convention An accounting technique that values an asset for balance sheet purposes at the price paid for the asset at the time of its acquisition. The asset could have risen or fallen in value since that time. *Opposite of* marking to market.

historical exchange rate An accounting term that refers to the exchange rate in effect at the time an asset or liability is acquired.

historical trading range The range of prices of a security or a commodity since trading began.

historical volatility The standard deviation of the asset's returns estimated from a historical time period.

historical yield A measure of a mutual fund's yield over a specific period of time, e.g., one year, two years, five years, or years to date.

hit the bid A dealer who agrees to sell at the bid price quoted by another dealer. *Opposite of* take the offer.

hit the tape When an executed trade crosses the ticker tape. *Also known as* print.

hold To maintain ownership of a security over a long period of time. "Hold" is also a recommendation of an analyst who is not positive enough about a stock to recommend a buy, but not negative enough to recommend its sale.

holder-of-record date The date on which holders of record in a firm's stock are designated as recipients of either dividends or stock rights. *Also called* date of record.

holding company A corporation that owns enough voting stock in another firm to control management and operations by influencing or electing its board of directors.

holding period Length of time a security is held.

holding the market The illegal practice of maintaining or placing a sufficient number of buy orders to create price support for a security or commodity in order to stop a downward trend.

holding-period return Rate of return on an investment over a given period.

holding-period yield The annual rate of return actually realized on a bond investment.

home run Large capital gain in a stock in a short period of time.

home-asset bias The tendency of investors to overinvest in their own country's assets.

home owner's equity account A credit line offered by mortgage lenders providing a home owner a second mortgage that uses the equity in the house as collateral.

home owner's insurance policy An insurance policy protecting a home owner against damage or loss to property.

homestead exemption Under state bankruptcy laws, a provision that protects the equity in a debtor's primary residence from claims by creditors when the debtor files for bankruptcy.

homogeneity The degree to which items are similar.

homogeneous Exhibiting a high degree of homogeneity.

Hong Kong Futures Exchange (HKFE) Established in 1976, the Hong Kong Futures Exchange operates futures and options markets in index, stock, interest rate, and foreign exchange products. www.hkex. com.hk

horizon analysis An analysis of securities' total return to assess performance over an investment time horizon.

horizon return Total return over a given time horizon.

horizontal acquisition Merger between two companies producing similar goods or services.

horizontal price movement Stock price movement within a narrow price range over an extended period of time that creates the appearance of a relatively straight line on a graph of the stock's price. *Also known as* flatliner.

horizontal spread The simultaneous purchase and sale of two options that differ only in their exercise dates.

hospital revenue bond A bond issued to finance construction of a hospital by a municipal or state agency.

host security The security to which a warrant is attached.

hostile takeover A takeover of a company against the wishes of the current management and the board of directors by an acquiring company or raider. Such takeovers were common in the 1980s, but most acquisitions and mergers in subsequent periods have been friendly. *Opposite of* friendly takeover.

hot In the context of general equities, active; usually with positive price implications.

hot money Money that moves quickly across country borders in response to interest rate differences and that moves away when the interest rate differential disappears.

house Firm that conducts business as broker/dealer in securities or in the investment banking field is characterized as a house.

house account A type of account at a brokerage firm that is given a high level of priority and is handled by the main office or an executive rather than a traditional salesperson.

house call Notification by a brokerage house that a customer's margin account is below the minimum level required by the firm. The client must provide more cash or equity or the account will be liquidated. *Also known as* maintenance call.

house maintenance requirement The internal rules of a brokerage house that govern the minimum amount of equity that must be present in a customer's margin account. If that level is not met, additional cash or assets must be deposited.

house of issue An investment banking firm that underwrites stock or bond issues and offers the securities to the public.

house poor People who are short on cash because most of their money is tied up in their homes.

house rules Internal rules of broker/dealer firm that govern the handling of its customers' accounts.

housing bond Bonds issued by a local housing authority to finance housing projects.

Hulbert rating A rating by *Hulbert Financial Digest* of how well the recommendations of various investment advisory newsletters have performed. www.hulbertdigest.com

human capital The unique capabilities and expertise of individuals. Technology firms rely heavily on human capital to keep their products from becoming obsolete.

hunkering down A term used to describe a trader selling off a big position in a stock.

hurdle rate The required return in capital budgeting. For example, if a project has an expected rate of return higher than the hurdle rate, the project may be accepted.

hybrid annuity A type of insurance company investment that combines the benefits of both a fixed annuity and a variable annuity.

hybrid security A convertible security whose underlying common stock is trading in a middle range, causing the convertible security to trade with the characteristics of both a fixed-income security and a common-stock instrument.

hyperinflation A period of rapid inflation that can make currency worthless. During hyperinflation, investors may shift their money to tangible assets.

hypothecation In banking, refers to the commitment of property to secure a loan. In securities, refers to the commitment of securities to serve as collateral for margin loans at a broker/dealer firm.

I

IDR *See* international depositary receipt.

IFC *See* International Finance Corporation.

illiquid Refers to a security that trades infrequently and is therefore difficult to convert into cash. Stocks are generally more liquid than bonds, but a stock with a small number of shares outstanding can be very hard to buy or sell without disrupting its price. With fewer investors willing to trade in an illiquid security, often the buyer or seller must engage a broker to conduct a search for someone interested in the trade. *Also known as* thinly traded.

imbalance of orders When too many buy or sell orders pile up in a stock without matching orders of the opposite kind. An imbalance usually follows a significant event such as a takeover, research recommendation, anomalous earnings announcement, or a government ruling that will significantly affect the company's business. If it occurs before the stock exchange opens, trading in the stock is delayed. If it occurs during the trading day, the specialist suspends trading until enough matching orders can be found to make an orderly market. Order imbalances do not stop trading on Nasdaq stocks.

IMF *See* International Monetary Fund.

immediate payment annuity An annuity contract purchased by an individual from an insurance company. The buyer makes a single payment and the insurance company begins paying out a specified annual amount immediately.

impaired credit Result of a borrower's reduced credit rating.

implied volatility The expected volatility in a stock's return derived from its option price, maturity date, exercise price, and risk-free rate of return, using an option pricing model such as the Black-Scholes.

import/export letters of credit Bank or financial institution issuance of funds to facilitate international trade.

imputation tax system Arrangement by which investors who receive a dividend also receive a tax credit for corporate taxes that the firm has paid.

imputed interest Interest that has effectively been paid to a bondholder, even though no money has actually been paid. Since bonds pay interest semiannually, imputed interest may be calculated in the month just prior to a payment.

imputed value The value of an asset, service, or company that is not physically recorded in any accounts but is implicit in the product.

in play Company that has become the target of a takeover, and whose stock has now become a favorite among speculative investors.

incentive fee Compensation paid to money managers who achieve above-average returns. Sometimes referred to as a performance fee.

incentive stock option An employee stock option plan that meets stringent IRS requirements so that taxes are not due on shares until they are sold. *Opposite of* nonqualified stock option.

income bond A bond whose payment of interest is contingent on the company generating enough earnings. These bonds are commonly used during the reorganization of a failed or failing business.

income fund A mutual fund that seeks to provide liberal current income from investments. Such a fund would typically invest in bonds or stock with hefty dividends and would sacrifice future growth in share prices for the receipt of current income.

income limited partnership A limited partnership investment whose main goal is income generation with limited liability.

income property Real estate purchased to generate income.

income statement (statement of operations) A financial statement showing a company's revenues and costs over a period of time. The difference between revenues and expenses is net income. Investors consult income statements to see that a company's sales are rising and that its costs are being kept under control. An income statement is also where investors go to check that a company's operations are generating enough money to cover the interest costs on its debt, for instance. When all costs, including taxes, are deducted from a company's sales, the resulting net income is divided by the number of shares outstanding to compute earnings-per-share.

income stock Common stock that pays a high dividend.

income tax A state or federal government's levy on individuals' income and on the earnings of corporations.

income-exclusion rule The IRS rule that excludes certain types of income from taxation, e.g., welfare payments.

incontestability clause Clause in a life insurance contract preventing the insurer from revoking the policy after it has been in force for a year or two if the life insurance company discovers any important facts that the policyholder may have concealed, such as health problems that would have prevented the policy from being written.

incorporation A legal process through which a company receives a charter, and the state in which it is based allows it to operate as a corporation.

incremental costs and benefits Costs and benefits that would occur if a particular course of action is taken, compared to those that would have obtained if that course of action had not been taken.

incremental internal rate of return The difference in the internal rate of return from choosing a larger instead of a smaller project.

indemnify To release a party to a contract from accountability for damage or loss. Typically used in insurance policy agreements.

indenture Agreement between lender and borrower that details specific terms of a bond issuance, such as the legal obligations of bond issuer and rights of bondholders.

independent auditor A certified public accountant operating outside a company who provides an accountant's opinion of the financial condition of the concern after scrutinizing its books.

independent broker NYSE member who executes orders for floor brokers and firms other than his or her own.

index Statistical composite that measures changes in the economy or in financial markets, often expressed in percentage changes from a specified period. Indexes often measure the ups and downs of stock and bond markets in terms of weighted market prices. The most well-known stock market index is the Dow Jones Industrial Average. *See also* S&P 500 Composite Index.

index arbitrage An investment strategy that exploits differences between actual prices and those expected by investors in the future. An example is the simultaneous buying (or selling) of stock-index futures (i.e., S&P 500) while selling (or buying) the underlying stocks of that index, capturing as profit any difference.

index fund Mutual fund designed to match the returns on a stock market index. The most common fund mirrors the broad-based S&P 500 Composite index.

index option A call or put option based on a stock market index.

indexed bond Bond whose interest payments are linked to an index. Bonds linked to the consumer price index, for example, will pay an interest rate that keeps up with the rate of inflation.

indexing A passive investment strategy calling for construction of a portfolio of stocks designed to track the total return performance of an index of stocks. Buying an index fund is a form of passive investing.

indexing-plus *See* enhanced indexing.

indicated dividend Total amount of dividends that would be paid to a shareholder of a stock over the next twelve months if each dividend were the same amount as the most recent dividend. Usually represented by the letter "e" in stock tables.

indicated yield The yield of a stock based on the most recent quarterly dividend rate times four. To determine the yield, divide the annual dividend by the price of the stock. The resulting number is represented as a percentage. *See also* dividend yield.

indication of interest A dealer's or investor's interest in purchasing securities that are expected to be issued publicly and are being registered with the Securities and Exchange Commission. An indication of interest is not, however, a commitment to buy.

indicator Technical or fundamental measurement that securities analysts use to forecast the overall market's direction, such as investment advisory sentiment, volume of stock trading, direction of interest rates, and buying or selling by corporate insiders.

individual retirement account (IRA) A retirement account that may be established by an employed person. IRA contributions have pre-established limits, are tax deductible, and the gains in the account are tax-deferred until they are removed. Withdrawals from IRAs before the age of fifty-nine and a half require payment of penalties and taxes.

individual retirement account (IRA) rollover A provision of the law governing IRAs that enables a retiree or anyone receiving a lump-sum payment from a pension, profit-sharing, or salary-reduction plan to transfer the amount into an IRA without incurring penalties or taxes.

individual tax return A tax return filed by an individual to account for his or her personal income and taxes payable.

industrial production A statistic determined by the Federal Reserve Board focusing on the total output of all U.S. factories and mines on a monthly basis. Used as an indicator of the economy's health.

industrial revenue bond (IRB) A bond issued by local government agencies on behalf of corporations.

industrials General term used in the financial markets to refer to companies manufacturing, producing, or distributing goods and services.

industry The category describing a company's primary business activity. This category is usually determined by the largest portion of revenue.

industry allocation Investment of certain proportions of a portfolio in certain industries. *Also known as* sector allocation; rotation.

inflation The rate at which the general level of prices for goods and services is rising, typically measured by the consumer price index. *Opposite of* deflation.

inflation accounting Accounting practices allowing for the effects of inflation.

inflation hedge Investments designed to hedge against inflation and the loss of value associated with it. Investing in gold is a common inflation hedge.

inflation risk The risk of which after adjusting an investment return for inflation, the realized gain will be negative. *Also called* purchasing power risk.

inflation-escalator clause A clause in a contract providing for increases or decreases in inflation depending on fluctuations in the cost of living or production costs.

inflation-indexed securities Securities such as bonds or notes that guarantee a return that is higher than the rate of inflation if the security is held to maturity.

information costs Cost of gathering information on a particular security, product, or deal.

infrastructure A country's fundamental system of transportation, communications, and other aspects of its physical capabilities.

ingot A bar of metal such as the type used by the Federal Reserve System to store gold reserves.

initial margin Amount of cash or securities required to be deposited with a broker before an investor can borrow money to buy stocks. The

Securities Exchange Act of 1934 gives the Board of Governors of the Federal Reserve the responsibility to set initial margin requirements, but individual brokerage firms are free to set higher requirements. Initial margin requirements of only 10 percent in the 1920s are now recognized as feeding the speculative frenzy leading up to the crash of 1929. More recently, the initial margin requirement has been 50 percent, requiring investors to put up half of the value of their stock purchase. Initial margins for futures trading are smaller and reflect the volatility of the underlying security.

initial public offering (IPO) A company's first sale of stock to the public. Securities offered in an IPO are often, but not always, those of young, small companies seeking outside investors and a public market for their stock. Investors purchasing stock in IPOs generally must be prepared to accept considerable risks for the possibility of large gains. In the stock market mania of the late 1990s, prices of IPOs surged fivefold on average in their first days of trading. However, the vast majority of these companies' shares subsequently fell below their offering prices, leaving many investors with large losses.

initiate coverage When research analysts at a particular securities house begin to follow a company, writing reports on its progress for investors.

in-line A corporate earnings announcement that adheres closely to Wall Street analysts' expectations.

inside market Refers to over-the-counter markets, such as the Nasdaq. Highest bid or lowest offer.

insider Director or senior officer of a corporation who may have access to inside information about the company. An insider is also someone who owns more than 10 percent of the voting shares of a company.

insider information Material information about a company that has not yet been made public. It is illegal for holders of this information to make trades based on it, however received.

insider trading Legal trading by officers, directors, major stockholders, or others who hold private information about the corporation that happens during special trading windows. Reports on trades are submitted to the SEC each month in form 4.

Insider Trading Sanctions Act of 1984 Act imposing civil and criminal penalties for insider-trading violations.

insolvency risk The risk that a firm will be unable to satisfy its debts. Also referred to as bankruptcy risk.

insolvent A firm that is unable to pay debts, meaning its liabilities exceed its assets.

installment sale The sale of an asset in exchange for a specified series of payments (installments).

institutional broker A broker who buys and sells securities for institutional investors such as banks, mutual funds, and pension funds.

Institutional Brokers' Estimate System (I/B/E/S) Service that assembles analysts' estimates of future earnings for thousands of publicly traded companies, detailing how many estimates are available for each company and the high, low, and average estimates for each.

institutional investor Organization that invests for the benefit of others, including insurance companies, pension funds, investment companies, mutual funds, and endowment funds. Institutional investors are the driving force in the market, currently accounting for over 50 percent of market capitalization and approximately 70 percent of trading volume. *Compare to* retail investor.

instrument Financial securities, such as a money-market instrument or capital-market instrument.

instrumentality Notes issued by a federal agency whose obligations are guaranteed by the full faith and credit of the U.S. government, even though the agency's responsibilities are not necessarily those of the U.S. government.

insurable interest An insurance term referring to the relationship between a policy's insured person or property and the potential beneficiary. The beneficiary must have an insurable interest in the insured person or property to receive payment of the policy if the insured died while the policy was in force.

insurance A contract that guards against property loss or damage. The entity buying insurance pays premiums to the insurer, which pays an agreed-upon sum to the insured in the event of loss.

insurance agent The insurance company representative and adviser who sells insurance policies.

insurance broker A broker, independent of any insurance company, who represents the interests of the buyer in searching for insurance coverage at the lowest cost and providing the highest benefit to the buyer.

insurance claim A claim for reimbursement from the insurance company when the insured has suffered a loss that is covered under its policy.

insurance policy A contract detailing what risks are insured, what insurance premiums are to be paid by the policyholder, what deductibles prevail, and all other strictures associated with a policy.

insurance premium Periodic payments calculated by the insurance company that must be made by the insured to guarantee protection of property loss under an insurance policy. The premiums are based on the risks the insurer feels it is taking on by writing the policy.

insured The property or persons covered by an insurance policy.

insured account A bank or financial account that is insured for the benefit of the depositor, protecting against loss to a limited amount in the event that the savings institution becomes insolvent. *See* Federal Deposit Insurance Corporation.

insured bond A municipal bond backed both by the credit of the municipal issuer and by a commercial insurance policy. These bonds typically pay a lower interest rate because the insurance feature reduces their risk.

intangible asset A type of asset belonging to a company that has value but no physical characteristics. Patents, copyrights, and trademarks are examples of intangible assets that are expected to generate cash in the future. The most common intangible asset is known as goodwill, which can represent the value of a well-known brand-name product, such as Coca-Cola or Tide. Goodwill also represents the premium over a company's net worth that an acquirer pays in a purchase. When too great a premium is paid and the acquired company's business does not produce the results that were expected of it, the goodwill associated with its purchase is written off as a loss.

intellectual property rights Patents, copyrights, and proprietary technologies and processes that may be the basis of a company's competitive advantage.

interbank market Financial institutions' exchange of currencies between and among themselves.

interbank rate *See* London Interbank Offered Rate.

intercompany loan Loan made by one unit of a corporation to another unit of the same corporation.

interest The price paid for borrowing money from a lender. It is expressed as a percentage rate over a period of time, usually annually, and fluctuates based on whether or not money is easily available for loans. When lenders are accommodating, interest rates are low; when money is scarce, rates are high.

interest coverage ratio The ratio of a company's earnings before interest and taxes to its annual interest expense. This ratio measures a firm's ability to pay interest costs.

interest coverage test A debt limitation that prohibits the issuance of additional long-term debt if the issuer's interest coverage would, as a result of the new debt, fall below a specified minimum.

interest deduction An interest expense, such as interest on a home mortgage, that is allowed as a deduction for individual income tax purposes.

interest expense Interest expense is the money the corporation or individual pays out in interest to its lenders.

interest in arrears Interest that is due only at the maturity date rather than periodically over the life of the loan.

interest on interest Interest earned on reinvestment of each interest payment on money invested. *See also* compound interest.

interest rate The rate, as a proportion of the principal, at which interest is computed. For example, the rate on a credit card with an 18 percent annual percentage rate is 1.5 percent per month.

interest rate agreement An agreement whereby one party, for an up-front premium, agrees to compensate the other at specific time periods if a designated interest rate, such as the federal funds rate, is different from a predetermined level.

interest rate cap An interest rate agreement in which payments are made when the rate exceeds a specified strike rate. Also referred to as interest rate ceiling.

interest rate floor An interest rate agreement in which payments are made when the reference rate falls below the strike rate.

interest rate futures contract A futures contract based on an interbank deposit rate or an underlying debt security. The value of the contract rises and falls inversely to changes in interest rates.

interest rate risk The chance that a security's value will change as a result of rising or falling interest rates. For example, a bond's price drops as interest rates rise because its previously assigned interest rate is lower than prevailing rates, making the bond less attractive to investors.

interest rate swap An agreement in which two parties agree to exchange periodic interest payments on some predetermined principal amount. For example, one party will pay a fixed rate while the other will pay a variable or floating rate. Interest rate swaps are bets on the future direction of rates and are entered into by large financial institutions or companies. *Compare to* equity swap.

interest-only (IO) A security based solely on the interest payments from a pool of mortgages, Treasury bonds, or corporate bonds. Once the principal on the mortgages or bonds has been repaid, interest payments stop, and the value of the IO falls to zero. When interest rates rise, the value of previously issued IOs declines because their interest rates are then below the prevailing market rate. Investors who buy IOs are making a bet that interest rates will remain static or decline. If rates fell, the previously issued IOs would have more value. *Compare to* principal-only (PO).

interest-only loan A loan in which payment of principal is deferred and interest payments are the only current obligation.

interest-sensitive stock Stocks whose earnings are dependent upon the direction of interest rates. For example, shares of home builders rise as interest rates decline because low interest rates reduce the cost of purchasing houses and increase demand for housing.

interim dividend The declaration and payment of a dividend prior to a company's annual earnings determination.

interim financing A short-term loan made to a company on the condition that long-term or intermediate financing will follow shortly.

interlocking directorate Describes cross-membership of directors on companies' board of directors. Such relationships can be a warning flag to investors because they may represent a lack of independence among directors.

Intermarket Surveillance Information System (ISIS) A database that distributes information from all the major stock exchanges in the United States.

Intermarket Trading System (ITS) Electronic communications network linking the trading floors of seven registered exchanges to permit trading among them in stocks listed on either the NYSE or AMEX and one or more regional exchanges. Through ITS, any broker or market maker on the floor of any participating exchange can reach other participants for an execution whenever the nationwide quote shows a better price available.

intermediary   *See* financial intermediary.

intermediate-term   Typically refers to a security with a maturity between one and ten years.

intermediated market   A market in which a financial institution stands between counterparties to financial transactions.

intermediation   Investment through a financial institution. *Opposite of* disintermediation.

internal auditor   An employee of a company who analyzes the company's accounting records to ensure that the company is following and complying with all regulations.

internal expansion   Growth of assets resulting from a company's own internal financing or internally generated cash flow.

internal growth rate   Maximum rate a firm can expand without using outside sources of funding. Growth generated by cash flows that are retained by a company.

internal measure   The number of days that a firm can finance operations without additional cash income.

internal rate of return (IRR)   The rate at which a company's future cash flows, discounted back to today, equal its price. Also computed on bonds and other income-generating investments.

Internal Revenue Code   The various statutes and regulations making up federal tax law.

Internal Revenue Service (IRS)   The U.S. federal agency responsible for the collection of federal taxes, including personal and corporate income taxes, Social Security taxes, and excise and gift taxes. www.irs.gov

Internal Revenue Service Restructuring and Reform Act of 1998   The legislation targeted at IRS reform, particularly related to taxpayer protection and rights. This law also changed the time period required to turn a short-term gain into a capital gain and therefore pay a lower tax rate on the profit incurred.

International Bank for Reconstruction and Development   *See* World Bank.

international bonds   Bonds of foreign issuers. Eurobonds are one type.

international depositary receipt (IDR)   A receipt issued by a bank as evidence of ownership of one or more shares of the underlying stock of a foreign corporation that the bank holds in trust. The advantage of the IDR structure is that the corporation does not have to comply with all the issuing requirements of the foreign country where the stock is to be traded. The U.S. version of the IDR is the American depositary receipt (ADR).

international diversification The attempt to reduce risk by investing in more than one nation. By diversifying across nations whose economic cycles are not perfectly correlated, investors can typically reduce the variability of their returns. However, as global economics have become more intertwined, this type of diversification has become less reliable.

International Finance Corporation (IFC) A corporation owned by the World Bank that produces a number of well-known stock indexes for emerging markets. Its major role is to provide financing for projects in less developed countries. www.ifc.org

international fund A mutual fund that can invest only outside the United States.

international market index An index listed on the American Stock Exchange tracking the performance of fifty American depositary receipts traded on the AMEX, NYSE, and Nasdaq.

International Monetary Fund (IMF) An organization founded in 1944 to oversee exchange arrangements of member countries and to lend foreign currency reserves to members with short-term cash needs. www.imf.org

international monetary system The global network of government and commercial institutions within which currency exchange rates are determined.

international mutual fund A mutual fund that invests strictly in securities markets throughout the world, excluding the United States. A global fund, on the other hand, invests in both foreign and U.S. securities.

inter vivos trust A trust created between living persons. *Opposite of* testamentary trust.

in-the-money option A put option that has a strike price higher than the underlying stock price, or a call option with a strike price lower than the underlying stock price. For example, if Microsoft is trading at $60 a share, a March Microsoft call option with a strike price of $55, which gives the option holder the right to purchase at $55, would be considered in-the-money by $5 a share. *Opposite of* out-of-the-money option.

intracompany trade Transactions between or among subsidiaries that are part of the same parent company.

intraday Term meaning "within the day," often to refer to the high and the low price of a stock.

intramarket sector spread The spread between two issues of the same maturity within a market sector. For instance, the difference in interest rates offered for a five-year industrial corporate bond and a five-year bond issued by an electric utility company.

intrastate offering A securities offering limited to just one state in the United States.

intrinsic value of a firm The present value of a firm's expected future net cash flows discounted by a required rate of return.

intrinsic value of an option The amount by which an option is in-the-money. An option that is not in-the-money has no intrinsic value.

inventory For companies, raw materials, items available for sale, or items in the process of being made ready for sale. They can be individually valued several ways, including their cost or their current market value. They can also be valued collectively by FIFO (first in, first out), LIFO (last in, first out), or other accounting techniques. The lower value is usually used to preclude overstating earnings and assets. For securities firms, inventory consists of securities bought and held by a broker or dealer for resale.

inventory financing Loans to companies that use inventory as collateral. Also referred to as an inventory loan.

inventory turnover ratio The ratio of annual sales to average inventory, which measures the speed at which inventory is being produced and sold. Low turnover is an unhealthy sign, indicating excess stock or poor sales. A rising inventory turnover is viewed as positive among investors.

inverse floater A derivative instrument whose coupon rate moves inversely to the market rate of interest.

inverse floating-rate note A variable-rate security whose coupon rate increases as a benchmark interest rate declines.

inverted yield curve When short-term interest rates are higher than long-term rates. An inverted or normal yield curve has presaged every economic recession over the past thirty-five years. *Opposite of* positive yield curve.

investment The creation of more money through the use of capital.

investment adviser A person or an organization that makes day-to-day decisions, regarding a portfolio's investments. *Also called* portfolio manager; investment manager; money manager.

Investment Advisers Act Legislation passed in 1940 requiring financial advisers to register with the SEC. The measure was enacted to protect the public from fraud or misrepresentation by investment advisers.

investment advisory service A business that specializes in providing investment advice for a fee. All advisers of an advisory service must be registered with the SEC.

investment analyst Research professional at an investment firm who analyzes company financial statements and industry trends with an eye to recommending that the company's securities be bought, sold, or avoided altogether. *Also known as* financial analyst.

investment bank Financial intermediary who performs a variety of services, including aiding in the sale of securities, facilitating mergers and other corporate reorganizations, acting as broker to both individual and institutional clients, and trading for his or her own accounts. *See also* underwriter.

investment climate Factors such as economic, monetary, and other conditions that affect the performance of investments.

investment club A group of people who combine their money into a larger pool, then invest collectively in stocks and bonds, making decisions as a group.

investment company A firm that invests the funds of investors in securities appropriate for their stated investment objectives in return for a management fee. *See also* mutual fund.

Investment Company Act of 1940 Legislation that requires investment companies to register with the SEC and outlines standards by which they must operate.

Investment Company Institute A national industry group of investment companies, including mutual funds, that was founded in 1940. www.ici.org

investment income The revenue from a portfolio of invested assets.

investment letter A letter of intent between the issuer of new securities and the buyer, in the private placement of these new securities. The letter of intent establishes that the securities are being bought for a minimum time period and are treated as an investment, not for resale. If no such letter exists, the securities must be registered with the SEC.

investment management The process of managing money. *Also called* portfolio management; money management.

investment manager The individual who manages a portfolio of investments. *Also called* portfolio manager; money manager; investment adviser.

investment objective What an investor hopes to achieve by investing his funds. One investor may require income while another wants capital appreciation or growth. The investor's objective governs the investment strategy.

investment philosophy The style and general ideology of investment practiced by an investor. For example, certain investors favor small-capitalization stocks, while others prefer large blue-chip stocks.

investment policy Statement of objectives and constraints for an individual's or organization's investing approach.

investment risk Uncertainty about the future gains or losses to be realized from an investment.

investment strategy A strategy used by an investor when deciding how to allocate capital among several options including stocks, bonds, cash equivalents, commodities, and real estate. The strategy should take into account the investor's tolerance for risk as well as when capital will be needed.

investment trust A closed-end fund regulated by the Investment Company Act of 1940. These funds have a fixed number of shares that are traded on the secondary markets. When many investors buy these shares, their prices may exceed the net asset values per share, in which case shares are selling at a premium. When the market price falls below the net asset value, the shares are selling at a discount. Many closed-end funds are of a specialized nature; these portfolios represent a particular industry or country. These funds are usually listed on U.S. and foreign exchanges.

investment valuation model (IVM) The basic mathematical technique of finance that calculates the value of an investment as the present value of all future cash flows expected to be generated by the investment.

investment-grade bond A bond that is assigned a rating in the top four categories by commercial credit-rating companies. Standard and Poor's classifies investment-grade bonds as BBB or higher, and Moody's classifies investment grade bonds as Baa or higher.

investment-strategy committee A committee within a brokerage firm that conducts research and makes recommendations on the firm's stated investment strategy.

investor The owner of a financial asset.

investor relations The process by which the corporation communicates with its investors.

investor's equity The credit balance in a customer's margin account at a brokerage firm. *See also* margin.

invoice Bill written by a seller of goods or services and submitted to a purchaser for payment.

IO *See* interest-only.

IPO *See* initial public offering.

IRA *See* individual retirement account.

IRR *See* internal rate of return.

IRS *See* Internal Revenue Service.

irrevocable letter of credit Assurance of funds issued by a bank that cannot be canceled or amended without the beneficiary's approval.

irrevocable trust A trust that cannot be amended, altered, or revoked by the person who established it.

ISIS *See* Intermarket Surveillance Information System.

issue A particular financial asset.

issuer An entity that sells a financial asset in the marketplace.

issuing bank Bank that issues a letter of credit.

Istanbul Stock Exchange The sole securities exchange in Turkey. www.ise.org

Italian Exchange (Borsa Italiana) Italy's major securities exhange. www.borsaitalia.it/eng/home

itemized deduction Specific deduction allowed by the IRS outlined in the tax return.

ITS *See* Intermarket Trading System.

J

Jakarta Stock Exchange Established in 1977, the largest securities exchange in Indonesia. www.jsx.co.id

January effect Refers to the historical pattern of stock prices rising in the first few days of January as investors put on new positions. Studies have suggested this holds only for small-capitalization stocks. In recent years, there is less evidence of a January effect.

Japanese Association of Securities Dealers Automated Quotation System (Jasdaq) Japanese equivalent of Nasdaq. Japanese language only. www.jasdaq.co.jp

J-curve Theory that says a country's trade deficit will initially worsen after its currency depreciates because higher prices on foreign imports will more than offset the reduced volume of imports.

jobber A term for a market maker used on the London Stock Exchange.

Johannesburg Stock Exchange (JSE) Established in 1886, the Johannesburg Stock Exchange is the only stock exchange in South Africa. Gold and mining stocks form the majority of shares listed. www.jse.co.za

joint account An agreement between two or more firms to share risk and financing responsibility in purchasing or underwriting securities, or an account owned jointly by two or more persons at a bank or brokerage house.

joint and survivor annuity A type of annuity, opened by and intended for two people, that makes payments for the entire lifetime of both beneficiaries, even if one dies.

joint bond A bond that is guaranteed by the issuer and another party.

joint clearing member Firm that clears on more than one exchange.

joint tax return Tax return filed by two people, usually spouses.

joint tenant with right of survivorship In the case of a joint account, on the death of one account holder, ownership of the account assets is transferred to the remaining account holder or holders.

joint venture An agreement between two or more firms to undertake the same business strategy and plan of action.

jointly and severally Municipal bond underwriting in which the account is undivided and syndicate members are responsible for unsold bonds in proportion to their participation, regardless of how many bonds they may have already sold. A firm with 20 percent of the account is responsible for selling 20 percent of the unsold bonds even if it has already sold 25 percent of the total debt issue, for example. *Compare to* severally but not jointly.

joint-stock company A form of business organization that falls between a corporation and a partnership. The company sells stock and its shareholders are free to sell their stock, but shareholders are liable for all debts of the company.

Jonestown defense An extreme defensive tactic employed by the management of a target corporation to prevent a hostile takeover. The defensive tactics are so extreme that they typically lead to the destruction of the target corporation. *Also known as* suicide pill.

jumbo certificate of deposit A certificate of deposit in increments of $100,000.

jumbo loan Mortgage loans that exceed the statutory size limit eligible for purchase or securitization by U.S. federal agencies. Super jumbo refers to mortgages over $1 million.

junior debt Debt whose holders have a claim on the firm's assets only after senior debt-holder claims have been satisfied. *Also known as* subordinated debt.

junior issue A debt or equity issue from one corporation over which the issue of another firm takes precedence with respect to dividends, interest, principal, or security in the event of liquidation.

junior mortgage A mortgage that will be satisfied only after more senior mortgages have been satisfied. A first mortgage will be satisfied prior to a second or a third mortgage.

junior refunding Issuing of new securities to refinance government debt that matures in one to five years.

junior security A security that has a lower-priority claim on a company's assets and income than a senior security. For example, common stock is junior in the capitalization structure to preferred stock.

junk bond A bond with a speculative credit rating of BB (Standard and Poor's) or Ba (Moody's) or lower. Junk or high-yield bonds offer investors higher yields than bonds of more financially sound companies.

just title A title with no encumbrances. *Also known as* clear title.

justified price The fair market price of an asset.

just-in-time inventory system System that schedules materials to arrive exactly when they are needed in the production process.

kaffirs South African gold-mining shares that trade on the London Stock Exchange.

kangaroos Australian stocks.

Kansas City Board of Trade A U.S.-based futures and options exchange. www.kcbt.com

Karachi Stock Exchange The major securities exchange of Pakistan. www.kse.com.pk

keiretsu A network of Japanese companies organized around a major bank.

Keogh plan A type of pension account in which taxes are deferred and that is available to those who are self-employed.

key man or woman insurance A life insurance policy purchased by a company to insure the life of a key executive. The company is the beneficiary in case of the executive's death.

Keynesian economics An economic theory of British economist John Maynard Keynes which proposes that active government intervention is necessary to ensure economic growth and stability.

"kick it out" To liquidate a position, selling a long or covering a short, without regard to price.

kickback Secret payment made to insure that the contract goes to a specific firm. An illegal activity.

kicker An additional feature of a debt obligation that increases its marketability and attractiveness to investors. May include warrants on the issuer's stock. *Also known as* sweetener.

kiddie tax Tax owed for the investment income of children under fourteen years of age if the amount is more than the annual exemption, currently $1,400. The tax is levied at the parent's or guardian's highest tax rate.

killer bees Those who help a company fend off a takeover bid; usually investment bankers who devise strategies to make the target less attractive or more difficult to acquire.

kiting The practice of depositing and drawing checks at two or more banks and taking advantage of the time it takes for the second bank to collect funds from the first bank. Also refers to illegally increasing the face value of a check by changing the numbers on the check. In the context of securities, refers to the manipulation and inflation of stock prices.

know your customer An ethical principle of securities laws that requires an adviser who recommends the purchase or sale of any security to a customer to believe that the recommendation is suitable for the customer, given the customer's financial situation. *Also known as* suitability rules.

Kondratieff wave An economic theory of the Soviet economist Nikolai Kondratieff stating that the economies of the Western world are susceptible to major up-and-down boom-and-bust "supercycles" lasting fifty to sixty years.

Korea Stock Exchange The major securities market of Korea. www.kse.or.kr/en_index.html

Krugerrand A gold coin minted by the Republic of South Africa that typically sells for a slightly higher price than the market value of the gold it contains.

Kuala Lumpur Stock Exchange Established in 1973, the only stock exchange in Malaysia. www.klse.com.my

L

ladder strategy A bond portfolio construction strategy that invests approximately equal amounts of money in every maturity within a given range.

Lady Macbeth strategy Strategy in which a third party poses as a white knight in a takeover bid, then joins forces with an unfriendly bidder.

Laffer curve A curve conjecturing that there is an optimal tax rate at which tax revenues to the government are maximized. Named after economist Arthur Laffer.

lagging indicators Economic indicators that follow rather than precede the country's overall pace of economic activity. *Compare to* leading indicators; coincident indicators.

laissez-faire A political doctrine according to which a government should not interfere with business and economic affairs.

land contract A method of real estate financing in which a mortgage-holding seller finances a buyer by taking a down payment and subsequent payments in installments, but holds the title until the mortgage is fully repaid.

landlord A property owner who rents property to a tenant.

lapsed option An option that no longer has any value because it has reached its expiration date without being exercised.

large-cap A stock with a high level of capitalization, usually at least $5 billion market value.

last in, first out (LIFO) An accounting treatment for the valuation of inventories. A company using LIFO assumes that any inventory sold was made from the last batch of inputs purchased, and the cost of manufacturing the product is valued accordingly. Choosing which type of valuation method will be followed can have an impact on a company's financial results in times of inflation when prices are rising rapidly. When prices are stable, whether LIFO or first in, first out (FIFO) is used is inconsequential. *Compare to* first in, first out (FIFO).

last sale The most recent trade in a security.

last trading day The final day under an exchange's rules during which trading may take place in a particular futures or options contract. Contracts outstanding at the end of the last trading day must be settled by delivery of underlying physical commodities or financial instruments, or by agreement for monetary settlement, depending on futures contract specifications.

late charge A fee a lender charges a borrower for a late payment.

late tape A delay in the display of price changes on the tape of a securities exchange because of heavy trading volume.

launder To move illegally acquired cash through financial systems so that it appears to be legally acquired.

lay off To eliminate all or part of a position by finding customers or other dealers to take the position.

lay up To execute a trade or order easily.

LBO *See* leveraged buyout.

lead manager The commercial or investment bank with the primary responsibility for bringing a security to the market. The lead manager recruits additional selling firms, negotiates terms of the security with the issuer, assesses market conditions, and advises on when it is best to make the offering. Also referred to as lead underwriter.

leader A stock or group of stocks that is the first to move in a market upsurge or downturn.

leading indicators Economic indicators that tend to rise or fall in advance of the rest of the economy. For example, initial claims for unemployment insurance are considered a leading indicator because they tend to rise at the beginning of an economic downturn. *Compare* to lagging indicators; coincident indicators.

leading the market A stock or group of stocks moving in advance of the general market.

leakage Release of information, selectively or not, before official public announcement. A violation of regulation FD, an SEC rule, if the company is responsible for the leak.

LEAPS *See* long-term anticipation securities.

lease A rental agreement, and a form of secured debt.

lease acquisition cost The legal fees and other expenses incurred when acquiring a lease.

lease rate The payment per period stated in a lease contract.

leaseback A transaction that involves the sale of some property, and an agreement by the seller to lease the property back from the buyer after the sale.

leasehold An asset providing the right to use property under a lease agreement.

leasehold improvement An improvement made to leased property.

lease-purchase agreement An agreement that allows for portions of lease payments to be used to purchase the leased property.

ledger cash A firm's cash balance as reported in its financial statements. *Also called* book cash.

leg A prolonged trend in stock market prices, such as a multiple-period bull market. Also, an option that is one side of a spread transaction. Finally, a portion of a larger trade. For example, someone who wants to purchase ten thousand shares might go into the market and purchase one thousand shares "per leg."

LEGAL A computerized database maintained by the NYSE to keep track of enforcement actions, audits, and complaints against member firms. This term is not an acronym but is spelled in capital letters.

legal bankruptcy A legal proceeding for liquidating or reorganizing a business.

legal defeasance The deposit of cash and permitted securities, as specified in the bond indenture, into an irrevocable trust sufficient to enable the issuer to fully discharge its obligations under the bond indenture.

legal entity A person or organization that can legally enter into a contract, and may therefore be sued for failure to comply with the terms of the contract.

legal investment Investment that a regulated entity is permitted to make under the rules and regulations that govern its conduct.

legal list A list of high-quality debt and equity securities chosen by a state agency that are acceptable holdings for fiduciary institutions.

legal monopoly A government-regulated firm that is legally entitled to be the only company offering a particular service in a particular area.

legal opinion A statement, usually written by a specialized law firm, required for many different types of securities issues. The opinion states that the issue is legally acceptable.

legal transfer A stock or bond transaction that requires special documentation in addition to standard stock or bond power to be legally valid.

legislative risk The risk that new or changed legislation will have a large positive or negative effect on an investment.

Lehman Brothers Aggregate Bond Index A benchmark index made up of the Lehman Brothers Government/Corporate Bond Index, Mortgage-Backed Securities Index, and Asset-Backed Securities Index, including securities that are of investment-grade quality or better, have at least one year to maturity, and have an outstanding par value of at least $100 million. www.lehman.com

Lehman Brothers Government Bond Index A benchmark index made up of the Treasury Bond Index and the Agency Bond Index as well as the 1–3 Year Government Index and the 20+ Year Treasury Index. www.lehman.com

lemon An investment with poor results.

lemon problem Refers to the problem of asymmetric or uneven information in markets. The classic example is the sale of a used car, in which the buyer questions the reasons the owner is selling the car: Was it a lemon? The seller has more information than the buyer and the car's price will be discounted to reflect this informational asymmetry.

lend To provide money temporarily on the condition that it or its equivalent will be returned, often with interest charged.

lender An entity that provides loans to others.

lender of last resort Traditionally the Federal Reserve Bank in the United States, which assists banks that face large withdrawals of funds and in so doing stabilizes the banking system.

lender-liability lawsuit Legal action of debtor against creditor that alleges unfair enforcement of loan covenant or violation of a loan agreement's terms.

lending agreement A contract regarding funds transferred between a lender and a borrower.

lending at a premium A loan from one broker to another of securities to cover a customer's short position, with a borrowing fee included.

lending at a rate Interest paid to a customer on the credit balance received from a short sale.

lending securities Securities borrowed from a broker's inventory, from another customer's margin account, or from another broker, when a customer is required to deliver on a short sale.

less-developed country Country whose per capita GDP is below a World Bank–determined level. Less-developed countries include Paraguay, Russia, and Vietnam. *Also known as* emerging market.

lessee An entity that leases an asset from another entity.

lessor An entity that leases an asset to another entity.

letter of comment A communication to a firm from the SEC that suggests changes to its registration statement.

letter of credit A form of guarantee of payment issued by a bank on behalf of a borrower that assures the payment of interest and repayment of principal on bond issues.

letter of intent An assurance by a mutual fund shareholder that a certain amount of money will be invested monthly, in exchange for lower sales charges. In mergers, a preliminary merger agreement between companies after significant negotiations.

letter stock Privately placed common stock, so-called because the SEC requires a letter from the purchaser stating that the stock is not intended for resale.

level debt service A municipal charter provision mandating that debt payments be relatively equal from year to year so that required revenue projections are easier.

level load A mutual fund that charges a permanent sales charge, usually at some fixed percentage. *See also* front-end load; back-end-load fund.

level pay Scheduling principal and interest payments due on a mortgage so that total monthly payment of both is the same. Different from the typical mortgage for which the principal payment component of the monthly payment becomes gradually greater while the monthly interest component shrinks.

level term insurance A life insurance policy with a fixed face value and increasing premiums.

level-coupon bond Bond with a stream of coupon payments that remain the same throughout the life of the bond.

leverage The use of debt to finance acquisitions, asset purchases, or operations. But in investing, the use of leverage makes an equity investment rise or fall at a proportionately greater rate than that without leverage. Some investments have leverage embedded in them. For instance, one might consider an option to have high leverage compared to the underlying stock because any given price change in the stock will result in a greater change in the option's value.

leverage ratio Value of a firm's debt to its total value, calculated as debt plus stockholder capitalization.

leverage rebalancing Making transactions to adjust or rebalance a firm's leverage ratio to a target ratio. For instance, a firm might retire some debt to improve its leverage ratios.

leveraged buyout (LBO) A transaction used to take a public corporation private that is financed through debt such as bank loans and bonds. Because of the large amount of debt relative to equity in the new corporation, the bonds are typically rated below investment-grade, properly referred to as high-yield bonds or junk bonds. Investors can participate in an LBO through either the purchase of the debt or the purchase of equity through an LBO fund that specializes in such investments.

leveraged company A company that has debt in its capital structure.

leveraged equity Stock in a firm that relies on financial leverage. Holders experience the benefits and costs of using debt.

leveraged investment company An investment company or mutual fund entitled to borrow capital for its operations. Also, an investment company that issues both income shares and capital shares.

leveraged lease A lease arrangement under which the lessor borrows a large proportion of the funds needed to purchase the asset. The lender has a lien on the assets and a pledge of the lease payments to secure the borrowing.

leveraged portfolio A portfolio that includes risky assets purchased with borrowed funds.

leveraged recapitalization When a public company takes on significant additional debt with the purpose of either paying an extraordinary dividend or repurchasing shares, leaving the public shareholders with a continuing interest in a more financially leveraged company. *Also called* shark repellent.

leveraged required return The required return on an investment when the investment is financed partially by debt.

liability A financial obligation, or the cash outlay that must be made at a specific time to satisfy the contractual terms of such an obligation.

liability funding strategy Investment strategy that selects assets that will throw off enough cash to equal or exceed the investor's obligations.

liability insurance Insurance guarding against damage or loss that the policyholder may cause another person in the form of bodily injury or property damage.

LIBID *See* London Interbank Bid Rate.

LIBOR *See* London Interbank Offered Rate.

license agreement The contract by which one company, the licensor, allows another, the licensee, to market its products in return for royalties, fees, or other compensation.

lien A security interest in one or more assets that lenders hold in exchange for secured debt financing.

life annuity An annuity that pays a fixed amount for the lifetime of the annuitant.

life cycle The lifetime of a product or business, from its creation to its demise or transformation.

life expectancy The length of time that an average person is expected to live, used by insurance companies to calculate benefit payouts.

life insurance An insurance policy that pays a monetary benefit to the insured person's survivors after death.

life insurance in force The dollar amount of life insurance that a company has issued, measured as the sum of policy face values and dividends paid.

life insurance policy The contract that sets out the terms of life insurance coverage.

lifetime reverse mortgage A type of mortgage in which a home owner borrows against the value of the home, while retaining title, and makes no payments while residing in the home. When the owner ceases living in the house, the property is sold and the loan repaid.

LIFO *See* last in, first out.

lifted Having an offer taken in a stock, followed by the market maker raising the offer price.

lifting a leg Closing out one side of a long-short arbitrage before the other is closed.

lighten up Selling some part of a stock or bond position in a portfolio to realize capital gains or losses or to increase cash assets.

Lima Stock Exchange Peru's major securities market. www.bvl.com.pe/homepage2.html

limit on close order An order to buy or sell stock at the closing price only if the price is at a predetermined level or better.

limit order An order to buy a stock at or below a specified price, or to sell a stock at or above a specified price. An investor instructs a broker to buy one hundred shares of a company at $8 or less or sell one hundred shares of the company at $10 or better. A conditional trading order designed to avoid the danger of adverse unexpected price changes. The more volatile a stock, the more advisable it is to use limit orders.

limit order book A record of unexecuted limit orders maintained by the specialist. These orders are treated equally with other orders in terms of priority of execution.

limit order information system The electronic system supplying information about securities traded on participating exchanges so that the best securities prices can be found.

limit up, limit down The maximum price change allowed for a commodity futures contract per trading day.

limitation on asset disposition A bond covenant that restricts a firm's ability to sell a major asset, thereby protecting bondholders.

limitation on conversion Applies mainly to convertible securities and refers to a possible delay in convertibility. More frequently, the right to convert may be terminable prior to a redemption date, preventing the holder from receiving a final coupon or dividend.

limitation on lien A bond covenant that restricts in some way a firm's ability to grant liens on its assets, thereby protecting bondholders.

limitation on merger, consolidation, or sale A bond covenant that restricts in some way a firm's ability to merge or consolidate with another firm.

limitation on sale-and-leaseback A bond covenant that restricts in some way a firm's ability to enter into a sale-and-leaseback transaction, a financing technique that could affect a creditor's standing.

limitation on subsidiary borrowing A bond covenant that restricts in some way a firm's ability to borrow at the level of firm subsidiary.

limited company A form of business commonly used in the United Kingdom comparable to incorporation in the United States.

limited discretion Permission from a client that allows a broker to make certain stock and option trades without first consulting the client about them.

limited flexibility exchange rate system The International Monetary Fund's name for an exchange rate system with a managed float.

limited liability Limitation of loss to what has already been invested. Investments in common stocks are said to have limited liability.

limited partner A partner who has limited legal liability for the obligations of the partnership. General partners have much greater liability.

limited partnership A partnership that includes one or more partners who have limited liability. Limited partnerships may invest in real estate, equipment, and other assets. Limited partnerships were sold in the 1980s to individual investors seeking tax benefits, but the Tax Reform Act of 1986 made such investments less attractive.

limited payment policy Life insurance providing full life protection but requiring premiums for only part of the customer's lifetime.

limited risk The risk inherent in purchasing options contracts, which is much lower than that of a futures contract, which has unlimited risk. The maximum loss in buying a call option, for example, is the premium paid for the option.

limited warranty A warranty with certain conditions and limitations on the parts of an object covered, type of damage covered, or time period for which the agreement is good.

limited-liability instrument A security, such as a call option, in which the owner can lose only the initial investment.

limited-tax general obligation bond A general obligation bond of a government backed by specified or constrained revenue sources.

line of credit An informal loan arrangement between a bank and a customer allowing the customer to borrow up to a prespecified amount.

Lipper Mutual Fund Industry Average The average level of performance for all mutual funds, as reported by Lipper Analytical Services. www.lipperweb.com

liquid asset Asset that is easily and cheaply turned into cash—notably cash itself and short-term securities.

liquid market A market allowing the buying or selling of large quantities of an asset at any time with low transaction costs and little disruption to the market.

liquid yield option note (LYON) A zero-coupon convertible bond developed by Merrill Lynch and Company.

liquidating dividend Payment by a firm to its owners from capital rather than from earnings. A return of capital is not taxed as income is.

liquidation A firm in liquidation is one whose business is terminated. Assets are sold, proceeds are used to pay creditors, and whatever is left is distributed to shareholders. Any transaction that offsets or closes out a long or short position. *See also* chapter 7 bankruptcy.

liquidation by assignment Sale or realization of a debtor firm's assets voluntarily agreed to by its creditors, who estimate that the firm's liquidation value exceeds its going-concern value.

liquidation rights The rights of a firm's security holders in the event the firm liquidates.

liquidation value Value of a firm's assets after paying its debts.

liquidator Person appointed by an unsecured creditor in the United Kingdom to oversee the sale of an insolvent firm's assets and the repayment of its debts. In the United States, the person overseeing a liquidation is appointed by the bankruptcy court and is called a trustee.

liquidity A high level of trading activity, allowing buying and selling with minimum price disturbance. Also, a market characterized by the ability to buy and sell with relative ease. *Opposite of* illiquid.

liquidity preference hypothesis The argument that greater liquidity is valuable in an asset because it eases trading. Also, the theory that the forward rate exceeds expected future interest rates.

liquidity premium The premium embedded in a security that is easily turned into cash. Also, in commodities, the forward rate minus expected future short-term interest rate.

liquidity ratio Ratio that measures a firm's ability to meet its short-term financial obligations, such as the ratio of current assets to current liabilities.

liquidity risk The risk that arises from the difficulty of selling an asset in a timely manner. It can be thought of as the difference between the "true value" of the asset and the likely price, less commissions to perform the trade.

Lisbon Stock Exchange (LSE) Exchange in Portugal for trading stocks, bonds, and unit trusts. www.bvl.pt

listed firm A company whose stock trades on a stock exchange and that conforms to listing requirements. Nasdaq companies are not considered listed firms.

listed option An option that has been accepted for trading on an exchange.

listed security Stock or bond that has been accepted for trading by one of the organized and registered securities exchanges.

listing In the context of real estate, written agreement between a property owner and a real estate broker that gives the broker permission to find a buyer or tenant for some property.

listing broker A licensed real estate broker who completes a listing of a property for sale.

listing requirements Requirements—including minimum shares outstanding, market value, and income—that are laid down by an exchange for any stock to be listed for trading. When a company that is listed no longer meets all these requirements, its shares are delisted or removed from the exchange.

living benefits Life insurance benefits from which the insured can draw cash while still living, usually in the case of a high-cost illness.

living trust Document designed to allow an individual to control property while alive and provide for its disposal after death. Such a trust can avoid probate. *Also known as* revocable trust; or inter vivos trust.

Lloyd's of London An association of insurance underwriting syndicates based in London.

load The sales fee charged to an investor when shares are purchased in a load fund or annuity. *See also* back-end-load fund; front-end load; level load.

load fund A mutual fund that sells shares with a sales charge—typically 4 percent to 8 percent of the net amount indicated. Some no-load funds also levy marketing fees permitted by article 12b-1 of the Investment Company Act; these are typically 0. 25 percent.

load-spread option A method of allocating the annual sales charge on load funds, often through percentage deductions from a customer's periodic fixed payments.

loan Temporary use of a sum of money.

loan amortization schedule The timetable for repaying the interest and principal on a loan.

loan commitment Assurance by a lender to make money available to a borrower on specific terms in return for a fee.

loan crowd A group of member firms in the 1920s that lent or borrowed securities needed to cover the positions of customers who had sold short securities.

loan syndication Group of banks sharing a loan. *See also* syndicate.

loan value The maximum percentage of the value of securities that a broker can lend to a margin account customer, as dictated by the Federal Reserve Board in regulation T.

loaned flat Securities lent interest-free between brokers to cover customers' short sale positions.

loan-to-value ratio The ratio of money borrowed on a property to its fair market value.

local A futures exchange member who trades securities for his or her own account.

local tax Property, sewer, school, or other community tax paid to a locality. Local taxes are usually deductible for federal income tax purposes.

locational arbitrage Attempt to exploit discrepancies in exchange rates between banks.

lock Make a market both ways (bid and offer) either on the bid, offering, or an in-between price only. Locking on the offering occurs to attract a seller, since the trader is willing to pay (and ask) the offering side when others only ask it. Locking on the bid side attracts buyers for similar reasons. Typically, the sell side requires a plus tick to comply with short sale rules. Locked markets are uncommon.

lockbox A collection and processing service, provided to firms by banks, that collects payments from a dedicated postal box to which the firm directs its customers. The banks make several collections per day, process the payments immediately, and deposit the funds into the firm's bank account.

lockup agreement An agreement between executives of companies issuing shares to the public that they will not sell their shares for a specified period, usually three months.

lockup option To discourage a hostile takeover, a privilege offered to a white knight (friendly acquirer) by a target company to buy crown jewels (a particularly profitable asset) or additional equity. *Compare to* shark repellent.

London Interbank Bid Rate (LIBID) The bid rate that a Euromarket bank is willing to pay to attract a deposit from another bank.

London Interbank Offered Rate (LIBOR) The rate of interest that major international banks in London charge each other for borrowings. Many variable interest rates in the United States are based on spreads to LIBOR. In contrast LIBID is quoted by banks seeking such deposits.

London International Financial Futures and Options Exchange (LIFFE) A leading market for trading options and futures on euro money market derivatives. www.liffe.com

London Metal Exchange (LME) A leading market for trading options and futures on base metals, based in London. www.lme.co.uk

London Stock Exchange (LSE) The United Kingdom's six regional exchanges joined together in 1973 to form the stock exchange of Great Britain and Ireland, later named the LSE. The FTSE 100 index (known as "the Footsie") is its dominant index. www.londonstockexchange.com

long Refers to practice of establishing a market position that has not yet closed out through a contract for an offsetting sale. *Compare to* short.

long bond Bond with longest current maturity. The long bond has traditionally been the thirty-year U.S. Treasury bond, which was discontinued in 2001.

long coupon Bond or note with a long current maturity or a bond on which one of the coupon periods, usually the first, is longer than the other periods or the standard period.

long hedge The purchase of a futures contract in anticipation of actual purchases in the cash market. Used by processors or exporters as protection against an advance in the cash price. *See also* hedge; short hedge.

long leg The part of an option spread in which an agreement to buy the underlying security is made.

long market value The market value of a security, excluding options, as of the close of the last business day.

long position Owning or holding securities. An owner of stock is said to "long the stock." *Opposite of* short position.

long position in an option Purchase of an option.

long straddle Taking a long position in both a put and a call option.

long-term In accounting terms, one year or longer.

long-term anticipation securities (LEAPS) Options on stocks that have longer terms than regular options.

long-term capital gain A profit on the sale of a security or mutual fund share that has been held for more than one year and is therefore taxed at a lower rate than income.

long-term debt An obligation having a maturity of more than one year from the date it was issued. *Also called* funded debt.

long-term debt ratio The ratio of long-term debt to total capitalization.

long-term debt/capitalization Indicator of financial leverage. Shows the long-term debt portion of a company's capital structure. Determined by dividing long-term debt by the sum of long-term debt, preferred stock, and common stockholders' equity. For most companies, this figure should not exceed 50 percent.

long-term debt-to-equity ratio A capitalization ratio comparing long-term debt to shareholders' equity.

long-term financial plan Financial plan covering two or more years of future operations.

long-term financing Liabilities repayable in more than one year plus equity.

long-term goals Financial goals expected to be accomplished in five years or longer.

long-term investor A person who makes investments for a period of at least five years in order to finance his or her long-term goals.

long-term liability Amount owed for lease, bond repayment, and other items due after one year.

long-term loss A loss on the sale of a capital asset held less than twelve months that can be used to offset a capital gain. Taxpayers can only offset $3,000 in losses each year.

look-back option An option that allows the buyer to choose as the strike price any price of the underlying asset that has occurred during the life of the option. For a call option, the buyer will choose the minimum price; for a put option, the buyer will choose the maximum price.

look-thru A method for calculating U.S. taxes owed on income from controlled foreign corporations, which was introduced by the Tax Reform Act of 1986.

loophole A technicality in some legislation or regulation that makes it possible to avoid certain consequences or circumvent a rule without breaking the law, such as the legal avoidance of taxes.

loose credit Policy by the Federal Reserve Board to make loans less expensive and more available by reducing interest rates through open-market operations.

loss When costs exceed revenue. *Opposite of* profit.

loss carry-back (carry-forward) A tax provision that allows operating losses to be used as a tax shield to reduce taxable income in prior and future years. Losses can be carried backward for up to three years and forward for up to fifteen years under current tax codes.

loss ratio The ratio of losses paid or accrued by an insurer to premiums collected over a specified period.

loss-control activity Action that an insured person or company takes at the instigation of an insurance company in order to prevent accidents or losses.

loss-of-income insurance Insurance coverage that will pay out for income lost as a result of a disability, injury, or business disruption.

lots Blocks or portions of equity trades. Can express a specific transaction in a stock at a certain time, often implying execution at the same price, such as trading forty thousand shares in two lots of ten and four lots of five.

low ball Slang for making an offer well below the fair value of an asset in hopes that the seller may be desperate enough to sell at that price.

low grade Bonds that fall below investment grade. *Also known as* high-yield bond; junk bond.

low price The day's lowest price of a security that has changed hands between a buyer and a seller.

low price-earnings ratio effect The tendency of portfolios of stocks with a low price-earnings ratio to outperform portfolios of stocks with high price-earnings ratios.

low-balance method A method of calculating interest owed based on the lowest balance of an account over the applicable period.

low-coupon bond refunding Refunding of a low-coupon bond with a new, higher-coupon bond.

low-load fund A mutual fund that charges a sales commission of 3.5 percent or less for the purchase of shares.

LYON *See* liquid yield option note.

lump sum A large one-time payment of money.

lump-sum distribution A single payment that represents an employee's interest in a qualified retirement plan. The payment must be prompted by retirement (or other separation from service), death, disability, or attainment of age fifty-nine and a half, and must be made within a single tax year to avoid the federal government's 10 percent penalty tax.

macaroni defense A tactic used by a corporation that is the target of a hostile takeover bid involving the issue of a large number of bonds that must be redeemed at a higher value than they were issued at if the company is taken over.

macro country risk Country risk or political risk that affects all foreign firms in a host country.

macroeconomics Analysis of an economy as a whole. *Compare to* microeconomics.

Madrid Stock Exchange (Bolsa de Madrid) The largest of Spain's four stock exchanges. www.bolsamadrid.es

mail float Time period that checks submitted for payment of bills spend in the postal system.

maintenance call A call for additional money or securities when a margin account falls below its exchange-mandated level. *Also known as* house call (because it is made by the customer's brokerage house).

maintenance fee A yearly charge to maintain brokerage accounts, such as asset-management accounts or IRAs.

maintenance margin The dollar amount required to be kept at the Options Clearing Corporation throughout the life of an option contract; percentage of the dollar amount of securities that must always be kept as margin or collateral for the loan.

maintenance margin requirement A sum, usually smaller than but part of the original margin, that must be maintained on deposit in a customer's brokerage account at all times. If a customer's equity in any futures position drops to or below the maintenance margin level, the broker must issue a margin call for the amount required to restore the customer's equity in the account to the original margin level. Maintenance requirements are set by brokerage firms and may vary.

majority shareholder A shareholder who is part of a group that controls more than half of the outstanding shares of a corporation.

majority voting Voting system under which a corporation's shareholders vote for each director separately. *Compare to* cumulative voting.

make a market Dealers are said to make a market when they quote bid and offered prices for securities at which they stand ready to buy and sell.

making delivery Refers to the seller actually turning over to the buyer the assets agreed upon in a forward contract.

Maloney Act Legislation from 1938 amending the Securities Exchange Act to regulate the over-the-counter market.

managed account An investment portfolio entrusted to a manager who decides how to invest it.

managed float Also referred to as a "dirty" float, a system of floating exchange rates with central bank intervention to reduce currency fluctuations.

management The people who administer a company, create policies, and provide the support necessary to implement the owners' business objectives.

management buying The acquisition of a controlling interest in a promising business by an outside investment group that retains existing management and places representatives on the board of directors.

management buyout A leveraged buyout whereby the acquiring group is led by the firm's management.

management contract An agreement by which a company will provide its organizational and management expertise in the form of services.

management fee An investment advisory fee charged by the financial adviser to a fund typically on the basis of the fund's average assets, but sometimes determined on a sliding scale that declines as the dollar amount of the fund increases.

management/closely held shares Percentage of shares held by persons closely related to a company, as defined by the SEC. Parts of these percentages often are included in "institutional holdings"—making the combined total of these percentages over one hundred. There is overlap as institutions sometimes acquire enough stock to be considered closely allied to the company by the SEC.

management's discussion and analysis (MD&A) A report from management to shareholders that accompanies the firm's financial statements in the annual report. It explains the period's financial results and allows management to discuss topics that may not be apparent in the financial statements in the annual report.

manager The person or persons responsible for the overall investment decisions of a mutual fund.

managerial decision Decision concerning the operation of the firm, such as the choice of firm size, firm growth rates, and employee compensation.

managing underwriter The leading brokerage firm in an underwriting group, which originates the securities offering and acts as an agent for the group.

mandatory redemption schedule Schedule according to which bond sinking fund or gradual retirement payments must be made.

manipulation Dealing in a security to create a false appearance of active trading in order to bring in more traders. Illegal.

manufactured-housing securities Loans on factory-built or prefabricated housing, including mobile homes.

maple leaf A gold, silver, or platinum coin minted in Canada that usually trades at slightly more than its current bullion value.

margin Allows investors to buy securities by borrowing money from a broker. The margin is the difference between the market value of a stock and the loan a broker makes. The initial margin requirement is set by the Federal Reserve and is one-half the purchase price of an investment in stock. Not all stocks are marginable; those with prices under $5 cannot be borrowed against.

margin account (stocks) A leverageable account in which stocks can be purchased for a combination of cash and a loan. The loan in the margin account is collateralized by the shares; if the value of the stock drops sufficiently, the owner will be asked to either put in more cash or sell a portion of the stock. Margin rules are federally regulated, but margin requirements and interest charges may vary among broker/dealers.

margin agreement The agreement governing customers' margin accounts that must be signed prior to their opening.

margin call A demand for additional funds because of adverse price movement. Margin calls require an investor to come up with more cash or additional securities or to sell some of the stock in question.

margin department The department in a brokerage firm that monitors customers' margin accounts, ensuring that all short sales, stock purchases, and other positions are adequately covered by the margin-account balance.

margin of profit Gross profit divided by net sales. Used to measure a firm's operating efficiency and pricing policies in order to determine how competitive the firm is within the industry. Profit margins are studied closely in financial statements. Rising profit margins are desired by investors.

margin security A security that may be bought or sold in a margin account as defined in regulation T. Also referred to as a marginable security.

margin trading Buying securities, in part, with borrowed money.

marginal Incremental.

marginal cost The increase or decrease in a firm's total cost of production as a result of changing production by one unit.

marginal efficiency of capital The percentage yield earned on an additional unit of capital.

marginal revenue The change in total revenue as a result of producing one additional unit of output.

marginal tax rate The tax rate that would have to be paid on any additional dollars of taxable income earned.

marital deduction A tax deduction that allows spouses to transfer unlimited amounts of property to one another.

marital trust A trust created to allow one spouse to transfer, during life or upon death, an unlimited amount of property to his/her spouse without incurring gift or estate tax.

markdown The amount subtracted from the selling price of a security when it is sold to a dealer in the over-the-counter market.

mark to market The valuing of securities at their current market price by brokerage firms, banks, mutual funds, so that investors can see the firm's or fund's profits or losses. Also, in futures trading, an arrangement whereby the profits or losses on a futures contract are settled each day.

market Usually refers to the equity market. "The market went down today" means that the value of a broad stock market index such as the S&P 500 Composite Index dropped that day.

market analysis An analysis of technical corporate and market data used to predict movements in the market or in a particular stock.

market break A significant decline in the overall market.

market capitalization The total dollar value of all outstanding shares based on current prices. Computed as shares times market price. Capitalization is a measure of corporate size. *Also known as* market value.

market conversion price The price that an investor effectively pays for common stock by purchasing a convertible security and then converting. This price is equal to the market price of the convertible security divided by the conversion ratio. *Also known as* conversion parity.

market correction A relatively short-term drop in stock market prices, generally viewed as bringing overpriced stocks back to a level closer to companies' actual values.

market cycle The period between the two latest highs or lows of the S&P 500 Composite Index, showing net performance of a fund through both an up and a down market. A market cycle is complete when the S&P is 15 percent below the highest point or 15 percent above the lowest point.

market index Market measure that consists of a list of companies that represent a wide variety of industries and therefore the overall market. The S&P 500 Composite Index is a relatively broad market index that includes shares in five hundred diverse companies. An even broader index is the Wilshire, which consists of most publicly traded companies.

market jitters Anxiety among many investors, causing them to sell stocks and bonds, pushing prices down.

market letter A newsletter analyzing the market that is written by an SEC-registered investment adviser who sells the letter to subscribers. *See also* Hulbert rating.

market maker A person or firm who maintains bid and offer prices in a given security by standing ready to buy or sell at least one hundred share lots at publicly quoted prices. *See also* dealer; specialist.

market model The market model says that the return on a security depends on the return on the market portfolio and the extent of the security's relative volatility, as measured by beta. The return also depends on conditions that are unique to the firm.

market opening　The start of formal trading on an exchange.

market order　An order to buy or sell a stated amount of a security at the most advantageous price obtainable after the order is represented in the trading crowd. You cannot specify special restrictions such as an all-or-none or good-'til-canceled order on market orders. Market orders placed in highly volatile stocks can be quite dangerous. *Opposite of* limit order.

market overhang　The theory that, in certain situations, institutions wish to sell their shares but postpone the sale because large orders under current market conditions would drive down the share price and the consequent threat of securities sales will tend to retard the rate of share-price appreciation. Support for this theory is largely anecdotal. One type of market overhang is the number of shares owned by a company's executives that are subject to lockup periods but once these periods are concluded will enter the market and possibly depress the stock price.

market penetration or share　Percent of trading volume in a stock that a particular market maker trades.

Market Performance Committee　A group of NYSE market oversight specialists who monitor specialists' efficiency in maintaining fair prices and orderly markets. www.nyse.com

market price　The amount of money that a willing buyer pays to acquire something from a willing seller when a buyer and seller are independent and when such an exchange is motivated only by commercial considerations. Market price also refers to the last reported price at which a security was traded on an exchange.

market price of risk　A measure of the extra return, or risk premium, that investors demand to bear risk. The reward-to-risk ratio of a market portfolio.

market research　A technical analysis of factors such as volume, price trends, and market breadth that are used to predict price movement.

market return　The return on the market portfolio.

market risk　Risk that cannot be diversified away. That is, the part of the stock return that is driven by the overall market return. *Opposite of* specific risk. *Also known as* undiversifiable risk; systematic risk.

market sector　Classification of stocks by industry groups. Classification of bonds by issuer characteristics, such as state government, corporate, or utility.

market share The percentage of total industry sales that a particular company controls.

market timer A money manager who assumes he or she can forecast when the stock market will go up or down.

market timing Asset allocation in which investment in the equity market is increased if one forecasts that the equity market will outperform T-bills and is decreased when the market is anticipated to underperform.

market timing costs Costs that arise from price movement of a stock during a transaction period but are attributable to other activity in the stock.

market tone The general state of a securities market, based mostly on trading activity; a bullish or bearish tone.

market value (1) The price at which a security is trading and could presumably be purchased or sold. (2) What investors believe a firm is worth; calculated by multiplying the number of shares outstanding by the current market price of a firm's shares. *Also known as* market capitalization.

marketability A negotiable security is said to have good marketability if there is an active secondary market in which it can easily be resold. *Compare to* liquidity.

marketable securities Securities that are easily convertible to cash because there is high demand allowing them to be sold quickly.

marketable title A clear, reasonably incontestable title to a piece of real estate that is good for transaction purposes.

marketed claim Claim that can be bought and sold in financial markets, such as those of stockholders and bondholders.

market-impact cost The combination of a bid/ask spread and a dealer's price concession that is paid by an investor. Cost that traders incur when purchases or sales of a security make that security's price change significantly. *Also called* price-impact cost.

market-on-close order An order to trade stocks, options, or futures as close as possible to the market close.

market-out clause A clause that may appear in an underwriting commitment that releases it from its purchase requirement if there are negative securities-market developments.

marketplace price efficiency The degree to which the price of assets reflects the available marketplace information. Marketplace price efficiency is sometimes estimated as the difficulty faced by active management of earning a greater return than passive management would, after adjusting for the risk associated with a strategy and the transactions costs associated with implementing a strategy.

market-required rate of return schedule The minimum return required by investors at each level of investment risk, beginning at the risk-free interest rate and rising as risk increases.

marking to market The practice of reporting the value of assets on a market value rather than book value or cost basis; settling or reconciling changes in the value of futures contracts on a daily basis. *Compare to* historical cost accounting convention.

marking up or down The amount by which a securities dealer raises or lowers the price of a stock or bond due to changes in demand and supply.

marriage penalty A tax that has the effect of penalizing a married couple because they pay more on a joint tax return than they would if they filed tax returns separately.

married put A put option bought at the same time as its underlying securities in order to hedge the price paid for the securities.

master limited partnership A publicly traded limited partnership.

match orders When a broker seeks to offset orders from other investors to maintain an orderly market.

matched book When the mix of maturities in a bank's or trading firm's assets and liabilities is equally distributed.

matched maturities The coordination by a financial institution of the maturities of assets (or loans) and liabilities (or deposits) in order to enable it to meet its obligations at the required times.

match-fund A bank is said to match-fund a loan or other asset by buying or taking a deposit of the same maturity. The term is commonly used in the Euromarket.

matching concept The accounting principle that requires the recognition of all costs that are associated with the generation of the revenue reported in the income statement.

material adverse change or effect Many mergers and acquisitions (M&A) contracts include a material adverse change clause that allows a company to renegotiate or walk away from a deal if the other company or its subsidiaries announce a significant event that may negatively affect its stock price or operations. *See also* materiality.

materiality The importance of an event or information in influencing a company's stock price or its operations. For example, a lawsuit filed against a company may have a material adverse effect on the company if it loses the suit, and therefore must be disclosed to investors. Companies must report any material events within one month by filing SEC form 8-K.

Matif SA The futures exchange of France. www.matif.fr

mature To cease to exist; to expire. Usually refers to fixed-income securities.

mature economy The economy of a nation with a stable population and slowing economic growth.

matured noninterest-bearing debt Outstanding savings bonds and notes that have reached final maturity and no longer earn interest. Includes all series A-D, F, G, I, J, and K bonds. Series E bonds (issued between May 1941 and November 1965), series EE (issued since January 1980), series H (issued from June 1952 through December 1979), and savings notes issued between May 1967 and October 1970 have a final maturity of thirty years. Series HH bonds (issued since January 1980) mature after twenty years.

maturity For a bond, the date on which the principal is required to be repaid. In an interest rate swap, the date that the swap stops accruing interest.

maturity date Usually used for bonds. Date that the bond is paid off. Date on which the principal amount of a note, draft, acceptance, bond, or other debt instrument becomes due and payable.

maturity factoring An arrangement that provides collection and insurance of accounts receivable.

maturity phase A stage of company development in which earnings grow at the rate of the general economy.

maturity spread The difference in returns between bonds of different life spans.

maturity value What a bondholder receives upon maturity. *Also known as* par value; face value.

maximum capital gains mutual fund A mutual fund whose objective is to produce capital gains by investing in small or risky rapid-growth companies.

maximum price fluctuation The greatest amount by which the contract price can change, up or down, during one trading session, as fixed by exchange rules in the contract specification.

maximum-expected-return criterion A standard by which the asset with the highest anticipated return is chosen for investment over other assets.

maximum-return criterion A standard by which the asset with the highest current return is chosen for investment over other assets.

May Day The date of May 1, 1975, after which brokers were allowed to charge any brokerage commission they wished rather than a mandatory rate.

may expand Warning that the size of the equity order/total may be increased.

M&A Mergers and acquisitions. Brokerage firm M&A departments help arrange mergers and acquisitions for corporate clients.

MD&A *See* management's discussion and analysis.

mean of the sample The arithmetic average: the sum of the observations divided by the number of observations.

mean return *See* expected return on investment.

mean-variance analysis Evaluation of risky prospects based on the expected value and variance of possible outcomes.

median market cap The midpoint of market capitalization, market price multiplied by the number of shares outstanding, of the stocks in a portfolio. Half the stocks in the portfolio will have higher market capitalizations; half will have lower.

medium-term bond A bond maturing in two to ten years.

medium-term note A corporate debt instrument that is continuously offered to investors over a period of time by an agent of the issuer. Investors can select from maturity bands of nine months to one year, one year to eighteen months, eighteen months to two years, etc., up to thirty years.

member bank A national- or state-chartered bank that is a member of the Federal Reserve System.

member firm Brokerage or trading firm that has at least one membership on a major stock exchange even though, by exchange rules, the membership is in the name of an employee and not of the firm itself.

member short-sale ratio The total shares sold short by NYSE members divided by total short sales; used to analyze market expectations and bullish or bearish trends. A higher ratio represents a potential bearish trend.

membership or a seat on the exchange A limited number of exchange positions that enable the holder to trade for the holder's own accounts and charge clients for the execution of trades for their accounts. *See also* member firm.

Merc Nickname for Chicago Mercantile Exchange.

mercantile agency An organization that supplies credit ratings and reports on firms that are prospective customers.

merchant bank A British term for a bank that specializes in providing various financial services such as accepting bills arising out of trade, underwriting new issues, and providing advice on acquisitions, mergers, foreign exchange, portfolio management, etc.

Mercosur The "Common Market of the South," which includes Argentina, Brazil, Paraguay, and Uruguay in a regional trade pact that reduces tariffs on intrapact trade by up to 90 percent.

merger (1) Acquisition in which all assets and liabilities are absorbed by the buyer. (2) More generally, any combination of two companies. A merger can be paid for in cash or stock.

method of payment The way a merger or acquisition is financed.

Mexican Stock Exchange (Bolsa Mexicana de Valores) The only stock exchange in Mexico. The Indice de Precios y Cotizaciones, or IPC index, consists of the thirty-five most representative stocks chosen every two months. www.bmv.com.mx

mezzanine bracket The members of an underwriting group with involvement large enough to be in the second participation tier from the top.

mezzanine financing The stage of financing that follows initial venture-capital financing.

mezzanine level The period in a company's development just before it goes public.

micro country risk Country or political risk that is specific to an industry, company, or project within a host country.

micro-cap stock Shares of a company with a very small market value.

microeconomics Analysis of the behavior of individual economic units such as companies, industries, or households. *Compare to* macroeconomics.

mid cap A company with a market capitalization of between $1 billion and $5 billion.

mid-cap SPDR Share that tracks the Standard & Poor's Mid-Cap 400

Index of mid-cap stocks. This SPDR (Standard & Poor's depositary receipt) trades on the AMEX, under the symbol MDY.

midmarket Price around which a market maker derives bid and ask prices.

Miller trust A trust funded with a person's income in order to ensure that he or she can receive Medicaid benefits in states where there is an income cap in addition to an assets cap to qualify for Medicaid assistance. The trust pays out monies under the income cap to the person during his or her lifetime, and the remaining money in the trust is paid to the state at the person's death. *Compare to* pooled trust; under-65 trust.

minimanipulation Trading in the underwriting security of an option contract in order to manipulate its price so that the options will become in-the-money.

minimum maintenance The lowest required equity level that must be held with a broker in a margin account.

minimum price fluctuation Smallest increment of price movement possible in trading a given contract. *Also called* point; tick.

minimum purchase For mutual funds, the amount required to open a new account (minimum initial purchase) or to deposit into an existing account (minimum additional purchase). These minimums may be lowered for buyers participating in an automatic purchase plan.

minority interest An outside ownership interest in a subsidiary that is consolidated with the parent for financial-reporting purposes.

minus tick A stock whose most recent trade was for a loss. *Also known as* downtick. *Opposite of* plus tick; uptick.

misery index An index that combines the unemployment and inflation rates, used as a political rating or measure of consumer confidence.

miss the price/market (1) Have an order in hand but fail to execute a transaction on terms favorable to a customer and, thus, be negligent as a broker; (2) receive an order just after a print has transpired.

mixed account A brokerage account holding both long- and short-positioned securities.

mob spread The yield spread between a tax-free municipal bond and a Treasury bond with the same maturity.

mock trading The simulated trading of securities used as a learning device to train investors and brokers.

modeling The process of creating a depiction of reality, such as a graph, picture, or mathematical representation.

modern portfolio theory Principals underlying the analysis and evaluation of rational portfolio choices based on risk-return trade-offs and efficient diversification.

momentum Acceleration of an economic, price, or volume movement. A trader that follows a momentum strategy will purchase stocks that have recently risen in price.

momentum fund A type of mutual fund in aggressive growth stocks. The fund has higher levels of risk and potential return.

momentum indicator Indicator used in market analysis to quantify the momentum of upward and downward price movements.

M1, M2, and M3 *See* money supply.

monetarist An economist who believes that changes in the money supply are the most important determinants of economic activity and economic cycles.

monetary assets and liabilities Assets and liabilities with contractual pay-offs.

monetary gold Gold held by governmental authorities as a financial asset.

monetary indicators Economic indicators of the effects of monetary policy, such as the condition of the credit market.

monetary policy Actions taken by the board of governors of the Federal Reserve System to influence the money supply or interest rates.

monetize the debt Financing the national debt by printing new money, which causes inflation due to a larger money supply.

money Currency and coin that are guaranteed as legal tender by the government.

money base Composed of currency and coin outside the banking system plus liabilities to the deposits held by money-center banks.

money management The management of money for gains; investment.

money manager Individual who makes investment decisions. *Also known as* investment adviser; investment manager; portfolio manager.

money market Money markets are for borrowing and lending money for three years or less. The securities in a money market can be U.S. government bonds, Treasury bills, and commercial paper from banks and companies.

money market demand account A bank account that pays interest based on short-term interest rates.

money market fund A mutual fund that invests only in short-term securities, such as bankers' acceptances, commercial paper, repurchase agreements, and government bills. The net asset value per share is maintained at $1. Such funds are not federally insured, although the portfolio may consist of guaranteed securities and/or the fund may have private insurance protection.

money market hedge The use of borrowing and lending transactions in foreign currencies to lock in the home currency value of a foreign currency transaction.

money market instruments Treasury bills, short-term corporate obligations, and other cash equivalents.

money market notes Publicly traded issues that may be collateralized by mortgages and mortgage-backed securities.

money market security Short-term investment usually of less than one year.

money order A financial instrument, backed by a deposit at a certain firm such as a bank, that can be easily converted into cash.

money purchase plan A defined benefit contribution plan in which the participant contributes some part and the firm contributes at the same or a different rate.

money rate of return Annual money return as a percentage of asset value.

money supply

> M1-A: Currency in circulation plus demand deposits.
>
> M1-B: M1-A plus other checkable deposits.
>
> M2: M1-B plus overnight government repurchase agreements, money market funds, savings, and small (less than $100,000) time deposits.
>
> M3: M2 plus large time deposits and longer-term government repurchase agreements.
>
> L: M3 plus other liquid assets.

money-center banks Large banks that raise most of their funds from the domestic and international money markets, relying less on depositors for funds.

monopoly Absolute control of all sales and distribution in a market by one firm, due to some barrier to entry of other firms, allowing the firm to sell at a higher price than the socially optimal price.

monopsony The existence of only one buyer in a market, forcing sellers to accept a lower price than the socially optimal price.

monthly investment plan A plan in which a certain amount is invested each month in order to benefit from dollar-cost averaging.

Montreal Exchange (Bourse de Montreal) The oldest stock exchange in Canada trading stocks, bonds, futures, and options. www.me.org

Moody's Investors Service A security and bond rating agency. www.moodys.com

moral hazard The risk that the existence of a contract will change the behavior of one or both parties to the contract, e.g., an insured firm will take fewer fire precautions or the risk that if the government bails out one troubled institution, investors will assume it will bail out all. With such a perception, investors would take on excessive risk because they feel certain they will be bailed out.

moral obligation bond A tax-exempt bond issued by a municipality or a state financial intermediary that is backed by the moral, but not legal, obligation of a state government to appropriate funds in case of default.

more behind it Indicates that more stock exists to be bought or sold by the same buyer or seller, respectively. Often, the buyer or seller does not disclose the full size of his or her buy or sell interest so as not to affect the market adversely. *See also* may expand.

more flexible exchange rate system The International Monetary Fund's name for an exchange rate system in which rates float freely.

Morningstar rating system A system used in rating and evaluating mutual funds and annuities by Morningstar Incorporated of Chicago. www.morningstar.com

mortality tables Tables of probability that individuals of various ages will die within one year.

mortgage A loan secured by the collateral of some specified real estate property that obliges the borrower to make a predetermined series of payments.

mortgage banker A company or individual that originates mortgage loans and sells them to investors, while taking care of borrowers' loan payments, records, taxes, and insurance.

mortgage bond A bond in which the issuer has granted the bondholders a lien against the pledged assets. *See also* collateral trust bond.

mortgage broker A company or individual that places mortgage loans with lenders, but does not originate or service loans like a mortgage banker.

mortgage duration A modification of the standard life of a mortgage to account for the impact of changes in prepayment speed that results from changing interest rates. For example, when rates fall, mortgage prepayments rise. As a result, the effective life of a pool of mortgages decreases.

mortgage life insurance A life insurance policy that pays off the remaining balance of the insured person's mortgage at death.

mortgage pass-through security Also called a pass-through, a security created when one or more mortgage holders form a collection of mortgages and sell shares or participation certificates in the pool. The cash flow from the collateral pool is "passed through" to the security holder as monthly payments of principal, interest, and prepayments. This is the predominant type of mortgage-backed security traded in the secondary market. *Also known as* collateralized mortgage obligation.

mortgage pipeline The period from the taking of applications from prospective mortgage borrowers to the marketing of the loans.

mortgage pool A group of mortgages with similar class, interest rate, and maturity characteristics.

mortgage rate The interest rate on a mortgage loan.

mortgage REIT A real estate investment trust (REIT) that invests in loans secured by real estate that derives income from mortgage interest and fees. *Opposite of* equity REIT.

mortgage servicing The collection of monthly payments and penalties, record keeping, payment of insurance and taxes, and possible settlement of default involved with a mortgage loan.

mortgage-backed securities Securities backed by a pool of mortgage loans.

Mortgage-Backed Securities Clearing Corporation (MBSCC) Founded in 1979, MBSCC is the sole provider of automated posttrade comparison, netting, risk management, and pool notification services to the mortgage-backed securities market. The organization is a registered clearing agency with the SEC and majority-owned by its members: mortgage-backed securities dealers, interdealer brokers, and other nonbroker/dealers. MBSCC provides its specialized services to major market participants active in programs of the Government National

Mortgage Association, Fannie Mae, and the Federal Home Loan Mortgage Corporation. www.mbscc.com

mortgagee   The lender of a loan secured by property.

mortgage-interest deduction   A federal tax deduction for interest paid on a mortgage used to acquire, construct, or improve a residence.

mortgage-pipeline risk   The risk associated with taking applications from prospective mortgage borrowers who may opt to decline to accept a quoted mortgage rate within a certain grace period.

mortgager   The borrower of a loan secured by property.

most-active list   The stocks with the highest volume of trading on a certain day.

most-distant futures contract   When several futures contracts are considered, the contract settling last. *See also* nearby futures contract.

moving average   Used in charts and technical analysis, the average of security or commodity prices constructed in a period as short as a few days or as long as several years and showing trends for the latest interval. As each new variable is included in calculating the average, the last variable of the series is deleted.

multifamily loan   Loan usually represented by conventional mortgage on multifamily rental apartments.

multilateral netting system   Elimination of offsetting cash flow between a parent and several subsidiaries.

multinational corporation   A firm that operates in more than one country.

multiple   Another name for a price/earnings ratio.

multiple listing   An agreement used by a real estate broker who is a member of a multiple-listing organization, providing the exclusive right to sell with an additional authority and obligation on the part of the listing broker to distribute the listing to the other brokers.

municipal bond   State or local governments issue municipal bonds to pay for special projects such as highways or sewers. The interest that investors receive is exempt from some income taxes. Also referred to as a muni bond.

municipal bond fund   A mutual fund that invests in tax-exempt bonds issued by state, city, and/or local governments. The interest obtained from these bonds is passed through to shareholders and is generally free of federal (and sometimes state and local) income taxes.

municipal bond insurance An insurance policy that guarantees payment on municipal bonds in the event of default.

municipal improvement certificate A certificate used to finance local government projects and services that is financed by a special tax assessment and provides tax-free interest.

municipal investment trust A unit investment trust that buys municipal bonds and usually holds them until maturity, passing the bond income on to shareholders, usually tax free.

municipal notes Short-term notes issued by municipalities in anticipation of tax receipts, proceeds from a bond issue, or other revenues.

municipal revenue bond A bond issued to finance a public project that is funded by the revenues of the project.

mutual association A savings and loan association organized as a cooperative, with members purchasing shares, voting on association affairs, and receiving income in the form of dividends.

mutual company A corporation that is owned by a group of members and that distributes income in proportion to the amount of business that members do with the company. Some insurance companies are owned by their policyholders and are mutual companies.

mutual exclusion doctrine The doctrine that ruled that municipal bond interest is federal-tax free. In return for this federal tax exemption, states and localities cannot tax interest generated by federal government securities.

mutual fund Mutual funds are pools of money managed by an investment company. They offer investors a variety of goals, depending on the fund and its investment charter. Some funds, for example, seek to generate income on a regular basis. Others seek to preserve an investor's money. Still others seek to invest in companies that are growing at a rapid pace. Funds can impose a sales charge, or load, on investors when they buy or sell shares. Many funds impose no sales charge (known as no load). Mutual funds are regulated by the Investment Company Act of 1940. *See also* open-end fund; closed-end fund.

mutual fund cash-to-assets ratio The portion of the assets of a mutual fund that exists in cash instruments.

mutual fund custodian A commercial bank or trust company that holds securities owned by a mutual fund and sometimes acts as transfer agent for the mutual fund.

mutual offset A system, such as the arrangement between the Chicago Mercantile Exchange (CME) and Singapore International Monetary Exchange (SIMEX), that allows trading positions established on one exchange to be offset or transferred on another exchange.

mutual savings bank A state-chartered savings bank that is owned by its depositors and managed by a fiduciary board of trustees.

mutually exclusive investment decisions Investment decisions in which the acceptance of a project precludes the acceptance of one or more alternative projects.

Nagoya Stock Exchange Established after World War II, one of the three major securities markets in Japan. www.nse.or.jp/index-e.htm

naked option Option position that is not hedged (balanced) with an investment in the underlying security. *Also known as* uncovered option. *Opposite of* covered option.

naked put Short put position that is not hedged (balanced) with a short investment in the underlying security. *Also known as* uncovered put. *Opposite of* covered put.

naked-option strategy An unhedged, extremely risky strategy, of which there are two kinds. First, selling short a call option, in which the speculator hopes to capitalize on a falling stock price. The investor sells a call option to another investor without owning the underlying stock, which is why it is called a naked option strategy. Second, selling put options, in which the investor hopes to capitalize on a stock's rise. Selling naked calls is much more dangerous than selling naked puts because calls have the potential for unlimited losses if the stock rises, and the investor must pay prevailing market prices to be able to supply the stock to the person who bought the call from him or her. *Opposite of* covered- or hedge-option strategy.

named-perils insurance An insurance policy that names specific risks covered by the policy.

narrowing the spread Reducing the difference between the bid and ask prices of a security. The more investors there are participating in the trading of a stock, the narrower the spread is likely to be. Stocks with little investor interest typically have very wide spreads.

NASD *See* National Association of Securities Dealers.

Nasdaq *See* National Association of Securities Dealers Automated Quotation System.

Nasdaq stock market The first electronic stock market, listing over four thousand companies. The Nasdaq stock market comprises two separate markets: the Nasdaq National Market, which trades large, active securities, and the Nasdaq Bulletin Board, which lists young companies or those whose shares are trading for less than $1. www.nasdaq.com

National Association of Investors Corporation A Michigan-based association that helps groups establish investment clubs. www.betterinvesting.org

National Association of Realtors (NAR) Lobbying organization for real estate salespeople. www.nar.realtor.com

National Association of Securities Dealers (NASD) Organization formed to comply with the Maloney Act, which provides for the regulation of the over-the-counter, including the Nasdaq, market. Located in Washington, D.C., the NASD is the largest self-regulatory investing organization in the United States, overseeing almost five thousand brokerage firms and their registered representatives. The organization conducts audits of firms and regulates its members. www.nasdr.com

National Association of Securities Dealers Automated Quotation System The computer system that provides both trading capability and information for over four thousand over-the-counter securities. *Also known as* Nasdaq. *See also* National Market System.

National Credit Union Administration Federal agency that oversees and insures the U.S. federal credit union system and is funded by its members. www.ncua.gov

national debt Treasury bills, notes, bonds, and other debt obligations that constitute the debt owed by the federal government.

National Foundation for Credit Counseling A nonprofit organization that seeks to help consumers who have taken on too much debt by helping them work out payment plans and supplying credit counseling. www.nfcc.org

National Futures Association (NFA) The self-regulatory organization established in 1982 that oversees the commodity futures industry. www.nfa.org

National Market System (NMS) Refers to Nasdaq stocks. System of trading under the sponsorship of the NASD. Companies must meet certain criteria for size, profitability, and trading activity in their shares before they can trade on the system. More comprehensive information is available for NMS stocks than for non-NMS stocks, including high, low, and last sale prices; cumulative volume figures; and bid-and-ask quotations throughout the day. This is due to the fact that market makers must report the actual price and number of shares in each transaction within ninety seconds versus a lag in reporting for non-NMS stocks (for which last sale prices and minute-to-minute volume updates are not available).

National Quotation Bureau (Pink Sheets LLC) A service that publishes bid-and-offer quotes from market makers in Nasdaq and other over-the-counter transactions. www.nqb.com

National Securities Clearing Corporation (NSCC) A clearing corporation that facilitates the settlement of accounts among brokerage firms, exchanges, and other clearing corporations. It is jointly owned by the New York Stock Exchange, the American Stock Exchange, and the National Association of Securities Dealers. www.nscc.com

National Stock Exchange of India (NSE) Established in 1993, the second-largest stock exchange in India. www.nseindia.com

nationalization A government takeover of a private company.

NAV *See* net asset value.

NDF *See* nondeliverable forward contract.

near money Assets that are easily convertible into cash, such as money market accounts and bank deposits.

nearby futures contract When several futures contracts are considered, the contract with the closest settlement date is called the nearby futures contract. The next (or the "next out") futures contract is the one that settles just after the nearby futures contract. The contract furthest away in time from settlement is called the most-distant futures contract.

nearest month The expiration date of an option or future contract that is closest to the present month. *Opposite of* far month.

negative amortization A loan repayment schedule in which the outstanding principal balance of the loan increases, rather than decreases, because the scheduled monthly payments do not cover the full amount required to retire the loan over a set period. The unpaid interest is added to the outstanding principal, to be repaid later.

negative carry Net financing cost to carry a security.

negative cash flow Occurs when a business spends more than it earns.

negative covenant A bond covenant that limits or prohibits certain actions unless the bondholders agree.

negative pledge clause A bond covenant that requires the borrower to grant lenders a lien equivalent to any liens that may be granted in the future to any other currently unsecured lenders.

negative working capital Occurs when current liabilities exceed current assets, which can lead to bankruptcy.

negative yield curve *See* inverted yield curve.

negotiable A security whose title is transferable by delivery and is free of any liens or disputes of ownership.

negotiable certificates of deposit Large-denomination bank certificates of deposit that can be traded.

negotiable instrument An unconditional order or promise to pay some amount of money, easily transferable from one party to another.

negotiable order of withdrawal (NOW) Demand deposits, usually held at a bank, that pay interest.

negotiated commission A broker's commission that is determined through negotiation, depending on the specifics of the trades performed.

negotiated market Market in which each transaction is separately negotiated between buyer and seller.

negotiated offering An offering of securities for which the terms, including underwriters' compensation, have been negotiated between the company issuing the securities and the underwriters offering them to investors.

negotiated sale Determining the terms of an offering by negotiation between the issuer and the underwriter rather than through competitive bidding by underwriting groups.

negotiated underwriting A securities-offering process in which the purchase price paid to the issuer and the public offering price are determined by negotiation rather than through competitive bidding.

net The gain or loss on a security sale as measured by the selling price of a security less the adjusted cost of acquisition.

net adjusted present value The adjusted present value of an investment minus its initial cost.

net advantage to leasing The net present value of entering into a lease-financing arrangement rather than borrowing the necessary funds and buying the asset.

net advantage of refunding The net present value of the savings from a refunding of debt.

net advantage to merging The difference in total post- and pre-merger market value minus the cost of the merger.

net after-tax gain Capital gain after income taxes have been paid.

net asset value (NAV) The value of a mutual fund's investments. The net asset value per share usually represents the fund's market price, subject to a possible sales or redemption charge. For a closed-end fund, which trades like a stock, the market price may vary significantly from the net asset value.

net assets The difference between total assets on the one hand, and current liabilities and noncapitalized long-term liabilities on the other hand.

net book value The current book value of an asset or liability, that is, its original book value net of any accounting adjustments such as depreciation.

net capital requirement SEC requirement that brokerage firms maintain enough capital so that the ratio of indebtedness to liquid capital never exceeds fifteen to one.

net cash balance Beginning cash balance at a company plus its cash receipts minus its cash disbursements.

net change The difference between a day's last trade and the previous day's last trade.

net currency exposure Exposure to foreign exchange risk after netting all intracompany cash flows.

net current assets The difference between current assets and current liabilities. *Also known as* working capital.

net financing cost The difference between the cost of financing the purchase of an asset and the asset's cash yield. Positive carry means that the yield earned is greater than the financing cost; negative carry means that the financing cost exceeds the yield earned. *Also called* cost of carry; carry.

net income A company's total earnings, reflecting revenues adjusted for costs of doing business, depreciation, interest, taxes, and other expenses. Investors want to see a company's net income rise year to year.

net income per share of common stock The net income of a company divided by its shares outstanding. *Also known as* earnings per share

net interest cost The total amount of interest that will be paid on a debt obligation by a corporate or municipal bond issuer.

net investment Gross, or total, investment minus depreciation.

net investment income per share Income received by an investment company from dividends and interest on investments less administrative expenses, divided by the number of shares outstanding.

net lease A lease arrangement under which the lessee is responsible for all property taxes, maintenance expenses, insurance, and other costs associated with keeping the asset in good working condition.

net operating loss Loss that a firm can take advantage of to reduce its taxes.

net operating loss carryback The application of losses to offset earnings in previous years.

net operating loss carryforward Application of losses to offset earnings in future years.

net operating margin The ratio of net operating income to net sales. *Also known as* operating profit margin.

net position The value of the position subtracting the initial cost of setting up the position. For example, if one hundred options were purchased for $1 each and the option is currently trading for $9, the value of the net position is $900 − $100 = $800.

net present value (NPV) The present value of the expected future cash flows that a company may generate, minus the cost of generating them.

net present value of future investments The present value of future cash flows, minus costs, expected to result from all of the firm's future investments.

net present value rule An investment is worth making if it has a positive net present value.

net proceeds Amount received from the sale of an asset after deducting all transaction costs.

net profit margin Net income divided by sales; the amount of each sales dollar left over after all expenses have been paid. If profit margins fall, investors grow concerned.

net quick assets Cash, marketable securities, and accounts receivable less current liabilities.

net realized capital gains per share Capital gains realized by an investment company minus any capital losses divided by the total number of the company's outstanding shares.

net sales Gross sales less returns and allowances, freight out, and cash discounts allowed.

net sales transaction Refers to Nasdaq and other over-the-counter trading. Securities deal in which the quoted prices include commissions.

net salvage value The after-tax net cash flow for terminating the project.

net tangible assets per share All of a company's assets except patents, trademarks, and other intangible assets, minus all liabilities and the par value of preferred stock, divided by the number of shares outstanding. This gives investors an idea of a company's net worth.

net working capital Current assets minus current liabilities. Often simply referred to as working capital and reflects a company's financial health and its ability to pay its bills.

net worth Common stockholders' equity, which consists of common stock, surplus, and retained earnings. *Also known as* owner's equity.

net yield The rate of return on a security minus purchase costs, commissions, or markups.

netting out To get or bring in as a net; to clear as profit.

neutral stock A stock with a beta of 1.0 that trades on average similar to the overall market.

new account report A broker's document including information about a new client.

New European Exchange (NEWEX) A trading market for Central and East European securities established by the Deutsche Börse (German Stock Market) and the Wiener Börse (Austrian Stock Market) in 2000.

new high/new low A stock valued at its highest or lowest price in the last year.

new issue Securities that are publicly offered for the first time, whether in an initial public offering (IPO) or as an additional issue of stocks or bonds by a company that is already public.

new listing A security that has just been entered on a stock or bond exchange for trading.

new money In a Treasuries auction, where the U.S. government borrows money by issuing new securities, the amount by which the par value of the securities offered exceeds that of those maturing.

New York Cotton Exchange (NYCE) Commodities exchange in New

York trading futures and options on cotton, frozen concentrated orange juice, and potatoes, as well as interest rate, currency, and index futures and options. www.nyce.com

New York Futures Exchange (NYFE) A wholly owned subsidiary of the NYSE that trades futures and futures options on the NYSE composite index. www.nyfe.com

New York Mercantile Exchange (NYMEX) The world's largest physical commodity futures exchange. www.nymex.com

New York Stock Exchange (NYSE) The nation's oldest stock exchange, founded in 1792. The NYSE is also a self-regulatory organization that oversees its members and insures that they abide by its rules. The NYSE has stringent requirements that companies must meet before their shares can be traded there: they must have two thousand shareholders or more, average monthly trading volume of one hundred thousand shares, and stock market value of $100 million or more. More than three thousand companies are currently listed on the exchange, which is located at Broad and Wall Streets in New York City. *Also known as* Big Board; the Exchange. www.nyse.com

New Zealand Stock Exchange Automated, screen-based national trading system based in Wellington. www.nzse.co.nz

new-issues market The market in which a new issue of securities is first sold to investors. This is not a separate market but refers to a niche of the overall market.

next futures contract The contract settling immediately after the nearby futures contract.

next-day settlement Transaction in which the contract is settled the day after the trade is executed. *See also* settlement date.

NFA *See* National Futures Association.

nifty fifty Refers to a group of fifty stocks popular among institutional investors in the late 1960s, including such glamour stocks as Avon, Polaroid, and Xerox. The nifty fifty fell on hard times in the bear market of 1974 and many of the companies and their stock prices never recovered. *Also known as* one-decision stocks.

Nikkei Stock Average Price-weighted average of 225 stocks on the Tokyo Stock Exchange, started in 1949. Japanese equivalent of the Dow Jones Industrial Average.

nine-bond rule A NYSE rule requiring that orders for nine bonds or fewer stay on the floor for one hour to seek a market.

19c3 stock A stock listed on a national securities exchange after April 26, 1979, that is exempt from the SEC rule that prohibits exchange members from participating in over-the-counter trading.

NM Stands for "not meaningful." For instance, when a stock has no earnings and its price/earnings multiple is therefore incalculable, its price/earnings will be listed in newspapers and other sources of investment information such as Web sites.

NMS *See* National Market System.

no-action letter A letter from the SEC agreeing that the commission will take no civil or criminal action against a party.

noise Price and volume fluctuations in a stock that can confuse interpretation of market direction. Stock market activity caused by program trades, dividend rolls, and other phenomena not reflective of general sentiment.

no-load mutual fund A mutual fund that does not impose a sales commission. The only fees an investor pays are marketing fees and management fees, as set out in rule 12b-1.

no-load stock Shares that can be purchased from the issuing companies themselves, so that broker fees and commissions can be avoided.

nominal In name only. Differences in compounding cause the nominal rate to differ from the effective interest rate. Inflation causes the purchasing power of money to differ from one time to another.

nominal annual rate An effective rate per period multiplied by the number of periods in a year. *Also known as* annual percentage rate.

nominal dollars Dollars that are not adjusted for inflation. *Compare to* constant dollars.

nominal exchange rate The actual foreign exchange quotation in contrast to the real exchange rate, which has been adjusted for changes in purchasing power.

nominal GDP Change over a period in the gross domestic product that is not adjusted to reflect equivalent buying power of an earlier period. *Compare to* real GDP (which takes inflation into account).

nominal income Income that has not been adjusted for inflation and decreasing purchasing power.

nominal interest rate The interest rate unadjusted for inflation. *Compare to* real interest rate.

nominal price Price quotations on futures for a period in which no actual trading took place.

nominal quotation Bid-and-offer prices given by a market maker for the purpose of valuation, but not as an invitation to trade; must be specifically identified as such by prefixing the quotes FYI (for your information) or FVO (for valuation only).

nominal yield The income received from a fixed-income security in one year divided by its par value. *See also* coupon rate.

nominee A person or firm to whom securities or other properties are transferred to facilitate transactions, while leaving the customer as the actual owner. When nominees are used to hide ownership, it can be a violation of securities laws.

nonaccredited investor Investors who don't have the net worth required by SEC regulation D. Accredited investors are deemed to require less protection because of large financial resources.

noncallable A preferred stock or bond that cannot be redeemed at the issuer's whim.

noncash charge A cost, such as depreciation, depletion, and amortization, that does not involve any cash outflow but that reflects accounting practices.

nonclearing member An exchange member firm that is not able to clear transactions, and must pay another member firm to carry out its clearing operations. Most small brokerages do not clear their own trades.

noncompete clause A provision in an employment contract that prohibits an employee from working for a competing firm for a specified period of time after the employee leaves the original employer.

noncompetitive bid In a Treasuries auction, bidding for a specific number of securities at the price, which will be set, equal to the average price of the accepted competitive bids.

noncompetitive tender Offer by an investor to purchase Treasury securities at a price equivalent to the weighted average discount rate or yield of accepted competitive bids in a Treasury auction. Noncompetitive tenders are always accepted in full.

noncontributory pension plan A pension plan that is fully paid for by the employer, requiring no employee contributions.

noncumulative Type of preferred stock on which unpaid or omitted dividends do not accrue. Omitted dividends are, as a rule, gone forever.

noncumulative preferred stock Preferred stock whose holders must forgo dividend payments when the company misses a dividend payment. *Opposite of* cumulative preferred stock.

noncurrent asset Any asset that is expected to be held, not sold or exchanged, for the whole year, such as real estate, machinery, or a patent.

noncurrent liability A liability due in one year.

nondeductible contribution A contribution to either a traditional individual retirement account (IRA) or Roth IRA that exceeds the amount that is deductible. Income tax is due on the contribution in the tax year for which the contribution is made.

nondeliverable forward contract (NDF) Agreement regarding a position in a specified currency, a specified exchange rate, and a specified future settlement date, that does not result in delivery of currencies. Rather, one party in the agreement makes a payment to the other party on the basis of the exchange rate at the future date.

nondiscretionary trust A personal trust whose trustee has no discretion in deciding how income will be distributed to the beneficiary.

nondiversifiable risk Risk that cannot be eliminated by having a large portfolio of diverse assets. For example, if the market as a whole falls sharply, it is likely that a diversified portfolio will also lose value. Hence, market risk is nondiversifiable.

nonfinancial assets Physical assets, such as real estate and machinery, as opposed to cash and securities.

nonfinancial services Services not related to investment or banking, such as freight, passenger services, and travel.

noninsured plans Defined benefit pension plans that are not guaranteed by life insurance products.

noninterest-bearing note A note without periodic interest payments, but selling at a discount and maturing at face value. *See also* zero-coupon bond.

nonintermediated debt market A financial market in which borrowers, such as governments and large corporations, appeal directly to savers to raise debt capital without using a financial institution as intermediary.

nonmarketable security Securities that cannot be easily bought and sold. Also referred to as an illiquid security.

nonmember firm Brokerage firm that is not a member of an organized exchange. Such firms execute trades either through member firms or on regional exchanges where they are members or in the third market (exchange traded stocks transacting in over-the-counter market).

nonparticipating life insurance policy Life insurance policy whose policyholders do not receive dividends, because they are not participants in the interest, dividends, and capital gains earned by the insurer on premiums paid.

nonperforming asset An asset that is not effectively producing income, such as a loan that is overdue on its interest payments.

nonpublic information Information about a company that is not known by the general public and will have a definite impact on the stock price when released. *See also* insider trading.

nonpurpose loan A loan with securities pledged as collateral but that is not to be used in securities trading or transactions.

nonqualified plan A retirement plan that does not meet the IRS requirements for favorable tax treatment.

nonqualified stock option An employee stock option that does not satisfy IRS qualifying rules and therefore is liable for taxation upon exercise. *Opposite of* incentive stock option (on which taxes are not due until shares covered by the option are sold).

nonqualifying annuity An annuity that does not fall under an IRS-approved pension plan. Contributions are made with after-tax dollars, but earnings can accumulate tax-deferred until withdrawal.

nonrated A bond that has not been rated by a large rating agency, usually because the issue is too small.

nonrecourse In the case of default, the lender has ability to claim assets over and above what the limited partners contributed. *Also known as* without recourse.

nonrecourse loan A loan taken by limited partners used to finance their portion of the partnership, which is secured by their ownership in the venture.

nonrecurring charge A one-time expense or credit shown in a company's financial statement. Usually has to do with an extraordinary event such as a restructuring in which plants are closed and employees laid off.

nonredeemable Not permitted, under the terms of a bond indenture, to be redeemed.

nonrefundable Not permitted, under the terms of a bond indenture, to be refunded.

nonreproducible assets A tangible asset with unique physical properties, like a parcel of land, a mine, or a work of art.

nonsystematic risk Nonmarket or firm-specific risk factors that can be eliminated by diversification. Systematic risk refers to risk factors common to the entire economy. *Also called* unique risk; diversifiable risk.

nonvoting stock A security that does not entitle the holder to vote on the corporation's resolutions or elections.

no-par-value stock A stock with no par value given in the charter or stock certificate. Par value has no relationship to market value.

normal portfolio A customized benchmark that includes all the securities from which a manager normally chooses.

normal random variable A random variable that has a normal probability distribution. This special distribution can be completely described by only two pieces of information: the average and the volatility.

normal retirement The age or number of working years after which a pension plan beneficiary can retire and receive unreduced benefits immediately.

normal yield curve *See* positive yield curve.

North American Free Trade Agreement (NAFTA) A regional trade pact that encourages the free flow of commerce between the United States, Canada, and Mexico.

not rated A rating-service indicator, neither positive nor negative, showing that a security or company has not been rated.

note Debt instruments with initial maturities longer than one year and shorter than ten years.

note agreement A contract for privately placed debt.

notes to the financial statements A detailed set of notes immediately following the financial statements in an annual report that explain and expand on the information in the financial statements. Also referred to as footnotes, these notes are crucial reading for investors wishing a comprehensive understanding of a company's financial circumstances and operations. Footnotes include details about how a company accounts for different aspects of its business and analyze certain elements contributing to earnings, such as gains in pension plans.

not-for-profit An organization established for charitable, humanitarian, or educational purposes that is exempt from some taxes.

notice day A day on which notices of intent to deliver, pertaining to a specified delivery month, may be issued.

notice of sale A notice advertising a new issue of municipal securities and inviting underwriters to submit competitive bids to the municipality.

notification date The day the option is either exercised or expires.

notional principal amount In an interest rate swap, the predetermined dollar principal on which the exchanged interest payments are based.

NOW *See* negotiable order of withdrawal.

NPV *See* net present value.

NSCC *See* National Securities Clearing Corporation.

NYSE *See* New York Stock Exchange.

NYSE composite index Composite index covering price movements of all common stocks listed on the New York Stock Exchange. It is based on the close of the market on December 31, 1965, at a level of 50.00, and is weighted according to the number of shares listed for each issue. Print changes in the index are converted to dollars and cents so as to provide a meaningful measure of changes in the average price of listed stocks. The composite index is supplemented by separate indexes for four industry groups: industrial, transportation, utility, and finance.

obligation A legal responsibility, such as to repay a debt.

obligor A person who has an obligation to pay off a debt.

OCC *See* Options Clearing Corporation.

odd lot A trading order for less than one hundred shares of stock. *Compare to* round lot.

odd-lot dealer A broker who combines odd lots of securities from multiple buy or sell orders into round lots and executes transactions in those round lots.

odd-lot short-sale ratio The percentage of total odd-lot sales that is composed of short sales. This supposedly indicates whether small investors are bearish—a large ratio would indicate so. The traditional view is that individual investors are not as savvy as institutional investors so a high ratio of odd-lot short sales would be a bullish sign. But few believe this.

odd-lot theory The theory that profits can be made by making trades contrary to odd-lot trading patterns, since odd-lot investors have poor timing. This theory is no longer popular.

OER Operating expense ratio. *See* expense ratio.

OEX options The symbol OEX represents the S&P 100 index, upon which options are traded.

off-balance-sheet financing Financing that is not shown as a liability on a company's balance sheet. Such financing can be troubling to investors because it is not required to be disclosed in securities filings and therefore cannot be measured.

off-board A trade in a NYSE stock that is made away from the exchange. After 9:30 A.M., if the stock has not opened due to the exchange's discretion, trading can occur elsewhere, but the trader must assume the role of a quasi specialist in the process.

offer Indicates a willingness to sell at a given price. *Opposite of* bid.

offer wanted Notice by a potential buyer of a security that he or she is looking for supply from a potential seller of the security, often requiring a capital commitment. *Opposite of* bid wanted.

offering date Date on which a new set of stocks or bonds will first be sold to the public.

offering memorandum A document that outlines the terms of securities to be offered in a private placement to high net worth investors.

offering scale The range of prices offered by the underwriter of a serial bond issue with different maturities.

offering statement A shortened registration statement required by the SEC on debt issues with less than a nine-month maturity.

offerings Often refers to initial public offerings (IPOs). When a firm goes public and makes an offering of stock to the market. Follow-on offerings of stock are called secondaries.

off-floor order An order to buy or sell a New York Stock Exchange or American Stock Exchange security that originates off the floor of the exchange. Also, customer orders originating with brokers, as distinguished from orders placed by floor members trading for their own accounts. Exchange rules require that off-floor orders be executed before orders initiated on the floor. *Also called* upstairs order (an order not handled on the floor but upstairs). *Opposite of* on-floor order.

Office of Thrift Supervision (OTS) An agency of the U.S. Treasury Department established in 1989 that is the primary regulator of all federal and many state thrift institutions. www.ots.treas.gov

official reserves Holdings of gold and foreign currencies by official monetary institutions.

official statement A statement published by an issuer of a new municipal security describing itself and the issue.

offset Elimination of a long or short position by making an opposite transaction.

offshore finance subsidiary A wholly owned affiliate incorporated overseas, usually in a tax haven country, whose function is to issue securities abroad for use in either the parent company's domestic or foreign business.

offshore fund A mutual fund based outside the United States.

off-the-run issue Usually refers to older Treasury securities which are not traded as heavily as more recent issues that have greater investor interest. *Opposite of* on-the-run issue.

"O.K. to cross" Legal to cross the buy and sell orders on the exchange floor because transactor is an agent and not a principal in the transaction.

old-line factoring An arrangement that provides collection, insurance, and financing for a company's accounts receivable.

oligopoly A market characterized by a small number of producers who often act together to control the supply of a particular good and its market price. OPEC is an oligopoly.

oligopsony A market characterized by a small number of large buyers who control all purchases and therefore the market price of a good or service.

omitted dividend A dividend that was scheduled to be declared, but is canceled by the board of directors probably because the company is experiencing financial difficulties and cannot pay it. When dividends are omitted, stock prices typically fall dramatically as investors sell the shares.

on board To own or to be long on equity.

on the money In line with, or at the same price as, the last sale.

on the opening order A market order that is to be executed at the price of the first trade of the day.

on the print To participate in a block trade of an exchange-listed stock that has already transpired, as if that customer had been part of the trade originally. Often used by a new party looking to participate in a trade that has just happened. *Also known as* open on the print.

on the sidelines An investor who decides not to invest due to market uncertainty.

on the take A stock price that is moving upward because more buyers are taking offerings, causing existing offerings to be replaced by higher ones. *Opposite of* come in, get hit.

on the tape Regarding stocks, refers to a trade printed on the ticker tape. Also, news displayed on Reuters, Dow Jones News Service, Bloomberg News, or other wire services.

one-decision stock A quality stock that is not actively traded, but that an investor buys and holds for its growth potential.

144 stock Shares of a company's stock that are given or sold to management, directors, venture capitalists, or other company insiders. The shares cannot be sold freely. They can only be sold according to SEC rule 144, which restricts insiders from selling unless certain volume measures and other requirements are met. Insiders who sell restricted or 144 stock must report their transactions to the SEC each month. Investors follow these trades closely.

one-share one-vote rule The principle that all shares should have equal voting rights in public companies and each share should have one vote. For instance, a shareholder owning four hundred shares would get four hundred votes, while a shareholder owning five shares would get five votes. *Opposite of* super-voting stock.

one-way market A market in which only one side, the bid or asked, is quoted by a market maker. Also, a market that is moving strongly in one direction.

on-floor order A security order originating with a member on the floor of an exchange when dealing with his or her own account, versus an upstairs order. *Opposite of* off-floor order.

on-the-close order A market order that is to be executed as close as possible to the closing price of the day.

on-the-run issue The most recently issued (and typically the most liquid) government bond in a particular maturity range. *Opposite of* off-the-run issue.

OPEC *See* Organization of Petroleum Exporting Countries.

open Having an interest in buying or selling a security at the indicated price level and side (buying or selling) of a preceding trade.

open contract Contract that has been bought or sold without completion of the transaction by subsequent sale or purchase, or by making or taking actual delivery of the financial instrument or physical commodity.

open interest The total number of derivatives contracts traded that have not yet been liquidated, either by an offsetting derivative transaction or by delivery.

open on the print Term for a block trade that has been completed with an institutional client and printed on the consolidated tape, but that leaves the block trader with stock available (because the trader has taken a long or short position to complete the trade) for new customers who are on the opposite side of the market to the initiating customer.

open order An order to buy or sell a security that stays active until it is completed or the investor cancels it. Open orders are often automatically canceled by brokerage firms after thirty days. *Also known as* good-'til-canceled order.

open position A net long or short position whose value will change with a change in prices.

open repo A repurchase agreement with no definite term. The agreement is made on a day-to-day basis, and either the borrower or the lender may choose to terminate. The rate paid is higher than on overnight repo and is subject to adjustment if rates move.

open-end credit Revolving line of credit that is extended with every purchase or cash advance.

open-end fund Mutual fund that continually creates new shares on demand. Mutual fund shareholders buy the funds at net asset value and may redeem them at any time at the prevailing market prices. *Opposite of* closed-end fund.

open-end lease A lease agreement that provides for an additional payment at the expiration of the lease to adjust for any change in the value of the property.

open-end mortgage Mortgage against which additional debts may be issued. *See also* closed-end mortgage.

opening The period at the beginning of the trading session officially designated by an exchange, during which all transactions are considered made "at the opening." *Opposite of* close.

opening price The range of prices at which the first bids and offers are made or the first transactions are completed on an exchange.

opening purchase Creation of or increase in a long position in a given series of options. Also, the first purchase of the day in a stock.

opening sale Creation of or increase in a short position in a given series of options. Also, the first sale of the day in a stock.

open-market operation Purchase or sale of government securities by the Federal Reserve Board to increase or decrease the domestic supply of money in circulation.

open-market purchase operation A systematic company program of repurchasing shares of stock in market transactions at current market prices, in competition with other prospective investors.

open-market rate Interest rate for Treasury bills, bonds, and notes that is determined by investors in the open market by supply and demand as opposed to being set by the Federal Reserve Board.

open-outcry The method of trading used at commodities and futures exchanges typically involving calling out the specific details of a buy or sell order, so that the information is available to all traders.

operating assets Another term for a company's working capital.

operating cash flow Earnings before depreciation minus taxes. Measures the cash generated from operations, not counting capital spending on equipment or working capital requirements.

operating cycle The average time between the acquisition of materials or services and the final cash realization from that acquisition.

operating earnings Revenues from a firm's regular activities less cost and expenses and before deduction of interest and taxes. *Also known as* earnings before interest and taxes; operating income; operating profit (or loss).

operating expenses The amount paid for asset maintenance or the cost of doing business. Earnings are distributed after operating expenses are deducted.

operating exposure Degree to which exchange rate changes, in combination with price changes, will alter a company's future operating cash flows.

operating in the red Describes a business that is losing money. Companies cannot continue such operations for long without taking on substantial debt.

operating income *See* operating earnings.

operating lease A type of lease in which the contract period is shorter than the life of the equipment, and the lessor pays all maintenance and servicing costs. An operating lease is accounted for by the lessee without showing an asset (for the equipment) or a liability (for the lease payment obligations) on the lessee's balance sheet.

operating leverage Fixed operating costs, which are characterized as leverage because they accentuate variations in profits.

operating profit margin The ratio of operating profit to net sales of a company.

operating profit (or loss) Revenue from a firm's regular activities less costs and expenses and before such deductions as taxes or interest. *Also called* operating earnings.

operating rate The percentage of total production capacity of a company, industry, or country that is being utilized. Total production capacity is the amount of goods that a company or country can produce if all of its plants are operating at maximum levels.

operating ratio A ratio that measures a firm's operating efficiency.

operating risk The inherent or fundamental risk of a firm that is unrelated to financial risk. *Also called* business risk.

operationally efficient market Market in which investors can obtain transaction services that reflect the true costs associated with furnishing those services. Also referred to as an internally efficient market.

operations department In reference to a brokerage firm, the department where securities trades are matched up, where checks go to pay for transactions, and where administration of accounts takes place. *Also known as* back office.

opinion shopping Attempts by a corporation with questionable accounting practices to attain a clean auditor's opinion by shopping for an auditor willing to sanction the practices. Prohibited by the SEC.

OPM Stands for "other people's money," which refers to borrowed funds used to increase the return on invested capital.

opportunity cost The cost of a missed investment opportunity. Also, the difference in the performance of an actual investment and a desired investment adjusted for fixed costs and execution costs. It is an opportunity cost when a trade cannot be implemented.

opportunity cost of capital Expected return that is forgone by investing in a project rather than in comparable financial securities.

optimal portfolio An efficient portfolio most preferred by an investor because its risk/reward characteristics approximate the investor's requirements. A portfolio that maximizes an investor's preferences with respect to return and risk.

optimal redemption provision Provision of a bond indenture that governs the issuer's ability to call the bonds for redemption prior to their scheduled maturity date.

optimum capacity The amount of manufacturing output that creates the lowest production cost per unit.

optimum leverage ratio The borrowing level that maximizes the value of a firm. The cost of capital to the firm is minimized at that same level.

option A security that gives the buyer the right, but not the obligation, to buy or sell an asset, typically stock, at a set price on or before a given date. Investors, usually not companies, issue options. Buyers of call options bet that a stock will rise above the option strike price, by more than they paid for the option. Buyers of put options bet that the stock's price will drop below the price set by the option. An option is part of a class of securities called derivatives, which derive their value from the worth of an underlying investment. Sellers of call options believe the underlying stock's price will fall, and they are obligated to supply the stock to the buyer of the option if exercised. Sellers of put options believe the underlying stock's price will rise and they are obligated to buy the stock from the put holder if the option is exercised.

option account A brokerage account that is approved to hold option positions or trades.

option agreement A form that an options investor opening an option account fills out requiring the investor to follow trading regulations and confirming the financial resources to settle possible losses.

option cycle The cycle of option expiration months. The most common cycles are: January, April, July, and October (JAJO); February, May, August, and November (FMAN); and March, June, September, and December (MJSD).

option elasticity The percentage increase in an option's value, given a 1 percentage point change in the value of the underlying security.

option holder A person who has an option that has not been exercised.

option margin The margin requirement for options stipulated by the Federal Reserve and in brokers' individual policies in regulation T.

option mutual fund A mutual fund that buys and sells options for aggressive or conservative investment.

option premium The option price paid by the buyer of a put or call, received by the seller. Also referred to as the option price.

option seller The party who grants a right to trade a security at a given price in the future. Also referred to as the option writer.

optional dividend A dividend that a shareholder can elect to receive either in cash or in stock.

optional payment bond A bond whose principal and/or interest may be paid in foreign or domestic currency at the discretion of the bond-holder.

Options Clearing Corporation (OCC) Financial institution that is the actual issuer and guarantor of all listed option contracts. www.occ.com

or better Indication on the order ticket of a limit order to buy or sell securities at a price better than the specified limit price if possible.

oral contract An agreement made with spoken words and either not recorded or only partially recorded on paper or on computer; it is usually enforceable.

order Instruction to a broker/dealer to buy, sell, deliver, or receive securities or commodities that commits the issuer of the order to whatever terms are specified.

order imbalance Orders for a stock not offset by opposite orders, which causes a wide spread between bid and offer prices. Trading is sometimes halted as a result of an order imbalance.

order room The brokerage firm department that receives and processes all orders to buy and sell securities.

order splitting The prohibited practice of breaking up orders so that they can be processed as small orders for automatic execution by a Nasdaq system designed for small investors known as the small order execution system, or SOES. Order splitting is forbidden by the NASD because it enables an institution to use a system specifically created for individuals.

order ticket A form detailing an order instruction from a customer that his account executive fills out.

ordering costs Costs that occur when an order is placed regardless of the size of the order.

ordinary income The income derived from the regular operating activities of a firm or individual. Income from investments, such as gains made when a stock is sold at a profit, are considered capital gains and may be taxed at a lower rate than ordinary income tax rates.

ordinary interest Interest calculated on a 360-day year instead of a 365-day year. *Compare to* exact interest.

ordinary shares Usually refers to common stock in British markets.

organization chart A chart showing the hierarchical interrelationships of positions within an organization.

Organization of Petroleum Exporting Countries (OPEC) A cartel of eleven oil-producing countries: Algeria, Indonesia, Kuwait, Libya, Nigeria, Iraq, Iran, Qatar, Saudi Arabia, the United Arab Emirates, and Venezuela. www.opec.org

organized exchange A securities marketplace where purchasers and sellers regularly gather to trade securities according to the formal rules adopted by the exchange. *Opposite of* an electronic communications network (ECN).

original face value The principal amount of a mortgage or a bond as of its issue date.

original issue discount debt securities Debt that is initially offered at a price below par.

original margin The security or cash deposit needed to cover a specific new trading position in a margin account.

original maturity Maturity at issue. For example, a five-year note has an original maturity of five years; one year later it has a maturity of four years.

origination The making of mortgage loans.

originator A savings and loan bank or mortgage banker that initially makes a mortgage loan that goes into a pool of mortgages. Also, an investment bank that has worked with the issuer of a new securities offering from the beginning and is usually appointed manager of the group of underwriters known as the syndicate.

orphan stock A stock that is ignored by research analysts and as a result may be trading at a low price/earnings ratio.

Osaka Securities Exchange Established after World War II, one of the three major securities markets in Japan. www.ose.or.jp/e

Oslo Børs An exchange in Norway, founded in 1819, which trades stocks, bonds, and stock options. www.ose.no/english/index.asp?lang= english

OTC *See* over-the-counter.

OTC bulletin board An electronic quotation listing of the bid-and-ask price of over-the-counter stocks that do not meet the requirements to be listed on the Nasdaq stock-listing system. Many of these stocks trade below $1 a share but some do not. These remain on the bulletin board because there is very little trading volume in them. www.otcbb.com

OTC margin stock Shares traded over-the-counter that can be used as margin securities under regulation T. Typically, shares trading at $5 or above are marginable, but each brokerage firm has its own rules about which stocks it will loan money on. Some stocks that are particularly volatile are not available for margin because their violent price moves could require a margin-account holder to put up more cash almost immediately if the stock fell.

other current assets Value of noncash assets, including prepaid expenses, due within one year.

other income Income from activities that are not undertaken in the ordinary course of a firm's business.

other long-term liabilities Value of leases, future employee benefits, deferred taxes, and other obligations not requiring interest payments, that must be paid over a period of more than one year.

other people's money Borrowed funds used to increase the return on invested capital. *Also known as* OPM.

other sources Amount of funds generated during a time period from operations by sources other than depreciation or deferred taxes. Part of the calculation used by investors to determine a company's free or unencumbered cash flow.

out of line A stock with a price that is too high or too low in comparison with similar-quality stocks in the same industry, according to its price/earnings ratio.

out-of-favor industry or stock An unpopular industry or stock that usually has a low price/earnings ratio. Some investors hunt for out-of-favor stocks because they believe that as the economic cycle turns, such companies may return to favor with investors.

out-of-the-money option A call option is out-of-the-money if the strike price is greater than the market price of the underlying security. That is, you have the right to purchase a security at a price higher than the market price, which has less value than an option with a strike price below the prevailing market. A put option is out-of-the-money if the strike price is lower than the market price of the underlying security, meaning that the stock must fall before the option becomes more valuable. *Opposite of* in-the-money option.

out-of-the-name When an investor or market maker no longer has an active trading profile or position in a stock.

outlays Payments on obligations in the form of cash, checks, the issuance of bonds or notes, or the maturing of interest coupons.

outside director A director of a company who is not an employee of that company and who has no conflict of interest with the company. Outside directors are considered a plus on a board because they can bring an independent view to the company and its operation.

outside market A quote on a stock that falls below the lowest offering and above the highest bid. This is not a quote that a knowledgeable investor would want to take.

outsourcing Purchasing a significant percentage of intermediate components from outside suppliers.

outstanding Shares outstanding refers to the total amount of stock held by shareholders. Shares held by the company, known as treasury stock, are not included in the outstanding.

outstanding share capital Issued share capital less the par value of shares that are held as the company's treasury stock.

overall FTC limitation A limitation on the foreign tax credit (FTC) equal to foreign source income times U.S. tax on worldwide income divided by worldwide income.

overbought Technically too high in price, and hence a technical correction is expected. *Opposite of* oversold.

overbought-oversold indicator An indicator that attempts to define when prices have moved too far and too fast in either direction and thus are vulnerable to reaction.

overcapitalization When a company has too much capital for the needs of its business.

overdraft Provision of instant credit by a lending institution.

overfunded pension plan A pension plan that has more assets than liabilities. This state ensures that pensioners will receive their pensions. However, since assets held in pensions can fluctuate, overfunded pensions can quickly dwindle. *Opposite of* underfunded pension plan.

overhang A sizable block of securities or commodities contracts that, if released on the market, would put downward pressure on prices. Examples include shares held in a dealer's inventory, a large institutional holding, a secondary distribution still in registration, and a large commodity position about to be liquidated. Related to share lockups, where managers have agreed not to sell shares for a period of time. Such holdings, because it is anticipated that they will hit the market at some time, are considered overhang.

overhanging bond A convertible bond issue that investors do not convert into common stock because the stock has not appreciated in value.

overhead The expenses of a business that are not attributable directly to the production or sale of goods.

overheating An economy that is growing very quickly, with the risk of high inflation.

overissue An excess of issued shares over authorized shares.

overlap the market To create a crossed market by expressing a willingness to sell on the bid side of the market and buy on the offer side.

overlapping debt The portion of debt of political subdivisions or neighboring special districts that a municipality is responsible for.

overnight delivery risk A risk brought about because differences in time zones between settlement centers require that payment or delivery on one side of a transaction be made without knowing until the next day whether the funds have been received in an account on the other side. Particularly apparent when delivery takes place in Europe for payment in dollars in New York.

overnight position A broker/dealer's position in a security at the end of a trading day. If a dealer has no position, he or she is considered "flat."

overnight repo A repurchase agreement with a term of one day.

overperform To appreciate at a rate faster than appreciation of the overall market.

overreaction hypothesis The supposition that investors overreact to unanticipated news, resulting in exaggerated movements in stock prices followed by corrections.

oversold Refers to an equity that is technically too low in price, and hence is expected to rise in price. *Opposite of* overbought.

oversubscribed issue Investors are not able to buy all the shares or bonds they want, so underwriters must allocate the shares or bonds among investors. This occurs when a new issue is underpriced or in great demand because of growth prospects.

oversubscription privilege In a rights issue, arrangement whereby shareholders are given the right to apply for any shares that are not taken up.

over-the-counter (OTC) With respect to equities, OTC refers to Nasdaq, a decentralized electronic market, not an exchange market, where geographically dispersed dealers are linked by telephones and computer screens. The market is for securities not listed on a stock or bond exchange and usually consists of newer or smaller companies than those on an exchange. The Nasdaq is also known as a dealer market rather than an auction market as the NYSE or AMEX are. In general, OTC trading takes place in many assets, such as bonds and options. OTC usually means not traded on an exchange.

overtrading Excessive broker trading, also referred to as churning, in a discretionary account. Also, when underwriters persuade brokerage clients to purchase some part of a new issue in return for the purchase by the underwriter of other securities from the clients at a premium. This premium is offset by the underwriting spread. The practice is illegal.

overvalued A stock price that is seen as too high according to the company's price/earnings ratio, expected earnings, or financial condition.

overwithholding Deducting and paying too much tax that may be refunded to the taxpayer or applied against the next period's obligation.

overwriting A speculative options strategy that involves selling call or put options on stocks that are believed to be overpriced or underpriced; the options are expected not to be exercised.

owner's equity Paid-in capital plus donated capital plus retained earnings less liabilities. *Also known as* shareholders' equity; net worth.

ownership-specific advantages Property rights or intangible assets, including patents, trademarks, organizational and marketing expertise, production technology, and management and general organizational abilities, that form the basis for a company's advantage over other firms.

P

PAC bond Planned amortization class bond. A class of securities in some collateralized mortgage obligations that has a sinking-fund schedule and an ability to make principal payments that are not subordinated or second to other classes.

Pacific Stock Exchange A regional equity securities exchange located in Los Angeles and San Francisco. www.pacificex.com

package mortgage A mortgage on a house and assets in the house.

Pac-Man strategy Takeover defense strategy in which the prospective target retaliates against the acquirer's tender offer by launching its own tender offer for the other firm.

paid up When all payments due have been made.

paid-in capital Capital received from investors in exchange for stock, but not capital generated from earnings or donated. This account includes capital stock and contributions of stockholders credited to accounts other than capital stock. It would also include surplus resulting from recapitalization. Also referred to as paid-in surplus.

paid-up policy A life insurance policy in which all premiums that are due have been paid.

painting the tape Illegal practice of traders who manipulate the market by buying and selling a security to create the illusion of high trading activity to attract other traders in order to push up the price.

paired off Matched buy-and-sell market orders, usually pertaining to the pre-opening market picture in a stock.

paired shares Stocks of two companies under the same management that are sold as one unit with one certificate.

pair-off A buyback to offset and effectively liquidate a prior sale of securities.

panic buying or selling Rapid trading of stocks or bonds in high volume in anticipation of sharply rising or falling prices, usually after unexpected news is released.

paper Usually refers to fixed-income securities such as money market instruments, commercial paper, or corporate bonds.

paper dealer A brokerage firm that buys and sells commercial paper to make a profit.

paper gain (loss) Unrealized capital gain (loss) on securities held in a portfolio based on a comparison of current market price to original cost.

par Equal to the nominal or face value of a security. A bond selling at par is worth an amount equivalent to its original issue value or its value upon redemption at maturity—typically $1,000 per bond. *Compare to* discount bond; premium.

par bond A bond trading at its face value.

par value The amount that a bond's issuer agrees to pay at the maturity date. Par value on stocks is unrelated to its market value. *Also known as* face value; maturity value.

par value of currency The official exchange rate between two countries' currencies.

parallel bond Fixed-income instrument denominated in the respective currencies of the countries where they are placed.

parallel loan A process whereby two companies in different countries borrow each other's currency for a specific period of time and repay the other's currency at an agreed maturity for the purpose of reducing foreign exchange risk. Also referred to as back-to-back loan.

parallel shift in the yield curve A shift in economic conditions in which the change in the interest rate on all maturities is the same number of basis points. In other words, if the three-month T-bill increases one hundred basis points, one percentage point, the six-month, one-year, five-year, ten-year, twenty-year, and thirty-year rates all increase by one hundred basis points as well.

parent company A company that controls subsidiaries through its ownership of voting stock and runs its own business.

Paris Interbank Offer Rate (PIBOR) The deposit rate on interbank transactions in the Eurocurrency market, quoted in Paris.

Paris Stock Exchange (Bourse de Paris) National stock market of France. www.euronext.com/fr

parity For convertibles, level at which a convertible security's market price equals the aggregate value of the underlying common stock. For international parity, the price in U.S. dollars of a foreign stock's last sale in an overseas market, as figured by taking the stock price in local currency, multiplying it with the current exchange rate and the ratio of American depositary receipts (ADRs) to foreign shares. For options parity, dollar amount by which an option is in-the-money. *Also called* conversion value. *See also* intrinsic value of an option.

parking Putting money into safe investments such as money market investments while deciding where to invest the money.

parking violation In risk arbitrage, the illegal holding of stock by a third party, or the financing of such a stock, in which the third party's sole reason for holding the stock is to conceal ownership or control of a raider, thus sidestepping the Williams Act requirements of disclosing holdings of 5 percent or more. *See* rule 13d.

part B prospectus *See* statement of additional information.

partial A trade whose size is only part of the customer's total order, usually made to avoid a compromise in price and also to get some business instead of losing the customer's order to a competitor.

partial compensation Incomplete payment for the delivery of goods to one party by buying back a certain amount of product from the same party.

participating convertible preferred stock Preferred stock that can be converted into common stock at the option of the holder. In contrast to the usual preferred stock, the value of the preferred stock is refunded to the holder. That is, one gets conversion plus the value of the stock.

participating dividend Dividend received from ownership of participating preferred stock.

participating fees The portion of total fees in a syndicated credit that goes to the participating banks.

participating GIC A guaranteed investment contract (GIC) whose policyholder is not guaranteed a certain rate of return, but instead receives return based on the actual performance of the portfolio managed by the life insurance company.

participating life insurance policies Life insurance that pays dividends to policyholders depending on the company's success as provided by few claims and profitable underwritings and investments.

participating preferred stock Preferred stock that provides the holder with a specified dividend plus the right to additional earnings under specified conditions.

participation loan A large loan made by a group of lenders that enables a borrower to obtain financing above the legal lending limit of an individual lender.

partner Business associate who shares equity in a firm.

partnership Shared ownership among two or more individuals, some of whom may, but do not necessarily, have limited liability with respect to obligations of the group. *See* general partnership; limited partnership; master limited partnership.

partnership agreement A written agreement among partners detailing the terms and conditions of participation in a business ownership arrangement.

party in interest An ERISA-specified individual—such as an administrator, officer, fiduciary, trustee, custodian, or counsel—who is prohibited from making certain transactions involving a retirement plan. A trustee, for example, would be prohibited from using a customer's IRA as collateral for a loan.

pass the book The process of transferring responsibility for a brokerage firm's trading account from one office to another around the world in order to benefit from trading twenty-four hours a day.

passive Income or loss from business activities in which a person does not materially participate, such as a limited partnership.

passive bond A bond that pays no interest.

passive income Income, such as that earned on investments, that does not come from active participation in a business. Such income is treated differently by the U.S. tax code.

passive investing Putting money into a profitable business opportunity that is deemed passive by the IRS and thus benefits from tax deductions.

passive investment management Buying a well-diversified portfolio to represent a broad-based market index without attempting to search out mispriced securities. Buying an index fund that mirrors a particular stock index is considered passive investment management. *Opposite of* active fund management.

passive investor An investor who does not play an active role in the management of the corporation. *Opposite of* active investor.

passive portfolio A market-index portfolio.

pass-through coupon rate The interest rate paid on a pool of securities, which is equal to the rate paid on the underlying loans minus the servicing and guaranteeing fees.

pass-through rate The net interest rate passed through to investors after deducting servicing, management, and guarantee fees from the gross mortgage coupon.

pass-through securities A pool of fixed-income securities backed by assets such as mortgages, where the holder receives the principal and interest payments. *See also* mortgage pass-through security.

patent The exclusive right to use documented intellectual property in producing or selling a particular product or using a process for a designated period of time.

path-dependent option An option whose value depends on the sequence of prices of the underlying asset rather than just the final price of the asset.

pattern A technical chart formation used to make market predictions by following the price movements of securities. A head and shoulders is such a trading pattern.

pay down In a Treasury refunding, the amount by which the par value of the securities maturing exceeds that of those sold. In the context of general equities, paying a lower price in an accumulation of stock.

pay up When an investor who wants to buy a stock at a particular price hesitates and the stock begins to rise, instead of letting the stock go, he "pays up" to buy the shares at the higher prevailing price. Also, to buy shares in a high-quality company at what is felt to be a high, but supportable, price due to its quality.

payable date The date when dividends or capital gains are paid to shareholders or reinvested in additional shares.

payables *See* accounts payable.

pay-as-you-go basis A method of paying income tax in which the employer deducts a portion of an employee's monthly salary to remit to the IRS.

payback The length of time it takes to recover the initial cost of a project, without regard to the time value of money.

payee A person receiving payment through any form of money transfer method.

payer The person making a payment to a payee.

paying agent An agent, usually a bank, that makes principal and interest payments to bondholders on behalf of the issuer.

payment date The date on which shareholders of record will be sent a check for the declared dividend.

payment float Company-written checks that have not yet cleared.

payment-for-order flow A dubious practice in Nasdaq stock trading where a dealer pays a firm to funnel its customers' trades to it. Under such an arrangement a customer's order is used by his firm as a profit source and the order is directed to the firm who paid for it even if that firm is offering a lower-than-market price to buy the shares or is offering a higher-than-market price to sell them. *Also known as* preference.

payment-in-kind (PIK) bond A bond that gives the issuer an option (during an initial period) either to make coupon payments in cash or in the form of additional bonds with the same coupon.

payments netting Reducing fund transfers between affiliates to only a netted amount. Netting can occur between pairs of affiliates or taking all affiliates together.

payments pattern Describes the typical collection pattern of a company's receivables. A pattern might describe the probability that a seventy-two-day-old account will still be unpaid when it is seventy-three days-old.

payout period The time period during which withdrawals from a retirement account or annuity can be made. In an IRA, for example, payouts cannot begin before age fifty-nine and a half.

payout ratio Generally, the proportion of earnings paid out to the common stockholders as cash dividends. More specifically, the firm's cash dividend divided by the firm's earnings in the same reporting period. If the ratio declines significantly, the company might have to suspend payment of its common stock dividend.

pay-to-play Attempts by municipal bond underwriting businesses to bribe political officials who decide which underwriters are awarded the municipality's business to try to influence their choices.

PBGC *See* Pension Benefit Guaranty Corporation.

p-coast Refers to the Pacific Stock Exchange.

P/E ratio *See* price/earnings (P/E) ratio.

peak The high point at the end of an economic expansion until the start of a contraction. Also the high point in a security's price.

pecking-order view (of capital structure) The argument that external financing transactions costs vary, so that companies have a preference, or pecking order of preferred sources, of financing. Internally generated funds are the most preferred, followed by new debt, and debt-equity hybrids. New equity is the most costly and therefore least preferred source because it represents ownership in the enterprise.

PEFCO *See* Private Export Funding Corporation.

PEG ratio *See* prospective earnings growth (PEG) ratio

pegged exchange rate Exchange rate whose value is pegged to another currency's value or to a unit of account.

pegging Making transactions in a security, currency, or commodity in order to stabilize or target its value through market intervention.

penalty clause A clause found in contract agreements that provides for a penalty in the event of default.

penalty tax A federal tax that can be applied if a plan holder does not meet certain requirements when making withdrawals from a tax-advantaged retirement plan. For instance, if the plan holder takes a payout before age fifty-nine and a half, he or she pays a penalty to the IRS of 10 percent. This penalty tax is owed in addition to any income taxes due.

pennant A chart pattern resembling a pointed flag, with the point facing to the right, which shows a diminishing variance of price.

penny stock Stock that typically sells for less than $1 per share, although it may rise to as much as $10 per share after the initial public offering, usually because of heavy promotion. All are traded over-the-counter (OTC), many of them on the OTC bulletin board or in the Vancouver or Salt Lake City local markets.

Pension Benefit Guaranty Corporation (PBGC) A federal agency that insures the vested benefits of pension plan participants. Established in 1974 by the ERISA legislation. www.pbgc.gov

pension fund A fund set up to pay the pension benefits of a company's workers after their retirement. Pension funds invest money hoping for gains that can be used to pay pensioners. Pension funds, particularly those for state and local workers, are among the largest institutional investors in the world.

pension liabilities Future liabilities resulting from pension commitments made by a corporation to its workers. Accounting for pension liabilities varies widely by country.

pension parachute A form of poison pill providing that in the event of a hostile takeover attempt, any excess pension plan assets can be used to benefit pension plan participants. This prevents the raiding firm from using the pension assets, which should be used to cover pension liabilities, to finance the takeover.

pension plan A fund that is established for the payment of retirement benefits. The most common is called a defined benefit pension plan where workers receive a set amount each year after they retire. These types of plans are rapidly being replaced at many companies by defined contribution plans, such as 401(k) plans, which only stipulate the contribution paid into the plan, not the benefit.

pension reversion Termination of an overfunded, defined benefit pension plan, that is, where pensioners will receive a set amount per year and replacement of it with a life insurance company–sponsored fixed annuity plan. Such plans also have set payment amounts.

pension sponsors Organizations that have established a pension plan. May include companies, universities, state and local governments.

people pill A form of poison pill providing that the entire management threatens to resign in the event of a takeover.

per capita debt The total bonded debt of a municipality divided by the population of the municipality.

per capita distribution A method for distributing the assets of a deceased individual equally among all surviving descendants. For example, if the individual has two children, the elder with five children and the younger with one child, and both of the person's children are already dead, one-sixth of the estate goes to each of the six grandchildren. From the Latin for "by the heads." *Compare to* per stirpes distribution.

per stirpes distribution A method for distributing the assets of a deceased individual equally along lines of descendance. For example, if the individual has two children, the elder with five children and the younger with one child, and both of the person's children are already dead, half of the estate goes to the elder's five children (one-tenth of the total estate each) and the other half of the estate goes to the younger's only child; hence, the younger descendant's child gets five times more of the estate. From the Latin for "by the roots." *Compare to* per capita distribution.

PERC *See* preferred equity redemption stock.

percent to double Percentage that the stock price has to rise or fall to double the price of the call or put option.

percentage premium Applies mainly to convertible securities. Premium over parity of a convertible bond divided by parity.

perfect capital market A market in which there are never any price discrepancies that would yield arbitrage opportunities.

perfect competition An idealized market environment in which every market participant is too small to affect the market price by acting on its own.

perfect hedge A situation in which the profit and loss from the underlying asset and the hedge position are equal. With a perfect hedge, an investor is not exposed to any financial, systemic, currency, or company risk. However, perfect hedges are almost impossible to find.

perfect market assumptions Conditions under which the law of one price holds. The assumptions include frictionless markets, which do not exist; rational investors, who are few; and equal access to market prices and information, which is rare. An economic theory that has little basis in reality.

perfect market view (of capital structure) Analysis of a firm's capital structure decision, which shows the irrelevance of capital structure in a perfect capital market. But since capital markets are imperfect, this view is dubious.

perfected first lien A first attachment on an asset that is duly recorded with the relevant government body so that the lender will be able to act on it should the borrower default.

perfectly competitive financial market Market in which no trader has the power to change the price of goods or services. Perfect capital markets are characterized by certain conditions: (1) Trading is costless, and access to the financial markets is free; (2) information about borrowing and lending opportunities is freely available; and (3) there are many traders, and no single trader can have a significant impact on market prices.

performance attribution analysis The decomposition of a money manager's performance results to explain why his results were achieved. This analysis seeks to answer questions such as: What were the major sources of added value? Was market timing statistically significant? Was security selection statistically significant?

performance bond A surety bond between two parties, insuring one party against loss if the terms of a contract are not fulfilled.

performance evaluation The assessment of a manager's results, which involves, first, determining whether the money manager added value by outperforming the established performance measurement, and second, determining how the money manager achieved the calculated return.

performance fund A growth-oriented mutual fund investing in growth stock and performance stock with low dividends and high risk.

performance index A risk-adjusted measure of how well a portfolio has performed.

performance measurement Calculation of the return a money manager realizes over some time interval.

performance shares Shares of stock given to managers on the basis of company performance as measured by earnings per share and similar criteria. A control device shareholders sometimes use to align management's interests with their own.

performance stock High-growth stock. For example, a company that retains earnings for further growth and therefore pays no dividends.

period of digestion The time period of often high volatility after a new issue is released when the trading price of the security is established by the market.

period-certain annuity An annuity that provides guaranteed payments to an annuitant for a specified period of time.

periodic call auction Selling stocks by bid at intervals throughout the day. Several stock-trading systems use these auctions.

periodic payment plan Accumulation of capital in a mutual fund by making regular payments on a monthly or quarterly basis.

periodic payments A series of payments from an annuity, qualified retirement plan such as a 401(k), or 403(b)(7) account made over a certain term of years. A payment from an IRA, even if over a period of years, is not considered a periodic payment for tax purposes.

periodic purchase deferred contract A fixed or variable annuity contract for which fixed-amount premiums are paid either monthly or quarterly, and one that does not begin paying out until a time elected by the annuitant.

periodic rate The effective interest rate for the period. For example, the monthly periodic rate on a credit card with an 18 percent annual percentage rate is 1.5 percent per month.

PERLS *See* principal exchange-rated-linked securities.

permanent assets Fixed assets such as plant and equipment and permanent current assets.

permanent current assets The minimum level of current assets, such as cash and securities, that a firm needs to operate. Because the level is always maintained, they are called permanent current assets. *Compare to* permanent spontaneous current liabilities.

permanent financing Long-term financing using either debt or equity.

permanent spontaneous current liabilities The minimum level of current liabilities always maintained by a firm. *Compare to* permanent current assets.

perpendicular spread Option strategy involving the purchase of options with similar expiration dates and different exercise prices.

perpetual bond Nonredeemable bond with no maturity date that pays regular interest rates indefinitely.

perpetual inventory Record-keeping system in which book inventory is updated daily.

perpetual warrants Warrants that have no expiration date.

perquisites Personal benefits, such as the use of a firm car or expense account for personal business, and indirect benefits, such as up-to-date office decoration.

personal exemption Amount of money a taxpayer can exclude from personal income for each member of the household when calculating his or her tax obligation.

personal income Total income received from all sources, including wages, salaries, rents, and tips.

personal inflation rate The inflation rate as it affects a specific individual.

personal property Any assets other than real estate.

personal tax view (of capital structure) A relationship between personal taxes and corporate financing decisions. Investors typically pay higher relative taxes on interest income than on equity income, and therefore, adjusting for risk, demand a higher pretax rate of return on interest income than on equity income. This means that corporations must pay higher interest rates on debt (i.e., higher coupon rates) than on equity returns, and this discourages firms from issuing debt, despite corporate tax advantages.

personal trust An interest in an asset held by a trustee for the benefit of another person.

personal-article floater Insurance policy attachment designed to cover specified personal valuables, such as jewelry or computer equipment worth more than $1,000.

petrodollars Deposits by countries that receive dollar revenues from the sale of petroleum to other countries. Commonly refers to OPEC deposits of dollars in the Eurocurrency market.

phantom bid A practice of putting in an order to buy or sell securities on electronic trading systems and immediately withdrawing the order in order to draw other investors into the market and push the price of the security up or down. The phantom bidder sells securities into the buying volume or buys securities as the price falls. *Also known as* spoof bid. *Opposite of* real market.

phantom income Income from a limited partnership that creates taxability without generating cash flow. Zero-coupon bonds, as they rise in value the closer they get to maturity, also throw off phantom income in the form of that increased value, which the IRS considers taxable.

phantom-stock plan An incentive scheme that awards management bonuses based on increases in the market price of the company's stock.

Philadelphia Board of Trade (PBOT) A subsidiary of the Philadelphia Stock Exchange that trades currency futures. www.phlx.com

Philadelphia Stock Exchange (PHLX) A securities exchange trading equity options and American and European foreign currency options on spot exchange rates. www.phlx.com

Philippine Stock Exchange Established in 1992 through the merger of the Manila Stock Exchange and the Makati Stock Exchange, the Philippines' only securities market. www.pse.org.ph

Phillips Curve A graph that supposedly shows the relationship between inflation and unemployment. It is conjectured that there is a simple trade-off between inflation and unemployment whereby when inflation is high, unemployment is low, and vice versa. Named after A. W. Phillips, a New Zealand–born economist. The relation between these important macroeconomic variables is more complex than this simple graph suggests.

phone switching Transferring money between funds in the same mutual fund family by telephone request. There may be a charge associated with these transfers. Phone switching is also possible among different fund families if the funds are held in street name by a participating brokerage firm.

physical asset Actual property such as precious metals or real estate. *Also called* real asset; tangible asset; hard asset. *Opposite of* intangible asset.

physical verification A procedure auditors use to ensure that inventory recorded in the book is correct by actually examining the physical inventory.

P&I Stands for principal and interest on bonds or mortgage-backed securities.

PIBOR *See* Paris Interbank Offer Rate.

pickup The gain in yield that occurs when a block of bonds is swapped for another block of higher-coupon bonds.

pickup bond A bond with a relatively high coupon that is close to the date at which it is callable, meaning that a fall in interest rates will most likely cause early redemption of the bond at a premium.

picture Describes bid and ask prices a broker quotes for a given security.

piece Increment of bonds that trade in portions of $1,000 minimum. Not all bonds can be traded in "pieces," and the increments can vary.

piggyback registration When a securities underwriter allows existing holdings of shares in a corporation to be sold in combination with an offering of new public shares.

piggybacking A broker who trades stocks, bonds, or commodities in a personal account following a trade just made for a customer. The broker assumes that the customer is making the trade on valuable inside information.

PIK *See* payment-in-kind (PIK) bond.

pink sheets Daily publication on long pink-colored paper of the National Quotation Bureau that reports the bid and ask prices of thousands of over-the-counter (OTC) stocks, as well as the market makers who trade each stock. The pink sheets have been replaced by the electronic or OTC bulletin board.

Pink Sheets LLC Formerly the National Quotation Bureau, a service that publishes bid-and-offer quotes from market makers in Nasdaq and other over-the-counter transactions. www.nqb.com

pip Smallest unit of a currency (i.e., cents for U.S. dollars).

pipeline The underwriting process that must be completed with the SEC before a security can be offered for sale to the public.

pit A specific area of the trading floor that is designed for the trading of commodities, individual futures, or option contracts.

pit committee A committee of the exchange that determines the daily settlement price of futures contracts.

PITI Stands for principal, interest, taxes, and insurance, the four main parts of monthly mortgage obligations.

pivot Price level in a market or security seen as being significant by the market's failure to penetrate or as being significant when a sudden increase in volume accompanies the move through the price level.

P&L Profit and loss statement.

place The marketing of new securities, usually through sales to institutional investors.

placement ratio The percentages of last week's new municipal bond offerings that have been bought from the underwriters, according to the newspaper *Bond Buyer.*

plain vanilla A term that refers to a relatively simple derivative financial instrument, usually a swap or other derivative that is issued with standard features.

plan agreement A document detailing the terms and conditions of a retirement plan such as an IRA.

plan for reorganization A plan for reorganizing a firm during the chapter 11 bankruptcy process.

plan participant Employee or other beneficiary who is eligible to receive benefits from a company's employee benefit plan.

plan sponsor The entity that establishes pension plans, including private business entity acting for its employees; state and local entity operating on behalf of its employees; union acting on behalf of its members; and individual representing himself.

planned amortization class (PAC) The class of a collateralized mortgage obligation (CMO) that has the most stable cash flows and the lowest prepayment risk of any other class, or a CMO bond class that stipulates cash flow contributions to a sinking fund. A planned amortization class directs principal payments to the sinking fund on a priority basis in accordance with a predetermined payment schedule, with prior claim to the cash flows before other CMO classes. Similarly, cash flows received by the trust in excess of the sinking-fund requirement are also allocated to other bond classes. The prepayment experience of the PAC is therefore very stable over a wide range of prepayment experience.

planned capital expenditure program Budgeted or projected outlays for major expenditures on permanent or fixed assets as outlined in the corporate financial plan.

planned financing program Budgeted or projected ways to obtain short-term and long-term financing as outlined in the corporate financial plan.

planning horizon The length of time a model or investor or plan will go into the future.

plant The assets of a business including land, buildings, machinery, and all equipment permanently employed.

player Customer or trader who is actively involved in a particular stock or the market in general.

playing the market Trading in undiversified portfolios, often with high or uncalculated risk. Sometimes refers to actions of amateur investors.

Plaza Accord Agreement among G-7 country representatives in 1985 to implement a coordinated program to weaken the American dollar. Held at the Plaza Hotel in New York, thus its name.

PLC *See* project loan certificate.

pledging *See* hypothecation.

plow back To reinvest earnings in a business rather than pay them out as dividends. Common practice in high-growth companies.

plowback rate Retention rate of earnings in a business.

plus Dealers in government bonds normally give price quotes in 1/32, but to quote a bid or offer in 1/64 they use pluses. A dealer who bids 4+ is bidding 4/32 + 1/64, which equals 9/64.

plus a match Floor indication that someone is on the floor with equal priority standing who wants to buy or sell at least the same number of shares at the same price as one's own order. *See* match orders.

plus tick Trade occurring at a price higher than the previous sale; uptick. Short sales must be made on an uptick. *Also known as* uptick. *Opposite of* minus tick; downtick.

plus-tick seller A short seller, referring to the regulation requiring a plus tick to put on a short position.

PMI *See* private mortgage insurance.

PO *See* principal-only.

point The smallest unit of price change quoted in a bond, or one one-hundredth of a percent.

poison pill Antitakeover device that gives a prospective acquiree's shareholders the right to buy shares of the firm or shares of anyone who acquires the firm at a deep discount to their fair market value. Named after the cyanide pill that secret agents are said to be instructed to swallow if capture is imminent.

poison put A covenant allowing the bondholder to demand repayment in the event of a hostile takeover.

policy asset allocation Way in which an investor seeks to assess an appropriate long-term mix of assets that represents an ideal blend of controlled risk and enhanced return.

policy limit The maximum dollar amount of coverage provided by an insurance company for a certain policy.

policy loan A loan often made at a below-market interest rate from an insurance company to a policyholder that is secured by the cash surrender value of his life insurance policy.

policyholder An individual who owns an insurance policy.

policyholder loan bonds Packaged loan acquired by policyholders that is secured by the cash surrender value of the policies and offered by a broker/dealer as bonds.

political risk Possibility of negative events such as expropriation of assets, changes in tax policy, restrictions on the exchange of foreign currency, or other changes in the business climate of a country that would make investing more risky.

Ponzi scheme A type of illegal money-raising plan in which funds from investors are used to pay returns to earlier investors. Named for Charles Ponzi, who perfected the fraud in a 1920s pyramid scheme in Boston.

pool In capital budgeting, the concept that investment projects are financed out of a pool of bonds, preferred stock, and common stock, and a weighted-average cost of capital must be used to calculate investment returns. In insurance, a group of insurers who share premiums and losses in order to spread risk. In investments, the combination of funds for the benefit of a common project, or a group of investors who illegally use their combined influence to manipulate prices.

pooled trust A trust established by a nonprofit organization that pools assets from individuals who therefore become eligible to receive Medicaid under asset caps. The organization, and not the individual or family member, must administer the trust's investments, and usually the individuals in the pooled trust are not related. When the person dies, the assets are either transferred to the accounts of other individuals in the pooled trust, or the state is reimbursed for Medicaid benefits paid, which can be substantially less than the cost of care through a private plan, and the remainder goes to family members or other beneficiaries. *Compare to* Miller trust; under-65 trust.

pooling of interests An accounting method for reporting acquisitions accomplished through the use of company stock. The combined assets of the merged entity are consolidated using book value, as opposed to the purchase method, which uses market value. The merging entities' financial results are combined as though the two entities have always been a single entity. Pooling-of-interest method does not result in goodwill, an asset that must be written off over time. Purchase-method accounting, because it records the acquisition at market value, generates "goodwill" which must be written off against earnings.

porcupine provision Some aspect of a company's capital structure or corporate structure that would repel a takeover. An example would be the issuance of additional shares of stock to current shareholders, making a takeover more difficult. *See* shark repellent.

portability The character of benefits that may be carried from a previous job to the next. Pensions may or may not be portable.

portfolio A collection of investments or assets.

portfolio allocation by region The distribution, by geographic region, of a portfolio's holdings.

portfolio asset allocation The distribution, by type of asset, of a portfolio's holdings. Stocks and bonds are different types of assets.

portfolio beta Portfolio beta describes the relative volatility of a securities portfolio, taken as a whole, measured by the individual stock betas of the securities making it up. A beta of 1.05 relative to the S&P 500 Composite Index implies that if the S&P's excess return increases by 10 percent the portfolio is expected to increase by 10.5 percent.

portfolio diversification Investing in different asset classes and in securities of many issuers in an attempt to reduce overall investment risk and to avoid damaging a portfolio's performance by the poor performance of a single security, industry, or country investment.

portfolio expected return A weighted average of individual assets' expected returns.

portfolio insurance A strategy designed to ensure that the value of the portfolio does not fall below a certain level. Can be achieved using hedges.

portfolio internal rate of return The rate of return computed by first determining the cash flows for all the bonds in the portfolio and then finding the interest rate that will make the present value of the cash flows equal to the market value of the portfolio.

portfolio management *See* investment management.

portfolio manager Professional responsible for the securities portfolio of an individual or institutional investor, such as a mutual fund, pension fund, profit-sharing plan, bank trust department, or insurance company. In return for a fee, the manager has the fiduciary responsibility to manage the assets prudently and choose which asset types are most appropriate over time. *Also known as* investment advisor; investment manager; money manager.

portfolio restructuring Recomposition of a portfolio by selling off undesired assets or specific types of securities while simultaneously buying other securities that are more desirable. For example, a portfolio heavily weighted to stocks may be restructured to give more weight to bonds.

portfolio transaction costs The expenses associated with buying and selling securities, including commissions, purchase and redemption fees, exchange fees, and other miscellaneous costs. In a mutual fund prospectus, these expenses are listed separately from the fund's expense ratio. *Also known as* trading costs.

portfolio turnover rate For an investment company, an annualized rate found by dividing the lesser of purchases and sales by the average of portfolio assets. High portfolio turnover is generally undesirable because of the costs associated with trading.

position A market commitment; the number of contracts bought or sold for which no offsetting transaction has been entered into. The buyer of a stock or other security is said to have a long position, and the seller has either no position or a short position.

position building Buying shares to build up a long position or selling shares to create a short position in a particular stock or other security or group of securities. Positions are built over time so as not to disrupt the market.

position sheet List of long and short positions for an individual trader or desk, at times accompanied by the trades from the previous trading session that brought these closing positions.

position trader Trader who takes a long-term approach in maintaining positions in the market.

positive carry When the yield on an investment outweighs the cost of financing it.

positive convexity A property of bonds whereby the price appreciation for a large downward change in interest rates will be greater (in absolute terms) than the price depreciation for the same upward change in interest rates.

positive covenant A bond covenant that specifies certain actions the firm must take to remain in good standing with lenders. *Also known as* affirmative covenant.

positive yield curve When long-term bond rates are higher than short-term debt rates because of the increased risk involved with long-term debt security. This is the most common slope of the yield curve, going from low in the left axis to higher on the right. *Opposite of* inverted yield curve.

possessions corporation A type of corporation permitted under the U.S. tax code whose branch operation in a U.S. possession can obtain tax benefits as though it were operating as a foreign subsidiary.

post Particular place on the floor of an exchange where transactions in stocks listed on the exchange occur. *Also known as* specialist's post.

postaudit A set of procedures for evaluating a capital budgeting decision after the fact.

postdated check A check that becomes payable and negotiable on a future specified date.

postponement option   The option of deferring a project without eliminating the possibility of undertaking it.

postponing income   Purposely delaying receipt of income to a later year in order to reduce current tax liability.

posttrade benchmark   Price after the decision to trade.

pot   The portion of stock or bond issue that is returned to the managing underwriter by the participating investment bankers for sale to institutional investors.

pot is clean   Phrase used when the managing underwriter has sold the entire pot.

power of attorney   A written authorization allowing a person to perform certain acts on behalf of another, such as moving assets between accounts or trading for a person's benefit.

PPI   *See* producer price index.

prearranged trading   Possibly fraudulent practice whereby commodities dealers carry out risk-free trades at predetermined prices to acquire tax advantages.

preauthorized electronic debit   Prearranged debit on a bank account. The payer's bank sends payment to the payee's bank through the automated clearing house (ACH) system.

preauthorized payment   Prearranged permission to make a payment by a bank account holder, thereby accelerating cash inflows.

precedence   The established system of priorities of trades in an exchange. For example, the highest bid and lowest offer have highest precedence; the first bid or first offer at a price has highest priority, and when bids or offers are simultaneous, large orders have priority over smaller orders. *See also* priority.

precious metal   Gold, silver, platinum, and palladium, which are used for their intrinsic value or for their value in production. These may be traded either in their physical state or by way of futures and options contracts, mining company stocks, bonds, mutual funds, or other instruments.

precompute   Method of charging interest in which the annual interest is either deducted from the face amount of the loan when the funds are distributed or added to the total amount and divided into the regular payments.

preemptive right   Common stockholders' right to anything of value distributed by the company.

preference   In Nasdaq trading, the selection of a dealer to handle a trade despite the dealer's market not being the best available. Sometimes the "preferenced dealer" will then move his market in line. The selection of a dealer is usually made because the dealer has paid to receive the order, making the practice dubious. *Also known as* payment-for-order flow.

preference share Preferred shares of a corporation that have first claim to preferred dividends.

preference stock A security that ranks junior to preferred stock but senior to common stock in the right to receive payments from the firm; essentially junior preferred stock.

preferred dividend coverage Net income after interest and taxes (before common stock dividends) divided by preferred stock dividends.

preferred equity redemption stock (PERC) Preferred stock that converts automatically into equity at a stated date. A limit is placed on the value of the shares the investor receives.

preferred shares or stock Shares that give investors a fixed dividend from the company's earnings and entitle them to be paid before common shareholders in the event of liquidation; the fixed dividend is usually stated in a dollar amount or as a percentage of par value. Preferred stock does not usually carry voting rights. Otherwise, preferred stock has characteristics of both common stock and debt.

preferred stock ratio Preferred stock at par value divided by total capitalization, which gives the portion of a company's capitalization that consists of preferred stock.

preliminary estimate Usually refers to the second estimate of GDP, released about two months after the measurement period.

preliminary prospectus An initial or tentative version of a prospectus. *Also known as* red herring (for the red print on the front of the prospectus stating that the document is preliminary).

premature distribution A distribution from an IRA before the owner reaches age fifty-nine and a half. Generally, a 10 percent penalty tax is owed to the IRS on such a distribution. Also referred to as an early distribution or an early withdrawal.

premium The amount above its par value that a bond trades at. The price of an option contract; also, in futures trading, the amount by which the futures price exceeds the price of the spot commodity. For convertibles, amount, usually expressed as a percentage, by which the price of a convertible exceeds parity. If a stock is trading at $45, and the bond convertible at $50 is trading at 105, the premium is $15, or 16.66 percent (15/90). If the premium is high, the bond trades like any fixed-income bond; if low, like a stock. For futures, excess of fair value over the spot index, which in theory will equal the Treasury bill yield for the period to expiration minus the expected dividend yield until the future's expiration. For options, price of an option in the open market (sometimes refers to the portion of the price that exceeds parity). For straight equity, price higher than that of the last sale or inside market.

premium bond A bond that is selling for more than its par value. If an investor buys such a bond and it is redeemed at par, the investor has a loss.

premium income The income received by an investor who sells an option.

premium raid An attempt to acquire a large portion of a company's stock to gain control by offering stockholders a premium over the market value for their shares.

prepackaged bankruptcy A bankruptcy in which a debtor and its creditors prenegotiate a plan of reorganization and then file it along with the bankruptcy petition. Much less time-consuming than a classic bankruptcy filing.

prepaid interest An asset account showing interest that has been paid in advance, which is expensed and charged to the borrower's P&L statement.

prepayment penalty A fee a borrower pays a lender when the borrower repays a loan before its scheduled time of maturity.

prepayment speed The estimated rate at which mortgagors pay off their loans ahead of schedule, critical in assessing the value of mortgage pass-through securities. *Also called* speed.

prepayments Payments made in excess of scheduled mortgage principal repayments.

prerefunded bond *See* refunded bond.

prerefunding Procedure of floating a second bond at a lower interest rate in order to pay off the bond paying higher rates at the first call date and to reduce overall borrowing costs.

presale order An order to purchase part of a new municipal bond issue that is accepted by an underwriting syndicate before an official public offering.

Prescribed Right to Income and Maximum Equity certificate *See* PRIME.

present value The amount of cash today that is equivalent in value to a payment, or to a stream of payments, to be received in the future. To determine the present value, each future cash flow is multiplied by a present value factor. For example, if the opportunity cost of funds is 10 percent, the present value of $100 to be received in one year is $100 × [1/(1 + 0.10)] = $91.

present value factor Factor used to calculate an estimate of the present value of an amount to be received in a future period. If the opportunity cost of funds is 10 percent over the next year, the factor is [1/(1 + 0.10)].

present value index (PVI) The ratio of the net present value of a project to the initial outlay required for it. The index measures the efficiency of investment decisions when capital is rationed.

present value of growth opportunities Net present value of investments the firm is expected to make in the future.

president Highest-ranking officer in a corporation after the chief executive officer.

presidential-election-cycle theory A theory that stock market trends can be predicted and explained by the four-year presidential election cycle.

presold issue An issue that is sold out before the coupon announcement.

pretax contribution Payment to an account, such as a 401(k) or personal medical account, made with funds from a worker's salary or wages before federal income taxes are applied.

pretax earnings or profit Net income before federal income taxes are deducted.

pretax rate of return Gain on a security before taxes.

pretrade benchmark Price occurring before or at the decision to trade.

previous-balance method Method of calculating finance charges based on the account balance at the end of the previous month.

price change Increase or decrease in the closing price of a security compared to the previous day's closing price.

price compression The limit on how much a callable bond's price might appreciate when the interest rate is falling, based on the expectation that the bond will be redeemed at the call price.

price continuity Minimal price changes in a stock or other security due to transactions.

price discovery process The process of determining the price of assets in the marketplace through the interaction of buyers and sellers.

price effect Impact of a change in interest rates on bond prices.

price elasticity The percentage change in quantity demanded divided by a percentage change in the price. Answers the question: How much will the demand for my product increase if I lower prices by 10 percent?

price gap When the price of a stock rockets or dives in a direction away from its last price range, such as a stock with a trading range of $10–$12 that closes at $12 one day and climbs to $14 the next.

price give Willingness of a buyer or seller to negotiate on the price of an asset he is interested in trading.

price immunization Portfolio protection strategy that focuses on the current market value of assets and liabilities.

price index *See* consumer price index; producer price index.

price leadership A price charged by the dominant producer that becomes the price adopted by all the other producers.

price momentum Securities that are rising in price. *See also* relative strength.

price range The interval between the high and low prices over which a stock has traded during a particular period of time.

price risk The risk that the value of a stock or other security will decline in the future. Or a type of mortgage-pipeline risk created when loan terms are set for the borrower in advance of setting terms for secondary-market sale of the mortgages. If the general level of rates rises during the production cycle, the lender may have to sell the loans at a discount.

price spread An options strategy that involves buying and selling two options on the same security with the same expiration month, but with different exercise prices.

price support Government intervention designed to aid producers by setting an artificially high price of a good through the use of a price floor.

price taker Individual who responds to rates and prices by acting as though prices have no influence on him or her.

price uncertainty Chance that the future price of an asset will change.

price value of a basis point (PVBP) Also referred to as the dollar value of a basis point; a measure of the change in the price of a bond if the required yield changes by one basis point.

price/book ratio Compares a stock's market value to the value of total assets less total liabilities or book value. Stocks that trade at many multiples to their book values are sometimes called glamour stocks or growth stocks. Stocks that trade below their book value are often called value stocks. *Also called* market-to-book.

priced in Means the market has already incorporated information, such as a low dividend, into the price of a stock.

price-earnings effect Refers to the fact that portfolios with low P/E stocks exhibit higher average risk-adjusted returns than those with high P/E stocks.

price/earnings (P/E) ratio A measure of the multiple of earnings at which a stock sells. Determined by dividing current stock price by current earnings per share. Earnings per share for the P/E ratio are determined by dividing earnings for the past twelve months by the number of common shares outstanding. A higher multiple may mean investors have higher expectations for future growth and have bid up the stock's price.

price-impact cost The cost that a trader incurs when his or her purchase or sale of a stock or other security makes the price of that security change significantly. *Also known as* market-impact cost.

price (of equity) Price of a share of common stock on the date shown. High and low prices are based on the highest and lowest intraday trading price.

price/sales ratio Determined by dividing current stock price by its revenue (or sales) per share. Revenue per share for the ratio is determined by dividing revenue for the past twelve months by number of shares outstanding. Stocks that trade at many times their revenues are viewed by some investors as having great promise.

price-volume relationship A relationship espoused by some technical analysts that signals continuing rises or falls in security prices that are related to changes in volume traded.

price-weighted index An index giving a greater influence to higher-priced stocks by weighting all component stocks by their prices.

pricing efficiency A market characteristic whereby prices always fully reflect all available information relevant to the valuation of securities. *Also called* external efficiency. *See also* efficient market.

primary dealer Usually refers to the select list of securities firms that are authorized to deal in new issues of U.S. government bonds.

primary distribution Sale of a new issue of stock or bonds, as distinguished from a secondary distribution. *Also known as* initial public offering (IPO).

primary earnings per (common) share Earnings available for the payment of dividends to common stockholders divided by the number of common shares outstanding.

primary market Where a newly issued security is first offered. All subsequent trading of the security is done in the secondary market.

primary offering Sale of a firm's newly issued shares by the firm to investors.

primary trend General movement in price data that lasts four to four and a half years.

PRIME Prescribed Right to Income and Maximum Equity, a certificate that entitles the owner to the dividend income from an underlying stock or other security, but not to the capital appreciation of that security. *Compare to* SCORE.

prime paper The highest-quality, investment-grade debt of corporations as determined by rating agencies such as Moody's.

prime rate The interest rate at which banks lend to their most creditworthy customers. More often than not, a bank's most creditworthy customers actually borrow at rates below the prime rate.

prime rate fund A mutual fund that buys portions of corporate loans from banks and pays the interest to shareholders.

primitive security An instrument such as a stock or bond for which payments depend only on the financial status of the issuer.

principal The total amount of money being borrowed or loaned. Alternatively, the party trading for his own benefit, rather than as an agent for someone else.

principal amount The face amount of debt; the amount borrowed or loaned. *Also called* principal.

principal exchange-rated-linked securities (PERLS) A debt instrument with its principal and interest denominated in U.S. dollars, but with principal repayment depending on the exchange rate of the U.S. dollar against a foreign currency.

principle of diversification The idea that portfolios of different types of assets (such as stocks and bonds) negatively correlated with one another will balance out risk. In other words, only market risks, those related to the particular assets in the portfolio, persist. *See also* diversification.

principal-only (PO) A mortgage-backed security whose holder receives only principal cash flows on the underlying mortgage pool. All the principal distribution due from the underlying collateral pool is paid to the registered holder of the security on the basis of the current face value of the underlying collateral pool. *Opposite of* interest-only (IO).

principal stockholder A stockholder who owns 10 percent or more of the voting stock of a company. Such stockholders must report all trading in the stock to the SEC using forms 3 and 4 pursuant to insider trading rules.

principal-agent relationship Occurs when one person, an agent, acts on behalf of another person, the principal.

print To execute a trade, evidenced by the printing of the trade on ticker tape. A print is a transaction. *Also known as* hit the tape; put on.

priority System used in an auction market, in which the first bid or offer price is executed before other bid and offer prices, even if subsequent orders are larger. NYSE rules stipulate that the bid made first should be executed first, or if two bids came in at once, the bid for the larger number of shares receives priority. The bid not executed is then turned to the broker, who informs the customer that the trade was not completed because there was stock ahead.

prior-lien bond A bond usually arising from a company reorganization with precedence over another bond of the same issuing company that is equally secured.

prior-preferred stock Preferred stock that has a higher claim on all dividends and assets in liquidation than claims of other preferred stock.

Private Export Funding Corporation (PEFCO) Private entity created and sponsored by the U.S. government to mobilize private capital for financing the export of big-ticket items by U.S. firms by purchasing at fixed interest rates the medium- to long-term debt obligations of importers of U.S. products. www.pefco.com

private limited partnership A limited partnership with no more than thirty-five participants that is not registered with the SEC. These are usually composed of wealthy individuals.

private market value The break-up value of all divisions of a company if divisions were each independent and established their own market stock prices.

private mortgage insurance (PMI) Policy protecting the holder against loss resulting from default on a mortgage loan.

private placement The sale of a bond or other security directly to a limited number of investors. For example, sale of stocks, bonds, or other investments directly to an institutional investor like an insurance company, avoiding the need for SEC registration if the securities are purchased for investment as opposed to resale. *Opposite of* public offering.

private-label pass-through *See* conventional pass-through.

private-letter ruling A ruling by the IRS in response to a request by a taxpayer for interpretation of a tax law.

private-purpose bond A municipal bond allowing more than 10 percent of the proceeds to go to private activities.

privatization The transfer of government-owned or government-run companies to the private sector, usually by selling them.

pro forma capital structure analysis A method of analyzing the impact of alternative capital structure choices on a firm's credit statistics and reported financial results, especially to determine whether the firm will be able to use projected tax shield benefits fully.

pro forma earnings An increasingly popular but dubious form of reported earnings that does not follow Generally Accepted Accounting Principles (GAAP). Companies reporting pro forma earnings may, for example, not include such things as interest expense, payroll taxes, or other costs. As a result pro forma earnings are not to be trusted.

pro forma financial statement A firm's financial statement as adjusted to reflect a projected or planned transaction such as an acquisition. Such statements are accepted practice, unlike reporting pro forma earnings, for attaining a "what-if" analysis.

probability The relative likelihood of a particular outcome among all possible outcomes.

probability distribution or function A measure that assigns a likelihood of occurrence to each and every possible outcome.

probate The procedure required to settle the estate of a deceased person.

proceeds Money received by the seller of an asset.

proceeds sale Nasdaq securities sale whose revenue is used to buy another security.

processing delay Time a selling firm takes to record receipt of a payment and deposit it.

producer price index (PPI) Index measuring wholesale prices, published by the U.S. Bureau of Labor Statistics every month. Investors watch this measure for signs of inflation. www.dol.gov

product cycle The time it takes to bring new or improved products to market.

product differentiation A source of competitive advantage that depends on producing some item that is regarded as having unique and valuable characteristics.

product risk A type of mortgage-pipeline risk that occurs when a lender has an unusual loan in production or inventory but does not have a sale commitment at a prearranged price.

production cost advantage A source of competitive advantage that depends on producing a product or service at the lowest cost.

production payment financing A method of asset-based financing in which a specified percentage of revenue realized from the sale of the project's output is used to pay debt service.

production possibilities schedule The maximum amount of goods that a country is able to produce given its labor supply.

productivity The amount of output per unit of input, such as the quantity of a product produced per hour of capital employed.

profit Revenue minus cost. The amount one makes on a transaction. *Also known as* bottom line.

profit center A division of an organization held responsible for producing its own profits.

profit forecast A prediction of future profits of a company, which may affect investment decisions.

profit margin Comparison of a company's earnings with its net sales, figured by dividing net income by revenue for the same twelve-month period. Result is shown as a percentage. Indicator of profitability. *Also called* net profit margin.

profit taking Action by short-term securities traders to cash in on gains created by a sharp market rise, which pushes prices down temporarily but implies an upward market trend.

profitability index The present value of the future cash flows divided by the initial investment. *Also called* cost/benefit ratio.

profitability ratio Ratio that focuses on how well a firm is performing. Profit margin measures performance in relation to sales. Rate of return ratio measures performance relative to some measure of size of the investment. *Also known as* return on investment (ROI).

profit-sharing plan An incentive program in which employees share in company profits through a cash fund or a deferred plan used to buy stock or bonds.

program trades Orders requiring the execution of trades in a large number of different stocks at as near the same time as possible. *Also called* basket trades.

program trading Trades of derivative products based on signals from computer programs, usually entered directly from the trader's computer into the market's computer system and executed automatically. A process of electronic execution of trading of a basket of stocks simultaneously, for index arbitrage, portfolio restructuring, or outright buy/sell interests. *See* super DOT.

progress payment Periodic payment to a supplier, contractor, or subcontractor for work as it is satisfactorily completed, in order to reduce working-capital requirements.

progress review A periodic review of a capital investment project to evaluate its continued economic viability.

progressive tax A tax system providing that the average tax rate rises relative to rises in taxpayers' incomes. *Opposite of* regressive tax.

project finance loan program Program under which commercial banks, the Export-Import Bank, or a combination of both extends long-term financing for capital equipment and related services for major projects.

project financing A form of asset-based financing in which a firm finances a discrete set of assets on a stand-alone basis.

project link An econometric model forecasting and describing the effects of changes in different economies on other economies.

project loan certificate (PLC) A primary program of Ginnie Mae for packaging and selling to investors Federal Housing Administration (FHA)–insured and coinsured multifamily, hospital, and nursing home loans. www.ginniemae.gov

project loans Usually Federal Housing Administration (FHA)–insured and U.S. Department of Housing and Urban Development (HUD)–

guaranteed mortgages on multiple-family housing complexes, nursing homes, hospitals, and other special development projects.

project notes Notes issued by municipalities, and guaranteed by the U.S. Department of Housing and Urban Development, to finance federally sponsored programs in urban renewal and housing.

projected benefit obligation A measure of a pension plan's liability or amount it owes retirees at the calculation date, assuming that the plan is ongoing and will not terminate in the foreseeable future.

projected maturity date With mortgage pools, the date at the end of the estimated cash flow window when final payment is made.

projection The use of econometric models using historical and current information to forecast the performance of a company, country, or other financial entity.

project-loan security Security backed by a variety of U.S. Federal Housing Administration (FHA)–insured loans—primarily multifamily apartment buildings, hospitals, and nursing homes.

promissory note Written pledge to pay a debt.

property inventory A list of personal property with corresponding values and initial costs, used to substantiate an insurance claim or tax loss.

property rights Rights of individuals and companies to own and use property as they see fit and to receive the stream of income that their property generates.

property tax A tax levied on real property based on its use and its assessed value.

proprietary trading Principal trading in which a firm risks its own money to make a profit rather than commission dollars.

proprietorship An unincorporated business that is owned and operated by only one person who has complete liability for all assets and complete rights to all profits.

prospective earnings growth (PEG) ratio Based on forecasts from analysts, a company's growth of earnings as forecast, minus current earnings divided by current earnings. Forward-looking measure rather than typical earnings-growth measure, which looks back in time.

prospectus Formal written document, filed with the SEC, that describes the plan for a proposed business enterprise, or the facts concerning an existing one that an investor needs to make an informed decision. Prospectuses are used by mutual funds to describe fund objectives, risks, and other essential information.

protectionism Notion that governments should protect domestic industry from import competition by means of tariffs, quotas, and other trade barriers. *Opposite of* free trade.

protective covenant A part of an indenture or loan agreement that limits certain actions a company may take during the term of the loan to protect the lender's interests.

protective put-buying strategy A strategy that involves buying a put option on the underlying security that is held in a portfolio to protect oneself if the security falls in price.

provision for income tax An amount on the income statement that estimates a company's total income tax liability for the year.

provisional call feature A stipulation in a convertible issue that allows the issuer to redeem or call the issue during the noncall period if the price of the stock reaches a certain level. In the case of convertible securities, right of an issuer to accelerate the first redemption date if the underlying common stock should trade at or above a certain level for a sustained period. Most typical terms are 150 percent of conversion price for twenty consecutive days. Note that under these circumstances the security has appreciated, at a minimum, 50 percent since being issued.

proxy Authorization, whether written or electronic, that shareholders' votes may be cast by others. Shareholders can and often do give management their proxies, delegating the right and responsibility to vote their shares as specified.

proxy contest A battle for the control of a firm in which a dissident group seeks, from the firm's other shareholders, the right to vote those shareholders' shares in favor of the dissident group's slate of directors. *See also* proxy fight.

proxy fight Technique used by an acquiring company to attempt to gain control of a takeover target. The acquirer tries to persuade the shareholders of the target company that the present management of the firm should be ousted in favor of a slate of directors favorable to the acquirer, thus enabling the acquiring company to gain control of the target company without paying a premium price.

proxy statement Document intended to provide shareholders with information necessary to vote in an informed manner on matters to be brought up at a stockholders' meeting. Includes information on closely held shares. Information required by the SEC that must be provided to shareholders who wish to vote for directors and on other company decisions by proxy. These filings are also where shareholders find out how much a company's top executives are being paid in cash, stock, and other perks.

proxy vote Vote cast by one person or entity on behalf of another.

prudent-man rule A common law standard against which those investing the money of others, known as fiduciaries, are judged. Fiduciaries must act prudently, under law.

P&S Purchase and sale statement. A statement provided by the broker showing change in the customer's net ledger balance after the offset of any previously established positions.

PSA *See* Public Securities Administration.

PSA prepayment rate The Bond Market Association's prepayment model for mortgage-backed securities based on an assumed rate of prepayment each month of the then unpaid principal balance of a pool of mortgages. The rate is used primarily to derive an implied prepayment speed of new production loans.

public debt Issues of debt by governments to compensate for a lack of tax revenues.

public limited partnership A limited partnership with an unlimited number of partners that is registered with the SEC and is available for public trading by brokers/dealers.

public offering Offering of securities to public investors after compliance with registration requirements of the SEC, usually by an investment banker or a syndicate made up of several investment bankers, at a price agreed upon between the issuer and the investment bankers. *Opposite of* private placement. *See also* primary distribution; secondary distribution/offering.

public offering price The price of a new issue of securities at the time that the issue is offered to the public.

public ownership The portion of a company's stock that is held by the public.

Public Securities Administration (PSA) The trade association for primary dealers in U.S. government securities. www.bondmarkets.com

public securities offering A securities issue placed with the public through an investment or commercial bank.

public, the Individual investors who trade single securities independently or invest in intermediaries such as mutual funds. *Also known as* retail investor. *Compare to* institutional investor.

Public Utility Holding Company Act of 1935 Legislation intended to eliminate many holding company abuses by reorganizing the financial structure of holding companies in the gas and electric utility industries and regulating their debt and dividend policies. Much of this regulation was amended in 1992 to allow nonutilities to build, own, and operate power plants.

public warehouse Storage facility operated by an independent warehouse company on its own premises.

public-housing-authority bond Bonds of local public housing agencies that are secured by the federal government and whose proceeds are used to provide low-rent housing.

publicly held Describes a company whose stock is held by the public, whether individuals or business entities.

publicly traded asset Asset that can be traded in a public market, such as stock.

public-purpose bond A specific type of municipal bond used to finance public projects such as roads or government buildings. Interest on municipal bonds is not subject to federal income tax.

puke Slang for a trader selling a position, usually a losing position, when others are selling at the same time.

pull To cancel a trade or order.

pullback The downward reversal of a prolonged upward price trend.

pulling in their horns Investors selling off positions after a stock or bond market has increased sharply or setting up hedging positions to guard against a negative turn in the market.

purchase Buy; be long; have an ownership position.

purchase accounting Method of accounting for a merger that treats the acquirer as having purchased the assets and assumed the liabilities of the acquiree, which are then written up or down to their respective fair market values.

purchase agreement Used in connection with project financing; an agreement to purchase a specific amount of project output per period.

purchase and sale A method of securities distribution in which a firm purchases securities from the issuer for its own account at a stated price and then resells them. *Opposite of* best-efforts sale.

purchase fee A charge assessed by an intermediary, such as a broker/dealer or a bank, for assisting in the sale or purchase of a security.

purchase fund Resembles a sinking fund except that money is used to purchase bonds only if they are selling below their par value.

purchase group *See* underwriting syndicate.

purchase method Accounting for an acquisition using market value for the consolidation of the two entities' net assets on the balance sheet. Generally, depreciation or amortization will increase under this method due to the creation of goodwill, which is the difference between an asset's cost basis and its usually higher purchase price. Compared to the pooling method of recording an acquisition, purchase accounting results in lower net income because the goodwill must be written off against earnings over time.

purchase order A written order to buy specified goods at a stipulated price.

purchase-money mortgage A mortgage given by a buyer in lieu of cash when the buyer is unable to borrow commercially for the purchase of property.

purchasing power The amount of credit available for securities trading in a margin account after taking margin requirements into consideration.

purchasing power of the dollar The amount of goods and services that can be exchanged for a dollar as compared with the amount at a previous time.

purchasing power parity The notion that the ratio between domestic and foreign price levels should equal the equilibrium exchange rate between domestic and foreign currencies.

purchasing power risk The risk that a consumer's purchasing power will diminish or that an investor's gain will be negative when adjusted for inflation. *Also called* inflation risk.

pure monopoly A market in which only one firm has total control over the entire market for a product due to some sort of barrier to entry for other firms, often a patent held by the controlling firm.

pure play A company involved in only one line of business, allowing investors a "pure play" on that business.

pure yield pickup swap Move investments to higher-yield bonds.

pure-discount bond A bond that makes only one payment of both the principal and interest, due at the bond's maturity date. *Also known as* zero-coupon bond; single-payment bond.

pure-index fund A mutual fund that is managed so as to perfectly replicate the performance of the overall market.

purpose loan A loan that is backed by securities and that is used to buy other securities under certain government regulations.

purpose statement A form filed by a borrower that describes the use of a loan backed by securities and guarantees that the funds will not be used illegally to buy securities against Federal Reserve regulations.

put an option To exercise a put option.

put bond A bond that the holder may choose either to exchange for par value at some date or to extend for a given number of years. If the exchange price is above par, the put is a "premium put."

put guarantee letter A bank's letter certifying that the person writing a put option has sufficient funds in an account to cover the cost of his or her counterparty-exercising option.

put on Trade, or cross, a block of stock listed on a securities exchange at the designated price and quantity. *See* print.

put option A security that gives investors the right to sell a fixed number of shares at a fixed price to an investor within a given period. An investor, for example, might wish to have the right to sell shares of a stock at a certain price by a certain time in order to protect, or hedge, an existing investment. *Opposite of* call option.

put price The price at which a stock or other asset will be sold if a put option is exercised. *Also called* strike price; exercise price.

put provision Gives the holder of a floating-rate bond the right to redeem the note at par on the coupon payment date.

put ratio backspread A complex options strategy adopted when one believes a stock price will decline but wants to protect against it rising.

put swaption A financial instrument giving the buyer the right, or option, to enter into a swap as a floating-rate payer, meaning he is making a bet that rates will change. The seller of the swaption therefore becomes the fixed-rate payer.

put to seller Exercise a put option; require that the option seller purchase the underlying stock at the strike price.

put-call parity Option-pricing principle that says, given a stock's price, a put and call of the same class must have a static price relationship because arbitrage activities will always reestablish such a relationship.

put-call parity relationship The relationship between the price of a put and the price of a call on the same underlying stock or other security with the same expiration date, which prevents arbitrage opportunities. Holding the underlying stock and buying a put will deliver the exact payoff as buying one call and investing the present value of the exercise price.

put/call ratio The ratio of the volume of put options traded to the volume of call options traded, which is used as an indicator of investor sentiment. More put options is bearish, more call options is bullish.

PVBP *See* price value of a basis point.

PVI *See* present value index.

pyramid scheme An illegal, fraudulent scheme in which a con artist convinces victims to invest by promising an extraordinary return; he or she embezzles the funds while using the minimum necessary to pay off any investors who insist on terminating their investment.

Q

Q A letter that is attached to a Nasdaq stock's symbol when a company is in bankruptcy proceedings.

Q ratio *See* Tobin's Q ratio.

Q-TIP *See* Qualified Terminable Interest Property Trust.

qualification period A period covering the first few months or weeks of a new insurance policy when the company will not reimburse a policyholder making a claim in order to allow the insurance company to discover if the application includes any fraudulent information.

qualified opinion An auditor's opinion expressing certain limitations of an accounting firm's audit of a company's books. Investors usually treat a qualified opinion as bad news. *See also* form 10-K.

qualified plan or trust A tax-deferred plan allowing employer and employee contributions that build up savings, which are paid out at retirement or on termination of employment. Tax is paid only when amounts are drawn from the trust.

qualified retirement plan A retirement plan established by employers for their employees that meets the requirements of Internal Revenue Code section 401(k) or 403(b) and is eligible for special tax considerations. The plan may provide for employer contributions, as in a pension or profit-sharing plan, as well as employee contributions. Employers can deduct plan contributions made on behalf of eligible employees on the business's tax return as business expenses. Plan earnings are not taxed to the employee until withdrawn.

Qualified Terminable Interest Property Trust (Q-TIP) A trust that allows a surviving spouse to receive income generated from the trust,

while the actual distribution of the trust's assets is made to other beneficiaries such as the grantor's children.

qualified total distribution A payment representing an employee's
interest in a qualified retirement plan. The payment must be
prompted by retirement (or other separation from service), death, disability, or attainment of age fifty-nine and a half. Payment can be in
installments as long as the complete distribution is made within a single tax year.

qualifying annuity An annuity allowable as investment for a qualified
plan or trust.

qualifying share Shares of common stock that a person must hold in
order to qualify as a director of the issuing corporation.

qualifying stock option A benefit usually associated with a pay package
granted by a corporation that allows employees to purchase shares at a
discount price to the prevailing market.

qualitative analysis An analysis of the qualities of a company that cannot be measured concretely, such as management quality or employee
morale.

quality of earnings Increased earnings at a company due to better sales
or cost controls, as compared to artificial profits created by inflation of
inventory or accounting gimmickry.

quality spread Difference between Treasury securities and non-Treasury
securities that are identical in all respects except for rating. For instance,
the difference between yields on Treasuries and those on single A-
rated bonds of a company. These spreads indicate the level of risk
investors are willing to take in corporations' bonds and also reflect
investor confidence. For example, if spreads widen, that indicates
investors lack confidence in corporate bonds and require that these
bonds yield significantly more than what is required of Treasury issues.
Also called credit spread.

quant A person with numerical and computer skills who carries out
quantitative analyses of companies.

quantitative analysis An assessment of specific measurable securities
or investment factors, such as a company's cost of capital; value of its
assets; and projections of sales, costs, earnings, and profits. Combined
with more subjective or qualitative considerations (such as management effectiveness), quantitative analysis can identify promising investments.

quantity risk Occurs when the quantity of an asset to be hedged is uncertain.

quarterly Occurring every three months.

quasi-public corporation A corporation that is operated privately but supported by the government in its operations and often traded publicly. An example is a government-sponsored enterprise such as Fannie Mae or Freddie Mac.

quick assets Current assets minus inventories.

quick ratio Indicator of a company's financial strength (or weakness). Calculated by taking current assets less inventories, divided by current liabilities. This ratio provides information regarding the firm's liquidity and ability to meet its obligations. *Also called* acid-test ratio.

quiet period Time period an issuer that is preparing to bring new securities to market is "in registration" with the SEC and may not promote the forthcoming securities issue.

quorum The minimum number of people who must be present or must provide a proxy to vote at a meeting in order to make a valid decision.

quotation Highest bid and lowest offer on a stock or commodity price currently available.

quotation board The electronic board at a brokerage firm displaying prices and other financial data.

quote rule Rule requiring market makers to publish quotations for any listed stock or other security when a quotation represents more than 1 percent of the aggregate trading volume for that security.

quoted price The price at which the last trade of a particular security or commodity took place.

Racketeer Influenced and Corrupt Organization Act *See* RICO.

radar alert Close monitoring of trading patterns in a company's stock by senior managers to uncover unusual buying activity that might signal a takeover attempt. *See also* shark watcher.

raider Individual or corporate investor who intends to take control of a company by buying a controlling interest in its stock and installing new management. Raiders who accumulate 5 percent or more of the outstanding shares in the target company must report their purchases to the SEC using form 3, the exchange of listing, and the target itself. *See* takeover.

rainmaker A valuable employee, manager, or subcontracted person who brings new business to a company and thus generates income.

rally An upward movement of prices following a decline. A recovery. *Opposite of* correction; reaction.

random variable A variable whose outcome cannot be predetermined.

random walk Theory that stock price changes from day to day are accidental or haphazard; price changes are independent of each other and have the same probability distribution. Many adherents of the random-walk theory believe that it is impossible to outperform the market consistently without taking additional risk. These people believe an investor could do just as well throwing a dart at the stock tables and investing in the company the dart landed on than by analyzing companies.

range The high and low prices, or high and low bids and offers, recorded during a specified time.

rate anticipation swap An exchange of bonds in a portfolio for new bonds that will achieve the target portfolio duration, given the investor's assumptions about future changes in interest rates.

rate base The value of a regulated public utility and its operations as defined by its regulators and on which the company is allowed to earn a particular rate of return.

rate covenant A provision governing a municipal revenue project financed by a revenue bond issue that establishes the rates that users of the new facility are to be charged.

rate lock An agreement between the mortgage banker and the loan applicant guaranteeing a specified interest rate for a designated period, usually sixty days.

rate of exchange The price of one country's currency expressed in another country's currency.

rate of interest The rate, as a proportion of the principal, at which interest is computed.

rate of return Calculated as the current value minus the value at time of purchase divided by value at time of purchase. For equities, dividends are included with the current value.

rate of return ratio Ratio that measures the profitability of a firm in relation to various measures of investment in the firm.

rate risk In banking, the risk that profits may drop or losses occur because a rise in interest rates forces up the cost of funding fixed-rate loans or other fixed-rate assets.

ratings An evaluation of credit quality of a company's debt issue by ratings agencies such as Moody's, Standard and Poor's, and Fitch. Investors and analysts use ratings to assess the riskiness of an investment.

ratio analysis A way of expressing relationships between a firm's accounting numbers and their trends over time that analysts use to establish values and evaluate risks.

raw material Materials a manufacturer converts into a finished product.

R&D *See* research and development.

reachback The ability of a tax shelter or limited partnership to deduct certain costs and expenses at the end of the year that were incurred throughout the entire year.

reaction A decline in prices following an advance. *Opposite of* rally.

reading the tape Judging the performance of stocks by monitoring changes in price as they are displayed on the ticker tape.

real appreciation/depreciation A change in the purchasing power of a currency.

real asset Asset, such as land and buildings, equipment, patent, and trademark, as distinguished from a financial investment. *Also known as* hard asset; physical asset; tangible asset. *Opposite of* intangible asset.

real cash flow Income expressed in current purchasing power terms.

real currency The purchasing power in today's currency of future nominal currency to be disbursed or received.

real dollars *See* constant dollars.

real estate A piece of land and the physical property on it.

real estate appraisal An estimate of the value of property arrived at by a professional appraiser.

real estate broker An intermediary who receives a commission for arranging and facilitating the sale of a property for a buyer or a seller.

real estate investment trust (REIT) A trust that invests directly in real estate or loans secured by real estate assets and issues shares in such investments. A REIT is similar to a closed-end mutual fund.

real estate mortgage investment conduit (REMIC) A pass-through tax entity that can hold mortgages secured by any type of real property and can issue multiple classes of ownership interests to investors in the form of pass-through certificates, bonds, or other legal forms. A financing vehicle created under the Tax Reform Act of 1986.

real exchange rate Exchange rate that has been adjusted for the inflation differential between two countries.

real gain or loss A gain or loss adjusted for increasing prices by an inflation index such as the consumer price index.

real GDP Inflation-adjusted measure of gross domestic product (GDP). *Compare to* nominal GDP (which does not take inflation into account).

real income The income of an individual, group, or country adjusted for inflation.

real interest rate The rate of interest excluding the effect of expected inflation; that is, the rate that is earned in terms of constant purchasing-power dollars. Put another way, the nominal interest rate adjusted for expected inflation.

real market The bid and offer prices at which a dealer could execute a trade for the desired quantity of shares. *Opposite of* phantom bid (which disappears when actual trades are about to be made).

real property Land plus all other property that is in some way attached to the land.

real rate of return The percentage return on some investments that has been adjusted for inflation.

real return The actual payback on an investment after removing the effect of inflation.

real time A stock or bond quote that states a security's most recent offer to sell or buy. Different from a delayed quote, which shows the same bid and ask prices fifteen minutes and sometimes twenty minutes after a trade takes place.

realistic on price In trading, an indication that the size of the transaction under consideration requires price concessions, especially with illiquid stocks.

realized compound yield Yield assuming that coupon payments are invested at the going market interest rate at the time of their receipt and thus held until the bond matures.

realized profit or loss A capital gain or loss that has been posted (become actual) due to the sale or other type of surrender of one or many of the stocks or other securities held in a portfolio.

realized return The return that is actually earned over a given time period.

realized yield The holding-period return actually generated from an investment in a bond.

realtor A designation given to members of real estate firms affiliated with the National Association of Realtors (NAR), who are trained and licensed to assist clients in buying and selling real estate.

rebalancing Realigning the proportions of assets in a portfolio as needed. When a type of asset changes dramatically in price, a rebalancing is usually required.

rebate Negotiated return of a portion of the interest earned by the lender of stock to a short seller. When a stock is sold short, the seller borrows stock from an owner or custodian and delivers it to the buyer. The proceeds are delivered to the lender. The borrower, who is short, often wants a rebate of the interest earned on the proceeds under the lender's control, especially when the stock can be borrowed from many sources. Note: The seller must pay the lender any dividends paid out or, in the case of bonds, interest that accrues daily during the term of the loan.

recalculation method A method of calculating required minimum distributions from a retirement plan using life expectancy tables. These tables allow a plan holder to determine the applicable life expectancy each year a distribution is required.

recapitalization proposal Plan by a target company to restructure its capital structure, consisting of debt and equity; usually used to ward off a hostile or potential suitor.

recapture A provision in a contract that allows one party to recover some degree of possession of an asset, such as a share of the profits derived from some property.

receipts Funds collected from selling land, capital, or services, as well as collections from the public, such as taxes, fines, duties, and fees.

receivables turnover ratio Total operating revenue of a company divided by its average receivables. Used to measure how effectively a firm is managing its accounts receivable. If receivables turn over less frequently at a company, investors may grow concerned that those receivables may become bad debts and require a write-off.

receive fixed counterparty The transactor in an interest rate swap who receives payments based on the fixed rate and makes payments based on the floating rate. *See also* fixed-for-floating swap.

receive versus payment An instruction that only cash will be accepted in exchange for delivery of securities. *See also* delivery versus payment.

receiver A bankruptcy practitioner appointed by the bankruptcy court to oversee the repayment of a company's debts.

receiver's certificate A debt instrument, issued by a receiver and serving as a lien on property, that provides funding to continue operations or to protect assets in receivership.

recession A temporary downturn in economic activity, usually indicated by two consecutive quarters of decline in gross domestic product.

recharacterization The reversal of a traditional IRA contribution or conversion into a Roth IRA, or vice versa.

reciprocal marketing agreement A strategic alliance in which two companies agree to market each other's products. Production rights may or may not be transferred.

reclamation A claim for the right to return or the right to demand the return of a stock or other security that has been previously accepted as a result of bad delivery or other irregularities in the settlement process.

record date (1) Date by which a shareholder must officially own shares in order to be entitled to a dividend. Stocks trade ex-dividend the second day before the record date since the seller will still be the owner of record and is thus entitled to the dividend. (2) The date that determines who is entitled to payment of principal and interest due to be paid on a security. The record date for most mortgage-backed securities is the last day of the month, although the last day on which such an asset may be presented for the transfer is the last business day of the month. The record dates for collateralized mortgage obligations and other asset-backed securities vary with each issue.

recourse Term describing a type of loan. With recourse, the lender has a general claim against the company if the collateral is insufficient to repay the debt. Without recourse, the lender has no claim.

recovery A rebound in the economy or the stock market. *See* rally.

red herring A preliminary prospectus providing information required by the SEC. It excludes the offering price and coupon of the new issue. It is called a red herring because of red print on the face of the prospectus stating that the document is preliminary, not final. *Also known as* preliminary prospectus.

redeemable A stock or other security that is eligible for redemption under the terms of the offering.

redemption Repayment of a debt security or preferred stock issue, at or before maturity, at par or at a premium price.

redemption charge The commission a mutual fund charges an investor who is redeeming shares. For example, a 2 percent redemption charge, also called a back-end load, on the sale of shares valued at $1,000 will result in payment of $980 (98 percent of the value) to the investor. The charge may decline or be eliminated as shares are held for longer time periods.

redemption cushion The percentage by which the conversion value of a convertible security exceeds the redemption price.

redemption date The date on which a bond matures or is redeemed.

redemption fee A fee some mutual funds charge when an investor sells shares within a specified short period of time.

redemption or call Right of the issuer to force holders on a certain date to redeem their convertibles for cash. The objective usually is to force holders to convert into common stock prior to the redemption deadline. Typically, an issue is not called away unless the conversion price is

15 percent to 25 percent below the current level of the common. An exception might occur when an issuer's tax rate is high, and the issuer could replace it with debt securities at a lower after-tax cost.

redemption price The price at which a bond will be redeemed. *Also known as* call price.

red-lining Illegal discrimination in making loans, insurance coverage, or other financial services available to people or property in certain areas because of poor economic conditions, high levels of fraudulent transaction, or frequent defaults.

reference rate A benchmark interest rate, such as the London interbank offered rate (LIBOR), used to specify conditions of an interest rate swap or an interest rate agreement.

refinancing An extension and/or increase in amount of existing debt. Or the assumption of a new mortgage, while retiring the old, to capture a lower interest rate.

reflation Government monetary action that causes a reversal of deflation.

refund To retire existing bond issues through the sale of a new bond issue, usually to reduce the interest rate being paid.

refundable Eligible for refunding under the terms of a bond indenture.

refunded bond A bond that originally may have been issued as a general obligation or revenue bond but is now secured (redeemed or refunded) by an escrow fund consisting entirely of direct U.S. government obligations that are sufficient for paying the bondholders. *Also called* prerefunded bond.

refunding Redeeming a bond with proceeds received from issuing lower-cost debt obligations with ranking equal to or superior to the debt to be redeemed.

regional bank A bank operating in a specific region of the country, taking deposits and offering loans.

regional fund A mutual fund that invests in a specific geographic area overseas, such as Asia or Europe.

regional stock exchange Organized national securities exchange located outside of New York City and registered with the SEC. They include: Boston, Cincinnati, Midwest, Pacific, and Philadelphia Stock Exchanges.

registered bond A bond whose issuer records ownership and interest payments. Differs from a bearer bond, which is traded without record of ownership and whose possession is the only evidence of ownership.

registered check A check issued and guaranteed by a bank for a customer who provides funds for payment of the check.

registered company A company that is listed with the SEC after submission of a required statement and compliance with disclosure requirements.

registered competitive market maker An NYSE- or NASD-registered dealer who acts as a market maker for a designated stock by buying and selling that stock to maintain stability in its price and provide liquidity for investors who want to buy or sell stock.

registered equity market maker Member firm of the American Stock Exchange registered as a trader in order to make stabilizing trades for its own account in particular securities.

registered investment adviser SEC-registered individual or firm that completes a course of education and work experience in the field and pays an annual membership fee.

registered investment company An investment firm registered with the SEC that complies with certain stated legal requirements. There are two types of registered investment companies: open-ended (mutual funds) and closed-ended (investment trusts).

registered options trader An AMEX specialist who monitors a certain group of options to help maintain a fair and orderly market.

registered retirement savings plan (RRSP) Tax-sheltered retirement plan for Canadian citizens, much like the IRA in the United States.

registered representative A person licensed to sell securities, registered with the SEC or the Commodity Futures Trading Commission, and employed by and soliciting business for a brokerage house or futures commission merchant. *Also known as* stockbroker.

registered secondary offering A reoffering of a large block of securities, previously publicly issued, by the holder of a large portion of some corporation. The offering is made through an investment firm and the proceeds go to the holder, not the issuing company.

registered security Securities whose owner's name is recorded on the books of the issuer or the issuer's agent, called a registrar.

registered trader A member of an exchange who executes frequent trades for his or her own account.

registrar Financial institution appointed to record issue and ownership of company securities.

registration The process set up pursuant to the Securities Exchange

Acts of 1933 and 1934 whereby securities that are to be sold to the public are reviewed by the SEC prior to their sale.

registration statement A legal document filed with the SEC to register securities for public offering that details the purpose of the proposed public offering. The statement outlines financial details, a history of the company's operations and management, and other facts of importance to potential buyers. *See also* offering statement.

regressive tax A tax system designed so that average tax rates decrease as an individual's income bracket increases. *Opposite of* progressive tax.

regular settlement Transaction in which a stock trade in the United States is settled and delivered on the third full business day following the date of the transaction. In Japan, regular settlement also occurs three business days after the trade date; in London, two weeks after the trade date (at times, three weeks); in France, once per month.

regular-way settlement In the money and bond markets, the basis on which some security trades are settled. The delivery of the securities purchased is made against payment in Fed funds on the day following the transaction.

regulated commodities The group of registered commodity futures and options contracts traded on organized U.S. futures exchanges.

regulated investment company An investment company allowed to pass capital gains, dividends, and interest earned on fund investments directly to its shareholders so that it is taxed only at the personal level and double taxation is avoided.

regulation Rule specifying the appropriate behavior of agencies, organizations, or individuals in the securities industry. Regulations are written into law by Congress and are enforced by the SEC and by self-regulatory organizations.

regulation A A Federal Reserve Board regulation that exempts small public offerings, valued at less than $1.5 million, from most registration requirements with the SEC.

regulation D Federal Reserve Board regulation that requires member banks to hold reserves against their net borrowings from foreign offices of other banks over a twenty-eight-day period. Regulation D has been merged with regulation M.

regulation FD SEC mandate of fair disclosure. When a firm chooses to release any information, it must be done in such a way that the general public has access to the information at the same time as institutional investors and analysts.

regulation G Federal Reserve Board regulation of lenders other than commercial banks, brokers, or dealers that provide credit for the purchase or carrying of securities.

regulation M Federal Reserve Board regulation that currently requires member banks to hold reserves against their net borrowings from their foreign branches over a twenty-eight-day averaging period. Regulation M also requires member banks to hold reserves against Eurodollars lent by their foreign branches to domestic corporations for domestic purposes.

regulation Q Federal Reserve Board regulation imposing caps on the rates that banks may pay on savings and time deposits. Time deposits with a denomination of $100,000 or more are exempt.

regulation T Federal Reserve Board regulation that deals with granting credit to customers by securities brokers, dealers, and exchange members. The regulation specifies initial margin requirements and which securities are covered under the rules. Regulation T requires margin borrowers to put up 50 percent of the purchase cost of a transaction. Regulation of margin requirements subsequently falls to the brokerage firm where the investor holds his account.

regulation U Federal Reserve Board limit on how much credit a bank can allow a customer for the purchase and carrying of margin securities.

regulatory accounting procedures Accounting principles required by the Federal Home Loan Banks (FHLB) that allow savings and loans to elect annually to defer gains and losses on the sale of assets and amortize these deferrals over the average life of the asset sold.

regulatory pricing risk Risk that arises when insurance companies are subject to regulation of the premium rates that they can charge.

rehypothecation Pledge to bank by securities broker of the amount in customer's margin account as collateral for broker loans. Such loans are used to cover margin borrowings of customers for stock purchases and selling short.

reimbursement Payment for out-of-pocket expenses incurred.

reinstatement The restoration of an insurance policy after it has lapsed for nonpayment of premiums.

reinsurance The spreading of risk and division of client premiums among insurance companies, thereby allowing the sharing of the burden of a large risk.

reinvestment Use of investment income to buy additional securities. Many mutual fund companies and investment services and some corporations offer investors automatic reinvestment in the fund or stock of dividends and capital gains distributions earned. *See also* dividend reinvestment plan (DRIP).

reinvestment date The date on which an investment's dividend or capital gains income is reinvested, if requested by the shareholder, to purchase additional shares. *Also known as* ex-dividend date.

reinvestment effect The impact of a change in interest rates on the amount earned on reinvestment.

reinvestment privilege A shareholder's right to reinvest dividends and buy more shares in the corporation or mutual fund.

reinvestment rate The rate at which an investor assumes interest payments made on a debt security can be reinvested over the life of that security.

reinvestment risk The risk that proceeds received in the future may have to be reinvested at a lower potential interest rate, thereby diminishing the reinvestment rate that has been assumed.

REIT *See* real estate investment trust.

rejection Refusal by a bank to grant credit, usually because of the applicant's financial history. Alternatively, the refusal to accept a security presented to complete a trade, usually because of a lack of proper endorsements or violation of a firm's rules.

relative strength Movement of a stock's or other security's price over the past year as compared to a market index such as the S&P 500 Composite Index. A value below 1.0 means the stock shows relative weakness in price movement or that it underperformed the market, while a value above 1.0 means the stock shows relative strength over the one-year period. Equation for relative strength: [current stock price/year-ago stock price] divided by [current S&P 500/year-ago S&P 500]. This measure of a stock's performance does not take risk into account, however.

relative value The attractiveness measured in terms of risk, liquidity, and return of one investment instrument relative to another or, for a given instrument, of one maturity relative to another.

relative yield spread The ratio of the yield spread on a bond to the yield itself.

release To relieve a party to a trade of any previously made obligation concerning that trade, hence allowing the would-be transactor to show the order to a new broker. In estates, the document that beneficiaries and heirs sign before receiving a bequest that releases the estate from challenges and other liabilities.

release clause A mortgage provision that releases a pledged asset after a certain portion of the total payments has been made.

remainderman Person who receives the principal of a trust when it is dissolved. Beneficiary.

remaining maturity The length of time remaining until a bond comes due.

remaining principal balance The amount of principal dollars remaining to be paid under a mortgage as of a given time.

remargining Putting up additional cash or securities after a margin call on an investor's margin account so that it meets minimum maintenance requirements.

Rembrandt market The foreign market in the Netherlands.

remit To pay for purchases by cash, check, or electronic transfer.

remote disbursement Technique that involves writing checks drawn on banks in remote locations so as to maximize the amount of time it takes the check to clear or be paid.

renewable term life insurance A policy for a stated period that may be renewed if desired at the end of the term.

renewal Placement of a day order identical to one not completed on the previous day.

rent Regular payments to owner for the use of leased property.

rent control Municipal regulation restricting the amount of rent that a building owner can charge.

rental lease *See* full-service lease.

reoffering yield In a purchase and sale, the yield to maturity at which an underwriter offers to sell bonds to investors.

reopen an issue The U.S. Treasury, when it wants to sell additional securities, will occasionally sell more of an existing issue, or reopen it, rather than offer a new issue.

reopening Treasury offering of additional amounts of outstanding issues, rather than an entirely new issue. A reopened issue will always have the same maturity date, CUSIP number, and interest rate as the original issue.

reorganization Creation of a plan to restructure a debtor's business, usually after it has been in bankruptcy, and restore its financial health. *See also* chapter 11 bankruptcy.

reorganization bond A bond issued by a company undergoing a reorganization process.

repatriation The return from abroad of the financial assets or currency of an organization or individual.

replacement cost Cost to replace a firm's assets.

replacement cycle The frequency with which an asset is replaced by an equivalent asset.

replacement value Current cost of replacing the firm's assets.

replacement-cost accounting An accounting method that includes as part of depreciation the difference between the original purchase price of an asset and its current replacement cost.

replacement-cost insurance Insurance that pays out the full amount required to replace damaged property with new property, without taking into account the depreciated value of the property.

replicating portfolio A portfolio constructed to match an index or benchmark.

repo An agreement in which one party sells a security to another party and agrees to repurchase it on a specified date for a specified price. *Also known as* repurchase agreement.

report Written or oral confirmation that all or part of the investor's order has been executed, including the price and size of the trade.

reporting currency The currency in which the parent firm prepares its own financial statements, e.g., U.S. dollars for a U.S. company.

reproducible assets A tangible asset with physical properties that can be matched or duplicated, such as a building or machinery.

repurchase agreement An agreement with a commitment by the seller or dealer to buy a security back from the purchaser (customer) at a specified price at a designated future date. It represents a collateralized short-term loan for which the collateral may be a Treasury security, money market instrument, federal agency security, or mortgage-backed security. *Also called* repo. From the purchaser's perspective, the deal is reported as a reverse repo.

repurchase of stock Technique to pay cash to a firm's shareholders that provides more preferential tax treatment for shareholders than dividends because capital gains are typically taxed at lower rates than income. A repurchase is achieved through either a Dutch auction, open market purchase, or tender offer.

required minimum distribution The minimum amount that the IRS requires to be withdrawn each year from all tax-advantaged retirement plans starting in the calendar year following the year in which the plan holder reaches age seventy and a half. Roth IRAs are exempt from this rule.

required rate of return The minimum yield expected by investors in order to select a particular investment.

required reserves The dollar amounts, based on reserve ratios, that banks are required to keep on deposit at a Federal Reserve Bank.

required return The minimum expected return you would need in order to purchase an asset, that is, to make an investment.

required yield Generally referring to bonds, the yield required by the marketplace to match available expected returns for financial instruments with comparable risk.

rescheduled loan Bank loan that is altered to have a longer maturity in order to assist the borrower in making the necessary repayments.

rescind To cancel (a contract) because of misrepresentation, fraud, or illegal procedure.

research and development Development of new products and services by a company in order to obtain a competitive advantage. *Also known as* R&D.

research and development limited partnership A partnership whose investors put up money to finance R&D in return for profits generated from the products.

research department The office in an institutional investing organization that analyzes markets and securities. Research analysts work in such groups.

reservation price The price below (or above) which a seller (or purchaser) is unwilling to go.

reserve An accounting entry that properly reflects contingent liabilities.

reserve currency A foreign currency held by a central bank or monetary authority for the purpose of exchange intervention and the settlement of intergovernmental claims. The U.S. dollar is considered the reserve currency of the world.

reserve ratio Specified percentage of deposits, established by the Federal Reserve Board, that banks must keep in a noninterest-bearing account at one of the twelve Federal Reserve Banks.

reserve requirements The percentage of different types of deposits that member banks are required to hold on deposit at the Federal Reserve.

reset bond Bond that allows the initial interest rates to be adjusted on specific dates in order that the bond trade at the value it had when it was issued. Such bonds carry little to no interest rate risk.

reset frequency The frequency with which a floating rate on a security or loan changes.

residential mortgage Mortgage on a residential property, the interest on which is tax-deductible for individuals with a mortgage value up to $1 million.

residential property Property that consists of homes, apartments, town houses, and condominiums.

residual assets Assets that remain after sufficient assets are dedicated to meet all senior debt-holders' claims in full. Similar to a residual claim or an equity claim.

residual dividend approach An approach that suggests that a firm pay dividends if and only if acceptable investment opportunities for the funds that would go toward the dividends are currently unavailable.

residual method A method of allocating the purchase price for the acquisition of another firm among the acquired assets.

residual risk *See* unsystematic risk.

resiliency Speed with which new orders respond to a change in prices.

resistance level A price level above which it is supposedly difficult for a security or market to rise. Price ceiling at which technical analysts note persistent selling of a commodity or security. *Opposite of* support level.

resolution A document that records a decision or action by a board of directors, or a bond resolution by a government entity authorizing a bond issue.

restricted Securities placed on a list that dictates that a brokerage-firm trader may not maintain positions, solicit business, or provide indications in a stock, but may serve as broker in an agency trade after being properly cleared. Traders are so restricted due to investment bank involvement with the company on nonpublic activity (i.e., mergers and acquisitions defense), affiliate ownership, or underwriting activities. A restricted list and the stocks on it should never be conveyed to anyone outside of the trading areas, much less outside the firm. *Also known as* gray list.

restricted account A margin account without enough equity to meet the initial margin requirement that is restricted from any purchases until the requirement is fulfilled.

restricted stock Stock that must be traded in compliance with special SEC regulations concerning its purchase and resale. These restrictions generally result from affiliate ownership, merger-and-acquisition activity, and underwriting activity but also apply to insider holdings that must comply with SEC rule 144, which limits the amount of stock that may be sold based on the typical trading volume in that stock.

restricted surplus A portion of retained earnings not allowed by law to be used for the payment of dividends.

restrictive covenant Provision that places constraints on the operations of borrowers, such as restrictions on working capital, fixed assets, future borrowing, and payment of dividends.

restrictive endorsement An endorsement signature on the back of a check that specifies the conditions under which the check can be transferred or paid out.

restructuring The reorganization of a company in order to attain greater efficiency and to adapt to new markets. Often involves layoffs. Restructuring happens in both healthy companies and distressed companies. However, if a firm is close to bankruptcy or has already filed, there is almost always a restructuring.

resyndication limited partnership The sale of existing properties to new limited partners, so that they can receive the tax advantages that are no longer available to the old partners.

retail credit Credit granted by a firm to consumers for the purchase of goods or services. *See also* consumer credit.

retail house A brokerage firm that caters to individual customers rather than large institutions. Some firms do both.

retail investor Individual investor who commits capital for a personal account rather than on behalf of a company. Although the number of retail investors in the market increased in the 1990s, most of the market capitalization and trading volume is driven by institutional investors. *Compare to* institutional investor.

retail price The total price charged for a product sold to a customer, which includes the manufacturer's cost plus a retail markup.

retained earnings Accounting earnings that are retained by the firm for reinvestment in its operations; earnings that are not paid out as dividends.

retained earnings statement A statement of all transactions affecting the balance of a company's retained earnings account.

retention rate The percentage of present earnings retained by a corporation. Also referred to as the retention ratio.

retire To extinguish a security, as in paying off a debt.

retirement Removal from circulation of stock or bonds that have been reacquired or redeemed.

Retirement Protection Act of 1994 Legislation designed to protect the pension benefits of workers and retirees by increasing required support of pension plans by employers.

retracement A price movement of a stock or other security that is in the opposite direction of the previous trend. Commonly expressed as a percentage decrease from a prior high or a percentage increase from a prior low.

return The change in the value of a portfolio over an evaluation period, including any distributions made from the portfolio during that period.

return of capital A cash distribution resulting from the sale of a capital asset, or securities, or tax breaks from depreciation. When shareholders in real estate investment trusts receive payments that are considered a return of capital they are not taxed as ordinary income as dividends would be.

return on assets (ROA) Indicator of profitability. A percentage determined by dividing net income for the past twelve months by total average assets. Can be decomposed into return on sales (net income divided by sales) multiplied by asset utilization (sales divided by assets). Banks are typically judged by their return on assets.

return on equity (ROE) Indicator of profitability. A percentage determined by dividing net income for the past twelve months by common stockholder equity. May be decomposed into return on assets multiplied by financial leverage or total assets divided by total equity. Investors use return on equity as a measure of how efficiently a company is using its money.

return on investment (ROI) Generally, income as a proportion of a company's net book value. *Also known as* profitability ratio.

return on sales A measurement, expressed as a percentage, of operational efficiency equaling net pretax profits divided by net sales.

return on total assets The ratio of net earnings to total assets of a company.

revaluation An increase in the foreign exchange value of a currency that is pegged to other currencies or gold.

revenue anticipation note A short-term municipal debt issue that will be repaid with anticipated revenues, such as sales taxes, from the project.

revenue bond A bond issued by a municipality to finance either a project or an enterprise in which the issuer pledges to the bondholders the revenues generated by the operation of the projects financed. Examples are hospital revenue bonds and sewer revenue bonds or bonds whose proceeds are used to build toll bridges. *Also known as* self-supporting debt.

revenue fund A fund accounting for all revenues from an enterprise financed by municipal revenue bonds.

revenue sharing The percentage split between the general partner and limited partners of profits and losses resulting from the operation of the business in question.

reversal A change in direction in the stock or commodity futures markets.

reverse leverage Occurs when the interest on borrowings exceeds the return on investment of the funds that were borrowed.

reverse leveraged buyout Bringing back into publicly traded status a company that had been taken private by way of a leveraged buyout.

reverse mortgage A mortgage agreement allowing a home owner to borrow against home equity and receive tax-free payments until the total principal and interest reach the amount of equity, and the lender is either repaid in full or takes the house.

reverse price risk A type of mortgage-pipeline risk that occurs when a lender commits to sell a loan to an investor at the rate prevailing at the time of the mortgage application but sets the note rates when the borrower closes. The lender is thus exposed to the risk of falling rates, which would make the mortgage less valuable.

reverse repo Refers to a repurchase agreement. From the customer's perspective, the customer provides a loan backed by collateral to the seller.

reverse stock split A proportionate decrease in the number of shares but not the total value of shares of stock held by shareholders. Shareholders maintain the same percentage of equity as before the split. For example, a one-for-three split would result in stockholders' owning one share for every three shares owned before the split. After the reverse split, the firm's stock price is, in this example, three times the prereverse split price. A firm generally institutes a reverse split to boost its stock's market price. Some think this supposedly attracts investors. Reverse stock splits, however, are usually carried out to reduce transaction costs from high proportional bid-ask spreads and to satisfy minimum price levels for trading on certain exchanges.

reverse-annuity mortgage (RAM) Bank loan for an amount equal to a percentage of the appraisal value of the home. The loan is then paid to the home owner in the form of an annuity.

reversing trade Entering the opposite side of a currently held futures position to close out the position.

revised estimate Generally, a modification of an economic number after the release of the initial estimate. Can refer specifically to the third estimate of GDP, released about three months after the measurement period.

revocable letter of credit Assurance of funds issued by a bank that can be canceled at any time without prior notification to the beneficiary.

revocable trust A trust that may be altered as many times as desired, in which income-producing property passes directly to the beneficiaries at the time of the grantor's death. Since the arrangement can be altered at any time, the assets are considered part of the grantor's estate and they are taxed as such.

revolving line of credit A bank line of credit on which the customer pays a commitment fee and can take and repay funds at will. Normally a revolving line of credit involves a firm commitment from the bank for a period of several years.

revolving-credit agreement A legal commitment in which a bank promises to lend a customer up to a specified maximum amount during a specified period.

rich Term for a security whose price seems too high in light of its price history or its earnings potential.

RICO Racketeer Influenced and Corrupt Organization Act. Legislation under which inside traders may be convicted. RICO allows for treble damages.

rider An addendum to an insurance policy that alters the policy's terms or coverage.

riding the yield curve Buying long-term bonds in anticipation of capital gains as yields fall with the declining maturity of the bonds.

rigged market Manipulation of prices in a market to attract buyers and sellers. This practice is illegal.

right Privilege granted shareholders of a corporation to subscribe to shares of a new issue of common stock before it is offered to the public. Such a right, which normally has a life of two to four weeks, is freely transferable and entitles the holder to buy the new common stock below the public offering price. *Also known as* warrant.

right of first refusal The right of a person or company to purchase something before the offering is made to others.

right of redemption The right to recover property that has been attached by paying off the debt.

right of rescission The right to void a contract without any penalty within three days as provided in the Consumer Credit Protection Act of 1968.

rights of setoff An agreement defining each party's rights should one party default on its obligation. A setoff is common in parallel-loan arrangements.

rights offering Issuance to shareholders that allows them to purchase additional shares, usually at a discount to market price. Holdings of shareholders who do not exercise rights are usually diluted by the offering. Rights are often transferable, allowing the holder to sell them on the open market to others who may wish to exercise them. Rights offerings are particularly common to closed-end funds, which cannot otherwise issue additional common stock.

rights-on The trading of shares with rights attached to them.

ring Trading arena, in which traders execute orders, located on the floor of an exchange. Sometimes called a pit.

"ring the cash register" Take a profit in stock trading.

Rio de Janeiro Stock Exchange (Bolsa do Rio) Brazil's major securities market. Portuguese language only. www.bvrj.com.br

rising bottom Chart pattern showing a rising trend in the daily low price of a security or commodity.

risk The total risk measures the degree of uncertainty of return on an asset. Systematic risk measures the sensitivity of the asset return to a change in economy-wide variables. There are many types of risk. For example, currency risk refers to the impact a rising or falling currency might have on an investment; interest rate risk is the risk associated with a rise or fall in interest rates.

risk arbitrage Traditionally, the simultaneous purchase of stock in a company being acquired and the sale of stock of the acquirer. Modern risk arbitrage focuses on capturing the spreads between the market value of an announced takeover target and the eventual price at which the acquirer will buy the target's shares.

risk aversion An investor's unwillingness to accept a decline in the price of an investment while waiting for it to increase in value.

risk classes Groups of investments that have approximately the same amount of risk.

risk lover Faced with two investments with the same expected return, a person who will choose the investment with the highest risk.

risk management The process of identifying and evaluating risks, and selecting and managing techniques to adapt to risk exposures.

risk premium Usually refers to the reward for holding a risky equity market portfolio rather than a risk-free asset. Could also refer to the spread between government and nongovernment bonds of comparable maturity.

risk seeker Investor who likes to take a risk and is even willing to pay for it. *Also called* risk lover.

risk tolerance An investor's ability or willingness to accept a decline in the price of an investment while waiting for it to increase in value.

risk transfer The shifting of risk through insurance or securitization of debt because of risk aversion.

risk-adjusted discount rate The rate established by adding an expected risk premium to the risk-free rate of return in order to determine the present value of a risky investment.

risk-adjusted return An adjustment to the asset return to reflect the riskiness of the asset. For example, one could subtract from the rate of return on an asset a rate of return from another asset that has similar risk. This gives an abnormal rate of return or a risk-adjusted return.

risk-averse Describes an investor who, when faced with two investments with the same expected return but different risks, prefers the one with the lower risk.

risk-based capital ratio Bank requirement that there be a minimum ratio of estimated total capital to an estimated risk-weighted asset.

risk-free interest rate Describes return available to an investor in a security somehow guaranteed to produce that return. The most common risk-free rate is that on Treasury securities. Note that while the normal return is risk-free, the real return (after inflation) is risky.

risk-free rate The rate earned on a riskless asset.

riskless arbitrage The simultaneous purchase and sale of the same asset to yield a profit.

riskless or risk-free asset An asset whose future return is known today with certainty. The risk-free asset is commonly defined as short-term obligations of the U.S. government, referred to as Treasury securities.

riskless rate The rate of return on a riskless investment, typically the rate earned on the ninety-day U.S. Treasury bill.

riskless transaction A transaction that is guaranteed a profit, such as the arbitrage of a temporary differential between commodity prices in two different markets. There are few riskless transactions available to investors.

risk-neutral Insensitive to risk.

risk-prone One who buys risk from others.

risk-return trade-off The concept that higher expected returns accompany greater risk, and lower returns accompany lower risk.

risk-reward ratio Relationship of expected reward corresponding to the amount of risk taken.

risky asset An asset whose future return is uncertain.

ROA *See* return on assets.

road show A promotional presentation by an issuer of securities to potential buyers about the desirable qualities of the investments. Road shows precede initial public offerings of stocks and are used to drum up interest in the offering.

rocket scientist An employee of an investment firm (often having a Ph.D. in physics or mathematics) that works on complex mathematical models to help the firm's trading desks make money or devise new types of securities.

ROE *See* return on equity.

ROI *See* return on investment.

roll down To move to an option position with a lower exercise price.

roll forward To move to an option position with a later expiration date.

roll over To reinvest funds received from a maturing security in a new issue of the same or a similar security.

roll up To move to an option position with a higher exercise price. In venture capital, refers to the venture capitalist forcing small firms to merge operations in order to reduce costs.

rolling of futures As financial futures have short-term maturities, often three to nine months, before or at maturity, the future must be sold and a new future (for the same asset but with a new maturity) must be repurchased.

rollover Means that a loan is periodically repriced at an agreed spread over the appropriate, currently prevailing, rate.

roll-over IRA A traditional individual retirement account holding money from a qualified plan or 403(b) plan. These assets, as long as they are not mixed with other contributions, can later be rolled over to another qualified plan or 403(b) plan. *Also known as* conduit IRA.

rotation An active asset-management strategy that tactically overweighs and underweighs certain investment sectors, depending on expected performance. Sometimes called sector rotation. *See also* industry allocation; sector allocation.

Roth IRA Individual retirement account that allows individuals to make annual contributions and to withdraw the principal and earnings tax free under certain conditions. Maximum annual contributions are $3,000 per year (phasing up to $4,000 in 2005 and $5,000 in 2008).

round lot A trading order typically of one hundred shares of a stock or some multiple of one hundred. *Also known as* even lot. *Compare to* odd lot.

round-trip trade The purchase and sale of a security within a short period of time.

round-trip transaction costs Costs of completing a transaction, including commissions, market-impact costs, and taxes on both buys and sells.

round-turn Procedure by which an individual's long or short position is offset by an opposite transaction or by accepting or making delivery of the actual financial instrument or physical commodity.

royalty Payment for the right to use intellectual property or natural resources.

rubber check A check that bounces for lack of funds.

rule 12b-1 SEC rule that allows mutual fund companies to charge miscellaneous fees, such as fees to cover a broker's commission fees or the cost of marketing or advertising a fund, to their customers. *See also* 12b-1 fees; 12b-1 funds; no-load mutual fund.

rule 13d Requirement under section 13d of the Securities Act of 1934 that a form must be filed with the SEC within ten business days of acquiring direct or beneficial ownership of 5 percent or more of any class of equity securities in a publicly held corporation. The purchaser of such stock must also file a form 13d with the stock exchange on which the shares are listed and with the company itself. Required information includes the way the shares were acquired, the purchaser's background, and future plans regarding the target company. The law is designed to protect against insidious takeover attempts and to keep the investing public aware of information that could affect the price of their stock. *See also* Williams Act.

rule 14d Regulations and restrictions covering public tender offers and related disclosure requirements.

rule 144 SEC rule restricting the number of shares an insider in a corporation can sell at any given time based on volume trends in the stock. All transactions under rule 144 must be reported to the SEC by the tenth day of the month following the month in which the trades were made.

rule 144a Rule that permits issuers of high-yield debt to sell securities to qualified investors such as mutual funds without registering them with the SEC.

rule 405 NYSE codification of "know your customer" rules, which require that a broker know his or her customers sufficiently well to assure an investment is suitable to their circumstances.

rule 415 Permits corporations to file a registration for securities they intend to issue in the future when market conditions are favorable. *See also* shelf registration.

rule of absolute priority A condition of bankruptcy proceedings under which junior (subordinated) claim holders can receive no payment until senior (priority) claim holders are paid in full.

rule of 72 A formula used to roughly estimate the amount of time in years it will take for invested money to double at a given compound interest rate, which is 72 divided by the interest rate.

rules of fair practice Rules established by the NASD that promulgate just and equitable principles of trade and business in securities markets which must be followed by NASD members.

rumortrage A term combining the words "rumor" and "arbitrage" used to describe trading that occurs on the basis of rumors of a takeover.

run A series of bid-and-offer quotes for different securities or maturities. Dealers give and ask for runs from each other.

rundown A summary of the amount and price of a serial bond issue that is still available for purchase.

running ahead The illegal practice of trading in a stock or other security for a broker's personal account before placing an order for the same security for a customer. *Also known as* trading ahead; going ahead.

runoff Series of trades printed on the ticker tape that occur on the NYSE before 4:00 P.M., but are not reported until afterward due to heavy trading, which makes the tape late.

Russell Indexes U.S. equity index, widely used by pension and mutual fund investors, in which each company's stock is weighted by its market capitalization; published by the Frank Russell Company of Tacoma, Washington. www.russell.com

Russell 1000 A market capitalization–weighted benchmark index made up of the one thousand largest U.S. stocks in the Russell 3000.

Russell 2000 A market capitalization–weighted benchmark index made up of the two thousand smallest U.S. companies in the Russell 3000.

Russell 3000 A market capitalization–weighted benchmark index made up of the three thousand largest U.S. stocks, which represent about 98 percent of the U.S. equity market.

Russian Exchange Russia's major securities market. www.re.ru/eng

S

safe harbor Interpretation of securities laws that allows company management to make projections about company operations with no fear of running afoul of regulations.

safekeep Holding by a bank or brokerage of bonds, stocks, or other securities.

SAI *See* statement of additional information.

SAIF *See* Savings Association Insurance Fund.

salary Regular wages and benefits an employee receives from an employer.

salary freeze A temporary halt to increases in salary due to financial difficulties experienced by a company.

salary-reduction plan A plan allowing employees to contribute pretax income to a tax-deferred retirement plan.

sale An agreement between a buyer and a seller on the price to be paid for a security, followed by delivery.

sale and leaseback Sale of an existing asset to a financial institution that then leases it back to the user.

sales charge The fee charged by a mutual fund at purchase of shares, usually payable as a commission to a marketing agent, such as a financial adviser, who is thus compensated for assistance to a purchaser. It represents the difference, if any, between the share purchase price and the share net asset value. *Also known as* load.

sales forecast A company's sales forecasts are based on historical experience, statistical analysis, and review of macroeconomic factors.

sales literature Material written by an institution selling a product that informs potential buyers of the product and its benefits.

sales tax A percentage tax on the selling price of goods and services.

sales-type lease The leasing out of a firm's own equipment, such as a printing company leasing its own presses, thereby competing with an independent leasing company.

Sallie Mae *See* Student Loan Marketing Association.

salvage value Scrap value of a company's plant and equipment.

same-day substitution Offsets in an investor's margin account during one trading day that result in no overall change in the balance of the account.

samurai bond A yen-denominated bond issued in Tokyo by a non-Japanese borrower.

samurai market The foreign market in Japan.

S&P Standard & Poor's, a provider of financial news and information. www.standardandpoors.com

S&P 500 Composite Index Index of five hundred widely held common stocks that measures the general performance of the market. This index is the benchmark against which many investment managers are judged. The mix of companies changes every year to reflect dominance of certain industries. Unlike the Dow Jones Industrial Average, the S&P 500 is a capitalization-weighted index, which means that as stocks rise in value they carry a heavier weighting in the index. As they fall, they hold less sway over the entire index.

S&P Mid-Cap 400 Index A market capitalization–weighted index made up of four hundred medium-sized companies' securities with market values between $200 million and $5 billion.

S&P phenomenon Tendency of stocks newly added to the S&P 500 Composite Index to rise in price due to a large number of buy orders as S&P-related index funds add the stock to their portfolios.

S&P Ratings Service Rating service provided by S&P that indicates the amount of risk involved with different securities, most commonly bonds.

S&P Small-Cap 600 Index A market capitalization–weighted index made up of six hundred small domestic companies' shares chosen for market size, liquidity, and industry group representation.

Santa Claus rally Seasonal rise in stock prices in the last week of the calendar year.

Saturday night special Sudden attempt by one company to take over another by making a public tender offer.

saucer Technical chart pattern depicting a security whose price has reached bottom and is moving up.

savings and loan association National- or state-chartered institution that accepts savings deposits and invests the bulk of the funds it receives in mortgages.

Savings Association Insurance Fund (SAIF) A government organization that replaced the Federal Savings and Loan Insurance Corporation as the provider of deposit insurance for thrift institutions.

savings bank An institution that primarily accepts consumer savings deposits to make home mortgage loans.

savings bond A government bond issued in face value denominations from $50 to $10,000, with local and state tax-free interest and semiannually adjusted interest rates.

savings deposit Account that pays interest, typically at below-market interest rates, that does not have a specific maturity and usually can be withdrawn upon demand.

savings element Used in the context of life insurance, the cash value built up in a policy, which equals the amount of premiums paid minus the cost of protection. This excess is invested by the insurance company, and the returns are tax-deferred inside the policy.

Savings Incentive Match Plan for Employees (SIMPLE) 401(k) A tax-deferred retirement savings plan similar to a conventional 401(k) plan, redesigned with specific rules to meet the needs of small employers. The Small Business Job Protection Act of 1996 created these plans for companies with fewer than one hundred employees. An employee's contributions are indexed for inflation, and employers must make annual matching contributions.

savings rate Personal savings of a person or a population expressed as a percentage of that individual's or population's disposable personal income. Sometimes savings rates can be negative when borrowing exceeds income.

scale Payment of different rates of interest on CDs of varying maturities. A bank is said to "post a scale." Commercial-paper dealers also post scales.

scale in Gradually taking a position in a security or market.

scale order Order to buy or sell a security that specifies the total amount to be bought or sold and the amount to be bought or sold at successively decreasing or increasing price intervals. Such orders are often placed to average the price paid overall.

scale-enhancing Describes a project that is in the same risk class as the whole firm. That is, the project allows the firm to grow larger in the context of its current business rather than diversify into new businesses.

scalp To trade for small gains. Scalping normally involves establishing and liquidating a position quickly, usually within the same day.

scalping In the context of stocks, buying up good initial public offerings. In a trading context, scalping is an attempt to eke out a small gain on a lot of transactions.

scattered Unconcentrated buy or sell interest in a listed stock or other security.

scenario analysis To examine the value of a project, firm, or asset under different assumptions about future outcomes.

schedule 13d Disclosure-of-ownership form required when more than 5 percent of any class of equity securities in a publicly held corporation is purchased. *See* form 13d.

scheduled cash flows The mortgage principal and interest payments due to be paid under the terms of the mortgage, not including possible prepayments.

scorched-earth policy Often used in risk arbitrage. Any technique a company that has become the target of a takeover attempt uses to make itself unattractive to the acquirer. For example, it may agree to sell off its key assets (*see* crown jewel) or schedule all debt to become due immediately after a merger.

SCORE Special Claim on Residual Equity, a certificate that entitles the owner to the capital appreciation of an underlying security, but not to the dividend income from the security. *Compare to* PRIME.

scrip A temporary document that represents a portion of a share of stock, often issued after a stock split or spin-off.

scripophily Collecting stock and bond certificates for their scarcity rather than for their value as securities.

search costs Costs associated with locating a counterparty to a trade, including explicit costs (such as advertising) and implicit costs (such as the value of time).

seasonally adjusted Statistically adjusted by moderating a macroeconomic indicator (e.g., oil prices/imports) so that relative comparisons can be drawn across various time periods. For instance, demand for oil is higher in winter, so comparisons from summer to winter months are not meaningful. By adjusting them for seasonality, comparisons can be accommodated.

seasoned In the case of equity, having gained a reputation for quality with the investing public and enjoying liquidity in the secondary market; in the case of convertibles, having traded for at least ninety days after issue in Europe, and thus available for sale legally to U.S. investors.

seasoned issue Issue of a security for which there is an existing market. *Opposite of* a unseasoned issue.

seasoned new issue A new issue of stock after the company's securities have previously been issued. A seasoned new issue of common stock can be made using a cash offer or a rights offer.

seat Position of membership on a securities or commodity exchange, bought and sold at prevailing market prices.

SEC *See* Securities and Exchange Commission.

SEC fee Small fee the SEC charges to sellers of equity securities on an exchange.

SEC form *See* form 8-K; form 4; form S-4; form 10-K; form 10-Q; form 13-D; form 3.

second market The Nasdaq market.

second round Stage of venture-capital financing following the start-up and first round stages and before the mezzanine level stage which precedes a public offering.

secondary distribution/offering Public sale of previously issued securities held by large investors, usually corporations or institutions, as distinguished from a primary distribution, where the seller is the issuing corporation. The sale is handled by a securities firm or a group of firms, and the shares are usually offered at a fixed price related to the current market price of the stock. Secondaries are often used by insiders to sell large blocks of stock they wish to liquidate.

secondary issue (1) Procedure for selling blocks of seasoned issues of stocks. (2) More generally, sale of already issued stock.

secondary market The market in which securities are traded after they are initially offered in the primary market. Most trading occurs in the secondary market. The New York Stock Exchange, as well as all other stock exchanges and the bond markets, are secondary markets. Seasoned securities trade in secondary markets.

secondary mortgage market Buying and selling existing mortgage loans, which are often pooled and traded as mortgage-backed securities.

secondary offering An offering in which privately held shares in a corporation are sold to the public.

secondary stocks Stocks with smaller market capitalization, lower quality, and more risk than blue chip issues. These stocks behave differently from larger corporations' stocks; for example, they are more volatile.

second-mortgage lending Loans secured by real estate previously pledged in a first mortgage.

second-preferred stock Preferred stock issue that has less priority in claiming dividends and assets in liquidation than another issue of preferred stock.

second-to-die insurance Insurance policy that, on the death of the spouse dying last, pays a death benefit to the heirs that is designed to cover estate taxes.

sector Used to characterize a group of securities that are similar in maturity, type, rating, industry, or yield.

sector allocation Investment of certain proportions of a portfolio in certain sectors (e.g., financial services, telecommunications). *Also known as* industry allocation; rotation.

sector diversification A portfolio of stocks that includes companies in each major industry group.

sector fund A mutual fund that invests in a relatively narrow industry sector. These funds can experience higher share price volatility than some diversified funds because sector funds are subject to common market forces specific to a given sector.

sector rotation An active asset-management strategy in which an investor overweighs or underweighs certain sectors depending on expected performance and risk. Sometimes called rotation.

secular Long-term time frame (ten to fifty years or more). A secular bull market is one that lasts a very long time as opposed to a cyclical bull market, which responds to the business cycle.

secured bond A bond backed by the pledge of collateral, a mortgage, or other lien, as opposed to an unsecured bond, called a debenture.

secured debt Debt that is backed by collateral. Sometimes the item purchased on credit will serve as collateral for the debt, and if payments are not made the creditor can take back the item. In the event of a default, secured debt has first claim on specified assets. *Compare to* unsecured debt.

Securities Act of 1933 First law designed to regulate securities markets, requiring registration of securities and disclosure.

Securities Acts Amendments of 1975 Legislation to encourage the establishment of a national market system together with a system for nationwide clearing and settlement of securities transactions.

securities analyst Investment professional who analyzes companies and their operations and recommends the purchase or sale of their shares by investors. *Also known as* financial analyst; investment analyst.

securities and commodities exchanges Exchanges on which securities, options, and futures contracts are traded by members for their own accounts and for the accounts of customers.

Securities and Exchange Commission (SEC) A federal agency that regulates the U.S. financial markets. The SEC also oversees the securities industry and promotes full disclosure in order to protect the investing public against malpractice in the securities markets. www.sec.gov

Securities and Exchange Commission rules Rules enacted by the SEC to assist in the regulation of U.S. financial markets.

Securities Exchange Act of 1934 Legislation that created the SEC, outlawing dishonest practices in the trading of securities.

Securities Exchange of Thailand (SET) The only stock market in Thailand, based in Bangkok.

Securities Industry Association (SIA) An association of broker/dealers that lobbies the government, records industry trends, and keeps records of broker profits. www.sia.com

Securities Industry Committee on Arbitration (SICA) A committee of the Securities Industry Association that makes recommendations on issues surrounding the arbitration of customer complaints against securities firms. www.sia.com/committees

Securities Investor Protection Corporation (SIPC) A nonprofit corporation that insures a certain amount of customers' securities and cash held by member brokerage firms against the failure of those firms. The SIPC is not to be confused with the FDIC, which insures bank deposits. Created in 1970, the SIPC will only consider certain claims and often acts like an insurance company, denying investor claims. It is funded by the brokerage industry.

securities loan The loan of securities between brokers, often to cover a client's short sale; or a loan secured by marketable securities.

securities markets Organized exchanges plus Nasdaq and other over-the-counter markets where securities are traded.

securitization Creating a more or less standard investment instrument, such as the mortgage pass-through security, by pooling assets to back the instrument. Also refers to the replacement of nonmarketable loans provided by financial intermediaries with negotiable securities issued in the public capital markets.

security Document that proves ownership of stocks, bonds, and other investments.

security deposit (initial) Used in a margin account, a cash amount that must be deposited with the broker for each purchase of stock, or in the futures market, a contract that guarantees fulfillment of the futures contract. It is not considered as part payment or purchase.

security deposit (maintenance) Additional funds required to keep the margin loan on good terms, to meet maintenance requirements.

security rating Commercial rating agencies' assessment of the credit and investment risk of securities.

security-selection decision Criteria used to choose the particular stocks or bonds or other investment instruments to include in a portfolio.

seed money The first contribution by a venture capitalist toward the financing of a new business, often using a loan or purchase of convertible bonds or preferred stock.

seek a market Search for a securities buyer or seller.

segmented market A market in which there are impediments to the free flow of labor, capital, and information.

segregation of securities SEC rules to dictate how customers' securities may be used by broker/dealers in broker loans. Certain securities may not be loaned from one customer's account and certain other securities cannot be loaned at all.

selected-dealer agreement The set of rules governing the selling group in a securities underwriting.

selective hedging Protecting investments during some time periods and not during others.

self-amortizing mortgage Mortgage whose entire principal is paid off in a specified period of time with regular interest and principal payments.

self-directed IRA An IRA that allows the account holder to carry out his or her investment instructions, albeit through a custodian manager or firm.

self-employed income Taxable income of a person involved in a sole proprietorship or other sort of freelance work.

self-employment tax A tax self-employed people must pay to qualify them to receive Social Security benefits at retirement.

self-liquidating loan Loan to finance current assets. The sale of the current assets provides the cash to repay the loan.

self-regulatory organization (SRO) Organization that enforces fair, ethical, and efficient practices in the securities and commodity futures industries, including all national securities and commodities exchanges and the NASD.

self-supporting debt Bonds sold to finance a project that will produce enough revenue through tolls or other charges to retire the debt. *Also known as* revenue bond.

sell the book Order to a broker by the holder of a large quantity of shares of a security to sell all that can be absorbed at the current bid price. The term derives from the specialist's book—the record of all the buy and sell orders members have placed in the stock one handles. In this scenario, the buyers potentially include those in the specialist's book, the specialist for its own account, and broker/dealers.

sell off Sale of securities under pressure. *Also known as* dumping.

sell order An order, which may take many different forms, by an investor to a broker to sell a particular stock, bond, option, future, mutual fund, or other holding.

sell out Liquidation of a margin account after a customer has failed to deposit new cash or assets to bring an account to a required level. This occurs after a margin call has gone out. Also the selling of securities by a broker when a customer fails to pay for them. Also the complete sale of all securities in a new issue.

seller financing Funding a purchase by a seller's loan to the buyer; the buyer takes full title to the property when the loan is fully repaid.

seller's market Market in which demand exceeds supply. As a result, the seller can dictate the price and the terms of sale. *Opposite of* buyer's market.

seller's option Delayed settlement or delivery in a transaction.

selling climax A sudden drop in securities prices as sellers dump their holdings.

selling concession The discount that underwriters offer the selling group on securities in a new issue.

selling dividends Inducing a prospective customer to buy shares in order to profit from a dividend scheduled to be paid in the near future.

selling, general, and administrative (SG&A) expenses Expenses such as salespersons' salaries and commissions, advertising and promotion, travel and entertainment, office payroll and expenses, and executives' salaries. These costs fall immediately below the cost of goods sold on the income statement.

selling group All brokerage firms involved in selling or marketing a new issue of stock or bonds.

selling on the good news A strategy of selling stock shortly after a company announces good news and the stock price rises. Investors believe that the price is as high as it can go and is on the brink of going down.

selling short The sale of a stock that is not actually owned. If an investor thinks the price of a stock is going down, the investor borrows the stock from a broker and sells it. Eventually the investor must buy the stock back on the open market. For instance, an investor borrows a thousand shares of a company on July 1 and sells them for $8 per share. Then on August 1 he or she purchases a thousand shares of the company at $7 per share. He or she has made $1,000 (less commissions and other fees) by selling short.

selling short against the box Selling short stock that is actually owned by the seller but held in the box, meaning it is held in safekeeping. The seller borrows securities needed to cover the stock in the box that is inaccessible. Or the seller may not wish to disclose ownership, and chooses to borrow stock to make a sale.

selling syndicate A group of underwriters that issues a firm's securities by buying them from the issuing firm and reselling them to a group of smaller brokerage firms for eventual sale to individual investors. *Also known as* underwriting syndicate; purchase group.

sell-limit order Conditional trading order that indicates that a security may be sold at the designated price or higher. *Opposite of* buy-limit order.

sell-plus order Market or limit order to sell a stated amount of stock provided that the price to be obtained is not lower than the last sale, if the last sale was on an uptick, or at the same price as the previous trade.

sell-side analyst A financial analyst who works for a brokerage firm and whose recommendations are passed on to the brokerage firm's customers. *Also called* Wall Street analyst; securities analyst. *Opposite of* buy-side analyst.

semistrong-form efficiency Theory that the price of a security fully reflects all public information (including, but not limited to, historical price and trading patterns). *Compare to* weak-form efficiency; strong-form efficiency.

senior debt Debt whose terms in the event of bankruptcy require it to be repaid before subordinated debt receives any payment.

senior mortgage bond A bond that, in the event of bankruptcy, will be paid off before any other bonds are repaid.

senior refunding Replacement of securities with five-to-twelve-year maturities with securities of fifteen-year or longer maturities, in order to delay, reduce, or consolidate payment made by the issuer.

senior security A security that in the event of bankruptcy will be redeemed before any other securities.

seniority The order of repayment. In the event of bankruptcy, senior debt must be repaid before subordinated debt is repaid.

sensitivity analysis Analysis of how changes in sales, cost, and other factors can affect a project's profitability.

sentiment indicators The general feeling of investors about the state of the market, such as whether they are bullish or bearish.

SEP *See* Simplified Employee Pension plan.

separate tax returns Tax returns of married persons who choose to file their returns individually, usually because this approach produces lower overall tax payments.

Separate Trading of Registered Interest and Principal Securities (STRIPS) Long-term notes and bonds divided into two components: principal and interest. Each component may be transferred among investors and sold in amounts as small as $1,000. STRIPS are sold at auction at a minimum par amount, varying for each issue and depending upon the issue's interest rate.

serial bond Corporate bond arranged so that specified principal amounts become due on specified dates.

serial entrepreneur Business person who successfully starts a number of different businesses and sells them.

serial redemption The redemption of a serial bond.

series Referring to options: all option contracts of the same class that also have the same unit of trade, expiration date, and exercise price. Referring to stocks: shares that have common characteristics, such as rights to ownership and voting, dividends, or par value. In the case of many foreign shares, one series may be owned only by citizens of the country in which the stock is registered.

series bond Bond that may be issued in several series under the same indenture document.

series E bond A local and state tax-free savings bond issued by the U.S. government from 1941 to 1979, which was then replaced by series HH bonds.

series EE bond *See* savings bond.

series HH bond *See* savings bond.

SET *See* Securities Exchange of Thailand.

set-aside A percentage of a municipal or corporate bond underwriting that is allocated for handling by a minority-owned brokerage firm.

settle price An average of the trading prices in the futures market during the last few minutes of trading.

settlement When payment is made for a trade.

settlement date The date on which payment is made to settle a trade. For stocks traded on U.S. exchanges, settlement is currently three business days after the trade. For mutual funds, settlement usually occurs in the United States the day following the trade. In some regional markets, foreign shares may require months to settle.

settlement options The various possibilities open to a beneficiary under a life insurance policy as to how the benefit will be paid out.

settlement price A figure determined by the closing range that is used to calculate gains and losses in futures-market accounts. Settlement prices are used to determine gains, losses, margin calls, and invoice prices for deliveries. *See also* closing range.

settlement rate The rate suggested in Financial Accounting Standards Board (FASB) 87 for assessing the obligations of a pension plan. The rate at which the pension benefits could be effectively settled if the company sponsoring the pension plan wishes to terminate its pension obligation.

settlement risk The risk that one party will deliver and the counterparty will not be able to pay or vice versa. *Also known as* counterparty risk.

settlor A person who creates a trust. *Also known as* grantor.

setup Applies mainly to convertible securities. A strategy involving buying the convertible bond and shorting a certain percentage of the underlying shares. *Opposite of* Chinese hedge.

severally but not jointly An agreement between members of an underwriting group to buy a new issue (severally) but not to assume joint liability for shares left unsold by other members. *Compare to* jointly and severally.

S-4 *See* form S-4.

SG&A expenses *See* selling, general, and administrative expenses.

shadow calendar A backlog of securities issues registered with the SEC that are awaiting the determination of an offering date.

shadow stock When a public company creates a second privately held stock that outstrips the marketwide movements in equities for the purpose of rewarding managers. That is, a way to compensate managers with stock even when the publicly traded stock plummets because the market as a whole has fallen. Or when a private company creates a phantom stock also for the purpose of performance evaluation and rewards.

shakeout A dramatic change in market conditions that forces speculators to sell their positions, often at a loss.

sham A business transaction, such as a limited partnership, that is entered into for the sake of avoiding tax.

Shanghai Stock Exchange One of two major securities markets in China. Chinese language only. www.sse.com.cn

share repurchase Program by which a corporation buys back its own shares in the open market. Companies often announce buybacks when stock prices have fallen. Since repurchase reduces the number of shares outstanding, earnings per share increase, which might seem to elevate the market value of the remaining shares held by stockholders. But such a tactic is not the same as earnings growth generated by rising sales, and investors must recognize this. Many share buybacks are performed solely to offset shares issued in option grants to employees.

shared appreciation mortgage A mortgage with a low rate of interest, offset by giving the lender some portion of the appreciation in the value of the underlying property.

shareholder Person or entity that owns shares or equity in a corporation. *Also known as* stockholder.

shareholders' equity This is a company's total assets minus total liabilities. *Also known as* net worth; owner's equity.

shareholders' letter A section of an annual report where one can find general overall discussion by management of successful and failed strategies.

shares Certificates or book entries representing ownership in a corporation or similar entity.

shares authorized The maximum number of shares of stock a company may issue as stated in its articles of incorporation, which may be changed only by a shareholder vote.

shark repellent A takeover defense strategy that may include golden parachutes, poison pills, or other tactics to make a takeover prohibitively expensive to an acquirer.

shark watcher Firm specializing in the early detection of corporate takeover activity. Such a firm, whose primary business is usually the solicitation of proxies for client corporations, monitors trading patterns in a client's stock and attempts to determine the identity of parties accumulating shares.

shelf offering Offering of registered securities covered by a prospectus whose distribution is not underwritten on a firm commitment basis. The shares may be sold in one block or in small amounts from time to time in agency or principal transactions. *See* rule 415.

shelf registration A procedure that allows firms to file one registration statement covering several issues of the same security. SEC rule 415, adopted in the 1980s, allows a corporation to comply with registration requirements up to two years prior to a public offering of securities. With the registration "on the shelf," the corporation, by simply updating regularly filed annual, quarterly, and related reports to the SEC, can go to the market as conditions become favorable with a minimum of administrative preparation and expense.

shell corporation An incorporated company with no significant assets or operations, often formed to obtain financing before beginning actual business, or as a front for tax evasion.

Shenzhen Stock Exchange One of two major securities markets in China. Chinese language only. www.sse.org.cn

shock absorber *See* circuit breakers.

shogun bond Dollar bond issued in Japan by a nonresident corporation.

shoot-out Refers to two or more venture capital firms fighting for a start-up.

shop Wall Street slang for a firm.

shopped stock Sell inquiry that has been seen by or shown to other dealers before coming to an investment bank.

shopping Seeking to obtain the best bid or offer available by calling a number of dealers and/or brokers.

short Refers to general practice of selling a security that you do not own. *Opposite of* long.

short bond Bond maturing relatively soon.

short book *See* unmatched book.

short coupon A bond payment covering less than six months' interest because the original issue date is less than six months from the first scheduled interest payment. A bond with a short time to maturity, usually two years or less.

short covering Purchase of securities by a short seller to replace those borrowed at the time of a short sale.

short exempt A special trading situation in which a short sale is allowed on a downtick in a stock. The owners of a convertible security trading at parity can sell the equivalent amount of common short on a minus tick, assuming they have the firm intention to convert.

short hedge The sale of futures contracts to eliminate or lessen the possible decline in value of an approximately equal amount of the actual financial instrument or physical commodity. *See also* hedge; long hedge.

short interest Total number of shares of a security that investors have sold short and that have not been repurchased to close out the short position. Usually, investors sell short to profit from price declines. As a result, the short interest is often an indicator of the amount of pessimism in the market about a particular security. However, there are other reasons to short that are not related to pessimism, such as hedging strategies for mergers or by holders of convertible securities.

short position When a person sells stocks he or she does not yet own. Shares must be borrowed, before the sale, to make delivery to the buyer. Eventually, the shares must be bought back to close out the transaction. This technique is used when an investor believes the stock price will drop. *Opposite of* long position.

short ratio (or short-interest ratio) Number of shares of a security that investors have sold short divided by average daily volume of the security measured over thirty days or ninety days. There are various interpretations of this ratio. When people short, it is usually (but not always) because they are pessimistic about the security's future performance. Shorting requires buying at some point, however. Hence, some would interpret a high short ratio as an indicator that there will be buying pressure on the security that would increase its price.

short sale Selling a security that the seller does not own but is committed to repurchasing eventually. It is used to capitalize on an expected decline in the security's price.

short selling Establishing a market position by selling a security one does not own in anticipation of the price of that security falling.

short settlement Trade settlement made prior to the standard three-day period due to a customer's request.

short squeeze When a lack of supply tends to force prices upward. In particular, when prices of a stock or commodity futures contracts start to move up sharply and many traders with short positions are forced to buy stocks or commodities in order to cover their positions and limit losses. This sudden surge of buying leads to even higher prices, further aggravating the losses of short sellers who have not covered their positions.

short straddle When one put and one call on the same underlying asset are sold with the same time to capitalization.

short tender Practice prohibited by SEC that involves the use of borrowed stock to respond to a tender offer.

shortfall risk The risk of falling short of any investment target.

short-form registration A procedure that allows a firm to condense its registration statement and prospectus by referencing financial data already on file with the SEC.

short-interest theory The theory that a large interest in short positions in stocks will precede a rise in the market, because the positions must eventually be covered by purchases of the stock.

short-run operating activities Events and decisions concerning the short-term finance of a firm, such as how much inventory to order and whether to offer cash terms or credit terms to customers.

short-sale rule An SEC rule requiring that short sales be made only in a market that is moving upward; this means either on an uptick from the last sale or showing no downward movement.

short-term Any investment with a maturity of one year or less.

short-term bond fund A bond mutual fund holding short- to intermediate-term bonds that have maturities of three to five years.

short-term capital gain A profit on the sale of a security or mutual fund share that has been held for less than twelve months. A short-term capital gain is taxed as ordinary income.

short-term debt A company's debt obligations, recorded as current liabilities, requiring payment within the year.

short-term financial plan A financial plan that covers the coming fiscal year.

short-term gain or loss A profit or loss realized from the sale of securities held for less than a year that is taxed at normal income tax rates if the net total is positive.

short-term investment service Service that assists firms in making short-term investments.

short-term reserves Investments in interest-bearing bank deposits, money market instruments, U.S. Treasury bills, and short-term bonds.

short-term solvency ratio Ratio used to judge the adequacy of a company's liquid assets for meeting short-term obligations as they come due. *See* current ratio; acid-test ratio; inventory turnover ratio; accounts receivable turnover ratio.

short-term tax exempt Short-term security issued by states, municipalities, and quasi-government entities such as local housing and urban renewal agencies.

short-term trend Erratic price movement in securities or the overall market that lasts less than three weeks.

show-and-tell list A list full of real customer indications of interest for securities in an offering.

showstopper A legal barrier, such as a shark repellent, that firms use to prevent being acquired.

shrinkage Discrepancy between a firm's actual inventory and its recorded inventory due to theft, deterioration, loss, or clerical problems.

shut out the book Exclude a public investor's bid or offer from being included in a trade.

SIA *See* Securities Industry Association.

SIC *See* standard industrial classification.

SICA *See* Securities Industry Committee on Arbitration.

side effects Effects of a proposed project on other parts of the firm.

side-by-side trading Trading a security and an option on the same underlying security on the same exchange.

sidelines Investors who are not involved in a stock or are merely watching it are on the sidelines.

sideways market Horizontal price movement in the overall market. Indecisive action.

sight draft Demand for immediate payment.

signal To convey information through a firm's actions. The more costly it is to provide a signal, the more credibility it has. For example, to call a press conference and tell everyone that the firm's prospects have improved is less effective than raising the dividend.

signaling approach Notion that insiders in a firm have information that the market does not have, and that the choice of capital structure and payout policy by insiders can signal information to outsiders and change the value of the firm. This theory is also referred to as the asymmetric information approach.

signature guarantee The authentication of a signature in the form of a stamp, seal, or written confirmation by a bank or member of a domestic stock exchange (or other acceptable guarantor). A notary public cannot provide a signature guarantee. A signature guarantee is a common requirement when transferring or redeeming shares or changing the ownership of an account.

signature loan A good-faith loan that requires only the borrower's signature on the loan application and is not secured by an asset.

significant influence The holding of a large portion of the equity of a corporation, usually at least 20 percent, which gives the holder a significant amount of control over the corporation. This degree of holding must be recorded in a firm's financial statements. Such holders are also known as control persons.

significant order An order to buy or sell a large enough quantity of securities that the price of the security may be affected. Institutional investors usually spread out such an order over a few days or weeks to avoid adverse pressures on the buy or sell price.

significant order imbalance A large number of buy or sell orders for a stock that cause an abnormally wide spread between bid and offer prices, and often cause the exchange to halt the sale of the stock until a better balance has been reestablished.

silent partner A partner in a business who has no role in management but shares in the liability, tax responsibility, and cash flow.

simple compound-growth method Calculating a growth rate by relating current value to initial value and assuming a constant percentage annual rate of growth between the two.

simple interest Interest calculated as a simple percentage of the original principal amount. *Opposite of* compound interest.

SIMPLE IRA A salary deduction plan for retirement benefits provided by some small companies with no more than one hundred employees. *See* Savings Incentive Match Plan for Employees (SIMPLE) 401(k).

simple prospect An investment opportunity in which only two outcomes are possible.

simple rate of return The return from an investment figured by dividing income plus capital gains by the amount of capital invested. The effect of compounding is not taken into account.

Simplified Employee Pension plan (SEP) A pension plan in which both the employee and the employer contribute to an individual retirement account. Also available to the self-employed.

simulation The use of a mathematical model to imitate a situation many times in order to estimate the likelihood of various possible outcomes.

single-country fund A mutual fund that invests in assets in an individual country outside the United States.

single-factor model A model of security returns that says that only one economy-wide factor, which is usually the market return, determines movements in the expected returns.

single-index model A model of stock returns that reduces influences on returns to one factor. The most common single factor is the overall market return.

single-life annuity An annuity covering one person. A straight life annuity provides payments until death, while a life annuity with a guaranteed period provides payments until death or continues payments to a beneficiary for a guaranteed term, such as ten years.

single-payment bond A bond that makes only one payment of both the principal and interest, due at the bond's maturity date. *Also known as* zero-coupon bond; pure-discount bond.

single-premium deferred annuity (SPDA) An IRA-like annuity into which an investor makes a lump-sum payment that is invested in either a fixed-return instrument or a variable-return portfolio, and is taxed only when distributions are taken.

single-premium life insurance A life insurance policy requiring one premium payment, which accrues cash value much more quickly than a policy paid in installments.

single-state municipal bond fund A mutual fund investing only in government obligations within a single state, with state tax-free dividends, but taxed capital gains.

sinker A bond with interest and principal payments coming from the proceeds of a sinking fund.

sinking fund A fund associated with a bond or preferred stock to which money is added on a regular basis to ensure investor confidence that promised payments will be made. The sinking fund is used to redeem the securities as well. *See also* purchase fund.

sinking-fund requirement A condition included in some corporate bond indentures that requires the issuer to retire a specified portion of debt each year. Any principal due at maturity is called the balloon maturity.

SIPC *See* Securities Investor Protection Corporation.

sit tight Directive from the trader to the customer to be patient, emphasizing that one's piece of business will be executed.

size Refers to a very large offering, order, or trade. Size is relative from market to market and security to security. Among institutional investors, small is less than 10,000 shares. Medium is 15,000 to 25,000 shares. Good is 50,000 shares. Size is 100,000 shares. Good six-figure size is 200,000 to 300,000 shares. Multiple six-figure size is more than 300,000 shares.

size out the book Overt action to exclude a public investor's bid or offer from participation in a print through trading a larger size ahead. One can never size out a market order.

skip-day settlement Settling a trade one business day beyond what is normal.

skip-payment privilege A mortgage contract clause giving borrowers the right to skip payments if they are ahead of schedule.

SLD last sale This shows up on the consolidated tape of transactions when a trade is reported out of order or late. It refers to a sold sale, and may be an attempt by a market maker to take advantage of a volatile market by printing a trade late at an advantageous price. For instance, if the stock has dropped significantly, a late sell order could be at the higher price that prevailed earlier.

sleeper Stock in which there is little investor interest but that has significant potential to gain in price once its attractions are recognized. *Opposite of* high flyer.

sleeping beauty Potential takeover target that has not yet been approached by an acquirer. Such a company usually has particularly attractive features, such as a large amount of cash, or undervalued real estate or other assets.

slippage The difference between estimated transaction costs and actual transaction costs, where these costs include fees, the bid-ask spread, and market impact.

slump A temporary fall in performance, often describing consistently falling security prices for several weeks or months.

small business policy Insurance coverage available to new exporters and small businesses.

small investor An individual investing in small quantities of stock or bonds, or mutual funds.

small order execution system (SOES) Three-tiered system of automatic execution of small orders of Nasdaq stocks at the best price. Size is either two hundred, five hundred, or, most often, one thousand shares. It was devised in the late 1980s in response to the dismal performance of Nasdaq market makers in the crash of 1987 when they refused to answer their phones and investors could not buy and sell stocks. SOES is restricted to individual investors and cannot be used by institutions.

small-capitalization fund A mutual fund that invests primarily in stocks of companies whose market value is less than $1 billion. Small-cap stocks historically have been more volatile than large-cap stocks, and often outperform the overall market.

small-capitalization (small-cap) stock The stock of a company whose market value is less than $1 billion. Small-cap companies tend to grow faster than large-cap companies and typically use any profits for expansion rather than to pay dividends. They also are more volatile than large-cap companies and have a higher failure rate.

small-firm effect The tendency of small firms (in terms of total market capitalization) to have higher returns than the overall stock market. Of course, these securities are often riskier than the market.

small-issues exemption Securities issues that involve less than $1.5

million are not required to file a registration statement with the SEC. Instead, they are governed by regulation A, for which only a brief offering statement is needed when they sell shares to investors.

snowballing Process by which the exercise of stop orders in a declining or advancing market causes further downward or upward pressure on stock prices, thus triggering more stop orders and more price pressure.

Social Security benefits Monthly government payments to retired workers or their families who have paid Social Security taxes for a total of forty quarters or ten years.

Social Security Disability Income Insurance Program financed by the Social Security tax to provide compensation for lost income to individuals who are expected to be disabled for at least one year.

socially conscious mutual fund A mutual fund that does not invest in companies that produce harmful products or by-products or have interests deemed to be socially unacceptable.

SOES *See* small order execution system.

soft currency A national currency that is expected to drop in value relative to other currencies.

soft dollars The value of research services that brokerage houses supply to investment managers "free of charge" in exchange for the investment manager's trades on which the brokerage charges commissions.

soft landing A term describing a growth rate high enough to keep the economy out of recession, but slow enough to prevent inflation and high interest rates.

soft market A buyer's market in which supply exceeds demand, causing little trading activity and wide bid-ask spreads.

soft spot Stocks or groups of stocks that remain weak in a strong market.

softs Tropical commodities such as coffee, sugar, and cocoa.

sole proprietorship A business owned by a single individual. A sole proprietor pays no corporate income tax but has unlimited liability for business debts and obligations.

solvency Ability to meet obligations.

sour bond A bond issue that has defaulted on interest or principal payments, and will thus trade at a large discount and carry a poor credit rating.

source and application of funds statement *See* statement of cash flow.

source-of-funds seller Customer seller of stock for the purpose of raising cash for other purchases. Such a seller will sell only at advantageous prices, and not aggressively.

sovereign risk The risk that a central bank will impose foreign exchange regulations that will reduce or negate the value of currency contracts in effect. Also refers to the risk of government default on a loan made to a country or guaranteed by it.

SPDA *See* single-premium deferred annuity.

SPDR An SPDR tracks the value of the Standard & Poor's 500 Composite Index. Stands for Standard & Poor's depositary receipt. They trade on the American Stock Exchange under the symbol SPY. One SPDR unit is valued at approximately one-tenth of the value of the S&P 500. Dividends are disbursed quarterly and are based on the accumulated stock dividends held in trust, less any expenses of the trust. *Also known as* spider. *See also* mid-cap SPDR.

special arbitrage account A margin account with lower cash requirements, reserved for transactions that are hedged by an offsetting position in futures or options.

special assessment bond A municipal bond with interest paid by the taxes of the community benefiting from the bond-funded project.

special bid A method of purchasing a large block of stock on the NYSE by advertising a client's large buy order and matching it up with a number of other traders' smaller sell orders.

special bond account A special broker margin account used only for transactions in U.S. government bonds, municipals, and eligible corporate bonds.

Special Claim on Residual Equity certificate *See* SCORE.

special dividend Also referred to as an extra dividend. Dividend that is unlikely to be repeated.

specialist On an exchange, the member firm that is designated as the market maker or, on Nasdaq, a dealer for a common stock. Member of a stock exchange who maintains a "fair and orderly market" in one or more securities. Only one specialist can be designated for a given stock, but dealers may trade several stocks. Major functions include executing limit orders on behalf of other exchange members for a portion of the floor broker's commission, and buying or selling for the specialist's own account to counteract temporary imbalances in supply and demand and thus prevent wide swings in stock prices.

specialist block purchase and sale Purchase of a large number of securities by a specialist for himself or to pass on to another floor trader or block buyer.

specialist market　Market in a stock made solely by the specialist, as no public orders exist in the market.

specialist unit　A specialist who maintains a stable market by acting as a principal and agent for other brokers in one or many stocks. Many specialist units are owned by brokerage firms.

specialist's book　Chronological record maintained by a specialist that includes the specialist's own inventory of securities, market orders to sell short, and limit orders and stop orders that other stock exchange members or investors have placed with the specialist.

specialist's post　*See* post.

specialist's short-sale ratio　The percentage of the total short sales of stock by specialists compared to total sales.

special-purpose entity　A financing technique in which a company decreases its risk by creating separate partnerships, rather than subsidiaries, for certain holdings and solicits outside investors to take on the risk. In order to qualify as a special-purpose entity, whose financial results are not carried on the company's books, the unit must meet strict accounting guidelines. *Compare to* subsidiary.

specific risk　Risk that is specific to an investment or company, not to the market as a whole, and one that can be eliminated through diversification. *Compare to* market risk.

speculation　Purchasing risky investments that present the possibility of large profits but also pose a higher-than-average possibility of loss. A profitable strategy over the long term if undertaken by professionals who hedge their portfolios to control the amount of risk.

speculative　Securities that involve a high level of risk.

speculative demand (for money)　The need for cash to take advantage of investment opportunities that may arise.

speculative motive　A desire to hold cash in order to be poised to exploit any attractive investment opportunity requiring a cash expenditure.

speculative stock　Very risky stock.

speculative-grade bond　Bond rated BA, BB, or lower by S&P, or an unrated bond. *Also known as* junk bond.

speculator　One who attempts to anticipate price changes and, through buying and selling contracts, aims to make profits. A speculator does not produce, process, market, or handle a product. For example, a speculator may purchase corn futures in a bet that bad weather in the future will bring corn yields down and thus raise the price of corn.

speed *See* prepayment speed.

spider *See* SPDR.

spike A sudden, sharp increase in a company's share price.

spin-off An independent company created from an existing part of another company by distributing new shares in the so-called spin-off.

split *See* stock split.

split commission A commission shared between a broker and a financial adviser or other professional who brought the customer to the broker.

split offering A municipal bond issue that is made up of serial bonds and term maturity bonds.

split order A large securities transaction that is divided into smaller orders that are spread out over some period of time to avoid large fluctuations in the market price.

split rating Two different ratings given to the same security by two important rating agencies.

split-coupon bond A bond that begins as a zero-coupon bond paying no interest and converts to an interest-paying bond at a later date.

sponsor An underwriting investment company that offers shares in its mutual funds, or an influential institution that highly values a particular security and thus creates additional demand for the security.

spontaneous current liabilities Short-term obligations that automatically increase and decrease in response to financing needs, such as accounts payable.

spontaneous liability Obligation that arises automatically in the course of operating a business when a firm buys goods and services on credit.

spoof bid *See* phantom bid.

spot commodity A commodity that is traded with the expectation of actual delivery, as opposed to a commodity future that is usually not delivered.

spot exchange rate Exchange rate on currency for immediate delivery. *Opposite of* forward exchange rate.

spot interest rate Interest rate fixed today on a loan that is made today.

spot market Price on commodities available for immediate delivery.

spot month The nearest delivery month on a futures contract.

spot price The current market price of the actual physical commodity. Current delivery price of a commodity traded in the spot market, in which goods are sold for cash and delivered immediately. *Also called* cash price. *Opposite of* futures price.

spot rate The theoretical yield on a zero-coupon Treasury security. Also refers to spot foreign exchange rate.

spot secondary Secondary distribution of stock that may not require an SEC registration statement and may be attempted without delay. An underwriting discount is normally included in these offerings.

spot trade The purchase and sale of a foreign currency, commodity, or other item for immediate delivery.

spousal IRA An individual retirement account in the name of an unemployed spouse.

spousal remainder trust A fixed-term trust from which income is distributed to the beneficiary (such as a child) to take advantage of a lower tax bracket and that at the end of the term passes to the grantor's spouse.

spread The gap between bid and ask prices of a stock or other security; the simultaneous purchase and sale of separate futures or options contracts for the same commodity for delivery in different months. Also referred to as a straddle, the difference between the price at which an underwriter buys an issue from a firm and the price at which the underwriter sells it to the public. Also referred to as the underwriter's discount or the price an issuer pays above a benchmark fixed-income yield to borrow money.

spread income The difference between income and cost. For a depository institution, the difference between the assets it invests in (loans and securities) and the cost of its funds (deposits and other sources). *Also called* margin income.

spread option A position consisting of the purchase of one option and the sale of another option on the same underlying security with a different exercise price and/or expiration date.

spread order An order listing the series of options that the customer wants to buy and sell and the desired spread between the premiums paid and received for the options.

spread strategy A strategy that involves a position in one or more options so that the cost of buying an option is funded entirely or in part by the income received from selling another option in the same underlying security. Also referred to as spreading.

spreadsheet A computer program that organizes numerical data into rows and columns in order to calculate and make adjustments based on new data.

sprinkling trust A trust in which the trustee decides how to distribute trust income among a group of designated people.

squeeze Period when stocks or commodities futures increase in price and investors who have sold short must cover their short positions to prevent loss of large amounts of money.

SRO *See* self-regulatory organization.

stability The relative steadiness or safety of a security or fund compared to the market as a whole. For example, money market funds and other short-term investments offer more stability than funds that invest in growth stocks.

stabilization The action undertaken by a country when it buys and sells its own currency to protect its exchange value. Action that registered competitive traders undertake on the NYSE to meet the exchange requirement that 75 percent of their trades be stabilizing, meaning that sell orders follow an uptick and buy orders a minus tick. Stabilization also refers to actions a managing underwriter undertakes so that the market price of a new issue does not fall below the public offering price during the offering period.

stag Speculator who buys and sells stocks to hold for short intervals to make quick profits.

stagflation A period of slow economic growth and high inflation or rising prices of goods.

staggered board of directors Occurs when a portion of directors are elected periodically, instead of all at once. Board terms are often staggered in order to thwart unfriendly takeover attempts since it could take years before potential acquirers could take control of a company's board through the normal voting process.

staggering maturities Hedging against interest rate movements by investment in short-, medium-, and long-term bonds.

stagnation A period of slow economic growth or, in securities trading, a period of inactive trading.

stakeholders All parties that have an interest, financial or otherwise, in a firm—stockholders, creditors, bondholders, employees, customers, management, the community, and the government.

stamp duty Tax on foreign transactions in international equities, usually a percentage of total transaction amount, which can be unilateral or bilateral in nature.

stamp tax Tax on a financial transaction.

stand up to Make a good-sized market in the trader's own bid and offering prices. Hence, "standing up" to the bid signifies the trader's willingness to buy good size volume at the advertised bid.

stand-alone principle Investment approach that advocates a firm should accept or reject a project by comparing it with securities in the same risk class.

standard deduction The IRS-specified amount by which a taxpayer is entitled to reduce income. An alternative to itemizing deductions.

standard deviation A measure of dispersion or deviation of a set of data from its mean or normal behavior.

standard error A measure of possible error in an estimate. Plus or minus two standard errors usually provides 95 percent confidence.

standard industrial classification (SIC) A code system that designates a unique business activity classified by industry.

Standard & Poor's *See* S&P.

Standard & Poor's depository receipt See SPDR.

standby agreement In a rights issue, agreement that the underwriter will purchase any stock not purchased by investors.

standby commitment An agreement between a corporation and investment firm that the firm will purchase whatever part of a stock issue offered in a rights offering is not subscribed to in the two- to four-week standby period.

standby fee Amount paid to an underwriter who agrees to purchase any stock that is not purchased by public investors in a rights offering.

standby letter of credit Agreement to guarantee invoice payments to a supplier; a standby letter of credit promises to pay the seller if the buyer fails to pay.

standing Level of priority in the trading crowd.

standstill agreement Contract in which the bidding firm in a takeover attempt agrees to limit its holdings of another firm.

start-up The earliest stage of a new business venture.

state bank A bank authorized in a specific state by a state-based charter, with generally the same functions as a national bank.

state tax–exempt income fund A mutual fund that seeks current income exempt from a specific state's income taxes.

stated annual interest rate The interest rate expressed as a per year percentage, by which interest payments are determined. For example, a credit card stated annual rate is often 18 percent, or 1.5 percent ($18 \div 12$) on overdue monthly balances. *Also known as* annual percentage rate.

stated conversion price At the time of issuance of a convertible security, the price the issuer effectively grants the security holder to purchase the common stock, equal to the par value of the convertible security divided by the conversion ratio.

stated value A monetary-worth figure that bears no relation to market value; it is assigned, for accounting purposes, to stock for use instead of par value.

statement billing Billing method in which the sales for a given period, such as a month (for which a customer also receives invoices), are collected into a single statement, and the customer must pay all the invoices on the statement.

statement of additional information (SAI) A document provided as a supplement to a mutual fund prospectus. It provides more detailed information about fund policies, operations, and risks. *Also known as* part B prospectus.

statement of cash flow A financial statement showing a firm's cash receipts and cash payments during a specified period.

statement of condition A document describing the status of assets, liabilities, and equity of a person or business at a particular time.

statement of financial accounting standards no. 52 The currency translation standard currently used by U.S. firms. It mandates the use of current rates.

statement-of-cash-flow method A method of cash budgeting that is organized along the lines of the statement of cash flow.

stationary time series A longitudinal measure in which the process generating returns is identical over time.

statistical tracking error A standard deviation of the difference between a portfolio's return and the desired investment benchmark return.

statutory debt limit The cap that Congress imposes on the amount of public debt that may be outstanding whether temporary or permanent. When this limit is reached, the Treasury may not sell new debt issues until Congress raises the limit.

statutory investment An investment that a trustee is authorized to make under state law.

statutory merger A merger in which one corporation remains as a legal entity, instead of a new legal entity being formed.

statutory surplus The surplus held by an insurance company determined by the accounting treatment of both assets and liabilities as established by state statutes.

statutory voting The standard rule in most corporations that there is one vote per share in elections of the board of directors.

staying power The ability of an investor to stay in the market and not sell out of a position when an investment goes awry.

steenth One-sixteenth of one full point in price or 6.25 cents. Often used in negotiations to compromise an eighth difference, and in options trading.

steepening of the yield curve A change in the yield curve where the spread between the yield on a long-term and short-term Treasury has increased. *Opposite of* flattening of the yield curve.

step aside Allow a block to trade at a price at which you do not care to participate in the trade.

step up To increase, as in "step up" the tax basis or cost basis of an asset.

step-down note A floating-rate note whose interest rate declines after a specified period of time.

step-up bond A bond that pays a lower coupon rate for an initial period and then increases to a higher coupon rate.

step-up swap An interest rate swap on which the notional principal or face amount increases according to a predetermined schedule.

sterilized intervention Foreign exchange market activity by which monetary authorities insulate their domestic money supplies from the foreign exchange transactions with offsetting sales or purchase of domestic assets.

sticky deal A new securities issue that may be difficult to sell because of problems in the market or underlying problems with the corporation.

stock Ownership of a corporation indicated by shares, which represent a piece of the corporation's assets and earnings.

stock ahead When two or more orders for a stock at a certain price arrive about the same time and the exchange's priority rules take effect. NYSE rules stipulate that the bid made first should be executed first or, if two bids come in at once, the bid for the larger number of shares receives priority. The bid that is not executed is then directed to the broker, who informs the customer that the trade was not completed because there was "stock ahead."

stock bonus plan A plan used as an incentive that rewards employee performance with stock in the company.

stock buyback A corporation's purchase of its own outstanding stock, usually in the hope that the purchase will raise the company's earnings per share or offset shares issued to executives in stock options. Investors must recognize growth in earnings per share that is a result of stock buybacks is not as promising as growth that results from rising sales. *See* share repurchase.

stock certificate A document representing the number of shares of a corporation owned by a shareholder.

stock dividend Payment of a corporate dividend in the form of stock rather than cash. The stock dividend may be additional shares in the company, or it may be shares in a subsidiary being spun off to shareholders. Stock dividends are often used to conserve cash needed to operate the business. Unlike a cash dividend, stock dividends are not taxed until sold.

stock exchange Formal organization, approved and regulated by the SEC, that is made up of members who use the facilities to trade certain common stocks. The two major American stock exchanges are the New York Stock Exchange (NYSE) and the American Stock Exchange (AMEX). The five regional stock exchanges are the Midwest, Pacific, Philadelphia, Boston, and Cincinnati. The Arizona Stock Exchange is an after-hours electronic marketplace where anonymous participants trade stocks via personal computers.

Stock Exchange of Thailand The major securities market of Thailand. www.set.or.th

stock index Index like the Dow Jones Industrial Average that tracks a portfolio of stocks.

stock insurance company An insurance company owned by a group of stockholders who are not necessarily policyholders.

stock jockey A stockbroker who frequently buys and sells shares in a client's portfolio.

stock list The department within a stock exchange that oversees compliance with listing requirements and exchange regulations.

stock market The market for trading equities.

stock option An option whose underlying asset is the common stock of a corporation. In the late 1990s, companies increased the use of stock options to managers and employees as compensation, which allows them to participate when the company's stock rises. However, when stocks fall options can become worthless.

stock power A power of attorney form giving ownership of a security to another person, brokerage firm, bank, or lender after it has been sold or pledged to that party.

stock purchase plan A plan allowing employees of a company to purchase shares of the company, often at a discount or with matching employer funds.

stock rating An evaluation by a rating agency of the expected financial performance or inherent risk of common stocks.

stock record The accounting a brokerage firm keeps of all securities held in inventory.

stock repurchase A firm's repurchase of outstanding shares of its common stock. *Also known as* stock buyback.

stock right Another less common term for a stock option.

stock screen To analyze various stocks in search of those that meet predetermined criteria. For example, a simple value screen would sort all stocks by their price-to-book ratio and pick the stocks with the lowest ratios as candidates for a value portfolio.

stock selection An active portfolio-management technique that focuses on advantageous selection of particular stock rather than on broad asset-allocation choices.

stock split Occurs when a firm issues new shares of stock and in turn lowers the current market price of its stock to a level that is proportionate to presplit prices. For example, if a company trades at $100 before a two-for-one split, after the split it will trade at $50, and holders of the stock will have twice as many shares as they had before the split. The investor's percentage of equity remains the same following the split.

stock symbol An abbreviation, usually three, four, or five letters long, assigned to a publicly traded security that allows transactions to be recorded quickly on the consolidated tape. *Also known as* ticker symbol.

stock ticker A letter designation assigned to securities and mutual funds that trade on U.S. financial exchanges.

stock watcher A computerized service that monitors and investigates trading activity on the NYSE in order to identify any unusual activity or security movement that might be caused by rumors or illegal activities.

stockbroker An investment professional who deals with investors, executing their trades and providing advice. *Also known as* registered representative; customer's man.

stockholder A person who owns shares in a company. *Also known as* shareholder.

stockholder books Set of books kept by firm management for its annual report that follows Financial Accounting Standards Board rules for presentation to shareholders. The tax books follow IRS tax rules.

stockholder of record Stockholder whose name is registered on the books of a corporation and thus will receive dividends from the corporation.

stockholder's equity The residual claims that stockholders have against a firm's assets, calculated by subtracting all current liabilities and debt liabilities from total assets. Also known as net worth.

stockholders' report The annual report and other reports given to stockholders to inform them of the company's financial standing and developments during the period.

Stockholm Stock Market (Stockholm Börsen) The major securities market of Sweden. www.stockholmsborsen.se/index.asp?lang=eng

stock-index future A security that uses composite stock indexes to allow investors to speculate on the performance of the entire market, or to hedge against losses in long or short positions. The settlement of the contract is in cash.

stock-index option An option in which the underlying security is a common-stock index.

stock-index swap A swap involving a stock index. The other asset involved in a stock index swap can be another stock index (a stock-for-stock swap), a debt index (a debt-for-stock swap), or any other financial asset or financial price index.

stockout Running out of inventory.

stop-limit order A stop order that designates a price limit. Unlike the stop order, which becomes a market order once the stop is reached, the stop-limit order becomes a limit order and can only be executed at the limit price or better.

stop-loss order An order to sell a stock when the price falls to a specified level. *Also known as* stop order.

stop order or stop An order to buy or sell when a definite price is reached, either above (on a buy) or below (on a sell) the price that prevailed when the order was given.

stop payment An order given a depository institution to not pay out cash for a check; often used when the check has been stolen or lost.

stop-out price The lowest auction price at which Treasury bills are sold.

stopped When a specific price on the customer's working order has been guaranteed while the dealer tries to obtain a better price. Stopped against one's self involves a customer order and a firm's own account, not two customers. One can cancel an order even after being stopped by another party.

stopped out A purchase or sale that is executed under an order at the stop price specified by the customer.

story stock/bond A complex security that requires a long "story" so that investors may understand the corporation and be persuaded of its merits. Also, pejorative term used to characterize stocks that feature more fluff than substance and are peddled aggressively by often unscrupulous stockbrokers.

straddle Purchase or sale of an equal number of puts and calls on the same underlying asset with the same time to capitalization. Similar to a spread.

straight bankruptcy *See* chapter 7 bankruptcy.

straight value Also referred to as investment value, the value of a convertible security without the conversion option.

straight voting Allows shareholder to cast all of the shareholder's votes for each candidate for the board of directors.

straight-line depreciation Amortizing or apportioning an equal dollar amount of depreciation on an asset in each accounting period.

straight-term insurance policy Term life insurance policy providing a fixed-amount death benefit over a certain number of years.

strangle Buying or selling an out-of-the-money put option and call option on the same underlying instrument, with the same expiration. Profits are made only if there is a drastic change in the underlying instrument's price.

strap *See* strip.

strategic alliance Collaboration between two or more companies designed to achieve some corporate objective. May include international licensing agreements, management contracts, or joint ventures.

strategic buyout Acquisition of another firm in order to realize some operational benefits that will result in increased earnings.

strategy The general or specific approach to investing that an individual, institution, or fund manager employs.

stratified equity indexing A method of constructing a replicating portfolio that classifies the stocks in the index into strata and represents each stratum in the portfolio.

Street, the Refers to Wall Street financial community: brokers, dealers, underwriters, and other knowledgeable participants.

street name Securities held by a broker on behalf of a client and registered in the name of the brokerage firm to make trading easier. Stocks held in street name can be loaned out to speculators selling shares short.

strike price The stated price per share for which the underlying stock or index may be purchased in the case of a call option or sold in the case of a put option by the owner of the option contract. Also referred to as the striking price or exercise price.

strike rate In an interest rate agreement, one party, for an upfront premium, agrees to compensate the other party at specific times if a designated interest rate is different from this predetermined level.

strip Variant of a straddle. A strip is two puts and one call on a stock. A strap is two calls and one put on a stock. The puts and calls have the same strike price and expiration date.

STRIPS *See* Separate Trading of Registered Interest and Principal Securities.

stripped bond Bond that is stripped of its coupons and can be subdivided into a series of zero-coupon bonds.

stripped mortgage-backed security Security that separates and redistributes the cash flows from the underlying mortgage-backed security collateral into the principal and interest components of the mortgage to enhance its attractiveness to different groups of investors. For example, investors who want to bet on the future direction of interest rates might buy the interest-only (IO) security.

stripped yield Applies mainly to convertible securities. Return on the debt portion of a bond unit after subtracting the value of the issued warrant or equity segment of the securities.

strong currency A currency whose value compared to other currencies is improving, as indicated by a decrease in the direct exchange rates for the currency.

strong dollar When the dollar can be exchanged for a large amount of foreign currency, benefiting American travelers but hurting exporters. *Opposite of* weak dollar.

strong-form efficiency A form of pricing efficiency that posits that the price of a security correctly reflects all information, both private and public. *Compare to* semistrong-form efficiency; weak-form efficiency.

structured debt Debt that has been customized for the buyer, often by incorporating unusual options.

structured portfolio strategy Designing a portfolio to achieve a level of performance that matches some predetermined liabilities that must be paid out in the future. Insurance companies use such strategies.

structured settlement An agreement in settlement of a lawsuit involving specific payments made over a period of time. Property and casualty insurance companies often buy life insurance products to pay the costs of such settlements.

stub Piece of equity security left over from a major cash or security distribution from a recapitalization.

Student Loan Marketing Association (SLMA) A publicly traded corporation established by federal regulation that increases availability of educational loans by guaranteeing student loans traded in the secondary market. *Also known as* Sallie Mae. www.salliemae.com

subchapter M An IRS regulation dealing with investment companies and real estate investment trusts that avoid double taxation by distributing interest, dividends, and capital gains directly to shareholders, who are taxed individually.

subchapter S IRS regulation that gives a corporation with thirty-five or fewer shareholders the option of being taxed as a partnership to escape corporate income taxes.

subject Refers to a bid or offer that cannot be executed without confirmation from the customer. In other words, a bid or an offer that needs additional information before becoming firm and is therefore still negotiable.

subject market Quote in which prices are subject to confirmation. Also referred to as fast market because quotes are changing quickly.

subject to opinion An auditor's opinion reflecting acceptance of a company's financial statements subject to pervasive uncertainty that cannot be adequately measured such as information relating to the value of inventories, reserves for losses, or other matters open to judgment.

subordinated A claim ranked lower in priority than other claims. Common-stock claims are always subordinated to debt.

subordinated bond Security that falls after others in priority of claims on a company in the case of financial distress.

subordinated debenture bond An unsecured bond that ranks after secured debt, after debenture bonds, and often after some general creditors in its claim on a company's assets and earnings.

subordinated debt Debt over which senior debt takes priority. In the event of bankruptcy, subordinated debt-holders receive payment only after senior debt claims are paid in full. *Also known as* junior debt.

subordination clause A provision in a bond indenture that restricts the issuer's future borrowing by subordinating future lenders' claims on the firm to those of the existing bondholders.

subpart F Special category of foreign-source "unearned" income that is taxed by the IRS whether or not it is remitted to the United States. Currently, however, there is an exemption, which means this income is not taxed.

subperiod return The return of a portfolio over a shorter period of time than the evaluation period.

subrogation An insurance process whereby a company that has paid out to a policyholder for a loss incurred recovers the amount of the loss from a party that is legally liable.

subscription Agreement to buy new issue of securities.

subscription agreement An application reviewed by the general partner to join a limited partnership.

subscription price Price that current shareholders pay for a share of stock in a rights offering.

subscription privilege The right of current shareholders of a corporation to buy newly issued shares before they are available to the public. Also referred to as subscription right.

subscription warrant Type of security, usually issued with another security, such as a bond or stock, that entitles the holder to buy a proportionate amount of common stock of the issue at a specified price, usually higher than the market price at the time of issuance.

subsidiary A wholly or partially owned company that is part of a large corporation. A foreign subsidiary is a separately incorporated entity under the host country's law. A subsidiary's financial results are carried on the parent company's books.

subsidized financing Funding provided by a government or other entity that is available at a below-market interest rate.

substantially equal periodic payments (SEPP) A method of distribution from IRA account assets that under certain conditions is not subject to the IRS's 10 percent premature withdrawal penalty for those under age fifty-nine and a half.

substitution swap A swap in which a money manager exchanges one bond for another bond that is similar in terms of coupon, maturity, and credit quality, but that offers a higher yield.

suicide pill A hostile takeover prevention tactic that could destroy the target company. Taking on a large amount of debt to prevent the takeover might cause bankruptcy, for example.

suitability rules Policies and guidelines that brokers must use to ensure that investors have the financial means to assume risks that they wish to undertake or that the securities they purchase are suitable to their financial position, needs, and goals. These are enforced by the NYSE, the NASD, and other self-regulatory organizations.

summary plan description (SPD) A document that explains the fundamental features of an employer's defined benefit or defined contribution plan, including eligibility requirements, contribution formulas, vesting schedules, benefit calculations, and distribution options. ERISA requires that the description be easy to understand and that each participant receive a copy within ninety days of joining the plan.

sunk cost Cost that has been incurred and cannot be reversed.

sunrise industry Growth industry in an economy that may become a leader in the market in the future.

Super Bowl indicator A conjecture that if a team from the old American Football League pre-1970 wins the Super Bowl, the stock market will decline during the coming year. If a team from the old pre-1990 National Football League wins the Super Bowl, stock prices will increase in the coming year.

super DOT An automatic computerized trading system introduced on the NYSE in 1984 that provides faster execution than regular designated order turnaround (DOT). The average order through super DOT is transmitted, executed, and reported back to the originating firm in twenty-two seconds.

super sinker bond Usually a home financing bond, but also any other bond that has long-term coupons but short maturity; the mortgages may be prepaid, and the holders may receive the long-term yield after a short period of time.

supermajority Provision in a company's charter requiring a majority of shareholders to approve certain changes, such as a merger.

supermajority amendment Corporate amendment requiring that a substantial majority (usually 67 percent to 90 percent) of stockholders approve important transactions, such as mergers.

supervisory analyst An analyst who is qualified to approve publicly distributed research reports.

supervisory board The board of directors that represents stockholders in the governance of the corporation.

super-voting stock Shares that carry more voting power than the traditional one-share, one-vote shares. Super-voting stock is often held by families that once controlled a company outright and may be used to thwart takeover attempts. A share of stock that has a disproportionate number of votes per share than other forms of stock for the same company. For example, Class A shares may have ten votes per share while Class B shares have only one vote per share.

Supplemental Security Income A Social Security program established to help the blind, disabled, and poor.

supplier credit Self-financing of a supplier's operations.

supply-side economics A theory of economics that reductions in tax rates will stimulate investment and, in turn, will benefit the entire society. This theory was the basis of Ronald Reagan's tax cuts in the 1980s.

support level A price level below which it is supposedly difficult for a security or market to fall. That is, the price level at which a security tends to stop falling because buyers will step in; can be identified on a technical basis by seeing where the stock has bottomed out in the past.

surcharge An additional levy added to a charge.

surety An individual or corporation that guarantees the performance or actions of another.

surplus funds Cash flow available after payment of taxes in a project.

surtax A tax added to the normal tax paid by corporations or individuals who have earned income above a certain level.

surveillance department of exchanges A department that monitors trading activity on an exchange in order to identify any unusual activity that may indicate illegal practices.

sushi bond A Eurobond issued by a Japanese corporation.

suspended trading Temporary halt in trading in a particular security, in advance of a major news announcement or to correct an imbalance of orders to buy and sell.

suspense account An account used temporarily to record receipts and disbursements that have yet to be classified.

sustainable growth rate Maximum rate of growth a firm can sustain without increasing financial leverage.

swap An arrangement in which two entities lend to each other on different terms, e.g., in different currencies, and/or at different interest rates, fixed or floating.

swap book A bank's portfolio of swaps, usually arranged by currency and maturity.

swap buyback The sale of an interest rate swap by one counterparty to the other, effectively ending the swap.

swap reversal An interest rate swap designed to end a counterparty's role in another interest rate swap, accomplished by counterbalancing the original swap in maturity, reference rate, and notional amount.

swap sale Also called a swap assignment, a transaction that ends one counterparty's role in an interest rate swap by substituting a new counterparty whose credit is acceptable to the other original counterparty.

swaption Options on interest rate swaps. The buyer of a swaption has the right to enter into an interest rate swap agreement by some specified date in the future. The swaption agreement will specify whether the buyer of the swaption will be a fixed-rate receiver or a fixed-rate payer. The writer of the swaption becomes the counterparty to the swap if the buyer exercises the options.

sweat equity An increase in equity created by the labor of the owner. Usually refers to home improvements.

sweep account Account providing that a bank invests all the excess available funds at the close of each business day.

sweetener A feature of a security that makes it more attractive to potential purchasers. For example, a bond sweetener may be an equity kicker attached to a bond purchase.

Swiss Exchange The major securities market of Switzerland. www.swx.com

swissy Slang for the Swiss franc.

switching Liquidating a position and simultaneously reinstating a position in another security of the same type. Mutual fund families allow investors to switch between funds.

symbol Letters used to identify companies on the consolidated tape and other locations.

synchronous data Information available at the same time.

syndicate A group of banks that act jointly, on a temporary basis, to loan money or to underwrite a new issue of bonds or stock.

syndicate manager The firm leading the syndicate. *Also known as* managing underwriter.

synergy Describes a combination whose value is greater than the sum of the separate parts.

synthetic convertible Combination of bonds and warrants (that expire on or after the bonds' maturity) that together resemble a convertible bond.

synthetic lease When a company creates a special-purpose entity to arrange for a loan to purchase property, and then leases the property from the entity. The synthetic lease therefore keeps the loan off the company's balance sheet, while the company provides enough income to the special-purpose entity to cover the interest rate on the loan. *See also* off-balance-sheet financing.

synthetics Customized hybrid instruments created by combining securities that mimic the price movement of another single security or portfolio.

systematic Common to all businesses.

systematic investment plan An approach involving regular investments in order to take advantage of dollar-cost averaging.

systematic risk *See* market risk.

systematic withdrawal plan A provision of certain mutual funds to pay out to the shareholder specified amounts after specified periods of time.

T

tactical asset allocation (TAA) Portfolio strategy that allows active departures from the normal asset mix according to specified objective measures of value. Often referred to as active asset management.

tailgating Purchase of a security by a broker after the broker places an order for the same security for a customer. The broker hopes to profit either because of information that the customer has or because the customer's purchase is of sufficient size to affect security prices. An unethical practice.

Taiwan Stock Exchange (TSEC) Established in 1961, the only centralized securities market in Taiwan. www.tse.com.tw/docs/eng_home.htm

take a bath To sustain a loss on either a speculation or an investment.

take a flier To speculate on highly risky securities.

take a position To buy or sell short; that is, to own or to owe some amount on an asset or derivative security.

take it down Reduce the offering price or hit others' bids to such an extent as to lower the inside market.

take off A sharp increase in the price of a stock, or a positive movement of the market as a whole.

take the offer Buy stock by accepting a floor broker's or dealer's offer at an agreed-upon volume. *Opposite of* hit the bid.

takedown The share of securities of each participating investment banker in a new or a secondary offering, or the price at which the securities are distributed to the different members of an underwriting group.

take-or-pay contract An agreement that obligates the purchaser to take any product that is offered (and pay the cash purchase price) or pay a specified amount if the product is not taken.

takeover General term referring to transfer of control of a firm from one group of shareholders to another. Change in the controlling interest of a corporation, either through a friendly acquisition or a hostile bid. A hostile takeover (with the aim of replacing current existing management) is usually attempted through a public tender offer.

takeover target A company that is the object of a takeover attempt, friendly or hostile.

takes price Requiring some price movement or concession on behalf of the initiating party before a trade can be consummated. *See* price give.

taking a view A British expression; means forming an opinion as to where market prices are headed and acting on it.

taking delivery When the buyer actually assumes possession from a seller of assets agreed upon in a forward contract or a futures contract.

tangibility Characteristic of a physical asset that can be used as collateral to secure debt.

tangible asset An asset whose value is based on particular physical properties. These include reproducible assets such as buildings or machinery and nonreproducible assets such as land, a mine, or a work of art. *Also called* real asset. *Opposite of* intangible asset.

tangible net worth A company's total assets minus its intangible assets, which include patents and copyrights, and total liabilities.

tape As in ticker tape: a service that reports prices and sizes of transactions on major exchanges. Also includes electronic news wire services. *See also* composite tape; consolidated tape.

tape is late When the trading volume is so heavy that trades are reported more than a minute behind the time they actually take place.

target cash balance Optimal amount of cash for a firm to hold, considering the trade-off between the opportunity costs of holding too much cash and the financing costs of holding too little cash.

target company A firm chosen as an attractive takeover candidate by a potential acquirer. The acquirer may buy up to 5 percent of the target's stock without public disclosure, but it must report all transactions and supply other information to the SEC, the exchange the target company is listed on, and the target company itself once the 5 percent threshold is hit.

target firm A firm that is the object of a takeover by another firm.

target investment mix The percentage mix of stocks, bonds, and short-term reserves that an investor considers appropriate based on personal objectives, time horizon, risk tolerance, and financial resources.

target leverage ratio The ratio of the market value of debt to the total market value of a firm that management seeks to maintain.

target payout ratio A firm's long-run dividends paid compared to earnings, expressed as a ratio. The firm's policy is to attempt to pay out a certain percentage of earnings, but it pays a stated dollar dividend and adjusts it to the target as increases in earnings occur.

target price In the context of takeovers, the price at which an acquirer aims to buy a target firm. In the context of options, the price of the underlying security at which an option will become in-the-money. In the context of stocks, the price that an investor hopes a stock will reach in a certain time period.

target zone Implicit boundary on exchange rates established by central banks.

targeted repurchase Buying back of a firm's stock from a potential acquirer, usually at a substantial premium, to forestall a takeover attempt. *See also* greenmail.

target-zone arrangement A monetary system under which countries pledge to maintain their exchange rates within a specific margin around agreed-upon, fixed central exchange rates.

tariff A tax on imports or exports.

tax and loan account An account at a private bank, held in the name of the district Federal Reserve Bank, which holds operating cash for the business of the U.S. Treasury.

tax anticipation bill (TAB) Special bill that the Treasury occasionally issues that matures on corporate quarterly income tax dates and can be used at face value by corporations to pay their tax liabilities.

tax anticipation note (TAN) Note issued by states or municipalities to finance current operations in anticipation of future tax receipts.

tax arbitrage Trading that takes advantage of a difference in tax rates or tax systems as the basis for profit.

tax audit Audit by the IRS or other tax-collecting agency to determine whether a taxpayer has paid the correct amount of tax.

tax avoidance Minimizing tax burden through legal means such as tax-free municipal bonds, tax shelters, IRA accounts, and trusts. *Compare to* tax evasion.

tax base The assessed value of the taxable property, assets, and income within a specific geographic area.

tax basis In the context of finance, the original cost of an asset less depreciation that is used to determine gains or losses for tax purposes. In the context of investments, the price of a stock or bond plus the broker's commission.

tax books Records kept by a firm's management that follow IRS rules.

tax bracket The percentage of tax obligation for a particular taxable income.

tax credit A direct dollar-for-dollar reduction in tax allowed for expenses such as child care and R&D for building low-income housing. *Compare to* tax deduction.

tax deductible The effect of creating a tax deduction, such as charitable contributions and mortgage interest.

tax deduction An expense that a taxpayer is allowed to deduct from taxable income.

tax evasion Reducing tax burden illegally by underreporting income, overstating deductions, or using illegal tax shelters.

tax haven A nation with a moderate level of taxation or generous tax incentives for undertaking specific activities such as exporting or investing.

tax haven affiliate A wholly owned entity in a low-tax jurisdiction that is used to channel funds to and from a multinational's foreign operations.

tax holiday A reduced tax rate that a government provides as an inducement to foreign direct investment.

tax liability The amount in taxes a taxpayer owes to the government.

tax lien The right of the government to enforce a claim against the property of a person owing taxes.

tax planning Devising strategies throughout the year in order to minimize tax liability.

tax rate The percentage of tax paid for different levels of income.

tax refund Money back from the government when too much tax has been paid or withheld from a salary.

tax schedule Tax form used to report itemized deductions, dividend and interest income, profit or loss from a business, capital gains and losses, supplemental income and loss, and self-employment tax.

tax selling Selling of securities to realize losses that will offset capital gains and reduce tax liability. *See* wash sale.

tax shelter Legal way to reduce tax liabilities. An example is the use of depreciation of assets.

tax shield The reduction in income tax that results from taking an allowable deduction from taxable income.

tax software Computer software designed to assist taxpayers in filling out tax returns and minimizing tax liability.

tax straddle Technique used in futures and options trading to create tax benefits. For example, an investor with a capital gain takes a position creating an artificial offsetting loss in the current tax year and postponing a gain from the position until the next tax year.

tax swap Selling one bond and buying another similar security to receive a tax benefit.

tax umbrella Tax-loss carryforwards from previous business losses that form a tax shelter for profits earned in current and future years.

taxable acquisition A merger or consolidation that is not a tax-free acquisition. The selling shareholders are treated as having sold their shares and must pay tax on any gains recorded.

taxable equivalent yield The return from a higher-paying but taxable investment that would equal the return from a tax-free investment. This depends on the investor's tax bracket.

taxable estate That portion of a deceased person's estate that is subject to transfer tax.

taxable event An event or transaction that has a tax consequence, such as the sale of stockholding that is subject to capital gains taxes.

taxable income Gross income minus a variety of deductions.

taxable municipal bond Taxed private-purpose bonds issued by the state or local government to finance prohibited projects such as sports stadiums.

taxable transaction Any transaction that is not tax-free to the parties involved, such as a taxable acquisition.

taxable year The twelve-month period an individual uses to report income for income tax purposes. For most individuals, their tax year is the calendar year.

tax-deferral option Allowing the capital gains tax on an asset to be payable only when the gain is realized by selling the asset.

tax-deferred income Dividends, interest, and unrealized capital gains on investments in an account such as a qualified retirement plan, where income is not subject to taxation until a withdrawal is made.

tax-deferred retirement plan Employer-sponsored and other plans that allow contributions and earnings to be made and accumulate tax-free until they are paid out as benefits.

tax-differential view (of dividend policy) The view that shareholders prefer capital gains over dividends, and hence low dividend payout ratios, because capital gains are effectively taxed at lower rates than dividends.

tax-equivalent yield The pretax yield required from a bond whose income is taxable in order to equal the tax-free yield of a municipal bond.

tax-exempt bond A bond usually issued by municipal, county, or state governments whose interest payments are not subject to federal and, in some cases, state and local income tax.

tax-exempt income Dividends and interest not subject to federal and, in some cases, state and local income taxes.

tax-exempt income fund A mutual fund that seeks income that is exempt from federal and, in some cases, state and local income taxes.

tax-exempt money market fund A money market fund that invests in short-term tax-exempt municipal securities.

tax-exempt sector The municipal bond market, where state and local governments raise funds. Bonds issued in this sector are exempt from federal income taxes.

tax-exempt security An obligation whose interest is tax-exempt, often called a municipal bond, offered by a country, state, town, or any political district.

tax-free acquisition A merger or consolidation in which the acquirer's tax basis on each asset whose ownership is transferred is generally the same as the acquiree's, or each seller who receives only stock does not have to pay any tax on the gain realized until the shares are sold.

tax-loss carryback, carryforward A tax benefit that allows business losses to be used to reduce tax liability in previous and/or following years.

tax-preference item Items that must be included when calculating the alternative minimum tax; a tax designed to ensure that tax deductions do not wipe out all tax liabilities.

tax-preparation service Firm that prepares tax returns for a fee.

tax-sheltered annuity A type of retirement plan under section 403(b) of the Internal Revenue Code that permits employees of public education organizations or tax-exempt organizations to make before-tax contributions via a salary reduction agreement to a tax-sheltered retirement plan. Employers are also allowed to make direct contributions on behalf of employees.

tax-status election The decision of the status under which to file a tax return. For example, a corporation may file as a C corporation or an S corporation.

tax-timing option The option to sell an asset and claim a loss for tax purposes or not sell the asset and defer the capital gains tax.

TBA *See* to be announced.

T-bill *See* Treasury bill.

teaser rate A low initial interest rate on an adjustable-rate mortgage or credit card to entice borrowers that is later eliminated and replaced by the market rate.

technical analysis Security analysis that seeks to detect and interpret patterns in the charts of past security prices.

technical analysts Also referred to as chartists or technicians, analysts who use mechanical rules to detect changes in the supply of and demand for a stock, and to capitalize on the expected change.

technical condition of a market Demand and supply factors affecting price, in particular the net position, either long or short, of the Wall Street community.

technical forecasting A forecasting method that uses securities' historical prices and trends.

technical insolvency Default on a legal obligation of the firm. Technical insolvency occurs when a firm doesn't pay a bill on time.

technical rally Short rise in securities or commodities futures prices in the face of a general declining trend. Such a rally may result because investors are bargain hunting or because analysts have noticed a particular support level at which securities usually bounce up. *Opposite of* correction.

technical sign A short-term trend in the price movement of a security that analysts recognize as significant.

technician One who performs technical analysis.

TED spread Difference between Eurodollar rate and U.S. Treasury bill rate; used by some traders as a measure of investor anxiety or credit quality of a particular security.

teeny One-sixteenth or 0.0625 of one full point in price. *Also known as* steenth.

Tel Aviv Stock Exchange Established in 1953, Israel's only stock exchange. www.tase.co.il

telephone switching Moving one's assets from one mutual fund or variable annuity to another by telephone.

temporary investment A short-term investment, such as a money market fund, Treasury bill, or short-term CD, which is usually held for one year or less.

ten largest holdings The percentage of a portfolio's total net assets or equity holdings in its ten largest securities positions. As this percentage rises, a portfolio's returns are likely to be more volatile because they are more dependent on the fortunes of fewer companies.

10-K *See* form 10-K.

10-Q *See* form 10-Q.

1040 form The standard individual tax return form of the IRS.

1099 A statement sent to the IRS and taxpayers by the payers of dividends and interest and by issuers of taxable original-issue discount securities.

tenant A partial owner of a security, or the holder of some property. *See also* lessee.

tenants in common Account registration in which two or more individuals own a certain proportion of an account. Each tenant's proportion is distributable as part of the owner's estate, so that if one of the account holders dies, his heirs are entitled to his share of the account.

ten-bagger A stock that grows in value tenfold.

tender To offer for delivery against futures, or to offer a security for sale in response to a tender offer.

tender offer General offer made publicly and directly to a firm's shareholders to buy their stock at a price well above the current market price.

tender-offer premium The premium offered above the current market price in a tender offer.

tenor Maturity of a loan.

term The period of time during which a contract is in force.

term bond Bond whose principal is payable at maturity. Often referred to as bullet-maturity bond or simply bullet bond.

term certificate A certificate of deposit with a longer time to maturity.

term Fed funds Fed funds sold for a period of time longer than overnight.

term life insurance A contract that provides a death benefit but no cash buildup or investment component. The premium remains constant only for a specified term of years, and the policy is usually renewable at the end of each term.

term loan A bank loan, typically with a floating interest rate, for a specified amount that matures between one and ten years, and requires a specified repayment schedule.

term premium Excess of the yield to maturity on a long-term bond over those of a short-term bond.

term repo A repurchase agreement with a term of more than one day.

term to maturity The time remaining on a bond's life, or the date on which the debt will cease to exist and the borrower will have completely paid off the amount borrowed. *See also* maturity.

term trust A closed-end fund that has a fixed termination or maturity date.

terminal value The value of a bond at maturity, typically its par value, or the value of an asset (or an entire firm) on some specified future valuation date.

terms of sale Conditions under which a firm proposes to sell its goods or services for cash or credit.

terms of trade The weighted average of a nation's export prices relative to its import prices.

territorial tax system A tax system that taxes domestic income but not foreign income. Territorial tax regimes are found in Hong Kong, France, Belgium, and the Netherlands.

test The event of a price movement that approaches a support level or a resistance level established earlier by the market. A test is passed if prices do not go below the support or above the resistance level, and the test is failed if prices go on to new lows or highs.

testamentary trust A trust created by a will, that is, scheduled to occur after the maker's death. *Opposite of* inter vivos trust.

testate Dying with a will.

theoretical value Mathematically determined value of a derivative instrument, such as an option, dictated by a pricing model such as the Black-Scholes model.

theta The change in an option price for a one day decrease in time to expiration. As expiration approaches, the value falls. *Also called* time decay.

thin market A market in which trading volume is low, and consequently bid and asked quotes are wide and the instrument traded is difficult to buy and sell. Very little stock to buy or sell.

thinly traded Infrequently traded. *Also known as* illiquid.

third market Exchange-listed securities trading in the over-the-counter market.

13-D *See* form 13-D.

thirty-day visible supply The total volume in dollars of municipal bonds with maturities of thirteen months or more, expected to come to the market within thirty days.

thirty-day wash rule IRS rule stating that losses on a sale of stock may not be taken as a tax benefit if equivalent stock is purchased thirty days or less before or after the sale of the stock.

three steps and a stumble rule A rule predicting that stock and bond prices will fall following three increases in the discount rate by the Federal Reserve. This is a result of increased costs of borrowing for companies and the increased attractiveness of money market funds and CDs over stocks and bonds as a result of the higher interest rates.

threshold for refinancing When the weighted-average coupon of a mortgage-backed security is at a level to induce home owners to prepay the mortgage in order to refinance to a lower-rate mortgage, generally reached when the weighted-average coupon of the security is two percentage points or more above currently available mortgage rates.

thrift institution An organization formed as a depository primarily for consumer savings. Savings and loan associations and savings banks are thrift institutions.

thrift plan A defined contribution plan in which an employee contributes, usually on a before-tax basis, toward the ultimate benefits that will be provided. The employer usually agrees to match all or a portion of the employee's contributions.

throughput agreement An agreement to put a specified amount of product per period through a particular facility. An example is an agreement to ship a specified amount of crude oil per period through a particular pipeline.

tick Refers to the minimum change in price a security can have, either up or down.

tick indicator A market indicator based on the number of stocks whose last trade was an uptick or a downtick. Used as an indicator of market sentiment or psychology to try to predict the market's trend.

ticker symbol An abbreviation, usually three, four, or five letters long, assigned to a publicly traded security that allows transactions to be recorded quickly on the consolidated tape. *Also known as* stock symbol.

ticker tape Computerized device that relays to investors around the world the stock symbol and the latest price and volume on securities as they are traded. For most stocks, recorded trades refer to one hundred shares bought or sold.

ticket Abbreviation of order ticket.

tick-test rules SEC-imposed restrictions on when a short sale may be executed, intended to prevent investors from accelerating the fall of a stock. A short sale can be made only when the sale price of the particular stock is higher than the last trade price (referred to as an uptick trade), or if there is no change in the last trade price of the particular stock, the previous trade price must be higher than the trade price that preceded it (referred to as a zero uptick).

TIGER Treasury investors growth receipt. U.S. government–backed bonds without coupons, meaning that the bondholders do not receive the periodic interest payments. The principal of the bond and the individual coupons are sold separately. *Compare to* zero-coupon bonds.

tight In line with or extremely close to the inside market or last sale in a stock (+/–0.1). *Also known as* on the money.

tight market A market in which volume in a security is high, trading is active and highly competitive, and consequently spreads between bid and ask prices are narrow.

tight money When the Federal Reserve restricts money supply, making credit difficult to secure. *Opposite of* easy money.

tilted portfolio An indexing strategy with an active management aspect through the emphasis of a particular industry sector; selected performance factors such as earnings momentum, dividend yield, price/

earnings ratio; or selected economic factors such as interest rates and inflation.

time decay *See* theta.

time deposit Interest-bearing deposit at a savings institution that has a specific maturity. *See also* certificate of deposit.

time draft Demand for payment at a stated future date.

time horizon The period, usually expressed in years, for which an investor expects to hold an investment.

time order Order for a stock that becomes a market or limited price order or is canceled at a specific time.

time premium The amount by which an option price exceeds its intrinsic value. The value of an option beyond its current exercise value representing the option holder's control until expiration, the risk of the underlying asset, and the riskless return. The more time an option holder has until the security expires, the greater the chance that the underlying stock will reach a price the holder desires. *Also known as* time value.

time to maturity The time remaining until a financial contract, such as a bond or option, expires. *Also called* time until expiration.

time until expiration The time remaining until a financial contract expires. *Also called* time to maturity.

time value *See* time premium.

time value of money The idea that a dollar today is worth more than a dollar in the future, because the dollar received today can earn interest up until the time the future dollar is received.

timeliness A source of competitive advantage that depends on being the first to enter a given market with a product or service.

time-series analysis Assessment of relationships between two or more variables such as two stocks over periods of time.

time-series model System that examines series of historical data; sometimes used as a means of forecasting.

times-interest-earned ratio A company's earnings before interest and taxes, divided by its interest payments.

time-spread strategy Buying and selling puts and calls with the same exercise price but different expiration dates, and trying to profit from the different premiums of the options.

timing *See* market timing.

timing option The seller's choice of what day in the delivery month to deliver a commodity in a futures contract.

tip Information given by one trader or investor to another, which is used in making buy or sell decisions but is not available to the general public.

TIPS *See* Treasury inflation-protected securities.

tired A security that has been strong for a while but will probably fall due to increased supply at current price level.

title insurance Insurance policy that protects a policyholder from future challenges to the title claim on a property that may result in loss of the property.

to be announced (TBA) A contract for the purchase or sale of a mortgage-backed security to be delivered at an agreed-upon future date but does not include a specified pool number and number of pools or precise amount to be delivered. Refers to most recent mortgage pools.

Tobin's Q ratio Market value of firm's assets divided by replacement value of the firm's assets used to analyze whether a stock is overvalued or cheap. A Tobin's Q ratio greater than one indicates the firm has done well with its investment decisions or can reflect a manic stock market phase. Named after Nobel Laureate for economics James Tobin. *Also called* Q ratio.

TOCOM *See* Tokyo Commodity Exchange.

toehold purchase Accumulation by an acquirer of less than 5 percent of the shares of a target company. Once 5 percent is acquired, the acquirer must file form 13-D with the SEC and other agencies to explain its intentions and notify the acquiree. A toehold allows the purchase to remain unknown.

Tokyo Commodity Exchange (TOCOM) Tokyo exchange for trading futures on gold, silver, platinum, palladium, rubber, cotton yarn, and woolen yarn. www.tocom.or.jp

Tokyo International Financial Futures Exchange Exchange that trades Euroyen futures and options, and futures on the one-year Euroyen, three-month Eurodollar, and U.S. dollar/Japanese yen currency. www.tiffe.or.jp

Tokyo Stock Exchange (TSE) Established after World War II, the largest stock exchange in Japan and one of the most active in the world. www.tse.or.jp/english/index.shtml

tolling agreement An agreement to put a specified amount of raw material per period through a particular processing facility. For example, an agreement to process a specified amount of alumina into aluminum at a particular aluminum plant.

toll-revenue bond A municipal bond that is repaid with revenues from tolls that are paid by users of the public project built with the bond revenue.

tom next Means "tomorrow next" or a transaction that settles on the next business day.

tombstone Advertisement in a newspaper or magazine listing the underwriters of a security issue that has recently been sold.

ton $100 million in bond trader's terms.

top Indicates the higher price one is willing to pay for a stock in an order.

top-down approach A method of security selection that starts with asset allocation and works systematically through sector and industry allocation to individual security selection.

top-down equity investment style Investment style that begins with an assessment of the overall economic environment and makes a general asset-allocation decision regarding various sectors of the financial markets and various industries. The bottom-up manager, in contrast, selects specific securities within the particular sectors.

top-heavy At a price level where supply is exceeding demand. *See also* resistance level.

topping out Denoting a market or a security that is at the end of a period of rising prices and can now be expected to stay on a plateau or even to decline.

Toronto Stock Exchange (TSE) Canada's largest stock exchange, trading approximately sixteen hundred company stocks. www.tse.com

total Complete amount of buy or sell interest, as opposed to having more behind it. *Opposite of* partial.

total capitalization The total long-term debt and all types of equity of a company, which constitutes its capital structure.

total cost The price paid for a security plus the broker's commission. In the case of a bond, any accrued interest that is owed to the seller is also part of total cost.

total debt-to-equity ratio A capitalization ratio comparing a company's current liabilities plus long-term debt to its shareholders' equity. The ratio reveals whether a company's debt is too onerous. Shareholders' equity should be three times that of its debt.

total return In performance measurement, the actual rate of return on an investment realized over some evaluation period. In fixed-income analysis, the potential return that considers all three sources of return: coupon interest, interest on coupon interest, and any capital gain or loss over some investment horizon.

total return for calendar year The profit or loss realized by an investment at the end of a specified calendar year, stated as the percentage gained or lost per dollar invested on January 1.

total revenue Total sales and other revenue for the period shown. Known as "turnover" in the United Kingdom.

total volume The total number of shares or contracts traded on national and regional exchanges in a stock, bond, commodity, future, or option on a certain day.

total-asset turnover The ratio of a company's net sales to its total assets.

total-dollar return The dollar return on a nondollar investment, which includes the sum of any dividend/interest income, capital gains or losses, and currency gains or losses on the investment.

total-market capitalization The total market value of all of a firm's outstanding securities, its stock, and its debt obligations.

tough on price Firm-price mentality at which one wishes to transact stock, often at a discount or premium that is not typically available.

tout To promote a security in order to attract buyers. Usually involves the use of questionable selling practices.

tracking error In performance evaluation, the standard deviation of the difference between the performance of the benchmark and the portfolio being evaluated.

tracking stock Shares of stock that track a company's assets or operations but do not give holders ownership in those assets or operations. Companies may issue a tracking stock when a unit in their company is competing against stand-alone companies in a specific sector, such as wireless communications, and the value of the stock in the whole company including that unit does not seem to reflect the market value assigned to the stock of competitors in the sector. Generally, existing shareholders in the company will be given shares of the tracking stock that are issued.

trade An oral (or electronic) transaction involving one party buying a security from another party. Once a trade is consummated, it is considered "done" or final. Settlement occurs one to three business days later.

trade acceptance Written demand that has been accepted by an industrial company to pay a given sum at a future date. *See also* banker's acceptance.

trade away Trade execution by a competitive broker/dealer when another firm was trying to do the trade.

trade balance Overall result of a country's exports.

trade credit Credit one firm grants to another firm for the purchase of goods or services.

trade date The date that the counterparties in an interest rate swap commit to the swap. Also, the day on which a security or a commodity future trade actually takes place. Trades generally settle (are paid for) one to five business days after a trade date. With stocks, settlement is generally three business days after the trade, but can vary depending on the transaction and method of delivery used.

trade debt Accounts payable at a company.

trade deficit or surplus The difference in the value of a nation's imports over exports (deficit) or exports over imports (surplus).

trade draft A draft addressed to a commercial enterprise.

trade flat For convertibles, trade without accrued interest. Preferred stock always "trades flat," as do bonds on which interest is in default or in doubt. In trading, to get in and out of a position at the same price, neither making a profit nor taking a loss.

trade house A firm that deals in actual commodities.

trade me out Work out of one's long position by selling stock. *Opposite of* buy them back.

trade on the wire Immediately give a bid or offer to a salesperson without checking the floor conditions on listed securities, dealer depth on Nasdaq, or customer interest. An aggressive trading posture.

trade on top of Trade at a narrow or no spread in basis points relative to some other bond yield, usually Treasury bonds.

trademark A distinctive name or symbol used to identify a product or company and build recognition. Trademarks are registered with the U.S. Patent and Trademark Office.

traders Individuals who take positions in securities and their derivatives with the objective of making profits. Traders can make markets by trading around other investors' order flow. When they do this, their objective is to earn the bid/ask spread. Traders can also take proprietary positions in which they seek to profit from the directional movement of prices or spread positions.

trades by appointment A stock that is very difficult to trade because of illiquidity.

trading Buying and selling securities.

trading ahead *See* running ahead.

trading authorization A document, also referred to a power of attorney, that a customer gives to a broker in order that the broker may buy and sell securities on behalf of the customer.

trading costs Costs of buying and selling marketable securities and of borrowing. Trading costs include commissions, the bid/ask spread, and market impact. *Also known as* transaction costs.

trading curb *See* fluctuation limit.

trading desk (dealing desk) Personnel at an international bank or brokerage firm who trade securities or commodities.

trading dividends Maximizing a firm's revenues by purchasing stock in other firms in order to collect the maximum amount of dividends of which 70 percent is tax-free.

trading halt When trading of a stock, bond, option, or futures contract is stopped by an exchange while news is being broadcast about the security. *See also* suspended trading.

trading index *See* TRIN.

trading paper CDs purchased by accounts that are likely to resell them. The term is commonly used in the Euromarket.

trading pattern Long-range direction of a security or commodity futures price, charted by drawing one line connecting the highest prices the security has reached and another line connecting the lowest prices at which the security has traded over the same period. *See also* technical analysis.

trading posts The positions on the floor of a stock exchange where the specialists stand and securities are traded.

trading price The price at which a security is currently selling.

trading profit The profit earned on short-term trades of securities held for less than one year, subject to tax at normal income tax rates.

trading range The difference between the high and low prices traded during a period of time; for commodities, the high/low price limit an exchange establishes for a specific commodity for any one day's trading.

trading symbol *See* ticker symbol.

trading unit The number of shares of a particular security that are considered the acceptable quantity for trading on the exchanges.

trading variation The increments to which securities prices are rounded up or rounded down.

trading volume The number of shares transacted every day. As there is a seller for every buyer, one can think of the trading volume as half of the number of shares transacted. That is, if someone sells one hundred shares to another (one hundred shares were sold and one hundred shares were bought, with a total of two hundred shares transacted), the volume is one hundred shares.

traditional IRA A tax-deferred individual retirement account that allows limited annual contributions for each income earner. Contributions are fully deductible for all individuals who are not active participants in employer-sponsored plans or for plan participants within certain income ranges.

traditional view (of dividend policy) An argument that investors prefer higher dividends to lower dividends because dividends are more certain than future capital gains.

tranche Pieces of a larger security that are traded separately. Tranches usually have different risk, reward, and/or maturity characteristics.

transaction The delivery of a security by a seller and its acceptance by the buyer.

transaction costs The time, effort, and money necessary, including such things as commission fees and the cost of physically moving the asset from seller to buyer. Transactions costs should also include the bid/ask spread as well as price-impact costs (for example, a large sell order could lower the price). *Also known as* trading costs. *See also* round-trip transaction costs; search costs.

transaction exposure Risk to a firm with known future cash flows in a foreign currency that arises from possible changes in the exchange rate. *See also* translation exposure.

transaction fee A charge an intermediary, such as a broker/dealer or a bank, assesses for assisting in the sale or purchase of a security.

transaction loan A loan extended by a bank for a specific purpose. By contrast, lines of credit and revolving credit agreements involve loans that can be used for various purposes.

transaction motive A desire to hold cash in order to conduct cash-based transactions.

transaction risk The risk of changes in the home currency value of a specific future foreign currency cash flow.

transaction tax Applies mainly to international equities. Levies on a deal that foreign governments sometimes charge.

transfer A change of ownership from one person or party to another.

transfer agent Individual or institution a company appoints to look after the transfer of securities.

transfer payment Payment from a government to its citizens, such as welfare and other government benefits.

transfer price The price at which one unit of a firm sells goods or services to another unit of the same firm.

transfer tax A small federal tax on the movement of ownership of all bonds, except obligations of the United States, foreign governments, states, municipalities, and all stocks.

transferable put right An option issued by a firm to its shareholders to sell the firm one share of its common stock at a fixed price within a stated period. The put right is "transferable" because it can be traded in the capital markets.

transition phase A stage of development when a company begins to mature and its earnings decelerate to the rate of growth of the economy as a whole.

translation exposure Risk of adverse effects on a firm's financial statements that may arise from changes in exchange rates. *See also* transaction exposure.

translation risk The risk of inconsistencies in the reported domestic currency accounting results of foreign operations due to changes in currency exchange-rate fluctuations.

transmittal letter A letter describing the contents and purpose of a transaction delivered with a security that is changing ownership.

travel and entertainment expense Funds spent on business travel and entertainment that qualify for a tax deduction of 50 percent of the amount claimed.

treasurer The corporate officer responsible for designing and implementing a firm's financing and investing activities. Sometimes a company's treasurer is also its chief financial officer.

treasurer's check A check issued by a bank to make a payment. Treasurer's checks outstanding are counted as part of a bank's reservable deposits and as part of the money supply.

Treasuries Treasury securities or obligations of the U.S. government.

Treasury U.S. Department of the Treasury, which issues all Treasury bonds, notes, and bills as well as overseeing agencies such as the IRS. At corporations, the department that oversees its financial operations, including the issuance of new shares.

Treasury bill (T-bill) Debt obligation of the U.S. Treasury that has maturity of one year or less. Maturities for T-bills are usually 91 days, 182 days, or 52 weeks.

Treasury bond Debt obligation of the U.S. Treasury that has maturity of ten years or more.

Treasury direct A system allowing an individual investor to make a non-competitive bid on U.S. Treasury securities and thus avoid broker/ dealer fees.

Treasury inflation-protected securities (TIPS) U.S. Treasury bonds and notes that are indexed to the inflation rate, as measured by the consumer price index. TIPS interest rates are adjusted every six months to reflect changes in inflation. Introduced in 1997, the securities help investors protect their portfolios from inflation.

Treasury investors growth receipt *See* TIGER.

Treasury note Debt obligation of the U.S. Treasury that has maturity of more than two years but less than ten years.

treasury stock Common stock that has been repurchased by the company and held in the company's treasury and that may be reissued.

treat me subject A conditional bid or offer in the equities market. A bid or offer that is not firm and is subject to confirmation between other parties and to market changes.

trend The general direction of the market.

trend line A technical chart line that depicts the past movement of a security and is used in an attempt to help predict future price movements.

trend ratio analysis The comparison of the successive values of each ratio for a single firm over a number of years. For instance, investors might compare a company's debt-to-equity ratios over time to assess whether leverage may become a problem at the firm.

T-rex fund A large venture capital fund with investments exceeding $1 billion. Such funds are known for imposing strong discipline on the firms they fund.

triangular arbitrage Making offsetting investments among three markets simultaneously to obtain an arbitrage profit. Usually refers to currency trades.

trickle down An economic theory that the support of businesses that allows them to flourish will eventually benefit middle- and lower-income people, in the form of increased economic activity and higher employment rates.

TRIN Short-term trading index that shows a minute-by-minute correlation of the ratio of advances to declines to the ratio of advancing volume to declining volume. Depicts whether changes in the relationship of advances and declines are taking place more quickly or more slowly than changes in the general volume movement of the market. A figure of less than one indicates a bull market, one is neutral, and greater than one indicates a bear market. *See also* A-D.

triple net lease A lease providing that the tenant pay for all maintenance expenses, plus utilities, taxes, and insurance. This results in lower risk for investors, who usually form a limited partnership.

triple tax-exempt Municipal bonds featuring federal, state, and local tax-free interest payments.

triple witching hour The four times a year that the S&P futures contract expires at the same time as the S&P 100 index option contract and option contracts on individual stocks. It is the last trading hour on the third Friday of March, June, September, and December, when stock options, futures on stock indexes, and options on these futures expire concurrently. Massive trades in index futures, options, and underlying stock by hedge strategists and arbitrageurs cause abnormal activity and volatility.

trough The low point between economic recession and recovery.

true interest cost For a security such as commercial paper that is sold on a discount basis, the coupon rate required to provide an identical return assuming a coupon-bearing instrument of like maturity that pays interest in arrears.

true lease A contract that qualifies as a valid lease agreement under the Internal Revenue Code.

trust A fiduciary relationship calling for a trustee to hold the title to assets for the benefit of the beneficiary. The person creating the trust, who may or may not also be the beneficiary, is called the grantor.

trust company An organization that acts as a fiduciary and administers trusts.

trust deed Agreement between trustee and borrower setting out terms of a bond.

Trust Indenture Act of 1939 A law that requires all corporate bonds and other debt securities to be issued subject to indenture agreements and comply with certain indenture provisions approved by the SEC.

trust receipt Receipt for goods that are to be held in trust for the lender.

trustee Agent of a bond issuer who handles the administrative aspects of a loan and ensures that the borrower complies with the terms of the bond indenture.

trustee in bankruptcy A trustee appointed by the bankruptcy court charged with supervising and administering the affairs of a bankrupt company or individual.

truth-in-lending act Legislation governing the granting of credit that requires lenders to disclose the true cost of loans and the actual interest rates and terms of the loans in a manner that is easily understood.

TSE *See* Tokyo Stock Exchange; Toronto Stock Exchange.

TSE 300 (Toronto Stock Exchange 300 Index) Canadian counterpart of the S&P 500 Composite Index, the most commonly followed stock index.

turkey A losing investment.

turn In the equities market, a reversal of a trend in prices.

turnaround Securities bought and sold for settlement on the same day. Also describes a firm that has been performing poorly, but changes its financial course and improves its performance.

turnaround time Time available or needed to effect a turnaround.

turnkey construction contract A type of construction contract under which the construction firm is obligated to complete a project according to prespecified criteria for a price that is fixed at the time the contract is signed.

turnover For mutual funds, a measure of trading activity during the previous year, expressed as a percentage of the average total assets of the fund. A turnover rate of 25 percent means that the value of trades represented one-fourth of the assets of the fund. The higher the turnover rate, the greater the transactions costs to fund holders. For corporate finance, the number of times a given asset, such as inventory, is replaced during the accounting period, usually a year. Also could refer to the ratio of annual sales to net worth. For markets, the volume of shares traded as a percent of total shares listed during a specified period, usually a day or a year.

turnover rate Measures trading activity during a particular period. Portfolios with high turnover rates incur higher transaction costs and are more likely to distribute capital gains, which are subject to taxes in any holdings that are not qualified retirement accounts, such as 401(k)s, IRAs, and Roth IRAs.

12b-1 fees The percent of a mutual fund's assets used to pay marketing and distribution expenses. The amount of the fee is stated in the fund's prospectus. The SEC recently proposed that 12b-1 fees in excess of 0.25 percent be classed as a load. A true no-load fund has neither a sales charge nor a 12b-1 fee.

12b-1 funds Mutual funds that do not charge an up-front or back-end commission, but instead take out up to 1.25 percent of average daily fund assets each year to cover the costs of selling and marketing shares, an arrangement allowed by the SEC's rule 12b-1.

twenty-bond index A benchmark indicator of the level of municipal bond yields. It consists of the yields on twenty general obligation municipal bonds with twenty-year maturities with an average rating equivalent to A-1.

twenty-day period The period during which the SEC inspects registration statement and preliminary prospectus prior to a new issue or secondary distribution.

20 percent cushion rule Guideline that revenues from facilities financed by municipal bonds should exceed the operating budget plus maintenance costs and debt service by at least 20 percent to allow for unforeseen expenses.

25 percent rule The guideline that bonded debt over 25 percent of a municipality's annual budget is excessive.

twisting Convincing a customer that trades are necessary in order to generate a commission. This is an unethical practice.

two-dollar broker Floor broker of the NYSE who executes orders for other brokers having more business at that time than they can handle with their own private floor brokers or who do not have their exchange member on the floor.

two-sided market A market in which both bid and ask prices, good for the standard unit of trading, are quoted. Likewise, when customers or market makers are lined up ready to buy and sell a stock.

two-tier bid Takeover bid in which the acquirer offers to pay more for the shares needed to gain control than for the remaining shares, or to pay the same price but at different times in the merger period. *Compare to* any-or-all bid.

two-tier tax system Taxation system that results in taxing the income going to shareholders twice.

type The classification of an option contract as either a put or a call.

UCC *See* Uniform Commercial Code.

UGMA *See* Uniform Gifts to Minors Act.

ultra vires activity Corporate action and operation that is not sanctioned by corporate charter, sometimes leading to shareholder lawsuits.

ultra-short-term bond fund A mutual fund that invests in bonds with very short maturity periods, usually one year or less.

umbrella personal liability policy A liability insurance policy that provides protection against damages not covered by standard liability policies, such as large jury awards in lawsuits.

umbrella policy Insurance for exports of an exporter whose issuer handles all administrative requirements.

unamortized premium on investment The unexpensed portion of the difference between the price paid for a security and its par value.

unbundling Separation of a multinational firm's transfers of funds into discrete flows for specific purposes. *See* bundling.

uncollected funds The amount of bank deposits in the form of checks that have not yet been paid by the banks on which the checks are drawn.

uncollectible account An account that cannot be collected by a company because the customer is not able to pay or is unwilling to pay.

uncovered call A short call–option position in which the writer does not own shares of underlying stock that would be needed to be delivered to the option holder in the case of the option's exercise. Uncovered calls are much riskier for the writer than a covered call because the writer of the uncovered call does not own the underlying stock. If the buyer of an uncovered call exercises the option to call, the writer would be forced to buy the asset at the current market price. *Also called* naked-option strategy.

uncovered option A call option in which the seller or a put option in which the buyer does not own the underlying security. *Also known as* naked option. *Opposite of* covered option.

uncovered put A short put–option position in which the writer does not have a corresponding short stock position or has not deposited, in a cash account, cash or cash equivalents equal to the exercise value of the put. The writer has pledged to buy the asset at a certain price if the buyer of the option chooses to exercise it. Uncovered put options limit the writer's risk to the value of the stock adjusted for premium received. *Also called* naked put. *Opposite of* covered put.

under the belt Long position in a stock.

underbanked When an originating investment banker cannot find enough firms to underwrite a new issue.

underbooked Describes limited interest by prospective buyers in a new issue of a security during the preoffering registration period.

undercapitalized A business that has insufficient capital to carry out its normal functions.

underfunded pension plan A pension plan with liabilities exceeding assets. Such a plan may not meet its obligations to pensioners. *Opposite of* overfunded pension plan.

underlying That which supports the instrument that parties agree to exchange in a derivative contract. In an option, the underlying is shares of stock.

underlying asset The security or property or loan agreement that an option gives the option holder the right to buy or to sell.

underlying debt Municipal bonds issued by government entities but under the control of larger government entities and for which the larger entity shares the credit responsibility.

underlying futures contract A futures contract that supports an option on that future, which is executed if the option is exercised .

underlying security For options, the security that is subject to purchase or sold upon exercise of an option contract. For example, a firm's stock is the underlying security for its options.

undermargined account A margin account that no longer meets minimum maintenance requirements, requiring a call for more cash from the investor.

underperform When a security is expected to, or does, appreciate at a slower rate than the overall market rate of performance.

underpricing Issuing securities at less than their market value.

undervalued A stock price perceived to be too low, as indicated by a particular valuation model. For instance, some might consider a particular company's stock price cheap if the company's price/earnings ratio is much lower than the industry average. Another method of valuation that would indicate a cheap stock might be if a company's shares are trading for a price below its asset value.

underwithholding When a taxpayer has withheld too little tax from salary and will therefore owe tax when filing a return.

underwrite To guarantee, as to guarantee the issuer of securities a specified price by entering into a purchase-and-sale agreement. To bring securities to market.

underwriter A firm, usually an investment bank, that buys an issue of securities from a company and resells it to investors. In general, a party that guarantees the proceeds to the firm from a security sale, thereby in effect taking ownership of the securities before they are sold.

underwriter's discount An amount that is received by the underwriter on an offering that reflects the difference on the shares' price between the offering price and that received by the company.

underwriting Acting as the underwriter in the issue of new securities for a firm.

underwriting agreement The contract between a corporation issuing new publicly offered securities and the managing underwriter as agent for the underwriting group. *See also* agreement among underwriters.

underwriting commission The fee investment bankers charge for underwriting a security issue. The portion of the gross underwriting spread that compensates the securities firms that underwrite a public offering for their services.

underwriting income For an insurance company, the difference between the premium earned and the cost of settling claims.

underwriting spread The income that is generated by the underwriting syndicate and the selling group, which is essentially the difference between the amount paid to the issuer of securities in a primary distribution and the public offering price.

underwriting syndicate A group of investment banks that work together to sell new security offerings to investors. The underwriting syndicate is led by a lead underwriter. *Also known as* purchase group; selling syndicate.

underwritten offering An offer of stocks or bonds in which the investment bank (underwriter) guarantees a minimum price to the company.

under-65 trust A trust established on behalf of a person under the age of sixty-five that allows the assets in the trust to be ignored for Medicaid eligibility; income is paid to the individual during his or her life. Usually, a family member administers the trust's investments. When the person dies, the state is reimbursed for Medicaid benefits paid, which can be substantially less than the cost of care through a private plan, and the remainder goes to family members or other beneficiaries. *Compare to* Miller trust; pooled trust.

undigested securities Newly issued securities that are not purchased because of lack of demand during the initial public offering.

undiversifiable risk *See* market risk.

unearned income (revenue) Income received in advance of the time at which it is earned, such as prepaid rent.

unearned interest Interest that has been received on a loan, but that cannot be treated as a part of earnings yet because the principal of the loan has not been outstanding long enough.

unemployment rate The percentage of a national population classified as unemployed as compared to the total labor force.

unencumbered Property that is not subject to any claims by creditors. For example, securities bought with cash instead of on margin and homes with mortgages paid off.

unfunded debt Debt maturing within one year (short-term debt). *Compare to* funded debt.

unfunded pension plan Provides for the employer to pay out amounts to retirees or beneficiaries as and when they are needed. There is no money put aside on a regular basis. Instead, it is taken out of current income.

unified tax credit A federal tax credit that reduces tax liability, dollar for dollar, on lifetime gifts and asset transfers at death.

Uniform Commercial Code (UCC) Collection of laws dealing with commercial business.

Uniform Gifts to Minors Act (UGMA) Legislation that provides a tax-effective manner of transferring property to minors without the complications of trusts or guardianship restrictions.

uniform practice code Standards of the NASD prescribing procedures for handling Nasdaq securities transactions, such as delivery, settlement date, and ex-dividend date.

uniform securities agent state law examination A test required in some states for registered representatives who are employees of member firms of the NASD or over-the-counter brokers.

Uniform Transfers to Minors Act (UTMA) A law similar to the Uniform Gifts to Minors Act that extends the definition of gifts to include real estate, paintings, royalties, and patents.

uninsured motorist insurance Insurance that covers the policyholder and family if they are injured by a hit-and-run or uninsured motorist, assuming the other driver is at fault.

unique diversification benefit Reduction in the likelihood of financial distress for a conglomerate firm that comes with its diversified investments.

unique risk Specific company risk that can be eliminated through diversification. *See also* unsystematic risk.

unissued stock Shares authorized in a corporation's charter but not issued.

unit More than one class of securities traded together; for instance, one common share and three subscription warrants.

unit benefit formula Method used to determine a participant's benefits in a defined benefit plan. Involves multiplying years of service by the percentage of salary.

unit investment trust Money invested in a portfolio whose composition is fixed for the life of the fund. Shares in a unit trust are called redeemable trust certificates and can be sold at a premium to net asset value.

unit trust In the United Kingdom and other foreign markets, an open-end mutual fund.

United States government securities Debt issues of the U.S. government, as distinguished from government-sponsored agency issues. *Also known as* Treasuries.

universal life A whole life insurance product whose investment component pays a competitive interest rate.

universe of securities A group of stocks having a common feature, such as similar market capitalization or product line.

unleveraged cost of equity The discount rate appropriate for an investment that is financed with 100 percent equity.

unleveraged program The use of borrowed funds to finance less than 50 percent of a purchase of assets. In a leveraged program borrowed funds are used to finance more than 50 percent.

unleveraged required return The required return on an investment when the investment is financed entirely by equity (i.e., no debt).

unlimited liability Full liability for the debt and other obligations of a legal entity. The general partners of a partnership have unlimited liability.

unlimited marital deduction An IRS provision that allows an individual to transfer an unlimited amount of assets to a spouse, during life or at death, without incurring federal estate or gift tax.

unlimited tax bond A municipal bond secured by the pledge to levy taxes until full repayment at an unlimited rate.

unlisted security A security traded on the Nasdaq or other over-the-counter market that is not listed on an organized exchange.

unloading Selling securities or commodities whose prices are dropping to minimize loss.

unmargined account A cash account held at a brokerage firm where all trades are paid for in full.

unmatched book If the average maturity of a bank's liabilities is shorter than that of its assets, it is said to be running an unmatched book. The term is commonly used with the Euromarket. Also refers to entering into derivatives contracts and not hedging by making trades in the opposite direction to another financial intermediary. In this case, the firm with an unmatched book usually hedges its net market risk with futures and options. *Also known as* short book.

unpaid dividend A dividend declared by the directors of a corporation that has not yet been paid.

unqualified opinion An independent auditor's opinion that a company's financial statements comply with accepted accounting procedures. *Opposite of* qualified opinion.

unrealized capital gain or loss A change in the value of a security that is not "real" because the security has not been sold. Once a security is sold by the portfolio manager, the capital gains or losses are "realized" by the fund, and any payment to the shareholder is taxable during the tax year in which the security is sold.

unseasoned issue Issue of a security for which there is no existing market. *Opposite of* seasoned issue.

unsecured debt Debt that is not backed by collateral. If payments are not made, the creditor may sue for assets or payment, but cannot take the debtor's assets. *Compare to* secured debt.

unsterilized intervention Foreign exchange market intervention in which the monetary authorities have not insulated their domestic money supplies from the foreign exchange transactions.

unsystematic risk The risk that is unique to a company such as a strike, the outcome of unfavorable litigation, or a natural catastrophe, which can be eliminated through diversification. *Also called* diversifiable risk; residual risk. *Compare to* market risk; systematic risk.

unwind a trade Reverse a securities transaction through an offsetting transaction in the market.

upgrading Raising the quality rating of a security because of new optimism about the prospects of a firm due to tangible or intangible factors. This can increase investor confidence and push up the price of the security.

upset price The minimum price at which a seller of property will accept a bid at an auction.

upside potential The amount by which analysts or investors expect the price of a security might increase.

upstairs market A network of trading desks for the major brokerage firms and institutional investors, which communicate with each other by means of electronic display systems and telephones to facilitate block trades and program trades.

upstairs order Off-floor order for listed equity securities.

upswing An upward turn in a security's price after a period of falling prices.

uptick When a security trades at a price that is higher than its previous price. *Also known as* plus tick. *Opposite of* downtick; minus tick.

uptick rule SEC rule that selling short is allowed only on an uptick.

uptick trade A transaction that takes place at a higher price than the preceding transaction involving the same security. *See also* tick-test rules.

useful life The expected period of time during which a depreciating asset will be productive.

U.S. Treasury bill *See* Treasury bill.

U.S. Treasury bond *See* Treasury bond.

U.S. Treasury note *See* Treasury note.

usury laws Laws limiting the amount of interest that can be charged on loans.

utility A power company that owns or operates facilities used for the generation, transmission, or distribution of electric energy, which is regulated at state and federal levels. Also refers to the benefits derived by a user of a product or service.

utility revenue bond A municipal bond issued to finance the construction of public utility services. These bonds are repaid from the operating revenues the project produces after the utility is finished.

UTMA *See* Uniform Transfers to Minors Act.

V

V formation A technical chart pattern that follows a letter V form, indicating that the security price has bottomed out and is now in a bullish trend.

valuation Determination of the value of a company's stock based on its earnings, both current and future, and the market value of its assets.

valuation opportunity cost The potential increase in firm value associated with investments that are forgone due to capital rationing.

valuation reserve An allowance to provide for changes in the value of a company's assets, such as depreciation.

value added The risk-adjusted return generated by an investment strategy: the return of the investment strategy minus the return of the benchmark. The value an active manager adds.

value additivity principle When the value of a whole group of assets exactly equals the sum of the values of the individual assets that make up the group of assets. Or the principle that the net present value of a set of independent projects is just the sum of the net present values of the individual projects.

value broker A discount broker whose rates are a percentage of the dollar value of each transaction.

value dating When value or credit is given for funds transferred between banks.

value investing An investing style that focuses on the fundamental worth of a company measured by its book value or dividend yield. *Compare to* growth investing.

Value Line investment survey A proprietary investment service that provides research on stocks and ranks them for timeliness and safety. www.valueline.com

value manager A manager who seeks to buy stocks that are at a discount to their "fair value" and to sell them at or in excess of that value. Often a value stock is one with a low price-to-book value ratio. *Opposite of* growth manager.

value maximization Increases in owners' wealth achieved by maximizing the value of a firm's common stock.

value stock Stock that trades at a low price compared to its earnings, book value, or dividend yield.

value-added tax Method of indirect taxation that levies a tax at each stage of production on the value added at that specific stage.

value-stock fund A mutual fund that buys stocks of companies whose shares are undervalued relative to the overall market or the company's assets. A value-stock company often pays regular dividend income to shareholders and sells at relatively low prices in relation to its earnings or book value.

vanilla issue A security issue that has no unusual features.

variable annuity Investment contract whose issuer pays a periodic amount linked to the investment performance of an underlying portfolio.

variable interest rate An interest rate on a loan that varies based upon prevailing interest rates. *Also known as* adjustable rate.

variable life insurance policy A life insurance policy that provides a death benefit dependent on the insured's portfolio market value at the time of death. Typically the company invests premiums in common stocks, so variable life policies are referred to as equity-linked policies.

variable-price security A stock, bond, or other security that sells at a fluctuating market-determined price.

variable-rate CD Short-term certificate of deposit that pays interest periodically on roll dates. On each roll date, the coupon on the CD is adjusted to reflect current market rates.

variable-rate demand note A note that is payable on demand and bears interest tied to a money market rate.

variable-rate loan Loan made at an interest rate that fluctuates depending on a base interest rate, such as the prime rate or London Interbank Offered Rate.

variable-rated demand bond Floating-rate bond that periodically can be sold back to the issuer.

variance-minimization approach to tracking An approach to indexing that uses historical data to estimate the variance of the tracking error.

variation margin An additional required deposit to bring an investor's equity account up to the initial margin level when the balance falls below the maintenance margin requirement.

vega The change in the value of an option for a 1 percent increase in volatility. Vega is positive for both calls and puts.

Velda Sue *See* Venture Enhancement and Loan Development Administration for Smaller Undercapitalized Enterprises.

velocity The number of times a dollar is spent, or turns over, in a specific period of time. Velocity affects the amount of economic activity generated by a given money supply.

vendor Seller or supplier.

venture capital An investment in a start-up business that is perceived to have excellent growth prospects but does not have access to capital markets. Type of financing sought by early-stage companies seeking to grow rapidly.

venture capital limited partnership A partnership between a start-up company and a brokerage firm or entrepreneurial company that provides capital for the new business often in return for stock in the company and a share of the profits.

Venture Enhancement and Loan Development Administration for Smaller Undercapitalized Enterprises (Velda Sue) A federal agency that buys and pools small business loans made by banks, and then issues securities that are bought by large institutional investors.

Venture Exchange The Canadian Venture Exchange, previously the Vancouver Stock Exchange, an exchange for securities in extremely risky small companies. www.cdnx.com

vertical acquisition *See* vertical merger.

vertical analysis Dividing each expense item in the income statement of a given year by net sales to identify expense items that rise more quickly or more slowly than a change in sales.

vertical merger When one firm acquires or merges with another firm that is in the same industry but at another stage in the production cycle. For example, the firm being acquired or merged serves as a supplier to the firm making the acquisition. *Also known as* vertical acquisition.

vertical spread Simultaneous purchase and sale of two options that differ only in their exercise price. *See also* horizontal spread.

vertical-line charting A form of technical charting that shows the high, low, and closing prices of a stock or a market on each day on one vertical line with the closing price indicated by a short horizontal mark.

vest When a holding in a derivative becomes applicable or exercisable. A term mainly used in the context of employee stock ownership or option programs. Employees might be given equity in a firm but they must stay with the firm for a number of years before they are entitled to the full equity. This vesting provision offers incentive for employee performance and retention.

vesting Nonforfeitable ownership or partial ownership by an employee of the retirement account balances or benefits contributed on the employee's behalf by an employer. The Tax Reform Act of 1986 established minimum vesting rights for employees based on their years of service—full vesting in five years or 20 percent vesting per year starting by the end of the third year.

Veterans Administration (VA) mortgage A home mortgage loan granted by a lending institution to U.S. veterans and guaranteed by the Veterans Administration.

Vienna Stock Exchange (VSX) One of the world's oldest exchanges, which accounts for approximately 50 percent of Austrian stock transactions; the balance are traded over-the-counter.

visible supply New municipal bond issues scheduled to come to market within the next thirty days.

volatility A measure of risk based on the standard deviation of an asset's return. Volatility is a variable that appears in option-pricing formulas, where it denotes the volatility of the underlying asset's return from the present to the expiration of the option.

volume The number of shares of a security that change hands daily between a buyer and a seller.

volume discount A reduction in price based on the purchase of a large quantity.

voluntary accumulation plan Arrangement allowing shareholders of a mutual fund to purchase shares over a period of time on a regular basis, and in so doing take advantage of dollar-cost averaging.

voluntary bankruptcy The legal proceeding that follows a petition of bankruptcy.

voluntary liquidation Liquidation proceedings that are supported by a company's shareholders.

voluntary plan A pension plan supported partially by the employee through pension contributions deducted from each paycheck.

voting certificate Certificate, which represents all the rights of common stock except voting rights, issued by a voting trust to stockholders in exchange for their common stock.

voting right The right to vote on matters that are put to a vote of security holders. For example, the right to vote for directors.

voting stock The shares in a corporation that entitle the shareholder to vote.

voting trust certificate A trust in which control of a corporation is given to a few individuals, usually to support reorganization of a corporation without interference.

wage assignment A loan agreement provision allowing a lender to deduct payments from an employee's wages in case of default on a debt.

wage-earner's bankruptcy *See* chapter 13 bankruptcy.

wage-push inflation Inflation caused by skyrocketing wages.

waiting period Time during which the SEC may study a firm's registration statement, which will offer securities to the public. During this time, the firm may distribute a preliminary prospectus to potential investors.

waiver of premium A provision in an insurance policy that allows payment of insurance premiums to be permanently or temporarily stopped in the event the policyholder becomes incapacitated.

Wall Street Generic term for securities industry firms that buy, sell, and underwrite securities and provide investment advice to institutional and individual investors.

Wall Street analyst A research professional who studies companies' financial statements and operations with an eye for recommending their securities to investors. *Also known as* sell-side analyst (referring to so-called sell-side brokerage firms, which use research to help generate commissions from clients).

wallflower Stock that has fallen out of favor with investors; stock that tends to have a low price/earnings ratio.

wallpaper A security with no monetary value.

wanted for cash A statement displayed on market tickers indicating that a bidder will pay cash for same-day settlement of a block of a specified security.

war babies Slang for the stocks and bonds of corporations in the defense industry.

war chest Cash kept on hand at a company for use in mounting a takeover or for defense against a takeover bid.

warehouse receipt Evidence that a firm owns goods stored in a warehouse.

warehousing The interim holding period from the time of the closing of a loan to its subsequent marketing to capital-market investors.

warrant A security entitling the holder to buy a proportionate amount of stock at some specified future date at a specified price, usually higher than the current market price. Warrants are traded as securities whose price reflects the value of the underlying stock. Corporations often bundle warrants with another class of security to enhance the appeal of the other security. Warrants are similar to call options, but with much longer time spans, sometimes years. Warrants are offered by corporations, while exchange-traded call options are not. *Also known as* right. *Compare to* ex-warrant.

warranty A guarantee by a seller to a buyer that if a product requires repair or remedy of a problem within a certain period after its purchase, the seller will repair the problem at no cost to the buyer. Can apply to a company being acquired.

Warsaw Stock Exchange The major securities market of Poland. www.gpw.com.pl/xml/indexe.xml

wash When an investor's gains equal his or her losses.

wash sale Purchase and sale of a security either simultaneously or within a short period of time, often to recognize a tax loss without altering one's position. *Also known as* tax selling.

wasting asset An asset that has a limited life and thus decreases in value over time. Also applies to consumed assets, such as oil or gas, and termed "depletion."

watch list A list of securities at a brokerage firm selected for special surveillance by the firm, an exchange, or regulatory organization; firms on the list are often takeover targets, companies planning to issue new securities, or stocks showing unusual activity. Companies on a watch list may appear there because the brokerage firm's investment banking department has knowledge of a pending deal or offering. Stocks on watch lists cannot be traded by the firm's professionals or recommended to investors as this could involve the use of nonpublic information.

watered stock A stock representing ownership in a corporation that is worth less than the actual invested capital, resulting in problems of low liquidity, inadequate return on investment, and low market value.

weak dollar A depreciated dollar with respect to other currencies, meaning that more dollars are needed to buy a unit of foreign currency. *Opposite of* strong dollar.

weak market A market with few buyers and many sellers and a declining trend in prices.

weak-form efficiency A theory that the price of a security reflects the past price and trading history. The theory implies that security prices follow a random walk, that is, price changes are unpredictable. *Compare to* semistrong-form efficiency; strong-form efficiency.

WEBS *See* World Equity Benchmark Series.

weekend effect The historical pattern of lower average returns from Friday to Monday in the stock market compared to other three-day periods.

weighted-average cost of capital Expected return on a portfolio of all a firm's securities. Used as a hurdle rate that must be attained to make a capital investment. Often the weighted average of the cost of equity and the cost of debt. The weights are determined by the relative proportions of equity and debt in a firm's capital structure.

weighted-average coupon The weighted average of the gross interest rates of mortgages underlying a pool as of the pool issue date; the balance of each mortgage is used as the weighting factor.

weighted-average life *See* average life.

weighted-average maturity The weighted-average maturity of a mortgage-backed security is the weighted average of the remaining terms to maturity of the mortgages underlying the collateral pool at the date issue, using as the weighting factor the balance of each of the mortgages as of the issue date.

weighted-average portfolio yield The weighted average of the yield of all the bonds in a portfolio.

weighted-average remaining maturity The average remaining term to maturity of the mortgages underlying a mortgage-backed security.

well-diversified portfolio A portfolio that includes a variety of securities so that the weight of any security is small. The risk of a well-diversified portfolio closely approximates the systematic risk of the overall market.

when distributed A term noting that a security is trading based on its pending issuance or the pending attachment of another security to it. *Also known as* when issued.

when issued (WI) Refers to a transaction made conditionally, because a security, although authorized, has not yet been issued. Treasury securities, new issues of stocks and bonds, stocks that have split, and in-merger situations after the time the proxy has become effective but before completion are all traded on a when-issued basis.

whipsawed Buying stocks just before prices fall and selling stocks just before prices rise in a volatile market, often as the result of misleading signals.

whisper number Unofficial earnings estimate of a company given to clients by a security analyst if there is more optimism or pessimism about earnings than shown in the published number.

whisper stock A stock rumored to be the target of a takeover bid, drawing speculators who hope to make a profit after the takeover is completed.

whistle-blower A person who has knowledge of fraudulent activities inside a firm or government agency and who is protected from the employer's retribution by federal law.

white knight A friendly potential acquirer sought out by a target firm that is threatened by a less-welcomed suitor.

white squire White knight who buys less than a majority interest.

White's rating A rating of municipal securities that uses market factors rather than credit considerations to find appropriate yields. Short for White's Tax-Exempt Bond Rating Service.

whitemail Sale of a large amount of stock by a company that is the target of a takeover bid to a friendly party at below-market prices, so that the raider is forced to buy more highly priced shares to accomplish the takeover.

white-shoe firm Old-line brokerage firm that disdains practices such as advising companies on hostile takeovers.

whole life insurance A contract with both insurance and investment components: (1) It pays off a stated amount upon the death of the insured; and (2) it accumulates a cash value that the policyholder can redeem or borrow against.

whole loan A term that distinguishes an investment representing an original mortgage loan from a loan representing a participation with one or more lenders.

wholesale mortgage banking The purchase of loans originated by others, for the acquisition of the servicing fees.

wholesaler An underwriter or a broker/dealer who trades with other broker/dealers, rather than with the retail investor.

wholly owned subsidiary A subsidiary whose parent company owns 100 percent of its common stock.

whoops A nickname for the Washington Public Power Supply System, which in the 1970s raised billions of dollars through municipal bond offerings. The projects never materialized and the bonds defaulted on the payments to bondholders.

WI *See* when issued.

wide opening Abnormally wide spread between the bid and asked prices of a security at the opening of a trading session.

widow-and-orphan stock A stock paying high dividends with low risk, and a noncyclical business—one that is not volatile and not susceptible to swings in the economy.

Wiener Börse (Austrian Stock Exchange) Established in 1771, the major securities market of Austria. www.wienerboerse.at/cms/2/

wild-card option The right of the seller of a Treasury bond futures contract to give notice of intent to deliver at or before 8:00 P.M. central time after the closing of the Chicago Board of Trade (3:15 P.M. Chicago time) when the futures settlement price has been fixed.

Williams Act Federal legislation enacted in 1968 and now constituting rules 13d and 14d of the Securities Exchange Act of 1934 that imposes requirements on companies that make public tender offers.

Wilshire indexes Widely followed performance-measurement indexes measuring performance of all U.S.-headquartered equity securities with readily available price data, created by Wilshire Associates Inc. The Wilshire 5000 Equity Index includes all stocks traded on the NYSE and AMEX, as well as many Nasdaq and other over-the-counter stocks. www.wilshire.com

windfall profit A sudden unexpected profit in an investment.

window A brokerage firm's cashier department, where delivery of securities and settlement of transactions take place.

window dressing Trading activity near the end of a quarter or fiscal year designed to improve the appearance of a portfolio to be presented to clients or shareholders. For example, a portfolio manager may sell losing positions so as to display only positions that have gained in value.

Winnipeg Commodity Exchange Canada's only agricultural futures and options exchange, located in Manitoba. www.telemium.ca

winner's curse Problem faced by uninformed bidders. For example, in an initial public offering uninformed participants are likely to receive larger allotments of issues that informed participants know are overpriced.

wire house A firm operating a private wire to its own branch offices or to other firms, commission houses, or brokerage houses.

wire room A department within a brokerage firm that receives customers' orders and transmits the orders to the exchange floor or the firm's trading department.

with dividend Purchase of shares that entitle the buyer to the forthcoming dividend. *Also known as* cum dividend. *Opposite of* ex-dividend.

with rights Shares sold accompanied by entitlement to the buyer to buy additional shares in the company's rights issue.

withdrawal plan Agreement that a mutual fund will disburse automatic periodic redemptions to the investor.

withholding Used in the context of securities, the illegal practice of a public offering participant keeping some shares in a private account or with a family member, employee, or dealer to profit from the higher market price of a hot issue. Used in the context of taxes, the withholding by an employer of a certain amount of an employee's income in order to cover the employee's tax liability.

withholding tax A tax levied by a host country when income is repatriated to another country.

without recourse Giving the lender no right to seek payment or seize assets in the event of nonpayment from anyone other than the party specified in the debt contract. *Also known as* nonrecourse.

working Attempting to complete the remaining part of a trade by finding either buyers or sellers for the rest.

working away Transacting with a competing broker/dealer.

working capital Defined as the difference between current assets and current liabilities, excluding short-term debt. Current assets may or may not include cash and cash equivalents, depending on the company.

working control Control of a corporation by a shareholder or share-holders having less than 51 percent voting interest because of the wide dispersion of share ownership.

working order Standing order in the marketplace through which a broker bids or offers to fill the order in a series of lots at opportune times in hopes of obtaining the best price.

working-capital management The deployment of current assets and current liabilities so as to maximize short-term liquidity and reduce the need for borrowing.

working-capital ratio Working capital at a company expressed as a percentage of its sales.

workout Informal repayment or loan forgiveness arrangement between a borrower and creditors.

workout market Market indicating prices at which it is believed a security can be bought or sold within a reasonable length of time.

workout period Realignment of a temporarily misaligned yield relationship that sometimes occurs in fixed-income markets.

World Bank A multilateral development finance agency created at the 1944 Bretton Woods Conference in New Hampshire. The bank makes loans to developing countries for specific projects. Borrower countries must meet certain conditions, often involving economic reform, in order to qualify for bank loans. *Also known as* International Bank for Reconstruction and Development.

World Equity Benchmark Series (WEBS) The World Equity Benchmark Series are similar to SPDRs. WEBS trade on the AMEX and track the Morgan Stanley Capital International (MSCI) country indexes.

world investable wealth The part of world wealth that is traded and is therefore accessible to investors.

World Trade Organization (WTO) A multilateral agency that administers world trade agreements, fosters trade relations among nations, and solves trade disputes among member countries. www.wto.org

wrap account An investment consulting relationship for management of a client's funds by one or more money managers that bills all fees and commissions in one comprehensive fee charged quarterly.

wraparound annuity An annuity that gives the holder the ability to choose the assets the annuity is invested in. Wraparound indicates tax-deferred status.

wraparound mortgage A second mortgage that leaves the original mortgage in force. The wraparound mortgage is held by the lending institution as security for the total mortgage debt. The borrower makes payments on both loans to the wraparound lender, which in turn makes payments on the original senior mortgage.

wrinkle A feature of a new product or security intended to entice a buyer.

write Sell an option on a derivative.

write down Reducing the book value of an asset if it is overstated compared to current market values. Such a write-down reduces shareholder equity or net worth.

write off Charging an asset amount to expense or loss, such as through the use of depreciation and amortization of assets.

writer Seller of an option. The individual, bank, or company that writes the option has the obligation to sell the asset, if a call, or buy the asset, if a put, if the option buyer exercises it.

writing cash-secured puts An option strategy to avoid using a margin account. Instead of depositing funds into a margin account with a broker, a put writer can deposit a cash balance equal to the option exercise price, and can avoid additional margin calls.

writing puts to acquire stock Selling a put option at an exercise price that would represent a good investment by an option writer who believes a stock's value will fall. If the stock price unexpectedly goes up, the option will not be exercised and the writer's profit is the amount of the premium received. If the stock loses value, as expected, the option will be exercised, and the writer has the stock at what he had earlier decided was a good price, and has the premium income in addition.

written-down value The book value of an asset after allowing for depreciation and amortization.

WTO *See* World Trade Organization.

W-type bottom A double-bottom pattern in a price history that looks like the letter W. *See also* technical analysis.

X or XD Symbol indicating that stock is trading ex-dividend, with no dividend.

XR Symbol indicating that a stock is trading ex-rights, with no rights attached.

XW Symbol indicating that a stock is trading ex-warrants, with no warrants attached.

Y

Yankee bond Foreign bond denominated in U.S. dollars and issued in the United States by foreign banks and corporations. These bonds are usually registered with the SEC. *See also* bulldog bond; samurai bond.

Yankee CD A certificate of deposit issued in the domestic market, typically New York, by a branch of a foreign bank.

Yankee market The foreign market in the United States.

yard Slang for one billion currency units. Used particularly in currency trading, e.g., for Japanese yen since one billion yen equals approximately U.S.$10 million. It is clearer to say "I'm a buyer of a yard of yen" than to say "I'm a buyer of a billion yen," which could be misheard as "I'm a buyer of a million yen."

year-end dividend A special dividend declared at the end of a fiscal year that usually represents distribution of higher-than-expected company profits.

year-to-date (YTD) The period beginning at the start of the calendar year up to the current date.

yellow sheets Sheets published by Pink Sheets, formerly the National Quotation Bureau, that detail bid and ask prices, plus those firms that are making a market in over-the-counter corporate bonds. www. pinksheets.com

yen bond Any bond denominated in Japanese yen.

yield The percentage rate of return paid on a stock in the form of dividends, or the effective rate of interest paid on a bond or note.

yield advantage The advantage gained by purchasing convertible securities instead of common stock, which equals the difference between the rates of return of the convertible security and the common shares.

yield burning A municipal bond financing method which can be illegal. Underwriters in advance refundings add large markups on U.S. Treasury bonds bought and held in escrow to compensate investors while waiting for repayment of old bonds after issuance of the new bonds. Since bond prices and yields move in opposite directions, when the bonds are marked up, they "burn down" the yield, which violates federal tax rules and diminishes tax revenues.

yield curb Applies mainly to convertible securities. Difference in current yield between the convertible and the underlying common.

yield curve The graphic depiction of the relationship between the yield on bonds of the same credit quality but different maturities. This usually refers to Treasury securities. Campbell Harvey, an economist at Duke University, finds that when the yield curve inverts, that is when yields on long-term issues are below those of shorter maturities, a recession follows. The yield curve indicator has correctly forecast the last six recessions.

yield equivalence The interest rate at which a tax-exempt bond and a taxable security of similar quality give the investor the same rate of return.

yield spread The difference in yield between different security issues with identical maturities, usually securities of different credit quality.

yield to average life A yield calculation in which bonds are retired routinely during the life of the issue. Since the issuer buys its own bonds on the open market because of sinking-fund requirements, if the bonds are trading below par this action provides automatic price support for these bonds and they will usually trade on a basis that reflects the yield to average life.

yield to call The percentage rate of a bond or note if the investor buys and holds the security until the call date. This yield is valid only if the security is called prior to maturity. Generally, bonds are callable over several years and normally are called at a slight premium. The calculation of yield to call is based on a bond's coupon rate, length of time to call, and market price.

yield to maturity The percentage rate of return paid on a bond, note, or other fixed-income security if the investor buys and holds it to its maturity date. The calculation is based on the bond's coupon rate, length of time to maturity, and market price. It assumes that coupon interest paid over the life of the bond will be reinvested at the same rate.

yield to worst The bond yield computed by using the lower of either the yield to maturity or the yield to call on every possible call date.

yield-curve strategies Investments that position a portfolio to capitalize on expected changes in the shape of the Treasury yield curve.

yield-spread strategies Investments that position a portfolio to capitalize on expected changes in yield spreads between sectors of the bond market.

yo-yo stock A highly volatile stock that moves up and down like a yo-yo.

YTD Year-to-date.

Z

Z bond A bond on which interest accrues but is not currently paid to the investor; it is added to the principal balance of the Z bond and becomes payable upon satisfaction of all prior bond classes.

Z score Statistical measure that quantifies the distance (measured in standard deviations) a data point is from the mean of a data set. Separately, Z score is the output from a credit-strength test that gauges the likelihood of bankruptcy, developed by Edward Altman, a professor at New York University.

zaibatsu Large family-owned conglomerates that controlled much of the economy of Japan prior to World War II.

zero-balance account A checking account in which zero balance is maintained by transfers of funds from a master account in an amount only large enough to cover checks presented.

zero-base budgeting Budgeting method that disregards the previous year's budget in setting a new budget, since circumstances may have changed. Each and every expense must be justified in this system.

zero-beta portfolio A portfolio constructed to have zero systematic risk, similar to the risk-free asset, that is, having a beta of zero.

zero-bracket amount The standard deduction portion of income which is not taxed for taxpayers choosing not to itemize deductions.

zero-coupon bond A bond in which no periodic coupon is paid over its life. Instead, both the principal and the interest are paid in a lump sum at the maturity date. However, for tax purposes, the value of the bond increases as it approaches maturity and this is taxable as income even though it is not actually received until the bond matures. For this reason, most individuals hold zero-coupon bonds in tax-deferred accounts, such as IRAs. *Also called* pure-discount bond; single-payment bond.

zero-coupon convertible security A zero-coupon bond convertible into the common stock of the issuing company after the stock reaches a certain price. Also refers to zero-coupon bonds, which are convertible into an interest-bearing bond at a certain time before maturity.

zero-minus tick Sale that takes place at the same price as the previous sale, but at a lower price than the last different price. For example, if the last three prices were 10, 9, and 9, the last price is zero-minus tick. *Opposite of* zero-plus tick.

zero-plus tick Transaction at the same price as the preceding trade, but higher than the preceding trade at a different price. For example, if the last three prices were 10, 11, and 11, the last price is a zero-plus tick. *Opposite of* zero-minus tick.

zero-prepayment assumption The assumption of payment of scheduled principal and interest with no prepayments of principal.

zero-sum game A type of transaction wherein one player can gain only at the expense of another player.

zombie Company that continues operations while it awaits merger or closure, even though it is insolvent and bankrupt.

APPENDIX

Major Stock Exchanges Around the World

American Stock Exchange (AMEX), United States, www.amex.com

Amman Stock Exchange, Jordan, www.ammanstockex.com

Arizona Stock Exchange, United States, www.azx.com

Athens Stock Exchange, Greece, Greek language only, www.ase.gr

Australia Stock Exchange (ASX), Australia, www.asx.com.au/asx/homepage/index.jsp

Bombay Stock Exchange (Mumbai Stock Exchange), India, www.bseindia.com

Budapest Stock Exchange, Hungary, www.bse.hu

Buenos Aires Stock Exchange (Bolsa de Comercio de Buenos Aires), Argentina, Spanish language only, www.bcba.sba.com.ar

Canadian Venture Exchange, including the Alberta Stock Exchange, Montreal Stock Exchange, Toronto Stock Exchange, and Vancouver Stock Exchange, Canada, www.cdnx.com

Caracas Stock Exchange, Venezuela, www.caracasstock.com/bvc-eng/index.jsp

Chicago Mercantile Exchange (CME), United States, www.cme.com

Chicago Stock Exchange (CHX), United States, chicagostockex.com

Cincinnati Stock Exchange (CSE), United States, www.cincinnatistock.com

Colombo Stock Exchange, Sri Lanka, www.cse.lk

Deutsche Börse Group, including the Frankfurt Stock Exchange, Germany, deutsche-boerse.com/INTERNET/EXCHANGE/index_e.htm

Easdaq, European Union, www.easdaq.com

Euronext, Europe, www.euronext.com

Helsinki Exchanges (HEX), Finland, www.hse.fi

Hong Kong Futures Exchange, China, www.hkex.com.hk

Istanbul Stock Exchange, Turkey, www.ise.org

Italian Exchange (Borsa Italiana), Italy, www.borsaitalia.it/eng/home

Jasdaq, Japan, Japanese language only, www.jasdaq.co.jp

Jakarta Stock Exchange, Indonesia, www.jsx.co.id

Johannesburg Stock Exchange, South Africa, www.jse.co.za

Karachi Stock Exchange, Pakistan, www.kse.com.pk

Korea Stock Exchange, Korea, www.kse.or.kr/en_index.html

Kuala Lumpur Stock Exchange (KLSE), Malaysia, www.klse.com.my

Lima Stock Exchange, Peru, www.bvl.com.pe/homepage2.html

Lisbon Stock Exchange, Portugal, Portuguese language only, www.bvl.pt

London International Financial Futures and Options Exchange (LIFFE), United Kingdom, www.liffe.com

London Metal Exchange (LME), United Kingdom, www.lme.co.uk

London Stock Exchange (LSE), United Kingdom, www.londonstockexchange.com

Madrid Stock Exchange (Bolsa de Madrid), Spain, www.bolsamadrid.es

Matif SA, France, www.matif.fr

Mexican Stock Exchange (Bolsa Mexicana de Valores), Mexico, www.bmv.com.mx/bmving/index.html

Nagoya Stock Exchange, Japan, www.nse.or.jp/index-e.htm

Nasdaq, United States, www.nasdaq.com

National Stock Exchange of India, India, www.nseindia.com

New European Exchange (NEWEX), Europe, www.newex.com

New York Cotton Exchange (NYCE), United States, www.nyce.com

New York Futures Exchange (NYFE), United States, www.nyfe.com

New York Mercantile Exchange (NYMEX), United States, www.nymex.com

New York Stock Exchange (NYSE), United States, www.nyse.com

New Zealand Stock Exchange, New Zealand, www.nzse.co.nz

Osaka Securities Exchange, Japan, www.ose.or.jp/e

Oslo Børs, Norway, www.ose.no/english/index.asp?lang=english

Paris Stock Exchange (Bourse de Paris), France, www.euronext.com/fr

Philadelphia Stock Exchange, United States, www.phlx.com

Philippine Stock Exchange, Philippines, www.pse.org.ph

Rio de Janeiro Stock Exchange, Brazil, Portuguese language only, www.bvrj.com.br

Russian Exchange, Russia, www.re.ru/eng

Shanghai Stock Exchange, China, Chinese language only, www.sse.com.cn

Shenzhen Stock Exchange, China, Chinese language only, www.sse.org.cn

Stock Exchange of Thailand, Thailand, www.set.or.th

Stockholm Stock Market, Sweden, www.stockholmsborsen.se/index.asp?lang=eng

Swiss Exchange, Switzerland, www.swx.com

Taiwan Stock Exchange (TSEC), Taiwan, www.tse.com.tw/docs/eng_home.htm

Tel Aviv Stock Exchange, Israel, www.tase.co.il

Tokyo Stock Exchange, Japan, www.tse.or.jp/english/index.shtml

Warsaw Stock Exchange, Poland, www.gpw.com.pl/xml/indexe.xml

Wiener Börse, Austria, www.wienerboerse.at.cms/2/

Acknowledgments

I originally created my dictionary of financial terms while teaching global financial management at both Duke University and the University of Chicago. Thanks to John Graham and Michael Bradley for their keen contributions. I am indebted to all of my students over the years for suggesting words for the project, and particularly wish to thank Harley Adams, Bill Bane Jr., Carol Bass, Onthida Boonpiamsak, John Bracchini, Jeff Chung, Tiago Elvo, Chris Foster, Andrew Frankel, Tommy Jacobs, Berkin Kologlu, Jeremy Krasner, Merrill Liechty, Van Menard, Christina Nitz, Peter O'Hara, Patricia Peat, Murray Spence, Lance Stover, Jon Walker, Chris Withers, and Jean Yu.—C. H.

We wish to thank our dedicated and meticulous copyeditor, Brooke Goode, as well as Robin Dennis and Chris O'Connell at Henry Holt and Mike Levitas at the *New York Times* for their great patience and perseverance in making this book possible.—C. H. and G. M.

About the Authors

Winner of the 2002 Pulitzer Prize for her coverage of Wall Street, **Gretchen Morgenson** is market watch columnist for the *New York Times*. She is author of *Forbes Great Minds of Business* and *The Woman's Guide to the Stock Market*, as well as a contributor to *The New Rules of Personal Investing: The Experts' Guide to Prospering in a Changing Economy* by the financial correspondents of the *New York Times*. Before joining the *Times*, she was senior editor at *Forbes* magazine. She lives in New York City.

Campbell R. Harvey, Ph.D., is J. Paul Sticht Professor of International Business at Duke University's Fuqua School of Business and a research associate of the National Bureau of Economic Research. An internationally recognized expert in global portfolio management and risk analysis, he has over one hundred published articles and books. He has earned four Graham and Dodd awards for excellence in financial writing. Currently, he edits the *Review of Financial Studies*. He lives in Chapel Hill, North Carolina.